The Windows® 2000
Device Driver Book
SECOND EDITION

ISBN 0-13-020431-5

90000

9 780130 204318

PRENTICE HALL PTR MICROSOFT® TECHNOLOGIES SERIES

NETWORKING

- Microsoft Technology: Networking, Concepts, Tools
  Woodard, Gattuccio, Brain

- NT Network Programming Toolkit
  Murphy

- Building COM Applications with Internet Explorer
  Loveman

- Understanding DCOM
  Rubin, Brain

- Web Database Development for Windows Platforms
  Gutierrez

PROGRAMMING

- The Windows 2000 Device Driver Book, Second Edition
  Baker, Lozano

- WIN32 System Services: The Heart of Windows 98 and Windows 2000, Third Edition
  Brain, Reeves

- Programming the WIN32 API and UNIX System Services
  Merusi

- Windows CE 3.0: Application Programming
  Grattan, Brain

- The Visual Basic Style Guide
  Patrick

- Windows Shell Programming
  Seely

- Windows Installer Complete
  Easter

- Windows 2000 Web Applications Developer's Guide
  Yager

- Developing Windows Solutions with Office 2000 Components and VBA
  Aitken

- Multithreaded Programming with Win32
  Pham, Garg

- Developing Professional Applications for Windows 98 and NT Using MFC, Third Edition
  Brain, Lovette

- Introduction to Windows 98 Programming
  Murray, Pappas

- The COM and COM+ Programming Primer
  Gordon

- Understanding and Programming COM+: A Practical Guide to Windows 2000 DNA
  Oberg

- Distributed COM Application Development Using Visual C++ 6.0
  Maloney

- Distributed COM Application Development Using Visual Basic 6.0
  Maloney

- The Essence of COM, Third Edition
  Platt

- COM-CORBA Interoperability
  Geraghty, Joyce, Moriarty, Noone

- MFC Programming in C++ with the Standard Template Libraries
  Murray, Pappas

- Introduction to MFC Programming with Visual C++
  Jones

- Visual C++ Templates
  Murray, Pappas

- Visual Basic Object and Component Handbook
  Vogel

- Visual Basic 6: Error Coding and Layering
  Gill

- ADO Programming in Visual Basic 6
  Holzner

- Visual Basic 6: Design, Specification, and Objects
  Hollis

- ASP/MTS/ADSI Web Security
  Harrison

BACKOFFICE

- BizTalk: Implementing Business-To-Business E-Commerce
  Kobielus

- Designing Enterprise Solutions with Microsoft Technologies
  Kemp, Kemp, Goncalves

- Microsoft Site Server 3.0 Commerce Edition
  Libertone, Scoppa

- Building Microsoft SQL Server 7 Web Sites
  Byrne

- Optimizing SQL Server 7
  Schneider, Goncalves

ADMINISTRATION

- Microsoft SQL Server 2000
  Fields

- Windows 2000 Cluster Server Guidebook
  Libertone

- Windows 2000 Hardware and Disk Management
  Simmons
- Windows 2000 Server: Management and Control,
  Third Edition
  Spencer, Goncalves
- Creating Active Directory Infrastructures
  Simmons
- Windows 2000 Registry
  Sanna
- Configuring Windows 2000 Server
  Simmons
- Supporting Windows NT and 2000 Workstation
  and Server
  Mohr
- Zero Administration Kit for Windows
  McInerney
- Tuning and Sizing NT Server
  Aubley
- Windows NT 4.0 Server Security Guide
  Goncalves
- Windows NT Security
  McInerney

CERTIFICATION

- Core MCSE: Windows 2000 Edition
  Dell
- Core MCSE: Designing a Windows 2000 Directory
  Services Infrastructure
  Simmons
- Core MCSE
  Dell
- Core MCSE: Networking Essentials
  Keogh

- MCSE: Administering Microsoft SQL Server 7
  Byrne
- MCSE: Implementing and Supporting Microsoft
  Exchange Server 5.5
  Goncalves
- MCSE: Internetworking with Microsoft TCP/IP
  Ryvkin, Houde, Hoffman
- MCSE: Implementing and Supporting Microsoft Proxy
  Server 2.0
  Ryvkin, Hoffman
- MCSE: Implementing and Supporting Microsoft SNA
  Server 4.0
  Mariscal
- MCSE: Implementing and Supporting Microsoft Internet
  Information Server 4
  Dell
- MCSE: Implementing and Supporting Web Sites Using
  Microsoft Site Server 3
  Goncalves
- MCSE: Microsoft System Management Server 2
  Jewett
- MCSE: Implementing and Supporting Internet Explorer 5
  Dell
- Core MCSD: Designing and Implementing Desktop
  Applications with Microsoft Visual Basic 6
  Holzner
- Core MCSD: Designing and Implementing Distributed
  Applications with Microsoft Visual Basic 6
  Houlette, Klander
- MCSD: Planning and Implementing SQL Server 7
  Vacca
- MCSD: Designing and Implementing Web Sites with
  Microsoft FrontPage 98
  Karlins

PRENTICE HALL PTR MICROSOFT® TECHNOLOGIES SERIES

The Windows 2000 Device Driver Book

A Guide for Programmers

SECOND EDITION

Art Baker

Jerry Lozano

Prentice Hall PTR, Upper Saddle River, NJ 07458
www.phptr.com

Library of Congress Cataloging-in-Publication Data

The Windows 2000 device driver handbook / Art Baker, Jerry Lozano.
   p. cm.
  Includes bibliographical references and index.
  ISBN 0-13-020431-5
   1. Device drivers (Computer programs) 2. Microsoft Windows (Computer file) I.
Lozano, Jerry. II. Title.

QA76.76.D49 W56 2001
005.4'4769--dc21

                                00-061968

Acquisitions editor: *Mike Meehan*
Cover designer: *Talar Agasyan*
Cover design director: *Jerry Votta*
Manufacturing manager: *Maura Zaldivar*
Marketing manager: *Bryan Gambrel*
Project coordinator: *Anne Trowbridge*
Compositor/Production services: *Pine Tree Composition, Inc.*

© 2001 by Prentice Hall PTR
Prentice-Hall, Inc.
Upper Saddle River, New Jersey 07458

Prentice Hall books are widely used by corporations and government agencies for training, marketing, and resale.

The publisher offers discounts on this book when ordered in bulk quantities. For more information contact:
    Corporate Sales Department
    Phone: 800-382-3419
    Fax: 201-236-7141
    E-mail: corpsales@prenhall.com

    Or write:

    Prentice Hall PTR
    Corp. Sales Dept.
    One Lake Street
    Upper Saddle River, New Jersey 07458

Printed in the United States of America
10 9 8 7 6 5 4 3 2

ISBN: 0-13-020431-5

Prentice-Hall International (UK) Limited, *London*
Prentice-Hall of Australia Pty. Limited, *Sydney*
Prentice-Hall Canada Inc., Toronto
Prentice-Hall Hispanoamericana, S.A., *Mexico*
Prentice-Hall of India Private Limited, *New Delhi*
Prentice-Hall of Japan, Inc., *Tokyo*
Pearson Education Asia Pte Ltd.
Editora Prentice-Hall do Brasil, Ltda., *Rio de Janeiro*

To my daughter, Sandra, for showing me the value of determination. Your accomplishments are already far greater than what I will ever achieve.

—Jerry

CONTENTS

Drivers are the most fundamental and technically difficult part of operating system development. As a reader of this book, you are probably well aware of the complexities involved. Even for the most seasoned software engineer the task can be daunting. Writing device drivers under Windows 2000 is a big challenge to learn. The most comprehensive, authoritative guide to Windows NT driver development, The *Windows NT Device Driver Book* by Art Baker is now a classic. I can not think of anyone better qualified to write the second edition of Art's outstanding book than Jerry Lozano. Jerry combines the qualities of strong technologist, excellent writer, and gifted educator. These qualities have translated into book form very well. Reading this book I felt I was taking one of Jerry's classes.

There are two kinds of books. Some books provide reference information that very much read like an encyclopedia. Such books are picked up occasionally to answer a specific question. Other books are tutorial in nature. They are designed to be read from front to back in order to transfer the knowledge and skill necessary to perform a task.

The Windows 2000 Device Driver Book, like its predecessor, falls clearly into the latter category. It is intended to be used as an instructional guide for device driver authors. Unlike other books on the subject, this book does not attempt to reproduce the DDK. The DDK stands as the definitive reference on the Windows 2000 device driver technology. Instead, *The Windows 2000 Device Driver Book* provides the guiding information needed to successfully master W2K driver development. This book gives developers the knowledge to design, write, and debug Windows 2000 devices, and is based on a course Jerry created and teaches for UCI. Based on feedback from the course, Jerry found that one of the biggest problems device driver and kernel-mode code developers face is the lack of clear, concise technical information on driver models, kernel mode programming, and hardware interfaces. In this book Jerry has succeeded in solving this problem with detailed examples and informative coverage in all areas, and presenting it with exceptional clarity.

As the book went to press, it was clear that another chapter was highly desirable. The chapter concerns USB and IEEE 1394 driver specifics. The revision author has generously agreed to include this chapter on the book's companion web site: www.W2KDriverBook.com. Readers that need this information should visit this informative site.

Andrew Scoppa
President
UCI Software Technical Training

This book explains how to write, install, and debug device drivers for Windows 2000. It is intended to be a companion to the Microsoft DDK documentation and software.

Windows 2000 represents a major improvement to previous versions of Windows NT. Device drivers for Windows 2000 may be designed for the new Windows Driver Model (WDM) architecture. If so, the driver will be *source* compatible with Windows 98. This book covers the new WDM specification.

This book will also prove useful to those studying the internals of Windows 2000, particularly the I/O subsystem and related components.

What You Should Already Know

All instruction assumes a base knowledge level. First, the reader should be familiar with Windows 2000 administration—security and setup, for example. Since experimentation with kernel-mode code can (and will) cause system problems, the reader should be prepared and able to restore a chaotic OS.

Second, the reader should be competent in the C programming language and somewhat familiar with C++. Only a little C++ is used in this book, and then only for the purpose of simplifying tedious code.

Third, experience with Win32 user-mode programming is useful. Knowing how user-mode code *drives* I/O devices is useful in designing and testing device driver code. The test code for the examples in this book rely on the console subsystem model for Windows. To review this topic, the reader is referred to the *Win32 Programmers Reference,* particularly the chapters on I/O primitives (CreateFile, ReadFile, WriteFile, and DeviceIoControl). The bibliography lists other references for this topic.

Finally, while no specific prior knowledge of hardware or device driver software design is assumed, it would be useful if the reader had experience with some aspect of low-level device interfacing. For example, knowledge of writing device drivers for a Unix system will prove quite useful when reading this book.

What's Covered

The focus of this book is to first explain the *architecture* of the hardware, environment, and device driver, and then to explain the *details* of writing code.

Chapters are grouped within this book as follows:

Chapters 1–5: The first five chapters of this book cover the foundation of what's needed to write a device driver. This includes coverage of the Windows 2000 architecture, hardware terminology and bus basics, and an in-depth view of the Windows 2000 I/O Manager and related services.

Chapters 6–13: The next eight chapters form the nucleus of this book. The chapters cover everything from the mechanics of building a driver to the specifics of instrumenting a driver to log errors and other events.

Chapters 14–15: These two chapters deal with somewhat more advanced topics within device driver construction. This includes the use of system threads, layering, filtering, and utilizing driver classes.

Chapters 16–17: The final chapters deal with the practical but necessary details of driver installation and debugging. The use of Windows 2000 INF files for "automatic" installation of a plug and play device driver is covered (as well as manual installation for legacy devices). The use of WinDbg is covered in sufficient detail so that the programmer can actually perform interactive debugging.

Appendices: The appendices cover reference information needed for driver development. The mechanics of Windows 2000 symbol file installation, bugcheck codes, and so on are listed.

What's Not

Since the purpose of this book is to cover driver development from "the ground up," some specific topics fall outside its scope. Specifically, the list of topics not covered includes

File system drivers: Currently, the construction of a full Windows 2000 Installable File System requires the acquisition of the Microsoft IFS kit. The bibliography of this book points to one source for more information on this topic. Potential users of the IFS kit will benefit greatly from this book, as the material covered is essential prerequisite knowledge.

Device-specific driver information: The construction of NIC (Network Interface Card), SCSI, video (including capture devices), printers, and multimedia drivers is not specifically covered in this book. Chapter 1 discusses the architectural implications of such drivers, but even individual chapters on each of these driver types would seriously shortchange the requisite knowledge.

Virtual DOS device drivers: The current wave of driver development is toward the WDM 32-bit model. Legacy 16-bit VDDs are no longer of interest.

About the Sample Code

Most chapters in this book include one or more sample drivers. All code is included on the accompanying CD. Samples for each chapter are in separate subdirectories on the CD, so installation of individual projects is straightforward.

The CD also includes a device driver application wizard for Microsoft Visual C++ version 6. This wizard configures the build environment so that code can be written, compiled, and linked within Visual Studio.

> **Platform dependencies:** The sample code included with this book has been targeted and tested on Intel platforms only. Since it appears that the last non-Intel platform (Alpha) was dropped from the final release of Windows 2000, this should come as no surprise. Be advised, however, that Windows 2000 is intrinsically a platform-independent OS. It is a straightforward process to port the OS to many modern hardware sets. Driver writers should consider designs that take advantage of the Windows 2000 abstractions that permit source compatibility with non-Intel platforms.

> **To build and run the examples:** Besides the Microsoft DDK (Device Driver Kit) (which is available on an MSDN subscription or, at present, free for download from the Microsoft web site at *www.microsoft.com/DDK),* the sample code assumes that Microsoft Visual C++ is installed. The device driver application wizard was built for Visual Studio version 6. Obviously, with some effort the sample code can be built using other vendors' compilers.

Of course, an installed version of Windows 2000 (Professional, Server, or Enterprise) is required. For interactive debugging using WinDbg, a second host platform is required.

History of this Book

The first version of this book was written by Art Baker, entitled *The Windows NT Device Driver Book*. By any account, the book was required reading for any NT driver author. The Microsoft driver model is a continuously moving target. As such, recently introduced books on this subject provided more and up-to-date information. The goal of this revision of the book is to carry forward the goals, style, and clarity of Art's original work while updating the material with the very latest information available from Microsoft.

If you are a previous reader of the original version of this book, I hope you will find this version just as useful. I have attempted to provide accurate, concise, and clear information on the subject of Windows 2000 device drivers. While I have relied heavily on Art's original work, any errors present in this book are entirely mine.

Training and Consulting Services

The material in this book is based on training and consulting performed for various companies within the industry.

The subject matter of this book is presented exclusively by UCI in the format of a five-day instructor-lead lecture/lab course. The course is available as public or on site classes. UCI provides comprehensive training in high-end programming, web development and administration, databases, and system technologies.

For more information please visit the UCI web site at *www.ucitraining.com* or use the address information below:

UCI Corporation
4 Constitution Way
Suite G
Woburn, MA 01801

1-800-884-1772

The revision author, Jerry Lozano, provides seminars and workshops on the topic of device drivers and other related subjects. For more information visit the web site: *www.StarJourney.com*

Acknowledgments

I am grateful to many people who helped me with this 2nd edition. First and foremost, I want to thank Art Baker for his original work. The structure and content of this revision is based on his initial efforts.

To my partner in life, Carol, who makes everything possible. I thank Carol for both her personal and professional support. Without your encouragement, I would never have started this project. Without your help, I would never have finished.

Thanks to Russ Hall, my development editor and friend, for making the book sound good.

Thanks to Patty Donovan and her staff at Pine Tree Composition for making the book look good.

The staff of Prentice Hall PTR, especially Mike Meehan and Anne Trowbridge, deserve considerable credit for their patience and encouragement in leading me through the entire process.

I wish to thank Bryce Leach of Texas Instruments who tried to correct my misunderstandings of IEEE 1394. Your comments and suggestions for Chapter 2 were invaluable.

Thanks to Ron Reeves, for several great technical comments on several chapters.

And finally, thanks to the many people who attend my seminars, workshops, and classes for asking all those wonderful, thought-provoking questions.

Introduction to Windows 2000 Drivers

CHAPTER OBJECTIVES

Device drivers on any operating system necessarily interact intimately with the underlying system code. This is especially true for Windows 2000. Before jumping into the world of Windows 2000 device drivers, this chapter presents the design philosophy and overall architecture of Windows 2000.

Overall System Architecture

Windows 2000 presents arguably the most aggressive attempt at operating system control in the history of computers. This section tours the Windows 2000 architecture, highlighting the features of significant interest to a device driver author.

Design Goals for Windows 2000

The original goals for Microsoft's NT ("New Technology") operating system took form in early 1989. Interestingly, the original concept for NT did not even include a Windows operating environment. While the NT OS has indeed come a long way since 1989, the five fundamental goals remain intact.

- **Compatibility.** The OS should support as much existing software and hardware as possible.
- **Robustness and reliability.** The OS should be resilient to inadvertent or intentional misuse. A user's application should not be able to crash the system.
- **Portability.** The OS should run on as many present and future platforms as possible.
- **Extendibility.** Since the market requirements will change (grow) over time, the OS must make it easy to add new features and support new hardware with minimal impact on existing code.
- **Performance.** The OS should provide good performance for a given capability of the hardware platform which hosts it.

Of course, goals are not reality, and over time, serious compromise of one goal may be necessary to achieve another. NT is an operating system and, as such, is subject to the same sorts of compromises that affect all systems. The remainder of this section describes the delicate balance of solutions that Microsoft OS designers chose to implement their goals.

Hardware Privilege Levels in Windows 2000

To achieve the robustness and reliability goal, the designers of NT chose a *client-server architecture* for its core implementation. A user application runs as a client of OS services.

The user application runs in a special mode of the hardware known generically as *user mode*. Within this mode, code is restricted to nonharmful operations. For example, through the magic of virtual memory mapping, code cannot touch the memory of other applications (except by mutual agreement with another application). Hardware I/O instructions cannot be executed. Indeed, an entire class of CPU instructions (designated *privileged*), such as a CPU Halt, cannot be executed. Should the application require the use of any of these prohibited operations, it must make a request of the operating system kernel. A hardware-provided *trap* mechanism is used to make these requests.

Operating system code runs in a mode of the hardware known as *kernel mode*. Kernel-mode code can perform any valid CPU instruction, notably including I/O operations. Memory from any application is exposed to kernel-mode code, providing, of course, that the application memory has not been *paged out* to disk.

All modern processors implement some form of *privileged* vs. *nonprivileged* modes. Kernel-mode code executes in this privileged context, while user-mode code executes in the nonprivileged environment. Since different processors and platforms implement privileged modes differently, and to help achieve the goal of portability, the OS designers provided an abstraction for user and kernel modes. OS code always uses the abstraction to perform privileged context switches, and thus only the abstraction code itself need be ported to a new platform. On an Intel platform, user mode is implemented using Ring 3 of the instruction set, while kernel mode is implemented using Ring 0.

This discussion is relevant to device driver writers in that kernel-mode drivers execute in a privileged context. As such, poorly written device driver code can and does compromise the integrity of the Windows 2000 operating system. Driver writers must take extra care in handling all boundary conditions to ensure that the code does not bring down the entire OS.

Portability

To achieve the portability goal, NT designers chose a layered architecture for the software, as shown in Figure 1.1.

The Hardware Abstraction Layer (HAL) isolates processor and platform dependencies from the OS and device driver code. In general, when device driver code is ported to a new platform, only a recompile is necessary. How can this work since device driver code is inherently device-, processor-, and platform-specific? Clearly, the device driver code must rely on code (macros) within the HAL to reference hardware registers and buses. In some cases, the device driver code must rely on abstraction code provided in the I/O Manager (and elsewhere) to manipulate shared hardware resources (e.g., DMA channels). Subsequent chapters in this book will explain the proper use of the HAL and other OS services so that device driver code can be platform-independent.

Extendibility

Figure 1.1 also shows an important design concept of Windows 2000—the kernel is separate from a layer known as the *Executive.*

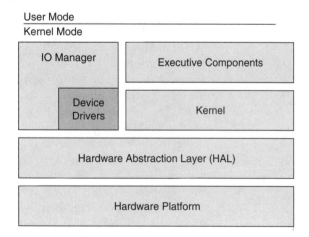

Figure 1.1   *The layers of the Windows 2000 operating system*

The Windows 2000 kernel is primarily responsible for the scheduling of all thread activity. A thread is simply an independent path of execution through code. To remain independent of other thread activity, a unique thread *context* must be preserved for each thread. The thread context consists of the CPU register state (including a separate stack and Program Counter), an ID (sometimes called a Thread ID or TID, internally known as a Client ID), a priority value, storage locations local to the thread (Thread Local Storage), and other thread-relevant information.

The scheduler's responsibility is to manage which thread should execute at any given time. In a single processor environment, of course, only one thread may actually gain control of the processor at a time. In a multiprocessor environment, different threads may be executing on the different available processors, offering true parallel execution of code. The scheduler assigns a processor to a thread for, at most, a fixed period of time known as the *thread time quantum*. Processors are assigned to threads primarily based on the thread's priority value. Higher priority threads that become ready to run will preempt a running thread.

Since the kernel's prime role is to schedule thread activity, other OS components perform the necessary work of memory, process, security, and I/O management. These components are collectively known as the *Executive*. The Executive components have been designed (though the I/O Manager itself is a significant exception) as modular software. Over the years, Microsoft has added, deleted, merged, and separated these components as improvements and compromises deemed necessary. A good example would be the addition of the Active Directory Services, which is relatively new to Windows 2000.

The notion of keeping the kernel itself small and clean, coupled with the modularization of Executive components, provides the basis for NT's claim to extendibility. The OS has now survived about ten years of revisions, maintenance, and significant feature improvement (a.k.a., *creeping elegance*).

Performance

While the layered approach to software design is often characterized by lackluster performance, attention to fast layer interaction has been a continual effort with the NT design group. First, it should be noted that all the layers described so far execute within the same hardware mode, kernel mode. Therefore, interlayer calls often involve nothing more than a processor CALL instruction. Indeed, HAL usage is often implemented with macros, thus achieving inline performance.

Second, there has been a concentrated effort to parallelize as many tasks as possible by allocating threads to different units of work. The Executive components are all multithreaded. Helper routines seldom *block* or *busy-wait* while performing their work. This minimizes true idle time on the processor.

The performance goals of Windows 2000 impact device driver writers. As user and system threads request service from a device, it is vital that the driver code not block execution. If the request cannot be handled immediately, perhaps because the device is busy or slow, the request must be queued for subsequent handling. Fortunately, I/O Manager routines facilitate this process.

Executive Components

Since the Executive components provide the base services for the Windows 2000 operating system (other than thread scheduling), their needs and responsibilities are fairly clear. These components are explained in the following sections.

SYSTEM SERVICE INTERFACE

This component provides the entry point from user mode to kernel mode. This allows user-mode code to cleanly and safely invoke services of the OS. Depending on the platform, the transition from user mode to kernel mode may be a simple CPU instruction or an elaborate Save and Restore context switch.

OBJECT MANAGER

Almost all services offered by the OS are modeled with an object. For example, a user-mode program that needs thread-to-thread synchronization might request a *mutex* service from the OS. The OS presents the mutex in the form of an OS-based object, referenced from user mode only through a *handle*. Files, processes, Threads, Events, Memory Sections, and even Registry Keys are modeled with OS-based objects. All objects are created and destroyed by a centralized Object Manager. This allows for uniform access, life spans, and security with all objects.

CONFIGURATION MANAGER

The Configuration Manager of Windows 2000 models the hardware and installed software of the machine. A database called the Registry is used to store this model. Device drivers utilize information in the Registry to discover many aspects of the environment in which they are executed. With the introduction of Plug and Play into Windows 2000, the role of the Registry for device drivers has been significantly reduced.

PROCESS MANAGER

A process is the environment in which threads execute in Windows 2000. Each process maintains a private address space and security identity. In Windows 2000, it is important to note that processes do not *run*; instead, threads are the unit of execution and the process is a unit of ownership. A process owns one or more threads.

The Windows 2000 Process Manager is the Executive component that manages the process model and exposes the environment in which process threads run. The Process Manager relies heavily on other Executive components (e.g., the Object Manager and Virtual Memory Manager) to perform its work. As such, it could be said that the Process Manager simply exposes a higher level of abstraction for other lower-level system services.

Device drivers seldom interact with the Process Manager directly. Instead, drivers rely on other services of the OS to touch the process environment. For example, a driver must ensure that a buffer residing with the private address space of a process remains "locked down" during an I/O transfer. Routines within the OS allow a driver to perform this locking activity.

VIRTUAL MEMORY MANAGER

Under Windows 2000, the address space of a process is a flat 4 gigabytes (4 GB) (2^{32}). Only the lower 2 GB is accessible in user mode. A program's code and data must reside in this lower half of the address space. If the program relies on shared library code (dynamic-link libraries or DLLs), the library code also must reside in the first 2 GB of address space.

The upper 2 GB of address space of every process contains code and data accessible only in kernel-mode. The upper 2 GB of address space is shared from process to process by kernel-mode code. Indeed, device driver code is mapped into address space above 2 GB.

The Virtual Memory Manager (VMM) performs memory management on behalf of the entire system. For normal user-mode programs, this means allocating and managing address space and physical memory below the 2 GB boundary. If the needed memory for a given process is not physically available, the VMM provides an illusion of memory by *virtualizing* the request. Needed memory is *paged* onto a disk file and retrieved into RAM when accessed by a process. In effect, RAM becomes a shared resource of all processes, with memory moving between files on the disk and the limited RAM available on a given system.

The VMM also acts a memory allocator in that it maintains heap areas for kernel-mode code. Device drivers can request the VMM to assign dedicated areas of pagable or nonpagable memory for its use. Further, devices that operate using DMA (direct memory access) can assign nonpagable memory as needed to perform data transfers between RAM and a device. Of course, these topics are covered in more detail in subsequent chapters.

LOCAL PROCEDURE CALL FACILITY

A Local Procedure Call (LPC) is a call mechanism between processes of a single machine. Since this *interprocess* call must pass between different address spaces, a kernel-mode Executive component is provided to make the action efficient (and possible). Device driver code has no need for the LPC facility.

I/O MANAGER

The I/O Manager is an Executive component that is implemented with a series of kernel-mode routines that present a uniform abstraction to user-mode processes for I/O operations. One goal of the I/O Manager is to make all I/O access from user mode device-independent. It should not matter (much) to a user process whether it is accessing a keyboard, a communication port, or a disk file.

The I/O Manager presents requests from user-mode processes to device drivers in the form of an I/O Request Packet (IRP). The IRP represents a work order, usually synthesized by the I/O Manager, that is presented to a device driver. It is the job of device drivers to carry out the requested work of an IRP. Much of the remainder of this book is devoted to the proper care and processing of IRPs by device driver code.

In effect, the I/O Manager serves as an interface layer between user-mode code and device drivers. It is therefore the most important block of code that a device driver must interact with during operation.

ACTIVE DIRECTORY SERVICE

The Active Directory Service is somewhat new to Windows 2000. It provides a network-wide namespace for system resources. Previously, the internal names used to identify system resources (disk drive names, printer names, user names, file names) were managed within a restricted space of the OS. It was the responsibility of other OS components (e.g., the networking services) to *export* names across different protocols.

The Active Directory is now a uniform, secure, and standard way to identify system resources. It is based on a hierarchical scheme (strictly defined by a schema) whereby entities are categorized into organization units (OUs), trees, and forests.

EXTENSIONS TO THE BASE OPERATING SYSTEM

Although the Executive components of Windows 2000 define and implement core services of the OS, it might be interesting to note that these services are not directly exposed to user-mode applications. Instead, Microsoft defines several Application Programming Interfaces (APIs) that user-mode code treats as abstractions of OS services. These APIs form different *environmental subsystems* that application code live within. Currently, the following environmental subsystems are included with Windows 2000.

- The Win32 subsystem is the native-mode API of Windows 2000. All other environmental subsystems rely upon this subsystem to perform their work. All new Windows 2000 applications (and indeed, most ported ones as well) rely on the Win32 subsystem for their environment. Because of its importance (and interesting implementation), this subsystem is described in more detail in the next section.

- The Virtual DOS Machine (VDM) subsystem provides a 16-bit MSDOS environment for old-style DOS applications. Despite its promise of compatibility, many existing 16-bit DOS programs do not operate properly. This is due to Microsoft's conservative and safe approach that *emulates* device (and other system resources) access. Attempts to directly access these resources results in intervention from the OS that provides safe, but not always faithful, results.
- The Windows on Windows (WOW) subsystem supports an environment for old-style 16-bit Windows applications (i.e., Windows 3.X programs). Interestingly, each 16-bit program runs as a separate thread within the address space of a single WOW process. Multiple WOWs can be spawned, but 16-bit Windows applications are then prohibited from sharing resources.
- The POSIX subsystem provides API support for Unix-style applications that conform to the POSIX 1003.1 source code standard. Unfortunately, this subsystem has not proved workable for hosting the ports of many (most) Unix-style applications. As such, most Unix applications are ported by rewriting for the Win32 environment.
- The OS/2 subsystem creates the execution environment for 16-bit OS/2 applications—at least those that do not rely on the Presentation Manager (PM) services of OS/2. This subsystem is available only for the Intel (x86) version of Windows 2000.

A given application is tightly coupled to exactly one environmental subsystem. Applications cannot make API calls to other environments. Also, only the Win32 subsystem is native—other subsystems emulate their environments and therefore experience various degrees of performance degradation compared to native Win32. Their purpose is compatibility, not speed.

Environmental subsystems are generally implemented as separate user-mode processes. They launch as needed to support and host user-mode processes. The environmental subsystem becomes the *server* for the user-mode *client*. Each request from a client is passed, using the Local Procedure Call Executive component, to the appropriate server process. The server process (i.e., the environmental subsystem) either performs the work to fulfill the request directly or it, in turn, makes a request of the appropriate Executive component.

THE WIN32 SUBSYSTEM

As the native API for Windows 2000, the Win32 environmental subsystem is responsible for

- The Graphical User Interface (GUI) seen by users of the system. It implements and exposes viewable windows, dialogs, controls, and an overall style for the system.
- Console I/O including keyboard, mouse, and display for the entire system, including other subsystems.
- Implementation of the Win32 API, which is what applications and other subsystems use to interact with the Executive.

Because the Win32 Subsystem holds special status within the system and because of its inherent requirement for high performance, this subsystem is implemented differently from any of the other subsystems. In particular, the Win32 subsystem is split into some components that execute in user mode and some that execute in kernel mode. In general, the Win32 function can be divided into three categories.

- USER functions that manage windows, menus, dialogs, and controls.
- GDI functions that perform drawing operations on physical devices (e.g., screens and printers).
- KERNEL functions, which manage non-GUI resources such as processes, threads, files, and synchronization services. KERNEL functions map closely to system services of the Executive.

Since NT 4.0, USER and GDI functions have been moved to kernel mode. User processes that request GUI services are therefore sent directly to kernel-mode using the System Service Interface, an efficient process. Kernel-mode code that implements USER and GDI functions resides in a module called WIN32K.SYS. The USER and GDI kernel components are illustrated in Figure 1.2.

Conversely, KERNEL functions rely on a standard server process, CSRSS.exe (Client-Server Runtime Subsystem), to respond to user process requests. In turn, CSRSS traps into Executive code to complete the request for such functions.

INTEGRAL SUBSYSTEMS

In addition to the Environmental Subsystems, there are also key system components that are implemented as user mode processes. These include

- The Security Subsystem, which manages local and remote security using a variety of processes and dynamic libraries. Part of the Active Directory work also resides within this logical subsystem.
- The Service Control Manager (affectionately called the *scum,* or SCM) manages services (daemon processes) and device drivers.
- The RPC Locator and Service processes give support to applications distributed across the network. Through the use of remote procedure calls, an application can distribute its workload across several networked machines.

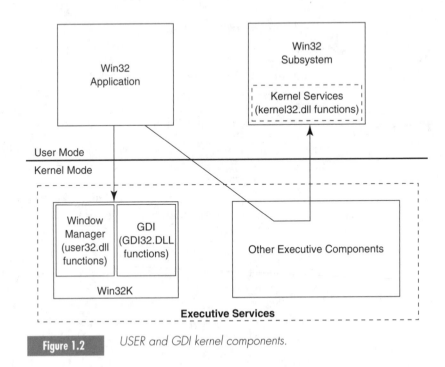

Figure 1.2   *USER and GDI kernel components.*

Kernel-Mode I/O Components

The purpose of this section is to describe the goals and architecture of the Windows 2000 I/O subsystem. Since different kinds of drivers perform wildly different kinds of service, the I/O Manager's categorization of drivers is also discussed.

Design Goals for the I/O Subsystem

The I/O subsystem of Windows 2000 added to the overall design goals of the operating system by including

- Portability, platform to platform.
- Configurability in terms of both hardware and software. For Windows 2000 drivers, this would include full support for Plug and Play buses and devices.
- Preemptable and interruptable. I/O code should never block and should always be written thread-safe.
- Multiprocessor-safe. The same I/O code should run on both uniprocessor and multiprocessor configurations.
- Object-based. The services provided by I/O code should be offered in encapsulated data structures with well-defined allowable operations.

- Packet-driven. Requests made of the I/O subsystem should be submitted and tracked using a distinct "work order" format, known as an *I/O Request Packet* (IRP).
- Asynchronous I/O support. Requests made of the I/O subsystem should be allowed to complete in parallel with the requestor's execution. When the request ultimately completes, a mechanism must exist to notify the caller of completion.

Besides these published goals, there is also strong emphasis placed on code reusability. This translates to heavy structuring of I/O code (including drivers) into logical layers. For example, bus-driving code should be layered separately from specific device code to allow for reuse of the bus code across multiple devices. In many cases, different vendors supply code for different layers. Only through careful *modularization* can this goal be achieved.

Kinds of Drivers in Windows 2000

There once was a time when a device driver author could understand the intricacies of the new hardware, learn the OS device driver interface, scope the work, and "just write the code." For better or worse, the days of monolithic device driver code have passed. Today, an author must understand the *architectures* of both complex hardware buses and heavily layered I/O subsystems just to scope the work statement. Deciding what *kind* of driver to write for Windows 2000 is itself an interesting challenge. Deciding whether to implement or to reuse a layer is yet another challenge. The purpose of this section is to describe where different kinds of drivers fit within the hardware world and the OS.

At the highest level, Windows 2000 supports two kinds of drivers, user-mode and kernel-mode. User-mode drivers, as the name implies, is system-level code running in user mode. Examples include a simulated, or *virtualized,* driver for imaginary hardware or perhaps a new environmental subsystem. Since Windows 2000 user mode does not allow direct access to hardware, a virtualized driver necessarily relies upon real driver code running in kernel mode. This book does not describe user-mode drivers. The purpose of this book is to describe *real* drivers, which in Windows 2000 are known as *kernel-mode drivers.*

Kernel-mode drivers consist of system-level code running in kernel mode. Since kernel mode allows direct hardware access, such drivers are used to control hardware directly. Of course, nothing prevents a kernel-mode driver from virtualizing real hardware—the choice between user and kernel mode is largely an implementer's choice. Again, however, the purpose of this book is to present the strategies for implementing true kernel-mode drivers for real hardware.

Moving down a level, kernel-mode drivers can be further decomposed into two general categories, legacy and Windows Driver Model (WDM). Legacy drivers were fully described in the first edition of this book. The techniques needed to discover hardware and interface with the I/O subsystem are well documented. Thankfully, most of the knowledge gained by understanding legacy Windows NT drivers is transportable to the Windows 2000 (and Windows 98) WDM world.

WDM drivers are Plug and Play compliant. They support power management, autoconfiguration, and hot plugability. A correctly written WDM driver is usable on both Windows 2000 and Windows 98, though at present, Microsoft does not guarantee binary compatibility. At most, a rebuild of the driver source is necessary using the Windows 98 DDK (Device Driver Kit).

Moving down yet another level, legacy and WDM drivers can be further decomposed into three categories, high-level, intermediate, and low-level. As the names imply, a high-level driver depends on intermediate and low-level drivers to complete its work. An intermediate driver depends on a low-level driver to complete its work.

High-level drivers include file system drivers (FSDs). These drivers present a nonphysical abstraction to requestors that, in turn, is translated into specific device requests. The need to write a high-level driver is apparent when the underlying hardware services are already provided by lower levels—only a new abstraction is required for presentation to requestors.

Microsoft supplies an Installable File System (IFS) kit, sold separately from MSDN or any other product. The IFS kit requires the DDK (and other products) for successful file system development. There are numerous restrictions on the types of file systems that can be developed using this kit. For pricing and ordering information, you can visit the HWDEV virtual site of Microsoft's Internet site. This book does not address file system development.

Intermediate drivers include such drivers as *disk mirrors, class drivers, mini drivers,* and *filter drivers*. These drivers insert themselves between the higher-level abstractions and the lower-level physical support. For example, a disk mirror receiving the request from the high-level FSD to write to a file translates such a request into two requests of two different low-level disk drivers. Neither the higher nor lower levels need to be aware that mirroring is, in fact, occurring.

Class drivers are an elegant attempt at code reuse within the driver model. Since many drivers of a particular type have much in common, the common code can be placed in a generic *class* driver separate from the physical, device-specific code. For example, all IDE disk drivers share considerable similarity. It is possible to write the common code once, placing it in a generic class driver that loads as an intermediate driver. Vendor and device specific IDE drivers would then be written as *mini drivers* that interact with the generic class driver.

Filter drivers are intermediate drivers that intercept requests to an existing driver. They are given the opportunity to modify requests before presentation to the existing driver.

Finally, within the WDM world, intermediate drivers can also consist of *Functional Drivers*. These drivers can be either class or mini drivers, but they always act as an interface between an abstract I/O request and the low-level

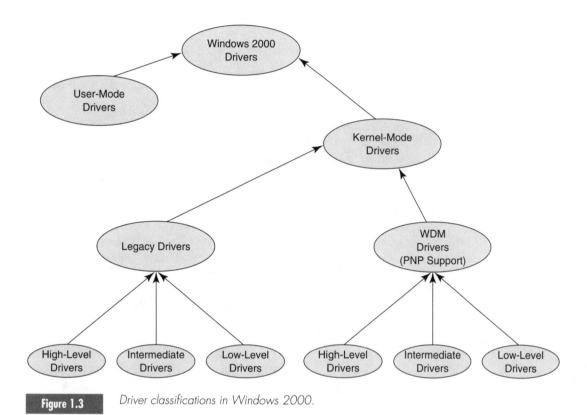

Figure 1.3   *Driver classifications in Windows 2000.*

physical driver code. Within the DDK documentation, the term *Functional Driver* is sometimes interchanged with Class or Mini Driver. The context determines the meaning.

Low-level drivers include controllers for the hardware buses. For example, the SCSI Host Bus Adapter is one such low-level driver. Such drivers interact with Windows 2000 HAL layer and/or the hardware directly. In the WDM world, low-level drivers include the notion of a *Physical Driver*. These Physical Drivers interact with one or more Functional Drivers.

Figure 1.3 shows the driver classifications in Windows 2000.

Special Driver Architectures

Building upon the intermediate driver strategy described in the last section, Microsoft supplies driver architectures for several types or classes of devices.

- Video drivers
- Printer drivers

- Multimedia drivers
- Network drivers

These architectures conform to the spirit, if not to the letter, of the classifications of the last section. Each architecture is described in more detail in the following sections.

Video Drivers

Video drivers in Windows 2000 present special requirements to the I/O subsystem. Because the graphical interface is constantly exposed to users, the apparent overall speed of the system is judged (often incorrectly) by the performance of this component. Competition among video adaptor hardware vendors has forced aggressive graphic accelerators to be included on high-end boards. The video driver architecture must exploit such hardware when it exists, yet provide full compatibility and capability when it does not. Finally, video drivers have evolved since the 16-bit world of Windows. There is a need to provide as much compatibility as possible with legacy drivers.

The video driver architecture of Windows 2000 is shown in Figure 1.4. The shaded components are provided with Windows 2000. Vendors of specific display adaptors supply the display driver. Since many display adaptors are designed using common chip sets, the chip set manufacturer supplies the video miniport *class driver* for its adaptor-manufacturing customers. For example, an ET4000 Miniport driver exists for all adaptors that utilize the ET4000 chip set. The extra hardware surrounding the chip set is driven with adaptor-specific display driver code.

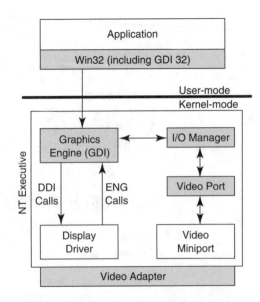

Figure 1.4   *Video driver architecture.*

Fundamentally, the video driver architecture differs from the standard I/O architecture in that user applications do not communicate directly with the I/O Manager when requesting drawing services. Instead, user-mode code interacts with a *Graphics Device Interface* (GDI) component of the kernel.

The GDI implements functions that allow the drawing of lines, shapes, and text in selected fonts. The GDI, therefore, is similar to a high-level driver. In turn, the GDI relies upon the services of the display driver and the I/O Manager to complete its work. Communication between the GDI and display driver is bidirectional. Where speed is paramount, the GDI can invoke functions in the display driver directly, bypassing the I/O Manager altogether. The display driver implements an interface known as the *Device Driver Interface* (DDI), which consists of functions prefixed with the **Drv** string. Conversely, the display driver relies on common graphics library routines implemented within the GDI. These GDI routines are known as *Graphics Engine calls* and are prefixed within the **Eng** string.

For less time-critical services, the GDI relies upon the traditional layered approach of the Windows 2000 I/O subsystem. The GDI uses the I/O Manager to invoke support routines of the video port and miniport intermediate drivers. An example of a function that would be implemented with port and miniport drivers would be a mode-switch command. Requests made by the I/O Manager of the video port driver are in the standard IRP format. The video port driver converts these IRPs into *Video Request Packets* (VRPs), which are then sent to and processed by the video miniport driver.

Printer Drivers

Printer drivers differ from standard Windows 2000 drivers in several ways. First, a print job may be directed to a spooling mechanism before being sent to a physical device. Second, the physical device is often connected to a remote machine, thus burdening the spool process with the use of RPC calls. Finally, the different printer stream protocols used by different printer devices (e.g., Postscript and HPCL) burden printer driver authors with yet another layer of integration.

The spooler components are shown in Figure 1.5. If spooling is enabled, an application's print job is first directed to a file by the spooler. The spooler then dequeues jobs as a printer (perhaps in a logical queue) becomes available. Data is passed to a print provider, which then directs the output to a local or remote printer.

The shaded components in Figure 1.5 are supplied with Windows 2000, as are several print providers. The client-side spooler component, *winspool.drv* or *Win32spl.DLL* (when remote printing), is simply an RPC-based client stub. It connects with a server-side RPC stub, *spoolsv.exe,* to implement a spooler API.

The server-side stub code relies on a routing service, *spoolss.dll,* which connects a specific print provider based on the target printer name. Finally,

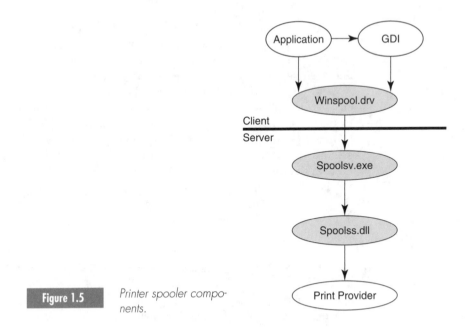

Figure 1.5   *Printer spooler components.*

the print provider acts as an abstract front-end for a specific print server or device. A specific device's job queue is created and managed by the print provider. A single print provider can serve the needs of an entire class of printers. Thus, the print providers supplied with Windows 2000 are usually sufficient to serve the needs of most applications and printers. A local, remote, and Internet print provider are included with Windows 2000.

Different print device characteristics, or perhaps different network protocols, sometimes require that a unique print provider be supplied. For example, Novell supplies a print provider for Windows 2000 that directs output to a NetWare print server.

Whether or not the spooling process is involved in a print job, it is the GDI which must ultimately render an application's drawing command into a printer-specific format. The GDI relies upon the services of the Printer Driver. The Printer Driver components consist of a Printer Graphics DLL and a Printer Interface DLL.

The printer graphics DLL is the component responsible for rendering data for a specific device. Depending on device capabilities, the work involved can range from *intense* for a bit-oriented device to *high-level* for a device supporting a full graphics engine (such as Postscript.) NT 4 required that this DLL reside in kernel mode, but the performance advantages of placing this code in the trusted category were not significant enough to outweigh the many disadvantages. In Windows 2000, the printer graphics DLL can reside in either user mode or kernel mode. Flexible configuration and higher system reliability result from placement of this DLL in user mode.

Each function exported by the printer graphics DLL is prefixed with the string **Drv.** The functions defined are invoked by the GDI when rendering is performed.

The printer interface DLL is responsible for configuration of device-specific parameters by providing a user interface for each device option. For example, a printer with multiple paper trays needs a way for a user to specify a default tray and paper size. The printer interface DLL provides user interfaces by building one or more property sheets. These sheets are a kind of Windows dialog, with standard Windows controls allowing selection of various options.

Multimedia Drivers

To support multimedia devices such as sound cards and TV tuners, Windows 2000 supports a new model known as *Kernel Streaming* (KS). Kernel Streaming consists of both Functional and Filter Drivers. Applications interact with a KS driver using Methods, Properties, and Events, familiar terms from the COM (Component Object Model) world. These mechanisms apply to four different kinds of KS objects exposed to an application: Filters, Pins, Clocks, and Allocators. Each KS object is exposed to an application as a standard I/O file object.

A filter object (which should not be confused with a filter driver) is the top-level entity exposed to an application performing multimedia operations. For example, an application might open a microphone filter on a sound card.

A pin object is a subobject of a filter. It represents a node (input or output) on a device. For example, the microphone filter might expose a single pin for input. An output pin could then be used to read, or acquire, the digitized signal.

A clock object exposes the real-time clock of a multimedia device, if equipped. The clock object may signal an application with an event when the clock timer expires or ticks.

Allocator objects represent the direct memory interface to a multimedia card. Memory on the card can be allocated or freed using this object.

Windows 2000 includes a generic class driver for streaming devices, *Stream.sys.* In most cases, it is only necessary to write a mini driver to support a specific device such as an audio card or video camera. The class driver implements the Windows 2000 Kernel Streaming abstraction, while the vendor-supplied mini driver utilizes the class driver's services, including buffer and DMA support, to support device-specific actions.

Network Drivers

Network drivers in Windows 2000 follow the Open Systems Interconnection (OSI) standard of ISO. This is a seven-layer model, with the top layer being the application software and the bottom layer being the physical hardware

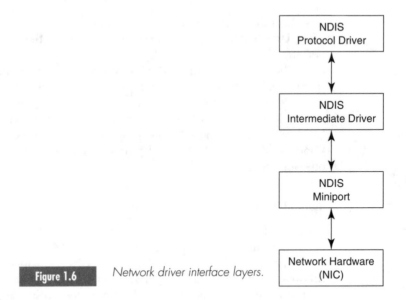

Figure 1.6	*Network driver interface layers.*

connection and topology of the network. Network Interface Cards (NIC) provide the hardware interface on most platforms for a given network. NIC drivers are written to support a specific device and Windows 2000 ships with popular NIC driver types. Separately, the OSI transport layer (the fourth layer up within the model) is provided by *protocol* drivers. It is possible to bind different protocols to the same physical NIC driver.

A Network Driver Interface Specification (NDIS) provides library support for NIC drivers that usually permits a NIC vendor to supply only an NDIS miniport driver to manage hardware specifics. Higher layers of NDIS, the NDIS intermediate driver and the NDIS protocol driver, provide media translations, filtering, and media-specific actions when required. The layering of NDIS is shown in Figure 1.6.

Windows 2000 includes a layer of kernel-mode software known as the Transport Driver Interface (TDI). This layer interfaces between the NDIS layer and higher-level software abstractions such as sockets and NetBIOS. The TDI layer makes the construction of Windows 2000 components such as the NetBIOS redirector and server easier and more portable.

Summary

Windows 2000 provides a rich architecture for applications to exploit. Of course, this richness comes at a price that device driver authors (among others) will have to pay. The I/O processing scheme of Windows 2000 is complex and the need to keep a view of the "big picture" is difficult, but necessary.

At this point, there should be a good understanding of what kinds of drivers exist (and where they fit) in Windows 2000. The next chapter begins a discussion of the hardware that drivers must control. An overview of the various buses that are supported by Windows 2000 is presented.

The Hardware Environment

CHAPTER OBJECTIVES

It is a fact of life that device drivers must interact with "real" hardware. Traditionally, first-generation device drivers were written as unit test code by the hardware designers. These early drivers were then passed to hardware-savvy software engineers to produce a fully-integrated driver.

As discussed in the previous chapter, the term *device driver* in Windows 2000 can describe a block of code miles away from any real hardware. Sooner or later, however, a device driver author must understand hardware and the terms sufficient to drive it. This chapter gives a gentle overview of hardware found on most systems.

Hardware Basics

Regardless of the type of device being driven, there are several basic items that must be known.

- How to use the device's control and status registers
- What causes the device to generate an interrupt

- How the device transfers data
- Whether the device uses any dedicated memory
- How the device announces its presence when attached
- How the device is configured, preferably through software

The following sections discuss each of these topics in a general way.

Device Registers

Drivers communicate with a peripheral by reading and writing registers associated with the device. Each device register generally performs one of the following functions:

Command. Bits in these registers *control* the device in some way—perhaps starting or aborting a data transfer or configuring the device—and are typically *written* by the driver.

Status. These registers are typically *read* by the driver to discover the current state of the device.

Data. These registers are used to transfer data between device and driver. Output data registers are *written* by the driver, while input data registers are *read* by the driver.

Simple devices (like the parallel port interface in Table 2.1) have only a few associated registers, while complex hardware (like graphics adapters) have many registers. The number and purpose of the registers is ultimately defined by the hardware designer and *should* be well documented in the Hardware Design Specification. Often, however, trial and error is required on the part of the driver author to determine the *real* behavior of bits in the various device registers. Further, experience shows that "reserved" bits in a register do not necessarily mean "don't care" bits. It is usually best to mask out these bits when reading, and to force them to zero when writing registers with reserved bits.

Accessing Device Registers

Once the hardware functions are known, there is still the small matter of knowing how to programmatically *reference* the device's registers. To do this, two additional pieces of information are required.

- The address of the device's first register
- The address *space* where the registers live

Usually, device registers occupy consecutive locations. Therefore, the address of the first register is a necessary clue in gaining access to all others. Unfortunately, the term *address* has varied meanings in a virtual address space on different platforms, so a complete discussion of this topic will have to wait until chapter 8. In general terms, however, device registers are ac-

Table 2.1	Parallel Port Interface Registers

Parallel port registers			
Offset	**Register**	**Access**	**Description**
0	Data	R/W	Data byte transferred through parallel port
1	Status	R/O	Current parallel port status
	Bits 0-1		Reserved
	Bit 2		0 - interrupt has been requested by port
	Bit 3		0 - an error has occurred
	Bit 4		1 - printer is selected
	Bit 5		1 - printer out of paper
	Bit 6		0 - acknowledge
	Bit 7		0 - printer busy
2	Control	R/W	Commands sent to parallel port
	Bit 0		1 - strobe data to/from parallel port
	Bit 1		1 - automatic line feed
	Bit 2		0 - initialize printer
	Bit 3		1 - select printer
	Bit 4		1 - enable interrupt
	Bits 5 – 7		Reserved

cessed by the CPU in one of two ways: through CPU-specific I/O instructions or through standard memory reference instructions. Figure 2.1 depicts the two methods. Each of these methods is explained briefly in the following sections.

I/O SPACE REGISTERS

Some CPU architectures (notably Intel x86) reference device registers using *I/O machine instructions.* These special instructions reference a specific set of pins on the CPU and therefore define a separate bus and address space for I/O devices. Addresses on this bus are sometimes known as *ports* and are completely separate from any memory address. On the Intel x86 architecture, the I/O address space is 64 KB in size (16 bits), and the assembly language defines two instructions for reading and writing ports in this space: **IN** and **OUT.**

Of course, as discussed in the first chapter, driver code should be platform-independent, so references to the actual IN and OUT instructions should be avoided. Instead, one of several HAL macros listed in Table 2.2 should be used.

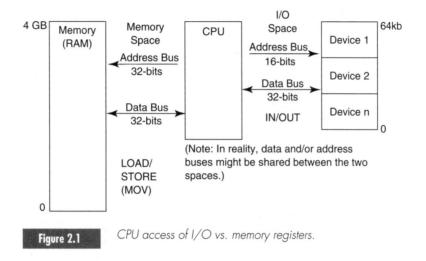

Figure 2.1   *CPU access of I/O vs. memory registers.*

MEMORY-MAPPED REGISTERS

Not all CPU architects see the need for a separate I/O address space, in which case device registers are mapped directly into the memory space of the CPU. Motorola processors are one such example. Similarly, it is possible (and common) to design hardware devices that interface to the memory address and data buses of a CPU even when that CPU supports separate I/O space. In some cases, devices (e.g., a video adapter) will touch *both* I/O and memory space.

Devices that expose large data buffers usually map into memory space. This allows fast and convenient access from high-level languages such as C. The simple and familiar dereferencing of a pointer permits direct access to a device's buffer.

As before, the HAL provides a set of macros for accessing memory-mapped device registers and these are listed in Table 2.3. Since these macros differ from the I/O space HAL macros, a device that must be supported on

Table 2.2   *HAL Macros to Access Ports in I/O Space*

HAL I/O Space Macros	
Function	**Description**
READ_PORT_XXX	Read a single value from an I/O port
WRITE_PORT_XXX	Write a single value to an I/O port
READ_PORT_BUFFER_XXX	Read an array of values from consecutive I/O ports
WRITE_PORT_BUFFER_XXX	Write an array of values to consecutive I/O ports

| Table 2.3 | *HAL Memory-Mapped Register Macros* |

HAL Memory-Mapped Register Macros

Function	Description
READ_REGISTER_XXX	Read a single value from an I/O register
WRITE_REGISTER_XXX	Write a single value to an I/O register
READ_REGISTER_BUFFER_XXX	Read an array of values from consecutive I/O registers
WRITE_REGISTER_BUFFER_XXX	Write an array of values to consecutive I/O registers

two different platforms (with different register access techniques) must be cleverly written. It is common to write a driver-specific macro that points to one of two HAL macros, depending on the presence of a unique compiler symbol. Techniques listed later in this book describe this process more fully.

Device Interrupts

Since devices typically perform their hardware actions in parallel with and asynchronous to normal CPU operation, it is common for devices to signal or generate an *interrupt* when CPU driver attention is required. Different CPUs have different mechanisms for being interrupted, but there is always one (or more) pin that can be driven or yanked by a device when service is needed. It is then the responsibility of the CPU to save the CPU state and context of the currently running code path before jumping into a driver-supplied Interrupt Service Routine.

Devices generate interrupts at strategic points in time, including

- When the device has completed a previously requested operation and is now ready for an additional request.
- When a buffer or FIFO of the device is almost full (during input) or almost empty (during output). This interrupt allows the driver an opportunity to empty (input) or refill (output) the buffer to keep the device operating without pause.
- When the device encounters an error condition during an operation. This is really just a special form of a completed operation.

Devices which do not generate interrupts can cause serious system performance degradation. Since the CPU is shared among many running threads on Windows 2000, it is not acceptable to allow a driver to steal precious cycles just waiting in a tight loop for a device operation to complete. Later chapters present some techniques that can be used when working with non-interrupting devices.

With the complex world of PC hardware, buses connect to other buses through an interface, or bridge. As a result, the source of an interrupt (e.g., a device) is often several hardware layers away from the CPU. The techniques for prioritization and signaling are therefore distorted along the real path to the CPU. Nevertheless, interrupts can be characterized as having several properties.

INTERRUPT PRIORITY

When several devices need attention at the same time, there needs to be a mechanism to describe which device is serviced first. Presumably the most important device or the device that can least afford to wait is given the highest priority. If a device can wait, it is assigned a lower interrupt priority. The assignment of an interrupt priority to a device is a configuration option. Hopefully, this priority can be assigned by software during device initialization.

Interrupt priority means that while the CPU is servicing a lower priority device (i.e., executing its Interrupt Service Routine) a higher priority device can still interrupt. In such a case, the CPU has taken, or accepted, two interrupts—the second on top of the first. Conversely, if a higher priority device is being serviced, lower priority interrupts are held off (and presumably not lost) until the higher priority interrupt service is completed and dismissed.

INTERRUPT VECTORS

Some devices and/or CPU architectures allow an interrupt to automatically dispatch (i.e., jump) to a software-defined function for servicing of the interrupt. Without interrupt vector capability, a common interrupt service routine must be supplied for all interrupt types. This common routine would then have to poll through a list of possible interrupting devices (in priority order) to determine the actual device requiring service. Since real systems handle tens to hundreds of interrupts per second, vectoring of interrupts can be considerably more efficient.

SIGNALING MECHANISMS

There are two basic strategies that devices use when generating an interrupt. An older, less desirable mechanism is known as *edge-triggered* or *latched* interrupts. Devices which generate edge-triggered interrupts signal their need for service by producing a *transition* on a hardware line, perhaps from 1 to 0. Once the transition has been generated, the device might release the line, restoring it to a logical 1 level. In other words, the interrupt line is *pulsed* by the device and it is the responsibility of the CPU to notice the pulse when it occurs.

Latched interrupts are subject to false signaling, since noise on the interrupt line may look like a pulse to the CPU. Much worse, however, is the problem that occurs when two devices attempt to share a single edge-triggered line. If the two devices signal simultaneously, the CPU recognizes only a single interrupt. Since the pulse occurs at an instant in time, the fact that two (instead of one) devices needed service is forever lost.

The classic example of lost edge-triggered interrupts occurred with old serial COM ports. Traditionally, COM1 and COM3 shared a single edge-triggered x86 interrupt, IRQ4. As a result, both ports could not be used simultaneously with interrupt-driven software. Attempts to use a mouse on COM1 with a modem on COM3 invariably led to a frozen situation for either the mouse or modem driver, which remained waiting for the lost interrupt to occur.

Such limitations do not occur when working with a level-sensitive, or level-triggered signaling mechanism. Devices using this technique signal their intent to interrupt by keeping a hardware line driven until their need is met. The CPU can detect an interrupt at any time since the line remains yanked until serviced. Thus, two or more devices can safely share a level-sensitive interrupt. When two interrupts occur simultaneously, the higher priority device can be safely serviced, knowing that the other device is continuing to signal its intentions by continually driving the line.

PROCESSOR AFFINITY

When a hardware system includes more than one processor, an issue of how interrupts are handled is raised. Is the device's interrupt line wired to only one CPU or to all? Usually, a special piece of hardware exists to allow for a driver's configuration and distribution of the interrupt signal. If a particular CPU can service a device's interrupt, those interrupts are said to have *affinity* to that CPU. Forcing interrupts to a specific CPU might be used as an attempt to control device load balancing among several CPUs and devices.

Data Transfer Mechanisms

There are three basic mechanisms that a device may use to move data to or from the CPU or memory.

- Programmed I/O
- Direct memory access (DMA)
- Shared buffers

The transfer mechanism selected by a hardware designer is largely dictated by the device's speed and the average size of data transfer. Of course, a device may choose to use more than one mechanism to transfer its data.

The following sections describe the differences between the three techniques.

PROGRAMMED I/O

Programmed I/O (PIO) devices transfer data directly through data registers of the device. Driver code must issue an I/O instruction to read or write the data register for each byte of data. Software buffer addresses and byte counts must be kept as state of the driver for larger transfers.

Since the actual device transfer rate is probably much slower than the time required by the CPU to write or read a data register, a PIO device typically interrupts once for each byte (or word) of data transferred. Serial COM ports are an example of PIO devices. Better hardware includes a FIFO in front of the real hardware, thus allowing one interrupt for every 4 or 16 bytes transferred. Still, the ratio of interrupts to bytes transferred remains high for PIO devices, and the technique is suitable only for slow devices.

Clever software design techniques can minimize the performance impact of PIO devices. Such techniques are discussed in chapter 8.

DIRECT MEMORY ACCESS

Direct memory access (DMA) devices take advantage of a secondary processor called a *DMA controller* (DMAC). A DMAC is a very limited auxiliary processor with just enough intelligence (and state) to transfer a specified number of bytes between a device and memory. The DMAC operates in parallel with the main CPU(s), and its operations typically have little effect on overall system performance.

To initiate an I/O operation, the driver must set up or program the DMAC by supplying a starting buffer address for the transfer along with a byte transfer count. When the order to start is given by the driver, the DMAC operates without further software intervention, moving bytes between device and system RAM. When the DMAC completes the entire transfer, an interrupt is generated. Thus, driver code executes only at the beginning of a transfer and at the completion of a transfer, freeing the CPU to perform other tasks.

High-speed devices that routinely need to transfer large blocks of data are well suited to utilize DMA. Interrupt overhead and driver activity is significantly reduced as compared to PIO operation. Disks, multimedia devices, and network cards are all examples of DMA devices.

It should be pointed out that the actual DMA transfer is not really transparent to other system operation. The DMAC secondary processor competes for memory bandwidth with the CPU(s) of the system. If the CPU is referencing main memory frequently, either the CPU or the DMAC must be held off while the previous memory cycle completes. Of course, with today's large CPU cache sizes, a CPU seldom places massive demand on memory bandwidth. A system with a large number of bus master DMA devices, however, may find that memory bandwidth is saturated as the devices compete with each other during simultaneous transfers.

DMA Mechanisms

Chapter 12 covers the details of DMA transfer, but to complete the overview of DMA now, there are two general types of DMA operation.

SYSTEM DMA

The original PC specification by IBM (and subsequent standards) included a mainboard (a.k.a. motherboard) with a set of community DMACs. Each DMAC is known as a DMA *channel,* and a given device can be configured to utilize one (or more) of the available channels. There were originally four channels, which expanded to seven with the introduction of the AT. System DMA is also known as *slave DMA.*

The advantage of using system DMA is that the amount of hardware logic for DMA on a device is reduced. The disadvantage is that when devices share a channel, only one at a time may actually participate in a DMA transfer. At any given time, the DMA channel is "owned" by a single device—others attempting to utilize the channel must wait their turn until the first device relinquishes ownership. This sharing situation would not work well for two high-speed, busy devices. The floppy controller in most PCs is an example of slave DMA operation.

BUS MASTER DMA

More complicated devices that do not wish to share DMAC hardware include their own customized DMA hardware. Because the hardware to perform DMA is on-board the controller itself, ownership is always guaranteed and transfers occur at will. SCSI controllers are often DMA bus masters.

Device-Dedicated Memory

The third type of data transfer mechanism that a device may use is *shared memory.* There are two general reasons why a device may wish to borrow (or own) system memory address space.

RAM or ROM might be a resource that is device-resident. For convenient, high-speed access by the driver code, it might make sense to *map* a view of the device's memory into CPU memory space. As an example, the device might contain a ROM with startup code and data. In order for the CPU to execute this code, it first must be mapped into the visible address space of the CPU.

The device may contain a high-speed specialized processor that relies on system memory for its buffer needs. A video capture card, for example, might make use of system memory to record the video image being streamed into it. Note that this second reason for borrowed address space is really a kind of DMA operation. In this case, the secondary processor is more intelligent and capable of more operation than a simple DMAC.

Devices generally take one of two approaches to deal with dedicated memory. Some specify a hard-coded range of physical addresses for their use. A VGA video adapter card, for example, specifies a 128 KB range of addresses beginning at 0xA0000 for its video buffer.

Other devices allow an initialization routine to specify the base address of the dedicated memory with software. This latter technique is more flexible, but Windows 2000 allows for either method to work with the operating system.

Auto-recognition and Auto-configuration

Every hardware device consumes PC resources. These resources consist of an I/O address range, an IRQ, a DMA channel, and perhaps a range of dedicated memory addresses. Since different devices are made at different times by different vendors, the possibility for conflict of resources is high—inevitable, in fact.

The first PCs required that an intelligent owner configure each device by setting jumpers, or DIP switches, to assign unique resources to each card within a system. The installation of a new device required knowledge of what system resources were already assigned to existing devices. Errors in this manual configuration process were common, with the net result being an unbootable system, a system with intermittent crashes, or unusable devices.

New bus architectures have been introduced that deal directly with the problem of automatic recognition and configuration. Autorecognition is necessary so new devices added to a system report their presence. This could happen at boot/reset time, or better yet, as soon as the new hardware is inserted. Buses and hardware that support hot plugability allow software to safely add and remove hardware without a reboot.

Auto-configuration allows software to assign available resources to software-configurable hardware. This feature allows naive users to install new hardware without first setting jumpers. The operating system ultimately remains in charge of assignment of resources to various devices, whether installed prior to or post-boot.

Considerable effort is spent in subsequent chapters describing the protocol Windows 2000 uses to support auto recognition and configuration. It should be apparent, however, that regardless of the device and bus type, a well-behaved device must support several features.

DEVICE RESOURCE LISTS

At a minimum, a device must identify itself and provide the system with a list of resources that it consumes. The list should include

- Manufacturer ID
- Device type ID
- I/O space requirements

- Interrupt requirements
- DMA channel requirements
- Device memory requirements

NO JUMPERS OR SWITCHES

To support auto-configuration, the device must allow authorized software to dynamically set and change port, interrupt, and DMA channel assignments. This permits Windows 2000 to arbitrate resource conflicts among competing devices.

CHANGE NOTIFICATION

The device, in conjunction with the bus to which it attaches, must generate a notification signal whenever the device is inserted or removed. Without this feature, it is not possible to support hot-plugability or auto-recognition.

Buses and Windows 2000

A *bus* is a collection of data, address, and control signal lines that allow devices to communicate. Some buses are wide, allowing simultaneous transmission of many bits of data and control. Others are nothing more than a single wire, allowing devices to transmit data and control in a serial fashion. Some buses allow any device to communicate with any other device on the bus. Others require the presence of a master controller (e.g., a CPU or I/O controller) that is the sole recipient or sender of data.

Buses gain and lose popularity over time. Trade-offs between speed, cost, extensibility, and ease of use change as bus technology advances. Device requirements change as new technologies are introduced into the PC world. For example, the common use of digital video on home PCs has produced a need for a simple, ultra-high speed bus.

The device driver architecture of Windows 2000 supports new buses easily and efficiently. Many popular buses are supported "out of the box." The remainder of this section describes the currently supported buses on Windows 2000. The descriptions are meant to provide an overview of the bus technology. For more detailed information, please refer to the bibliography.

ISA: The Industry Standard Architecture

This is the bus that IBM specified for the PC/AT in the early 1980s. It supports 8-bit and 16-bit devices. Because its origins are two decades old, ISA is neither fast nor simple. The bus clock rate is 8.33 MHz. Since even 16-bit transfers take at least two clock cycles, the maximum transfer rate is only about 8 MB/second. Since current CPU speeds are two orders of magnitude faster,

ISA is no longer a relevant bus. Its inclusion in Windows 2000 and this book are for backward compatibility reasons only.

REGISTER ACCESS

ISA is the bus by which the need for autorecognition and autoconfiguration were defined. That is, ISA provides the definition for bus chaos. No standards exist for register usage, so devices may grab any I/O address. Generally, I/O addresses between 0x0000 and 0x00FF belong only to devices on the mainboard. Territory between 0x0100 and 0x03FF is available for plug-in cards. Each card is typically assigned a 32-byte contiguous range of register addresses.

Sadly, many legacy ISA cards do not decode all 16 I/O address lines. Instead, they decode only the first 10 bits of address. Such cards respond to alias addresses in multiples of 0x400. A device at address 0x300 also responds at address 0x700. When such devices are present in a system, the 64 KB I/O address range diminishes quickly.

INTERRUPT MECHANISMS

Interrupts on an ISA bus are traditionally handled with two Intel 8259A programmable interrupt controller (PIC) chips (or an emulation thereof.) Each PIC provides eight levels of interrupt priority which, in essence, multiplex eight lines into one. One of the eight input lines (line 2, to be precise) from the first (master) chip routes to the output of the other (slave) PIC, which cascades the sixteen inputs from both chips into a single output. Of course, since one input is lost to the cascade configuration, only 15 lines are left for devices to utilize. Table 2.4 lists the ISA priority levels and their typical assignments.

The 8259A chip can be programmed to respond to either edge-triggered or level-sensitive interrupts. This choice must be made for the entire chip, not on a line-by-line basis. Traditional BIOS code initializes both PICs to use edge-triggered interrupts. Therefore, on typical systems, ISA cards may not share IRQ lines. Some main boards that perform custom emulation of the 8259A do allow IRQ-by-IRQ programming for edge vs. level triggering.

DMA CAPABILITIES

The standard implementation of ISA DMA uses a pair of Intel 8237 DMAC chips (or an emulation thereof). Each of these chips provides four independent DMA channels. As with the PICs, the standard configuration cascades the two chips, routing the output of the master DMAC through the first channel of the slave DMAC. As before, the cascading technique results in the loss of one channel, leaving seven free for DMA devices. Table 2.5 describes the channel configurations for the two DMACs.

When more than one DMA channel is in simultaneous use, the DMAC chips follow a software-selected scheme for prioritization. Typically, highest priority is given to channel 0 and lowest to channel 7. Also note that only the

Table 2.4	Interrupt Priorities on ISA Systems

ISA Interrupt Priority Sequence

Priority	IRQ Line	Controller	Use for...
Highest	0	Master	System timer
	1	Master	Keyboard
	2	Master	(Unavailable—pass through from slave)
	8	Slave	Real-time clock alarm
	9	Slave	(Available)
	10	Slave	(Available)
	11	Slave	(Available)
	12	Slave	(Available—usually the mouse)
	13	Slave	Error output of numeric coprocessor
	14	Slave	(Available—usually the hard disk)
	15	Slave	(Available)
	3	Master	2nd serial port
	4	Master	1st serial port
	5	Master	2nd parallel port
	6	Master	Floppy disk controller
Lowest	7	Master	1st parallel port

slave DMAC can be used to transfer words (16 bits). These upper channels can transfer data at twice the rate of the lower channels, since they move two bytes per cycle.

Finally, the ISA bus has only 24 address lines. This restricts DMA transfers to only the first 16 MB of system memory. This artifact leaves Windows 2000 with a special problem when dealing with ISA DMA transfers, and chapter 12 discusses the resolution to this complication.

Table 2.5	DMA Channel Usage on the ISA Bus

ISA DMA Channels

Channel	Controller	Transfer Width	Max Transfer
0–3	Master	8 bits (bytes)	64 KB
4	Slave	(Unavailable)	N/A
5–7	Slave	16 bits (words)	128 KB

AUTOMATIC RECOGNITION AND CONFIGURATION

As already mentioned, ISA is the poster child for highlighting the need for dynamic configuration of devices. ISA devices don't announce themselves, they don't provide a resource requirements list, and they are not required to provide software dynamic configuration. Configuration is manual and typically performed with jumpers or DIP switches.

Newer ISA devices attempt to correct this problem by conforming to a Plug and Play extension to the ISA standard. These devices gained considerable popularity with the introduction of the Windows 95 operating system. Versions of NT prior to Windows 2000 did not really support Plug and Play, so these devices relied on a special installation program to operate properly with NT. Windows 2000, however, correctly supports these newer ISA devices and exploits their capabilities.

EISA: The Extended Industry Standard Architecture

The EISA bus is an industry standard extension to the original ISA bus architecture. The attempt of EISA was to remove the ISA limitations without causing undue compatibility problems with legacy ISA cards.

Of course, this compatibility requirement necessarily limits the architecture in several ways. For example, while the data bus width was widened to 32 bits, the clock rate remains at 8 MHz. The maximum transfer rate is only about 32 MB/sec. Also, since EISA sockets had to accept ISA cards, it was impossible to fix some electrical noise problems caused by the layout of ISA wiring.

REGISTER ACCESS

The EISA bus contains up to 15 slots or sockets. Each slot is assigned a fixed range of 4 KB I/O addresses, thus minimizing port resource conflict. Table 2.6 lists the I/O address ranges assigned to each socket. Since ISA presents an aliasing problem (ISA devices respond to addresses in multiples of 0x400), only 256 bytes of register address space is guaranteed to be unique.

INTERRUPT MECHANISMS

EISA's interrupt capabilities are a superset of the ISA scheme. While EISA interrupt controllers provide the same 15 levels available on the ISA bus (see Table 2.4), each IRQ line can be individually programmed for edge-triggered or level-sensitive operation. This allows both ISA and EISA cards to coexist on the same bus.

DMA CAPABILITIES

As with ISA systems, two ganged DMAC's provide seven independent system DMA channels, numbered 0 through 7. (Channel 4 remains unavailable as it is the tie point for the two devices.)

Table 2.6	*I/O Space Used by EISA Systems*

EISA I/O Address Ranges

Address Range	Used by...
0x0400 – 0x04FF	EISA system board devices
0x0800 – 0x08FF	EISA system board devices
0x0C00 – 0x0CFF	EISA system board devices
0x1000 – 0x1FFF	EISA card slot 1
0x2000 – 0x2FFF	EISA card slot 2
:	:
0xF000 – 0xFFF	EISA card slot 15

The EISA architecture extends the ISA DMA model in several ways. First, any of the seven channels can perform 8-bit, 16-bit, or 32-bit data transfers. Thus, any device can use any channel.

EISA DMA channels can also be individually programmed to use a variety of different bus cycle formats. This permits new devices to run faster while still maintaining compatibility with legacy ISA cards. Table 2.7 describes the EISA DMA bus cycles.

Table 2.7	*The EISA DMA Bus Cycles*

EISA DMA Bus Cycle Formats

Bus Cycle	Transfer Size	Transfer Rate	Compatible with
ISA compatible	8-bit	1.0 MB/sec	Any ISA
	16-bit	2.0 MB/sec	Any ISA
Type A	8-bit	1.3 MB/sec	Most ISA
	16-bit	2.6 MB/sec	Most ISA
	32-bit	5.3 MB/sec	EISA only
Type B	8-bit	2.0 MB/sec	Some ISA
	16-bit	4.0 MB/sec	Some ISA
	32-bit	8.0 MB/sec	EISA only
Type C (Burst)	8-bit	8.2 MB/sec	EISA only
	16-bit	16.5 MB/sec	EISA only
	32-bit	33.0 MB/sec	EISA only

Another enhancement is the EISA DMAC's 24-bit count register. For 8-bit, 16-bit, and 32-bit devices, this register counts bytes, thus allowing a single transfer operation to move up to 16 MB. For compatibility, the DMAC can be programmed to use this as a word counter for 16-bit transfers.

Finally, since EISA DMAC's generate full 32-bit addresses, they can access the entire 4 GB physical address space of the system. There is no restriction placed on DMA transfers occurring in the first 16 MB range as there is with ISA.

DEVICE MEMORY

The EISA bus has 32 address lines. Device-dedicated memory can live anywhere within the system's 4 GB address range. This also applies to any on-board ROM the device might have.

AUTO RECOGNITION AND CONFIGURATION

Several components take part in the EISA configuration process. First, each card is required to implement a 4-byte ID register at location 0xnC80, where n is the EISA slot number from 1 to 0xA. This register identifies the manufacturer, the device type, and the revision level of the card placed in that slot.

Second, designers can use the remaining 124 bytes (from 0xnC84 to 0xnCFF) to implement other registers that configure the card. For example, there might be a configuration register for the DMA channel number the card should use, and another for setting its IRQ level. Storing values into these registers is the equivalent of setting DIP switches and jumpers on legacy ISA cards.

The third component is a script file that contains the card's resource list and defines the location and usage of any device-specific configuration registers on the card. This file is written in a standard EISA scripting language, and its name is based on the contents of the card's ID register. This script usually comes on a floppy disk supplied by the card's manufacturer.

The final piece of the puzzle is an EISA configuration program that runs when a system boots. The program scans the EISA slots, looking for cards in previously empty locations. If it finds one, it uses the contents of the slot's ID register to construct the name of a configuration script and then asks the user for the floppy containing that script. Once the disk is inserted, the configuration program assigns resources to the card. It also copies these assignments to nonvolatile CMOS memory associated with the slot, so it won't be necessary to ask for the script file with each boot.

Windows 2000 auto-detects many kinds of EISA cards. To gain access to EISA slots directly, the HAL provides **HalGetBusData** and **HalSetBusData.**

PCI: The Peripheral Component Interconnect

Fast networks, full-motion video, and 24-bit pixel displays all require extremely high data transfer rates. The PCI bus is an attempt to satisfy the needs of such demanding hardware. Although the initial design came from Intel,

PCI is relatively processor-neutral. PCI has been incorporated into Alpha (DEC) and PowerPC (Motorola) systems. Figure 2.2 shows a typical PCI system.

By using a fast bus clock (33 MHz) and a number of clever tricks, the PCI architecture can reach 132 MB/second for sustained 32-bit transfers and twice that rate for 64-bit operations. Some things that contribute to this zippy performance include:

- The PCI protocol assumes that every transfer is going to be a burst operation. This results in higher throughput rates for fast devices trying to move large amounts of data.
- PCI supports multiple bus masters and permits direct device-to-device transfers (with no intermediate stops in memory). This can result in much more overlap between I/O and CPU operations.
- A central bus arbiter reduces latency by overlapping arbitration with data transfers. This allows the next owner to start on operation as soon as the current owner releases the bus.
- An intelligent bridge between the host CPU and the PCI bus performs various caching and read-ahead functions. This helps to reduce the amount of time the CPU spends waiting for data.

The PCI architecture allows 32 physical units (called *devices*) to be plugged into one bus. Each of these physical units can contain up to eight

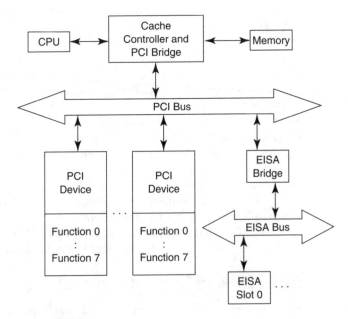

Figure 2.2   *Typical PCI bus system.*

separate functional units (called *functions*). After taking away one function address for generating broadcast messages, there can be up to 255 addressable functions on a single PCI bus. Furthermore, one system can have up to 256 separate PCI buses.

REGISTER ACCESS

Although the PCI uses 32-bit addresses, I/O register space on 80x86 machines is still limited to 64 kilobytes, so any PCI registers have to be squeezed into I/O space along with everything else. Furthermore, on systems with an EISA or ISA bridge, designers still need to avoid any I/O addresses being used by legacy hardware.

Along with I/O space and memory addresses, PCI defines a range of addresses known as *configuration space*. The discussion of PCI autoconfiguration explains how configuration space works.

INTERRUPT MECHANISMS

The PCI bus has four equal-priority interrupt request lines (INTA-INTD) which are active-low, level-triggered, and shareable. A single-function PCI device has to use INTA, while a multifunction device can use any sequential combination of the four beginning with INTA. The only restriction is that each function can be connected to only one request line.

The PCI specification is relatively neutral when it comes to interrupt priorities. Instead, it depends on an external controller to redirect PCI interrupt requests to the proper system interrupt line. For example, on a PC the redirector converts a given PCI function's request on INTA-INTD into a request on one of the IRQ0-IRQ15 lines. To make this work, any PCI function that generates interrupts must implement the following two configuration registers:

- **Interrupt pin register.** This read-only register identifies the PCI signal line (INTA-INTD) used by this function.
- **Interrupt line register.** This read-write register specifies the priority and vector that the interrupt redirector should assign to this function. On a PC system, the values 0x00-0x0F correspond to IRQ0-IRQ15.

This is a very flexible scheme because it doesn't impose any specific interrupt policies on the system designer. This makes it easier to support processor environments other than the 80x86.

DMA CAPABILITIES

The PCI specification doesn't include the notion of slave DMA. Instead, the native PCI functions are either bus masters doing their own DMA or they use programmed I/O. The only devices that perform slave DMA on a PCI machine are non-PCI boards plugged into the system's EISA bridge.

In a native PCI DMA operation, the participants are referred to as *agents*, and there are always two of them involved in any transaction.

- **Initiator.** This is a bus master that has won access to the bus and wants to set up a transfer operation.
- **Target.** This is the PCI function currently being addressed by the initiator with the goal of transferring data.

Because any PCI bus master can be an initiator, it is possible to transfer data directly between two PCI devices with no intermediate stops in memory. This powerful capability lends itself well to high-speed networking and video applications.

It's also worth mentioning that the PCI specification doesn't define the policy to be used for arbitrating access to the bus. It only defines the timing of the arbitration signals on the bus. The method used to determine who should go next is system-specific.

DEVICE MEMORY

Dedicated memory used by PCI functions can live anywhere within the 32-bit address space. This feature must be enabled on a function-by-function basis, however, before the PCI device's memory can be seen by the host CPU.

An interesting feature of PCI is that a single function can have multiple on-board ROM images, each for a different CPU architecture. This gives vendors the ability to sell the same product in several different markets. The PCI specification defines a standard header format for ROM blocks. Thus, the initialization software can locate the proper chunk of ROM and load it into memory for execution.

AUTOCONFIGURATION

The PCI specification dictates that each individual function on the bus must have its own 256-byte storage area for configuration data. This area is referred to as the PCI function's *configuration space*.

The first 64 bytes of any PCI function's configuration space (called the *header*) have a predetermined structure, while the remaining 192 bytes belong to the card designer. System software can use the header to identify a PCI function and assign resources to it. The header area includes

- Information about the vendor, the device type, and its revision level.
- A standard pair of command status registers for enabling various features and reporting errors.
- A resource list that specifies the function's memory and I/O space requirements.
- The interrupt pin and line registers described above.
- Pointers to device-specific ROM.

At 256 bytes per function, the configuration space for a PCI system could easily grow quite large—certainly much larger than the 64 KB I/O space available on x86 processors. Mapping it into memory is always an option, but that too would consume a lot of address space. Instead, PCI functions may access configuration data using the following two registers:

- **Configuration address register.** This identifies the bus number, the device, the function, and the address in configuration space accessed.
- **Configuration data register.** This acts as a data buffer between the CPU and configuration space. After setting the address register, writing or reading this register transfers information to or from configuration space.

Fortunately, Windows 2000 provides HAL functions to simplify access to configuration data. The **HalGetBusData, HalSetBusData,** and **HalAssignSlotResources** functions provide a simple way to access this data.

USB: The Universal Serial Bus

A consortium of companies (including Intel and Microsoft) developed the Universal Serial Bus specification. It was intended to provide a low-cost, medium-speed bus for such areas as digital imaging, PC telephony, and multimedia games. The current USB specification is revision 1.1, and the list of member companies which participate in the consortium continues to grow. A much higher-speed USB proposal is set forth in revision 2.0.

Full-speed USB devices transfer data at a rate of 12 Mb/second. Low-speed devices use a slower transfer rate of 1.5 Mb/second. USB version 2.0 should allow data transfer at the rate of 480 Mb/sec. Data is transferred serially over a pair of data wires. Power for some devices is available via separate power and ground wires.

Interestingly, USB devices can transfer data at about one-fifth the rate of ISA cards, but without the limitation of needing a mainboard slot. Devices can be connected over a distance of about 5 meters, but USB hubs are also available which extend the range and provide for multiple device connections to a single USB bus. Up to five hubs can be chained together, providing a possible connection distance of almost 30 meters. An example topology of USB devices and hubs is shown in Figure 2.3.

REGISTER ACCESS

Device registers are accessed using specific USB *commands*, 8-bit to 64-bit streams that are used to configure, control power, and retrieve small amounts of device data. Up to 127 USB devices can be connected to a host, with a bus-relative address assigned dynamically as devices are added. The transmission

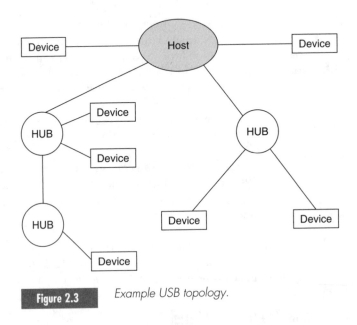

| **Figure 2.3** | *Example USB topology.* |

of command data is largely device-specific, so the number and meaning of device commands is defined by each device.

Separately, block data is transferred using an isochronous mechanism. Up to 1023 bytes of data can be transferred in a single USB *frame*. A frame occupies a fixed time interval of 1 millisecond. Command and block data access occurs over a logical abstraction defined by USB as a *pipe*. The *default pipe* is used to convey command data, while any number of *stream* and *message* pipes can be used to transfer data directly to higher software layers.

INTERRUPT MECHANISMS

For USB, true interrupts do not actually exist. Instead, the host USB interface polls devices for *interrupt data* at fixed intervals, usually every 16 to 32 millisecond. The device is allowed to send up to 64 bytes of data to the host when polled.

From a driver's perspective, the interrupt and DMA capabilities of USB are in fact defined by the host adapter that contains the physical USB interface. Considerable effort has been placed on the standardization of the host interface, and two have emerged: the Open Host Controller Inter-face (OpenHCI) and the Universal Host Controller Interface (UHCI). The host controller provides a conventional interrupt and DMA transfer mechanism.

DMA CAPABILITIES

USB devices have no direct access to system memory. They are isolated from system resources by the host USB interface. USB devices do not support DMA.

Nevertheless, the USB host interface provides an illusion of DMA for each logical pipe connected to a device. As the host interface collects data from a USB device, it uses DMA to place the received data into system memory. Thus, it is the host interface, not the USB device itself, which provides DMA capability. The bus type to which the host interface connects defines the DMA rules.

AUTOMATIC RECOGNITION AND CONFIGURATION

USB was designed to support Plug and Play directly and intelligently. Each USB device attaching to a USB port or hub signals its presence and reports manufacturer ID and device descriptor. Windows 2000 supports Plug and Play of USB devices by detecting their presence, locating, and then installing the appropriate driver for the device.

IEEE 1394: The Firewire™ Bus

Originally proposed and implemented by Apple Computers, the Institute of Electrical and Electronic Engineers (IEEE) defined a high-speed, peer-to-peer serial bus to accommodate applications where the lower speed of USB proved inadequate. IEEE 1394 (currently IEEE 1394a-2000) describes a bus standard that supports three transfer rates, 100, 200, and 400 Mb/sec. (IEEE 1394b will support faster rates). Even at the slowest rates, more than 10 MB/sec are transferred, faster than with the original ISA mainboard bus.

The name *Firewire* remains a trademark of Apple Computers. The term *1394* is typically used to describe the bus on PC hardware. Sony and other camcorder companies are using the term "i.Link™" for their implementation of 1394.

Each 1394 device can connect to its host using a 4.5 meter, 6- or 4-wire cable. Up to sixty-three devices can be daisy-chained over a total distance of 72 meters. Bridges are devices that span buses and thus allow the connection of up to 62 additional devices. Up to 1024 buses may be bridged together. The theoretical number of devices allowed in the 1394 topology is 64 K. A 16-bit Node ID is assigned when a new device is attached.

The 6-wire cable includes two twisted pairs for separate data transfer and clocking of data, and one pair for device power. The entire cable is shielded and jacketed and terminates with a Nintendo Gameboy-derived connector.

Typical uses for 1394 interfaces are found on digital cameras that must transfer large amounts of data from device memory to a PC. Digital video editing typically requires significant bandwidth, and new equipment with this capability now includes a Firewire interface.

REGISTER ACCESS

IEEE 1394 conforms to the IEEE 1212 standard of Control and Status Register (CSR) architecture. The CSR standard defines a 64-bit fixed addressing scheme, which includes a 10-bit bus number, a 6-bit Node ID with the remaining 48 bits left for device use. While recommendations for proper usage are given in the 1212 spec, the 256 TB (terabyte) address range for device registers is sufficient for most needs.

As with the USB scheme, device register usage is reserved for control and status and limited data transfer (up to 64 bytes). Isochronous clocking is used when bandwidth must be guaranteed (e.g., camera data) while asynchronous clocking is used for guaranteed arrival (e.g., hard disk data).

INTERRUPT MECHANISMS

As with USB, 1394 simulates device interrupts. A device must send a packet of data to announce its status or state when host intervention is required. The driver for the device must respond to the data placed in the system address space by the 1394 interface.

The 1394 family of standards includes an Open Host Controller Interface. The OHCI specification is the standard of most significance to a driver author. It provides a conventional interrupt and DMA mechanism for 1394 devices. The 1394 Trade Association provides a convenient link to the OHCI spec and other relevant information: www.1394.ta.org.

DMA CAPABILITIES

The host interface adapter uses DMA to transfer data and commands to and from system memory. The 1394 devices cannot directly access system memory. OHCI adapters provide a range of addresses that are routed by software and the DMAC of the host interface directly into system memory. Thus, an illusion of DMA is provided for each device.

AUTOMATIC RECOGNITION AND CONFIGURATION

The 1394 was designed to support Plug and Play directly and intelligently. Each device that attaches to the bus signals its presence with a bus reset. The host (or other nodes) then enumerates the device's configuration ROM to discover it.

The PC Card (PCMCIA) Bus

About ten years ago, several companies jointly developed a standard bus architecture for mobile devices. Initially, the focus was on memory cards and the group became the Personal Computer Memory Card International Association (PCMCIA). The mobile environment is short on size and power resources, so a small form factor was developed with heavy emphasis on power management. Today, more than 300 companies are members of PCMCIA.

The original PC Card standard defined a 68-pin interface with one of three card thicknesses, Type I, Type II, and Type III. The standard defined bus speeds comparable to ISA—again, the emphasis was on power and size, not performance.

The term *PCMCIA card* is often used interchangeably with *PC Card*. This terminology creates confusion; PCMCIA is an organization, while PC Card defines a bus interface. Today PCMCIA defines (at least) three bus interfaces: PC Card, DMA, and CardBus. Thus, a PCMCIA card does not signify which kind of card is being discussed.

The original PC Card bus clocked at ISA speeds, 8 MHz, and allowed for 8-bit or 16-bit devices. Thus, the maximum transfer rate for a 16-bit card was 16 MB/sec. The CardBus architecture allows for 32-bit devices. It clocks at the PCI bus speed of 33 MHz, thus allowing a maximum transfer rate of more than 128 MB/sec.

REGISTER ACCESS

The PC Card standard defines a 26-bit address range for its I/O access (64 MB). Otherwise, addressing is similar to the ISA scheme. For CardBus, a full 32-bit address range is defined, similar to the PCI bus.

INTERRUPT MECHANISMS

The PC Card and CardBus standards define a single pin for interrupts, IREQ or CINT. It is level-sensitive and can therefore be shared with other cards on the same bus. However, multifunction PCMCIA cards must arbitrate in software for sharing of the single interrupt wire.

DMA CAPABILITIES

The original PC Card standard did not allow for any DMA access. A newer standard released in 1995 added DMA to a PC Card extension, aptly titled just *DMA*. The DMA standard allows for byte or 16-bit word transfers in a manner similar to ISA. The standard assumes that devices will be bus slaves (of shared DMACs) and, like ISA, bus master DMA cards are difficult to implement.

The CardBus standard allows DMA much like the PCI bus. Bus mastering is a straightforward addition to a CardBus device, although the limited form factor requires considerable component integration. Sixteen-bit and 32-bit data transfers are allowed up to the CardBus clock speed of 33 MHz.

AUTOMATIC RECOGNITION AND CONFIGURATION

The intended uses of the PC Card bus mandated that complete Plug and Play capabilities be included. PC Cards continue to set the standard for hot plugability and autoconfiguration.

Software for the PC Card or CardBus standards is layered in two major pieces: Socket Services and Card Services. The Socket Service is BIOS-level software that manages one or more sockets on a system. It is responsible for detection and notification of device insertion or removal.

The Card Service software layer manages hardware resources for a given card.

Hints for Working with Hardware

Working with new hardware can be a real challenge. Hardware engineers follow a different design methodology than do software engineers. (Consider the user interface on a VCR.) The following hints may help make it easier to work with a new piece of hardware.

Learn about the Hardware

Before starting a new driver, learn as much as possible about the hardware itself. Most of the information needed should be in the hardware documentation. At the very least, ensure that information is available for

- bus architecture
- control registers
- error and status reporting
- interrupt behavior
- data transfer mechanisms
- device memory

BUS ARCHITECTURE

The hardware's bus architecture will have a big impact on the design of the driver. Auto recognition and configuration information must be clear. New drivers will be expected to participate in the Plug and Play mechanisms offered by Windows 2000.

CONTROL REGISTERS

The size and addressing scheme of the device's registers must be known. The purpose of each register and contents of any control, status, and data registers must be fully described. Odd behavior must be identified. For example:

- Some device registers may be read-only or write-only.
- A single register address may perform different functions on a read than it does on a write.
- Data or status registers may not contain valid information until some fixed time interval after a command is issued.
- Register access in a specific order may be required.

ERROR AND STATUS REPORTING

Determine any protocols used by the device for reporting hardware failures and device status.

INTERRUPT BEHAVIOR

Find out exactly what device conditions cause the hardware to generate an interrupt, and whether the device uses more than one interrupt vector. If working with a multidevice controller, interrupts may come from the controller itself, and there must be a mechanism to identify the actual device that wants attention.

DATA TRANSFER MECHANISMS

Drivers for programmed I/O devices are very different from DMA drivers. Some devices are capable of doing both kinds of I/O. In the case of a DMA device, find out if the DMA mechanism is bus master or bus slave, and whether there are any limitations on the range of physical buffer addresses it can use.

DEVICE MEMORY

If the device uses dedicated memory, find out how to access it. It could be mapped at a fixed physical location or there may be a register that must be initialized, pointing to the mapped address.

Make Use of Hardware Intelligence

Some peripherals contain their own processors that perform both diagnostic and device control functions. The processor may be running under the control of some firmware, or it may be possible for the driver itself to download code to on-board RAM at initialization time.

When working with a smart peripheral, it makes sense to take full advantage of the device's intelligence. Proper use of hardware features can result in significantly better driver performance and improved diagnostic capabilities.

Test the Hardware

New hardware is seldom delivered bug-free. Hardware should be tested early and tested often. Besides providing an opportunity to discover design errors, it also provides a discovery process for the device author to learn about a device's behavior.

BASIC TESTS

Make sure the device and any associated cables are all compatible with the development machine. Power up everything and try a simple boot. At a gross level, this ensures that the device isn't interfering with anything else in the box.

STANDALONE TESTS

If possible, write some standalone code that tests the board and any firmware it may contain. This will usually be a program that runs without the benefit of an operating system, or perhaps under DOS. With luck, the hardware vendor will provide some sort of exerciser for this purpose.

Finally, remember to test any on-board diagnostics by putting the hardware into an illegal state. The on-board firmware should detect and report the problem.

Summary

This chapter presented a cursory look at hardware issues. A driver needs to find the devices it will be controlling and determine the system resources required. Some bus architectures make this easy, some hard. Later chapters describe the services provided by Windows 2000 to make this job easier.

The next chapter provides an overview of the Windows 2000 I/O process.

Kernel-Mode I/O Processing

CHAPTER OBJECTIVES

With the hardware issues covered in the previous chapter, this chapter introduces the role of the Windows 2000 Executive components in processing I/O requests.

This chapter covers three areas. First, in sections 3.1 through 3.4, it introduces key concepts and techniques important to I/O processing.

Next, the chapter describes the purpose of the various routines that make up a driver. The details of each routine are covered in subsequent chapters.

Finally, the entire life cycle of an I/O request is examined. A good understanding of the I/O flow of control is probably the most important piece of knowledge a driver author can have.

How Kernel-Mode Code Executes

The kernel-mode parts of Windows 2000 (including a device driver) consist of massive amounts of code. But just what causes this code to execute? All code executes within a hardware and software *context*. A context, as used here, describes the state of the system while a CPU instruction executes. It includes the state of all CPU registers (including the stack), the processor mode (user or kernel), and significantly, the state of the hardware page tables. This last item describes what memory can be seen by executing code, and where within the address space that memory is located.

Clearly, code must make assumptions about the context in which it executes. Windows 2000 defines three execution contexts for kernel-mode execution. In other words, kernel-mode driver code executes in one of three contexts.

Trap or Exception Context

Chapter 1 described how user-mode code can request an OS service by trapping into kernel mode. When a kernel-mode routine executes, it may be because a user-mode application or service caused a hardware or software exception, or trap, to occur. In this case, the context of the kernel-mode code is largely that of the user code that caused the exception. The memory seen by kernel-mode code includes the same view as seen by the requesting user-mode thread.

When a user-mode thread makes a direct request of the I/O Manager, the I/O Manager executes within the context of the requester. In turn, the I/O Manager may call a dispatch routine within a device driver. Dispatch routines of a driver therefore execute within this exception context.

Interrupt Context

When the hardware (or software) generates an acknowledged interrupt, whatever code is executing within the system is stopped dead in its tracks. The executing context is saved and control is promptly handed over to a service routine appropriate for the kind of interrupt that occurred.

Clearly, the context of the executing code at the time of the interrupt is irrelevant and arbitrary. Kernel-mode code servicing the interrupt cannot make any assumptions about the state of the page tables. User-mode buffers must be considered unavailable in this context. Code running in interrupt context (which includes the bulk of driver routines) can make no assumptions about the current process or thread.

Kernel-Mode Thread Context

The final possibility is that a piece of code runs in the context of a separate kernel thread. Some drivers spawn separate threads to deal with devices that require polling or to deal with specialized timeout conditions. These kernel-mode threads are not significantly different from user-mode threads described in Win32 programming books. They execute when scheduled by the kernel's scheduler, in accordance with the assigned thread priority.

Like the interrupt context, kernel-mode thread context can make no assumption about the current process or thread. The state of the page tables is largely arbitrary as seen by the thread. Chapter 14 discusses the use of kernel-mode threads.

Use of Interrupt Priorities by Windows 2000

The last chapter introduced the concept of interrupt priorities as a means of arbitrating among different I/O devices competing for CPU service. This section presents a scheme implemented by Windows 2000 that not only takes into account hardware interrupt prioritization, but extends the concept to include prioritization of execution context.

CPU Priority Levels

Since different CPU architectures have different ways of handling hardware interrupt priorities, Windows 2000 presents an idealized, abstract scheme to deal with all platforms. The actual implementation of the abstraction utilizes HAL routines that are platform-specific.

The basis for this abstract priority scheme is the *interrupt request level* (IRQL). The IRQL (pronounced *irk-al*) is a number that defines a simple priority. Code executing at a given IRQL cannot be interrupted by code at a lower or equal IRQL. Table 3.1 lists the IRQL levels used in the Windows 2000 priority scheme. Regardless of the underlying CPU or bus architectures,

Table 3.1 *IRQL Level Usage*

IRQL Levels

Generated By	IRQL Name	Purpose
Hardware	HIGHEST_LEVEL	Machine checks and bus errors
	POWER_LEVEL	Power-fail interrupts
	IPI_LEVEL	Interprocessor doorbell for MP systems
	CLOCK2_LEVEL	Interval clock 2
	CLOCK1_LEVEL	Interval clock 1
	PROFILE_LEVEL	Profiling timer
	DIRQLs	Platform-dependent number of levels for I/O device interrupts
Software	DISPATCH_LEVEL	Thread schedule and deferred procedure call execution
	APC_LEVEL	Asynchronous procedure call execution
	PASSIVE_LEVEL	Normal thread execution level

this is how IRQL levels appear to a driver. It is important to understand that at any given time, instructions execute at one specific IRQL value. The IRQL level is maintained as part of the execution context of a given thread, and thus, at any given time, the current IRQL value is known to the operating system.

The actual hardware interrupt levels fall between DISPATCH_LEVEL and PROFILE-LEVEL of the IRQL abstraction. These hardware interrupt levels are defined as the device IRQLs (DIRQLs).

Interrupt Processing Sequence

When an interrupt reaches the CPU, the processor compares the IRQL value of the requested interrupt with the CPU's current IRQL value. If the IRQL of the request is less than or equal to the current IRQL, the request is temporarily ignored. The request remains pending until a later time when the IRQL level drops to a lower value.

On the other hand, if the IRQL of the request is higher than the CPU's current IRQL, the processor performs the following tasks:

1. Suspends instruction execution.
2. Saves just enough state information on the stack to resume the interrupted code at a later time.
3. Raises the IRQL value of the CPU to match the IRQL of the request, thus preventing lower priority interrupts from occurring.
4. Transfers control to the appropriate interrupt service routine for the requested interrupt.

When finished, the service routine executes a special instruction that dismisses the interrupt. This instruction restores the CPU state information from the stack (which includes the previous IRQL value) and control is returned to the interrupted code.

Notice that this scheme allows higher-IRQL requests to interrupt the service routines of lower-IRQL interrupts (an interrupt of an interrupt). Because the whole mechanism is stack-based, this doesn't cause confusion. It does, however, raise synchronization issues addressed in chapter 5.

Software-Generated Interrupts

The lower entries in the IRQL list of Table 3.1 are tagged as being software-generated. Some interrupt processing is initiated by kernel-mode code by the execution of a privileged instruction. Windows 2000 uses these software interrupts to extend the interrupt prioritization scheme to include thread scheduling. It can be used to synchronize activity among competing threads by arbitrarily raising the IRQL of one thread to prevent interruption by the others. The next section describes the use of software interrupts and IRQL levels to schedule medium-priority driver tasks.

Deferred Procedure Calls (DPCs)

While a piece of kernel-mode code is running at an elevated IRQL, nothing executes (on the same CPU) at that or any lower IRQL. Of course, if too much code executes at too high an IRQL, overall system performance will degrade. Time-critical event handling could be deferred and cause more disastrous results.

To avoid these problems, kernel-mode code must be designed to execute as much code as possible at the lowest possible IRQL. One important part of this strategy is the *Deferred Procedure Call* (DPC).

Operation of a DPC

The DPC architecture allows a task to be *triggered*, but not *executed*, from a high-level IRQL. This *deferral of execution* is critical when servicing hardware interrupts in a driver because there is no reason to block lower-level IRQL code from executing if a given task can be deferred. Figure 3.1 illustrates the

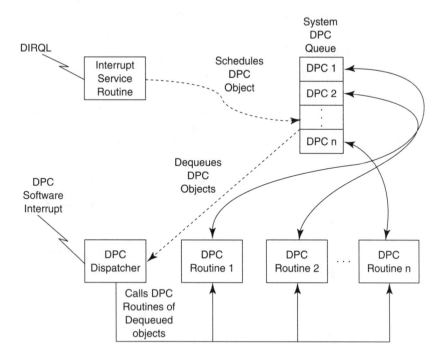

Figure 3.1   *Deferred Procedure Call flow.*

operation of a DPC. Subsequent chapters present more specific information about the use of a DPC in a driver, but an overview is presented below.

1. When some piece of code running at a high (e.g., hardware) IRQL wants to schedule some of its work at a lower IRQL, it adds a DPC object to the end of the system's DPC dispatching queue and requests a DPC software interrupt. Since the current IRQL is above DISPATCH_LEVEL, the interrupt won't be acknowledged immediately, but instead remains pending.

2. Eventually, the processor's IRQL falls below DISPATCH_LEVEL and the previously pended interrupt is serviced by the DPC dispatcher.

3. The DPC dispatcher dequeues each DPC object from the system queue and calls the function whose pointer is stored in the object. This function is called while the CPU is at DISPATCH_LEVEL.

4. When the DPC queue is empty, the DPC dispatcher dismisses the DISPATCH_LEVEL software interrupt.

Device drivers typically schedule cleanup work with a DPC. This has the effect of reducing the amount of time the driver spends at its DIRQL and improves overall system throughput.

Behavior of DPCs

For the most part, working with DPCs is easy because Windows 2000 includes library routines that hide most details of the process. Nevertheless, there are two frustrating aspects of DPCs that should be highlighted.

First, Windows 2000 imposes a restriction that only one instance of a DPC object may be present on the system DPC queue at a time. Attempts to queue a DPC object that is already in the queue are rejected. Consequently, only one call to the DPC routine occurs, even though a driver expected two. This might happen if two back-to-back device interrupts occurred before the initial DPC could execute. The first DPC is still on the queue when the driver services the second interrupt.

The driver must handle this possibility with a clever design. Perhaps a count of DPC requests could be maintained or a driver might choose to implement a separate (on the side) queue of requests. When the real DPC executes, it could examine the count or private queue to determine exactly what work to perform.

Second, there is an issue of synchronization when working with multiprocessor machines. One processor could service the interrupt and schedule the DPC. However, before it dismisses the interrupt, another parallel processor could respond to the queued DPC. Thus, the interrupt service code would be executing simultaneously with the DPC code. For this reason, DPC routines must synchronize access to any resources shared with the driver's interrupt service routine.

The DPC architecture prevents any two DPCs from executing simultaneously, even on a multiprocessor machine. Thus, resources shared by different DPC routines do not need to worry about synchronization.

Access to User Buffers

When a user-mode thread makes an I/O request, it usually passes the address of a data buffer located in user space. Since user-mode addresses are referenced through the lower half (< 2 GB) of the page tables, a driver must cope with the possibility that the page tables will change before the request can be completed. This would occur if the driver code executed at Interrupt Context or Kernel-Mode Thread context. As previously discussed, the lower half of the page tables are changed with each process switch. Thus, code executing with an arbitrary page table state cannot assume that any user-mode address is valid.

Worse, the user buffer may be paged out of RAM and exist only on the system's swap file on disk. User memory is always subject to swap-out if the system needs RAM for other processes.

In general, user memory is pagable, and by rule, pagable memory may not be accessed at DISPATCH_LEVEL_IRQL or higher. This rule is necessary since the tasks providing page-in service of the requested memory might need a device at a lower DIRQL than that which needed the page.

Buffer Access Mechanisms

Now that the problem is defined, a solution is needed. Fortunately, the I/O Manager provides drivers with two different methods for accessing user buffers. When a driver initializes, it tells the I/O Manager which strategy it plans to use. The choice depends on the nature and speed of the device.

The first strategy is to ask the I/O Manager to copy the entire user buffer into dedicated system RAM, which remains fixed (i.e., not paged) in both the page tables and physical memory. The device uses the copy of the buffer to perform the requested I/O operation. Upon completion, the I/O Manager conveniently copies the system buffer back to the user buffer. Actually, only one copy operation is performed. On I/O write requests, the user buffer is copied before presentation to the driver. On I/O read requests, the system buffer is copied after the driver marks the request as completed. Standard read or write requests do not require bidirectional copying.

The first technique is known as *buffered I/O* (BIO). It is used by slower devices that do not generally handle large data transfers. The technique is simple for driver logic, but requires the somewhat time-consuming job of buffer copying.

The second technique avoids the buffer copy by providing the driver with direct access to the user's buffer in physical memory. At the beginning of the I/O operation, the I/O Manager "locks down" the entire user buffer into memory, thus preventing the block from swap-out and causing a deadly page fault. It then constructs a list of page table entries that are mapped into slots above 2 GB and are thus not subject to process context switches. With the memory and page table entries locked for the duration of the I/O request, driver code may safely reference the user buffer. (Note, however, that the original user address is translated into another logical address, valid only from kernel-mode code. The driver must use the translated address.)

This second technique is well-suited for fast devices that transfer large blocks of data. It is known as *direct I/O* (DIO). DMA devices almost always use this technique and it is further discussed in chapter 12.

Structure of a Kernel-Mode Driver

A kernel-mode driver looks very different from conventional applications. In general, a driver is just a collection of routines that are called by operating system software (usually the I/O Manager). Flow charts don't provide much benefit when diagramming control paths of a device driver. The routines of the driver sit passively until they are invoked by routines of the I/O Manager.

Depending on the driver, the I/O Manager might call a driver routine in any of the following situations:

- When a driver is loaded
- When a driver is unloaded or the system is shutting down
- When a device is inserted or removed
- When a user-mode program issues an I/O system service call
- When a shared hardware resource becomes available for driver use
- At various points during an actual device operation

The remainder of this section briefly describes the major categories of routines that make up a kernel-mode driver. The details of each of these kinds of driver routines are discussed in subsequent chapters.

Driver Initialization and Cleanup Routines

When a driver loads into the system, various tasks must be performed. Similarly, drivers need to clean up before they are unloaded. There are several routines that a driver may supply to perform these operations.

DriverEntry ROUTINE

The I/O Manager calls this routine when a driver is first loaded, perhaps as early as boot time, but drivers may be dynamically loaded at any time. The DriverEntry routine performs all first-time initialization tasks, such as announcing the addresses of all other driver routines. It locates hardware that it will control, allocates or confirms hardware resource usage (ports, interrupts,

DMA), and provides a device name visible to the rest of the system for each hardware device discovered. For WDM drivers participating in Plug and Play, this hardware allocation step is deferred to a later time and routine, the Add-Device function.

REINITIALIZE ROUTINE

Some drivers may not be able to complete their initialization during Driver-Entry. This could occur if the driver was dependent on another driver that had yet to load, or if the driver needed more support from the operating system than had booted at the time DriverEntry was initially called. These kinds of drivers can ask that their initialization be deferred by supplying a Reinitialize routine during DriverEntry.

UNLOAD ROUTINE

The I/O Manager calls the Unload routine of a driver when a driver is unloaded dynamically. It must reverse every action that DriverEntry performed, leaving behind no allocated resource. This includes removing the system-wide device name supplied during initialization for all controlled devices. For WDM drivers, device resources (and names) are removed as each device is removed, during RemoveDevice.

SHUTDOWN ROUTINE

Surprisingly, the Unload routine is not invoked during a system shutdown. Since the system is "going away" anyway, a perfect cleanup is not required. Instead, the I/O Manager invokes a driver's Shutdown routine to provide an opportunity to place hardware into a quiescent state.

BUGCHECK CALLBACK ROUTINE

If a driver needs to gain control in the event of a system crash, it can provide a Bugcheck routine. This routine, when properly registered, is called by the kernel during an orderly "crash" process (truly an oxymoronic phrase).

I/O System Service Dispatch Routines

When the I/O Manager receives a request from a user-mode application, the type of request (read, write, etc.) is converted into a function code. The I/O Manager identifies the appropriate driver to handle the request, then calls one of several Dispatch routines in the driver. There is one Dispatch routine per function code supported by a driver.

The driver's appropriate Dispatch routine verifies the request and, if necessary, requests that the I/O Manager queue a device request to perform the real work. It then returns to the I/O Manager, marking the request as pending.

OPEN AND CLOSE OPERATIONS

All drivers must provide a CreateDispatch routine that handles the Win32 **CreateFile** request. Drivers that must perform cleanup on the Win32 **Close-Handle** call must supply a CloseDispatch routine.

DEVICE OPERATIONS

Depending on the device, a driver may have individual Dispatch routines for handling data transfers and control operations. The Win32 functions **Read-File, WriteFile,** and **DeviceIoControl** are dispatched to supplied routines in the driver by the I/O Manager. Again, a driver need only supply routines for those operations it supports.

If a user program makes a request of an I/O device for which the driver does not supply a Dispatch routine, the program receives an error indicating that the requested function is not supported.

Data Transfer Routines

Device operations involve a number of different driver routines, depending on the nature and complexity of the device.

START I/O ROUTINE

The I/O Manager calls the driver's Start I/O routine each time a device should begin the start of a data transfer. The request is generated by the I/O Manager each time an outstanding I/O request completes and another request is waiting in the queue. In other words, the I/O Manager (by default) queues and serializes all I/O requests, restarting the affected device only after the previous request completes. (Complex devices capable of dealing with simultaneous requests may choose not to utilize this serialized approach.)

The start I/O routine, supplied by the driver, allocates resources needed to process the requested I/O and sets the device in motion.

INTERRUPT SERVICE ROUTINE (ISR)

The Kernel's interrupt dispatcher calls a driver's Interrupt Service routine each time the device generates an interrupt. The ISR is responsible for complete servicing of the hardware interrupt. By the time the ISR returns, the interrupt should be dismissed from a hardware perspective.

As described earlier, only the most minimal of servicing should be performed within the ISR itself. If additional, time-consuming activities are required as a result of servicing the interrupt, a DPC should be scheduled within the ISR. The remaining work of the ISR can then be completed at an IRQL below DIRQL.

DPC ROUTINES

A driver can supply zero or more DPC routines that perform or complete routine device operations. This might include the release of system resources (such as a DMA page descriptor), reporting error conditions, marking I/O requests as complete, and starting the next device operation, as necessary.

If only one DPC is required for completion of interrupt servicing, the I/O Manager supports a simplified mechanism called a DpcForIsr routine. However, some drivers may wish to provide many DPCs for varied purposes. Perhaps two different DPCs, one that completes a write operation and one that completes a read operation, is convenient. DPCs can be scheduled simply to perform work at an IRQL of DISPATCH_LEVEL. A driver can have any number of custom DPC routines.

Resource Synchronization Callbacks

Recalling the design goals of Windows 2000, all kernel-mode code (including device driver code) must be reentrant. Driver code must consider that multiple threads in one or more processes may make simultaneous I/O requests. Contention issues between the two simultaneous requests must be handled safely and correctly by the reentrant driver code.

The I/O Manager provides several synchronization services to deal with the issue of shared resources among simultaneous requests. These synchronization routines operate differently than those provided to Win32 programmers. In particular, the Win32 model assumes that if a resource is unavailable due to its use by another thread, it is perfectly acceptable to block the execution of the second requester. In kernel mode, it is completely unacceptable to block the execution of an arbitrary thread. A caller must be guaranteed that a return will be prompt, even if the request must be queued for later completion.

The technique employed to synchronize within kernel-mode code is to supply the address of a callback routine dedicated to synchronization of a specific resource. When a driver needs access to a shared resource, it queues a request for that resource with the assistance of the I/O Manager. When the resource becomes available, the I/O Manager invokes the driver-supplied callback routine associated with the request. Of course, this means that multiple requests for the resource are serialized and that at any given time, only one thread context may "own" the resource.

There are three types of synchronization callback routines supported by the I/O Manager. These are discussed in the following sections.

ControllerControl ROUTINE

Sometimes a single controller (card) supports more than one function. Further, the functions may share a single set of controller registers. Thus, only one function on such cards may be in operation at a time. Typically, the Start I/O routine requests exclusive ownership of the controller. When granted, the

ControllerControl callback routine executes. When the I/O completes, the driver releases the controller, usually within a DpcForIsr routine.

AdapterControl ROUTINE

DMA hardware is another shared resource that must be passed from driver to driver. Before performing DMA, the driver requests exclusive ownership of the proper DMA hardware—typically a DMA channel. When ownership is granted, the AdapterControl callback routine executes.

SynchCritSection ROUTINES

Interrupt service occurs at a device-specific DIRQL while remaining driver code operates at DISPATCH_LEVEL or below. If the lower IRQL sections of code ever touch resources used by the ISR, that operation must execute inside of a SynchCritSection routine. Resources in this category include all device control registers and any other context or state information shared with the Interrupt Service routine.

SynchCritSection routines operate somewhat differently than other synchronization techniques. Once the callback occurs, the IRQL level is raised to the device's DIRQL level. Thus, lower IRQL sections of code temporarily operate at device DIRQL, preventing interruption by the ISR. When the SynchCritSection completes, the IRQL is restored to its original value.

Other Driver Routines

In addition to the basic set of routines just described, a driver may contain any of the following additional functions.

Timer routines. Drivers that need to keep track of time passage can do so using either an I/O Timer or a CustomTimerDpc routine. Chapter 11 describes both mechanisms.

I/O completion routines. A higher-level driver within layers of drivers may wish to be notified when a request sent to a lower-level driver completes. The higher-level driver may register an I/O Completion routine for this purpose. Chapter 15 discusses the details of this process.

Cancel I/O routines. Drivers must consider the possibility that a device request may be canceled by the requester. This could happen during a long device operation (or because an unanticipated device error leaves the driver in a waiting state). The driver may provide a Cancel I/O routine that is called by the I/O Manager when the requester "gives up."

I/O Processing Sequence

It is important to understand the complete life cycle of an I/O request. This section describes the flow of a request—from user-mode code to I/O Manager to device driver.

An I/O request goes through several stages during its life.

- Preprocessing by the I/O Manager
- Preprocessing by the device driver
- Device start and interrupt service
- Postprocessing by the driver
- Postprocessing by the I/O Manager

The following sections describe the stages in more detail.

Preprocessing by the I/O Manager

This phase performs device-independent preparation and verification of an I/O request.

1. The Win32 subsystem converts the request into a native system service call. The system service dispatcher traps into kernel mode and into the I/O Manager.

2. The I/O Manager allocates a data structure known as an *I/O Request Packet* (IRP). The next chapter describes an IRP in more detail, but an IRP can be thought of as a work order presented to a driver and its device. The IRP is filled with necessary information, including a code which identifies the type of I/O request.

3. The I/O Manager performs some validation of the arguments passed with the request. This includes verifying the file handle, checking access rights to the file object, ensuring that the device supports the requested function, and validating the user buffer addresses.

4. If the device requests a buffered I/O (BIO) operation, the I/O Manager allocates a nonpaged pool buffer, and for a write request, copies data from user space into the system buffer. If the device requests direct I/O (DIO), the user's buffer is locked down and a list of page descriptors is built for use by the driver.

5. The I/O Manager invokes the appropriate driver dispatch routine.

Preprocessing by the Device Driver

Each driver builds a dispatch table of entry points for each supported I/O function request. The I/O Manager uses the function code of the I/O request to index into this table and invoke the appropriate driver Dispatch routine. The routine performs the following tasks:

1. It performs additional parameter validation. The device driver can detect device-specific limitations unknown to the I/O Manager. For example, a user might request a data transfer size in violation of the capabilities of a specific device (or driver).

2. If the request can be handled without device activity (e.g., reading zero bytes), the Dispatch routine simply completes the request and sends the IRP back to the I/O Manager, marked as complete.

3. If (as is usual) device operation is required, the Dispatch routine marks the request (IRP) as pending. The I/O Manager is instructed to queue a call to the driver's Start I/O routine as soon as the device is free. (It is possible the device is handling a previous request.)

Device Start and Interrupt Service

Data transfers and other device operations are managed by the driver's Start I/O and Interrupt Service routines.

START I/O

When a Dispatch routine requests that the I/O Manager start a device, the I/O Manager first checks to see whether a device is already busy. The I/O Manager detects this condition by checking whether or not there is an IRP outstanding for the device (i.e., still marked as pending). If so, it queues the request to start the device. Otherwise, the driver's Start I/O routine is called directly. The Start I/O routine performs the following tasks:

1. It checks the IRP function (read, write, etc.) and performs any setup work specific to that type of operation.

2. If the device is part of a multifunction controller, a ControllerControl routine requests exclusive ownership of the controller hardware.

3. If the operation requires DMA, an AdapterControl routine requests exclusive ownership of the appropriate DMA channel hardware.

4. It uses a SynchCriticalSection routine to safely access device registers and start the device.

5. It returns control to the I/O Manager and awaits a device interrupt.

ISR

When an interrupt occurs, the kernel's interrupt dispatcher calls the driver's ISR. The ISR would typically perform the following steps:

1. Check to see if the interrupt was expected.

2. Dismiss the hardware device interrupt.

3. If programmed I/O was in progress and the total data transfer was still incomplete, the ISR would start another byte or word of data and await another interrupt.

4. If DMA was in progress and more data remained to be transferred, a DPC would be scheduled to set up the DMA hardware for the next chunk of data.

5. If an error occurred or the data transfer was complete, a DPC would be queued to perform postprocessing at a lower IRQL.

Postprocessing by the Driver

The kernel's DPC dispatcher eventually calls the driver's DPC routine to perform the driver's postprocessing chores. These would typically include

1. If a DMA operation just occurred and more data remains to be transferred, it sets up the DMA hardware, starts the device, and waits for another interrupt. It then returns to the I/O Manager with the IRP left as pending.

2. If there was an error or timeout, the DPC routine might record the event and then either retry or abort the I/O request.

3. It releases any DMA and controller resources being held by the driver.

4. The DPC routine puts the size of the transfer and final status information into the IRP.

5. Finally, it tells the I/O Manager that the current request has completed by marking the pending IRP as complete. This instructs the I/O Manager to restart the device (by calling Start I/O) with the next IRP, if one is waiting.

Postprocessing by the I/O Manager

Once the driver's DPC marks an IRP as complete, the I/O Manager performs cleanup operations. These include

1. If this was a buffered I/O write operation, the I/O Manager releases the nonpaged pool buffer used during the now completed transfer.

2. If this was a direct I/O operation, it unlocks the user's buffer pages.

3. It queues a request to the original requesting thread for a kernel-mode *asynchronous procedure call* (APC). This APC will execute I/O Manager code in the context of the requesting thread.

4. When the kernel-mode APC runs, it copies status and transfer-size information back into user space.

5. If this was a buffer I/O read operation, the APC copies the contents of the nonpaged pool buffer into the caller's original user-space buffer. It then frees the system buffer.

6. If the original request was for a Win32 overlapped operation, the APC routine sets the associated event and/or file object into the signaled state.

7. If the original request included a completion routine (e.g., **ReadFileEx**), the APC schedules a user-mode APC to execute the completion routine.

Figure 3.2 shows a summary of the I/O processing sequence just described.

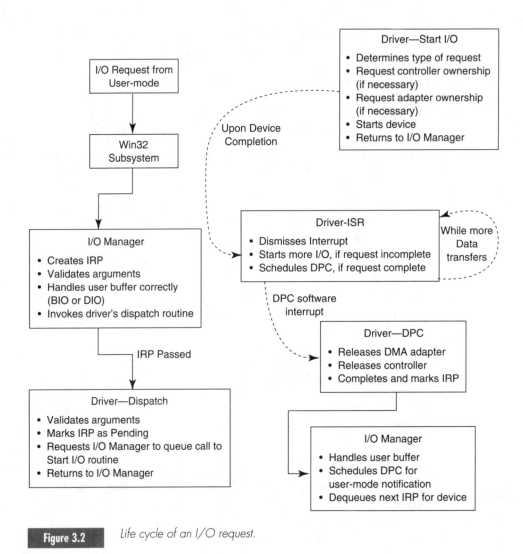

Figure 3.2   *Life cycle of an I/O request.*

Summary

The quick tour of the Windows 2000 I/O subsystem is now complete. The structure of a Windows 2000 basic device driver should be clear—only the details remain.

The next chapter deals with some of these details: the data structures created and used by the I/O Manager and the device driver.

Drivers and Kernel-Mode Objects

CHAPTER OBJECTIVES

Data structures are the lifeblood of most operating systems as well as most complicated applications, and Windows 2000 is no exception. Windows 2000 is different from most operating systems because it uses a taste of object technology to manage its data structures. This chapter examines the Windows 2000 approach to data structures and objects, then introduces the major structures involved in processing I/O requests.

Data Objects and Windows 2000

Object-oriented programming (OOP) is a proven software design technique to provide overall organization of code and high-level encapsulation of major design concepts. In this scheme, a data structure is grouped with the code that modifies it. Together, the code and its associated data are called *objects*. The data of the object remains opaque to the users of the object. Using code must invoke methods of the object to manipulate its state. The methods of an object form a strict interface for its use.

The overall goal of the object-orientation technique is to improve the reliability, robustness, and reusability of software by hiding implementation details from the users of an object.

Windows 2000 and OOP

Using a strict definition of OOP, the design of Windows 2000 isn't truly object-oriented. Rather, it can be thought of as object-based because it manages its internal data structures in an object-like way. In particular, Windows 2000 defines not only necessary data structures, but also groups of access functions that are allowed to manipulate those data structures. All other modules are expected to access functions to manipulate the contents of the structures.

In practice, not all elements of all data structures are completely opaque. In fact, since kernel-mode driver code is trusted code, there is no real way to enforce the object boundary. Additionally, the I/O Manager treats device drivers as trusted components of itself. A driver is required to read and write some offsets within some I/O Manager data structures directly.

Windows 2000 Objects and Win32 Objects

The Win32 API also defines kernel objects. These user-mode objects differ from internal OS objects in two important ways. First, in almost all cases, internal objects have no external name. This is because these objects aren't exported to user mode and, therefore, don't need to be managed by the Object Manager.

Second, user-mode code uses *handles* to reference the objects it creates or opens. Internal objects are referenced with a direct memory pointer. This pointer is routinely passed between I/O Manager and device driver. In some cases, the driver itself will allocate and initialize memory for the object.

I/O Request Packets (IRPs)

Almost all I/O under Windows 2000 is packet-driven. Each separate I/O transaction is described by a work order that tells the driver what to do and tracks the progress of the request through the I/O subsystem. These work orders take the form of a data structure called an *I/O Request Packet* (IRP), and this section describes their use and purpose.

1. With each user-mode request for I/O, the I/O Manager allocates an IRP from nonpaged system memory. Based on the file handle and I/O func-

tion requested by the user, the I/O Manager passes the IRP to the appropriate driver dispatch routine.

2. The dispatch routine checks the parameters of the request, and if valid, passes the IRP to the driver's Start I/O routine.

3. The Start I/O routine uses the contents of the IRP to begin a device operation.

4. When the operation is complete, the driver's DpcForIsr routine stores a final status code in the IRP and returns it to the I/O Manager.

5. The I/O Manager uses the information in the IRP to complete the request and send the user the final status.

The procedure just described is, in fact, a simplified model of IRP processing. It only applies in a flat driver model. When drivers are layered, one upon the other, the procedure is more complex. A single IRP may travel through several layers of drivers before the request is completed. Additionally, higher-level drivers can create new IRPs and disperse them to other drivers.

Layout of an IRP

An IRP is a variable-sized structure allocated from nonpaged pool. Figure 4.1 shows that an IRP has two sections.

- A header area containing general bookkeeping information
- One or more parameter blocks called *I/O stack locations*

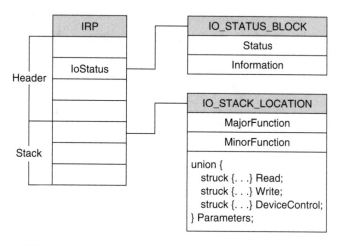

Figure 4.1   *Structure of an IRP.*

IRP HEADER

This area of the IRP holds various pieces of information about the overall I/O request. Some parts of the header are directly accessible to the driver, while other pieces are the exclusive property of the I/O Manager. Table 4.1 lists the fields in the header that a driver is allowed to touch.

The **IoStatus** member holds the final status of the I/O operation. When a driver is ready to complete the processing of an IRP, it sets this **Status** field of this block to a STATUS_XXX value. At the same time, a driver should set the information field of the status block either to 0 (if there is an error) or to a function code-specific value (for example, the number of bytes transferred).

The **AssociatedIrp.SystemBuffer, MdlAddress,** and **UserBuffer** fields play various roles in managing the driver's access to data buffers. Later chapters explain how to use these fields if a driver performs either Buffered or direct I/O.

I/O STACK LOCATIONS

The main purpose of an I/O stack location is to hold function code and parameters of an I/O request. By examining the **MajorFunction** field of the stack locations, a driver can decide what operation to perform and how to interpret the **Parameters** union. Table 4.2 describes some of the commonly used members of an I/O stack location.

For requests sent directly to a lowest-level driver, the corresponding IRP has only one I/O stack location. For requests sent to a higher-level driver, the I/O Manager creates an IRP with separate I/O stack locations for each driver layer. In other words, the size of an I/O stack is really the number of I/O layers that participate in an I/O request. Every driver in the hierarchy is allowed to touch only its own stack location. If a driver chooses to call a lower-layer driver, it must ensure that a new stack location has been correctly created beneath it.

| **Table 4.1** | *Externally Visible Fields of an IRP Header* |

IRP Header Fields	
Field	**Description**
IO_STATUS_BLOCK IoStatus	Contains status of the I/O request
PVOID AssociatedIrp.SystemBuffer	Points to a system space buffer if device performs buffered I/O
PMDL MdlAddress	Points to a Memory Descriptor List for a user-space buffer if device performs direct I/O
PVOID UserBuffer	User-space address of I/O buffer
BOOLEAN Cancel	Indicates the IRP has been canceled

Table 4.2	*Selected Contents of IRP Stack Location*

IO_STACK_LOCATION, *PIO_STACK_LOCATION

Field	Contents
UCHAR MajorFunction	IRP_MJ_XXX function specifying the operation
UCHAR MinorFunction	Used by file system and SCSI drivers
union Parameters	Typed union keyed to MajorFunction code
struct Read	Parameters for IRP_MJ_READ
	● ULONG Length
	● ULONG Key
	● LARGE_INTEGER ByteOffset
struct Write	Parameters for IRP_MJ_WRITE
	● ULONG Length
	● ULONG Key
	● LARGE_INTEGER ByteOffset
struct DeviceIoControl	Parameters for IRP_MJ_DEVICE_CONTROL
	● ULONG OutputBufferLength
	● ULONG InputBufferLength
	● ULONG IoControlCode
	● PVOID Type3InputBuffer
struct Others	Available to driver
	● PVOID Argument1-Argument4
PDEVICE_OBJECT DeviceObject	Target device for this I/O request
PFILE_OBJECT FileObject	File object for this request, if any

When a driver passes an IRP to a lower-level driver, the I/O Manager automatically *pushes* the I/O stack-pointer so that it points at the I/O stack location belonging to the lower driver. When the lower driver releases the IRP, the I/O stack pointer is *popped* so that it again points to the stack location of the higher driver. Chapter 15 explains in detail how to work with this mechanism.

Manipulating IRPs

Some IRP access functions operate only on the IRP header. Others deal specifically with the IRP's I/O stack locations. It is important to know whether an access function needs the pointer to the entire IRP or a pointer to

Table 4.3	Functions that Work with the Whole IRP	
IRP Access Functions		
Function	**Description**	**Called by...**
IoStartPacket	Sends IRP to Start I/O routine	Dispatch
IoCompleteRequest	Indicates that all processing is done	DpcForIsr
IoStartNextPacket	Sends next IRP to Start I/O	DpcForIsr
IoCallDriver	Sends IRP to another driver	Dispatch
IoAllocateIrp	Requests additional IRP	Dispatch
IoFreeIrp	Releases driver-allocated IRP	I/O Completion

an IRP stack location. The following sections describe each group of access functions.

IRPS AS A WHOLE

The I/O Manager exports a variety of functions that work with IRPs. Table 4.3 lists the most common ones. Later chapters explain how to use them.

IRP STACK LOCATIONS

The I/O Manager also provides several functions that drivers can use to access an IRP's stack locations. These functions are listed in Table 4.4.

Driver Objects

DriverEntry is the only driver routine with an exported name. When the I/O Manager needs to locate other driver functions, it uses the Driver object associated with a specific device. This object is basically a catalog that contains pointers to various driver functions. The life of a driver object is explained below.

1. The I/O Manager creates a driver object whenever it loads a driver. If the driver fails during initialization, the I/O Manager deletes the object.

2. During initialization, the DriverEntry routine loads pointers to other driver functions into the driver object.

3. When an IRP is sent to a specific device, the I/O Manager uses the associated driver object to find the right Dispatch routine.

4. If a request involves an actual device operation, the I/O Manager uses the driver object to locate the driver's Start I/O routine.

Table 4.4	*IO_STACK_LOCATION Access Functions*

IO_STACK_LOCATION Functions

Function	Description	Called by...
IoGetCurrentIrpStackLocation	Gets pointer to caller's stack slot	(Various)
IoMarkIrpPending	Marks caller's stack slot as as needing further processing	Dispatch
IoGetNextIrpStackLocation	Gets pointer to stack slot for next lower driver	Dispatch
IoSetNextIrpStackLocation	Pushes the I/O stack pointer one location	Dispatch
IoSetCompleteRoutine	Attaches I/O Completion routine to the next lower driver's I/O stack slot	Dispatch

5. If the driver is unloaded, the I/O Manager uses the driver object to find an Unload routine. When the Unload routine returns, the I/O Manager deletes the Driver object.

Layout of a Driver Object

There is a unique driver object for each driver currently loaded in the system. Figure 4.2 illustrates the structure of the driver object. As you can see, the driver object also contains a pointer to a linked list of devices serviced by this driver. A driver's Unload routine can use this list to locate any devices it needs to delete.

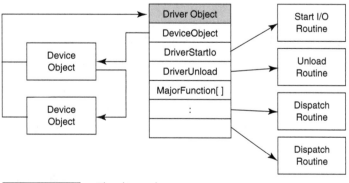

Figure 4.2	*The driver object.*

Table 4.5	*Externally Visible Fields of a Driver Object*
Driver Object Fields	
Field	**Description**
PDRIVER_STARTIO DriverStartIo	Address of driver's Start I/O routine
PDRIVER_UNLOAD DriverUnload	Address of driver's Unload routine
PDRIVER_DISPATCH MajorFunction[]	Table of driver's Dispatch routines, indexed by I/O operation code
PDEVICE_OBJECT DeviceObject	Linked list of device objects created by this driver

Unlike other objects, there are no access functions for modifying driver objects. Instead, the DriverEntry routine sets various fields directly. Table 4.5 lists the fields a driver is allowed to touch.

Device Objects and Device Extensions

Both the I/O Manager and a driver need to know what's going on with an I/O device at all times. *Device objects* make this possible by keeping information about the device's characteristics and state. There is one device object for each virtual, logical, and physical device on the system. The life cycle of a device object is shown below.

1. The DriverEntry routine creates a device object for each of its devices. For WDM drivers, the Device object is created by the AddDevice Plug and Play routine.

2. The I/O Manager uses a back-pointer in the device object to locate the corresponding driver object. There it can find driver routines to operate on I/O requests. It also maintains a queue of current and pending IRPs attached to the device object.

3. Various driver routines use the device object to locate the corresponding device extension. As an I/O request is processed, the driver uses the extension to store any device-specific state information.

4. The driver's Unload routine deletes the device object when the driver is unloaded. The act of deleting the device object also deletes the associated device extension. For WDM drivers, RemoveDevice performs the task of deleting the Device object.

Physical device drivers are not alone in their use of device objects. Chapter 15 describes the way higher-level drivers use device objects.

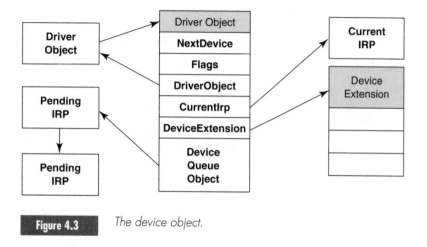

Figure 4.3 The device object.

Layout of the Device Object

Figure 4.3 illustrates the structure of the device object and its relationship to other structures. Although the device object contains a lot of data, much of it is the exclusive property of the I/O Manager. A driver should limit its access to only those fields listed in Table 4.6.

Manipulating Device Objects

Table 4.7 lists many of the I/O Manager functions that operate on device objects. The I/O Manager also passes a device object pointer as an argument to most of the routines in a driver.

Table 4.6 Externally Visible Fields of a Device Object

Device Object Fields	
Field	**Description**
PVOID DeviceExtension	Points to device extension structure
PDRIVER_OBJECT DriverObject	Points to driver object for this device
ULONG Flags	Specifies buffering strategy for device
	DO_BUFFERED_IO
	DO_DIRECT_IO
PDEVICE_OBJECT NextDevice	Points to next device belonging to this driver
CCHAR StackSize	Minimum number of I/O stack locations needed by IRPs sent to this device
ULONG AlignmentRequirement	Memory alignment required for buffers

Table 4.7	Access Functions for a Device Object	

Device Object Access Functions		
Function	**Description**	**Called by...**
IoCreateDevice	Creates a device object	DriverEntry or AddDevice
IoCreateSymbolicLink	Makes device object visible to Win32	DriverEntry or AddDevice
IoAttachDevice	Attaches a filter to a device object	DriverEntry or AddDevice
IoAttachDeviceByPointer	Attaches a filter to a device object	DriverEntry or AddDevice
IoGetDeviceObjectPointer	Layers one driver on top of another	DriverEntry or AddDevice
IoCallDriver	Sends request to another driver	Dispatch
IoDetachDevice	Disconnects from a lower driver	Unload or RemoveDevice
IoDeleteSymbolicLink	Removes device object from the Win32 namespace	Unload or RemoveDevice
IoDeleteDevice	Removes device object from system	Unload or RemoveDevice

Device Extensions

Connected to the device object is another important data structure, the *device extension*. The extension is simply a block of nonpaged pool that the I/O Manager automatically attaches to any device object created. The driver author specifies both the size and contents of the device extension. Typically, it is used to hold any information associated with a particular device.

The use of global or static variables violates the requirement that a driver must be fully reentrant. By keeping device state in the device extension, a single copy of driver code can manage multiple devices. The device extension typically includes

- A back-pointer to the device object
- Any device state or driver context information
- A pointer to the interrupt object and an interrupt-expected flag
- A pointer to a controller object
- A pointer to an adapter object and a count of mapping registers

Since the device extension is driver-specific, its structure must be defined in a driver header file. Although the extension's exact contents depend on what a driver does, its general layout looks something like the following:

```
typedef struct _DEVICE_EXTENSION {
    PDEVICE_OBJECT DeviceObject;  // back pointer
    :
    // other driver-specific declarations
    :
} DEVICE_EXTENSION, *PDEVICE_EXTENSION;
```

The code samples throughout this book will use the device extension in many ways.

Controller Objects and Controller Extensions

Some peripheral adapters manage more than one physical device using the same set of control registers. The floppy disk controller is one example of this architecture. This kind of hardware poses a synchronization dilemma. If the driver tries to perform simultaneous operations on more than one of the connected devices without first synchronizing its access to the shared register space, the control registers receive confusing values. To help with this problem, the I/O Manager provides *controller objects*.

The controller object is a kind of mutex that can be owned by only one device at a time. Before accessing any device registers, the driver asks that ownership of the controller object be given to a specific device. If the hardware is free, ownership is granted. If not, the device's request is put on hold until the current owner releases the hardware. By managing the controller object, the I/O Manager guarantees that multiple devices will access the hardware in a serial fashion. The life cycle of a typical controller object is described below.

1. The DriverEntry (or AddDevice) routine creates the Controller object and usually stores its address in a field of each device's Device Extension.
2. Before it starts a device operation, the Start I/O routine asks for exclusive ownership of the controller object on behalf of a specific device.
3. When the controller object becomes available, the I/O Manager grants ownership and calls the driver's ControllerControl routine. This routine sets up the device's registers and starts the I/O operation. As long as this device owns the controller object, any further requests for ownership block at step 2 until the object is released.
4. When the device operation is finished, the driver's DpcForIsr routine releases the Controller object, making it available for use by other pending requests.
5. The driver's Unload routine deletes the controller object when the driver is unloaded.

Obviously, not all drivers need a controller object. If an interface card supports only one physical or virtual device, or if multiple devices on the same card don't share any control registers, then there is no need to create a controller object.

Layout of the Controller Object

Figure 4.4 shows the relationship of a Controller object to other system data structures. The only externally visible field in a Controller object is the **PVOID ControllerExtension** field, which contains a pointer to the extension block.

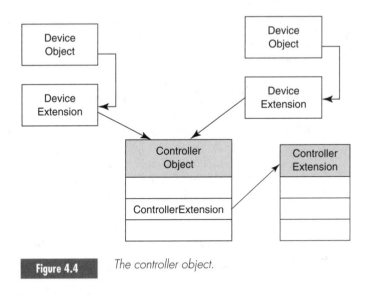

| **Figure 4.4** | *The controller object.* |

Manipulating Controller Objects

The I/O Manager exports four functions that operate on controller objects. These functions are listed in Table 4.8.

Controller Extensions

Like device objects, controller objects contain a pointer to an extension structure that can be used to hold any controller-specific data. The extension is also a place to store any information that's global to all the devices attached to a controller. Finally, if the controller (rather than individual devices) is the source of interrupts, it makes sense to store pointers to Interrupt and Adapter objects in the *Controller Extension*.

Table 4.8	*Access Functions for a Controller Object*	
Controller Object Access Functions		
Function	**Description**	**Called by...**
IoCreateController	Creates a Controller object	DriverEntry or AddDevice
IoAllocateController	Requests exclusive ownership of controller	Start I/O
IoFreeController	Releases ownership of controller	DpcForIsr
IoDeleteController	Removes Controller object from the system	Unload or RemoveDevice

Since the controller extension is driver-specific, its structure must be defined in a driver header file. Although the extension's exact contents depend on what a driver does, its general layout looks something like this:

```
typedef struct _CONTROLLER_EXTENSION {
    // back pointer
    PCONTROLLER_OBJECT ControllerObject
    :
    // other driver-specific declarations
    :
} CONTROLLER_EXTENSION, *PCONTROLLER_EXTENSION;
```

Adapter Objects

Just as multiple devices on the same controller need to coordinate their hardware access, so it is that devices that perform DMA need an orderly way to share system DMA resources. The I/O Manager uses adapter objects to prevent arguments over DMA hardware. There is one adapter object for each DMA data transfer channel on the system.

Like a controller object, an adapter object can be owned by only one device at a time. Before starting a DMA transfer, the Start I/O routine asks for ownership of the adapter object. If the hardware is free, ownership is granted. If not, the device's request is put on hold until the current owner releases the hardware. Obviously, if the device supports only programmed I/O, it has no need for an adapter object. The life cycle of the adapter object is described below.

1. The HAL creates Adapter objects for any DMA data channels detected at boot time.

2. The DriverEntry or AddDevice routine locates the adapter object for its device and stores that pointer in the device or controller extension. Adapter objects for nonsystem (i.e., bus master) DMA hardware may be created on the fly.

3. The Start I/O routine requests ownership of the adapter object on behalf of a specific device.

4. When ownership is granted, the I/O Manager calls the driver's adapter Control routine. This routine then uses the adapter object to set up a DMA transfer.

5. The driver's DpcForIsr routine may use the adapter object to perform additional operations in the case of a split transfer. When a transfer is finished, DpcForIsr releases the adapter object.

Another important function of the adapter object is to manage *mapping registers.* The HAL uses these registers to map the standard physical pages of a

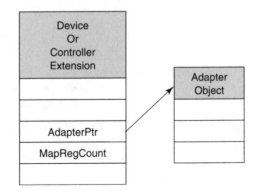

Figure 4.5   *The adapter object.*

user's buffer onto the contiguous range of addresses required by most DMA hardware. The complete mechanics of DMA transfers are covered in detail in chapter 12.

Layout of an Adapter Object

Figure 4.5 illustrates the relationship of adapter objects to other structures. As the diagram shows, the adapter object is completely opaque and has no externally visible fields. When working with DMA devices, the pointer to the adapter object, as well as the number of mapping registers it supports, should be stored in the device extension or controller extension structure.

Table 4.9   *Access Functions for an Adapter Object*

Adapter Object Access Functions		
Function	**Description**	**Called by . . .**
IoGetDmaAdapter	Gets a pointer to an adapter object	DriverEntry or AddDevice
AllocateAdapterChannel	Requests exclusive ownership of DMA hardware	Start I/O
MapTransfer	Sets up DMA hardware for a data transfer	Adapter Control/DpcForIsr
FlushAdapterBuffers	Flushes data after partial transfers	DpcForIsr
FreeMapRegisters	Releases map registers	DpcForIsr
FreeAdapterChannel	Releases adapter object	DpcForIsr

Manipulating Adapter Objects

Both the HAL and the I/O Manager export functions that can be used to manipulate adapter objects. Table 4.9 lists the more common adapter functions.

Interrupt Objects

The last kernel object described in this chapter is the interrupt object. Interrupt objects simply give the kernel's interrupt dispatcher a way to find the right service routine when an interrupt occurs. The life cycle of an interrupt object is described below.

1. The DriverEntry or AddDevice routine creates an interrupt object for each interrupt vector supported by the device or the controller.

2. When an interrupt occurs, the kernel's interrupt dispatcher uses the Interrupt object to locate the Interrupt Service routine.

3. The Unload or RemoveDevice routine deletes the interrupt object after disabling interrupts from the device.

A driver does not interact with interrupt objects other than to create and delete them. A pointer to the interrupt object is typically stored in the device extension or controller extension.

Layout of an Interrupt Object

Figure 4.6 illustrates the structure of an interrupt object. Like adapter objects, they are completely opaque and have no externally visible fields.

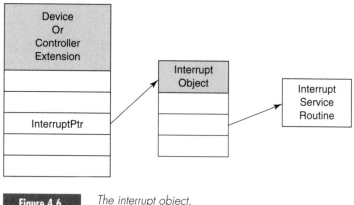

Figure 4.6   *The interrupt object.*

Table 4.10	*Access Functions for an Interrupt Object*

Interrupt Object Access Functions		
Function	**Description**	**Called by...**
HalGetInterruptVector	Converts bus-relative interrupt vector to systemwide value	DriverEntry
IoConnectInterrupt	Associates Interrupt Service routine with an interrupt vector	DriverEntry or AddDevice
KeSynchronizeExecution	Synchronizes driver routines that run at different IRQLs	(Various)
IoDisconnectInterrupt	Removes interrupt object	Unload or RemoveDevice

Manipulating Interrupt Objects

Several system components export functions that work with interrupt objects. Table 4.10 lists the most common ones.

Summary

Although it may seem as if there are a lot of objects involved in I/O processing, all are necessary and important. With this chapter, the background material explanation is complete. The next chapter begins the fun work of writing some actual driver code.

General Development Issues

CHAPTER OBJECTIVES

Writing kernel-mode code is not the same as writing an application program because the driver is a trusted component of the system. Code must be carefully written and follow special rules. This chapter is a short manual of good and sometimes required etiquette for driver writers.

Driver Design Strategies

Like most software, drivers benefit from an organized approach to development. This section gives some guidelines that may help shorten development time.

Use Formal Design Methods

Traditionally, writing a device driver implied a license to code without a design strategy. In the haste to test brand new hardware, the unit test code became the basis for the ultimate driver. Perhaps, too, many device drivers were written by programmers unfamiliar with the operating system. The first driver written is really a journey of discovery as the driver author learns the overall I/O architecture of the system.

Fortunately (or perhaps sadly, depending on one's perspective), the days of software cowboys are over. Between complicated hardware and operating systems, there is no longer room for design-as-you-go coding. Writing Windows 2000 drivers certainly entails a steep learning curve. Good software engineering and practices are required for success.

A short list of design techniques, some of which are borrowed from real-time design methodology, are listed below.

- Data flow diagrams can help break a driver into discrete functional units. These diagrams make it easier to visualize how the functional units in a driver relate to each other, and how they transform input data into output data.
- State-machine models are another good way to describe the flow of control in a driver—especially one that manages an elaborate hardware or software protocol. In the process of verifying the state machine, potential synchronization issues can be identified.
- An analysis of expected data arrival rates or mandatory input-to-output response will give a set of quantitative timing requirements. These are important to establish the overall performance goals of the driver.
- Another useful tool is an explicit list of external events and the driver actions that these events should trigger. This list should include both hardware events from the device and software I/O requests from users.

Using these techniques helps decompose a driver into well-defined functional units. In some cases, this might mean breaking a single, monolithic driver into a pair of port and class drivers that handle hardware-dependent and hardware-independent functions. In any event, the time spent analyzing the design of a driver at the start of the project more than pays for itself in reduced debugging and maintenance.

Use Incremental Development

Once an initial analysis and design is completed, it's time to start the actual development. Following the steps below can reduce debugging time by helping to detect problems while they're still easy to find.

1. Decide which kinds of kernel-mode objects a driver needs.

2. Decide what context or state information a driver needs, and decide where it will be stored.

3. Write the DriverEntry and Unload routines first. Do not initially add Plug and Play support. This allows for testing the driver manually using the Computer Management Console.

4. Add driver dispatch routines that process IRP_MJ_CREATE and IRP_MJ_CLOSE operations. These routines typically do not require device access. The driver can then be tested with a simple Win32 program that calls **CreateFile** and **CloseHandle.**

5. Add code that finds and allocates the driver's hardware, as well as code to deallocate the hardware when the driver unloads. If the hardware supports Plug and Play detection, this step tests the hardware and the driver's ability to automatically load.

6. Add dispatch routines that process any other IRP_MJ_XXX function codes. Initially, these dispatch routines should complete each I/O request without starting the physical device. Again, these new code paths can be tested with a simple Win32 program that makes **ReadFile** and **WriteFile** calls, as appropriate.

7. Finally, implement the real Start I/O logic, the Interrupt Service routine, and the DPC routine. Now the driver can be tested using live data and real hardware.

Another useful tip: When the exact behavior of hardware is unknown, add a **DeviceIoControl** function that gives direct access to the device registers. This allows a simple Win32 program to manipulate the device registers directly. Remember to disable this function before shipping the final version of the driver.

Examine and Use the Sample Drivers

The Windows 2000 Device Driver Kit (DDK) contains a considerable amount of sample code. There are many ways to use this code to make driver development easier. Microsoft encourages cutting and pasting from their sample source code. Of course, as usual, no warranty is implied or should be assumed when using this code.

Coding Conventions and Techniques

Writing a trusted kernel-mode component is not the same as writing an application program. This section presents some basic conventions and techniques to make it easier to code in this environment.

General Recommendations

First of all, here are some general guidelines to follow when writing a driver.

Avoid the use of assembly language in a driver. It makes the code hard to read, nonportable, and difficult to maintain. The C programming language is only a small step away from assembly language, anyway. Further, the HAL macros provide the only safe mechanism to access I/O device registers. Therefore, the use of assembly language in a driver should be extremely rare. Be sure to isolate such code into its own module.

For platform-specific code, provide a separate module, or at the very least, bracket it with **#ifdef/#endif** directives.

A driver should not be linked with the standard C runtime library. Besides being wasteful of memory space (each of 20 drivers should not include the same C runtime library support), some library routines are stateful or hold context information that is not thread-safe or driver-safe.

This particular guideline is perhaps the most uncomfortable aspect of writing device drivers. C programmers who live with their runtime environment day in and day out, often do not make a clear distinction between the C language and the C runtime library. The C runtime library requires initialization. It attempts to initialize a heap area and, in the case of C++, invoke constructors of global objects. All of these tasks interfere with proper driver operation.

Windows 2000 provides its own environmental support for kernel-mode code. This support includes **RtlXxx** functions (RunTime Library) to provide many of the common C runtime library services. Many of these routines are described later in this chapter.

Driver projects should be managed with source-code control. Microsoft Visual Source Safe® is a popular choice. For large projects that span multiple platforms, ClearCase® from Rational Software should also be considered.

Naming Conventions

All large software projects should adopt some standard naming convention for routines and data defined throughout the code. Device driver projects are no exception. Naming conventions improve the efficiency of development, debugging, testing, and maintenance of the driver.

Microsoft provides a naming convention for use with the DDK. A header file, **NTDDK.h,** defines all the data types, structures, constants, and macros used by base-level kernel-mode drivers. By DDK convention, all of these types of names are capitalized. Even native C-language data types are provided a corresponding DDK name. For example, the C data type **void*** is given the name **PVOID** by NTDDK.h. These definitions make future ports to 64-bit platforms easier.

Microsoft recommends that a driver-specific prefix be added to each of the standard driver routines. For example, if writing a mouse class driver, the Start I/O routine might be named **MouseClassStartIo.** Similarly a shorter two or three character prefix should be applied to internal names. This yields a name such as **MouConfiguration.** This recommendation is often, but not always, followed by driver authors.

Regardless of what convention is chosen for a driver project, it is important to establish a consistent way of naming entities within the entire project. It pays to spend a few hours making this decision early in the development life cycle.

Header Files

Besides including NTDDK.h or WDM.h, a driver should use private header files to hide various hardware and platform dependencies. For example, register access macros should be provided in a private header file. These macros should be surrounded by **#ifdef** compiler directives that allow for simple platform-to-platform porting. This technique, of course, solves the issue of register access differences between I/O space and memory space.

Even if portability were not a concern, register access macros make the driver easier to read and maintain. The following code fragment is an example of some hardware beautification macros for a parallel port device. The example assumes that some initialization code in the driver has put the address of the first device register in the **PortBase** field of the device extension.

```
//
//   Define device registers as relative offsets
//
#define PAR_DATA          0
#define PAR_STATUS        1
#define PAR_CONTROL       2
//
//   Define access macros for registers. Each macro
//   Takes a pointer to a Device Extension
//   as an argument.
//
#deinfe ParWriteData( pDevExt, bData )   \
(WRITE_PORT_UCHAR(                        \
    pDevExt->PortBase + PAR_DATA, bData ) )

#define ParReadStatus( pDevExt )         \
(READ_PORT_UCHAR(                         \
    pDevExt->PortBase + PAR_STATUS ))

#define ParWriteControl( pDevExt, bData )   \
(WRITE_PORT_UCHAR(                          \
    pDevExt->PortBase + PAR_CONTROL, bData ) )
```

Status Return Values

The kernel-mode portion of Windows 2000 uses 32-bit status values to describe the outcome of a particular operation. The data type of these codes is NTSTATUS. There are three situations in which this status code is used.

- When using any of the internal Windows 2000 functions, the success or failure of the call is reported by an NTSTATUS value.

- When the I/O Manager calls a driver-supplied callback routine, that routine usually has to return an NTSTATUS value to the system.
- After completing the processing of the I/O request, a driver must mark the IRP with an NTSTATUS value. This value ultimately is mapped onto a Win32 ERROR_XXX code. It is worth noting that NTSTATUS values and Win32 error codes are not identical. The I/O Manager provides a mapping between the two. A DDK topic describes how the mapping occurs and is often not logical.

NTSTATUS.h describes symbolic names for a large number of NTSTATUS values. These names all have the form STATUS_XXX, where XXX describes the actual status message. STATUS_SUCCESS, STATUS_NAME_EXISTS, and STATUS_INSUFFICIENT_RESOURCES are all examples of these names.

When a system routine that returns an NTSTATUS value is called, the DDK header file provides a convenient macro to test for the success or failure of the call. The following code fragment illustrates this technique:

```
NTSTATUS status;
    :
status = IoCreateDevice ( … );
if ( !NT_SUCCESS( status )) {
        // clean up and exit with failure
        :
}
```

Always, always, always check the return value from any system routine called. Failure to follow this rule allows an error to propagate into other areas of the driver code and perhaps system code. Catching errors early is a cardinal rule of software engineering. (Of course, the examples supplied with this book are exempt from this rule for the sake of clarity. ☺)

Windows 2000 Driver Support Routines

The I/O Manager and other kernel-mode components of Windows 2000 export a large number of support functions that a driver can call. The reference section of the DDK documentation describes these functions, and this book includes many examples of their use. For the moment, it's enough to point out that the support routines fall into specific categories based on the kernel module that exports them. Table 5.1 gives a brief overview of the kinds of support that each kernel module provides.

The ZwXxx functions require more explanation. These are actually an internal calling interface for all the NtXxx user-mode system services. The difference between the user and kernel-mode interfaces is that the ZwXxx functions don't perform any argument checking. Although there are a large number of these functions, the DDK reference material describes only a few of them. Use of undocumented functions is always a risk because Microsoft reserves the right to change or delete any of these functions at a future time.

Table 5.1 *Driver Support Routine Categories*

Windows 2000 Driver Support Routines

Category	Supports...	Function names
Executive	Memory allocation Interlocked queues Zones Lookaside lists System worker threads	ExXxx()
HAL	Device register access Bus access	HalXxx()
I/O Manager	General driver support	IoXxx()
Kernel	Synchronization DPC	KeXxx()
Memory Manager	Virtual-to-physical mapping Memory allocation	MmXxx()
Object Manager	Handle management	ObXxx()
Process Manager	System thread management	PsXxx()
Runtime library	String manipulation Large integer arithmetic Registry access Security functions Time and date functions Queue and list support	RtlXxx() (mostly)
Security Monitor	Privilege checking Security descriptor functions	SeXxx()
(Miscellaneous)	Internal system services	ZwXxx()

One final point to make life easier: The I/O Manager provides several convenience functions that are nothing more than wrappers around one or more lower-level calls to other kernel modules. These wrappers offer a simpler interface than their low-level counterparts, and should be used whenever possible.

Discarding Initialization Routines

Some compilers support the option of declaring certain functions as discardable. Functions in this category will disappear from memory after a driver has finished loading, making the driver smaller. If the development environment offers this feature, it should be used.

Good candidates for discardable functions are DriverEntry and any subroutines called only by DriverEntry. The following code fragment shows how to take advantage of discardable code in the Microsoft C environment:

```
#ifdef ALLOC_PRAGMA
#pragma alloc_text( init, DriverEntry )
#pragma alloc_text( init, FuncCalledByDriverEntry )
#pragma alloc_text( init, OtherFuncCalledByDriverEntry )
:
#endif
```

The **alloc_text** pragma must appear after the function name is declared, but before the function itself is defined—so remember to prototype the function at the top of the code module (or better yet, in a suitable header file). Also, functions referenced in the pragma statement must be defined in the same compilation unit as the pragma.

Controlling Driver Paging

Nonpaged system memory is a precious resource. A driver can reduce the burden it places on nonpaged memory by defining appropriate routines in paged memory. Any function that executes only at PASSIVE_LEVEL IRQL can be paged. This includes Reinitialize routines, Unload and Shutdown routines, Dispatch routines, thread functions, and any helper functions running exclusively at PASSIVE_LEVEL IRQL. Once again, it is the **alloc_text** pragma that performs the declaration. An example follows.

```
#ifdef ALLOC_PRAGMA
#pragma alloc_text( page, Unload )
#pragma alloc_text( page, Shutdown )
#pragma alloc_text( page, DispatchRead )
#pragma alloc_text( page, DispatchHelper )
:
#endif
```

Finally, if the entire driver is seldom used, it can be temporarily paged out. The system routine **MmPageEntireDriver** overrides a driver's declared memory management attributes and makes the entire module temporarily paged. This function should be called at the end of the DriverEntry routine and from the Dispatch routine for IRP_MJ_CLOSE when there are no more open handles to any of its devices. Be sure to call **MmResetDriverPaging** from the IRP_MJ_CREATE Dispatch routine to ensure that the driver's page attributes revert to normal while the driver is in use.

When using this technique, beware of the inherent dangers. First, make sure there are no IRPs being processed by high-IRQL portions of the driver before calling **MmPageEntireDriver**. Second, be certain that no device interrupts arrive while the driver's ISR is paged.

Driver Memory Allocation

An important aspect of programming concerns the need to allocate storage. Unfortunately, drivers don't have the luxury of making simple calls to **malloc** and **free,** or **new** and **delete.** Instead, care must be taken to ensure that memory of the right type is allocated. Drivers must also be sure to release any memory they allocate, since there is no automatic cleanup mechanism for kernel-mode code. This section describes techniques a driver can use to work with temporary storage.

Memory Available to Drivers

There are three options for allocating temporary storage in a driver. The criteria used to select the right storage type depends on factors such as duration, size, and from what IRQL level the code which accesses it will be running. The available options are

- **Kernel stack.** The *kernel stack* provides limited amounts of non-paged storage for local variables during the execution of driver routines.
- **Paged pool.** Driver routines running below DISPATCH_LEVEL IRQL can use a heap area called *paged pool.* As the name implies, memory in this area is pagable, and a page fault can occur when it is accessed.
- **Nonpaged pool.** Driver routines running at elevated IRQLs need to allocate temporary storage from another heap area called *nonpaged pool.* The system guarantees that the virtual memory in nonpaged pool is always physically resident. The device and controller extensions created by the I/O Manager come from this pool area.

Because a driver must be reentrant, global variables are almost never declared. The only exception occurs for read-only data. Otherwise, the attempt by one thread of execution to store into the global variable interferes with another thread's attempt to read or write the same data.

Of course, local static variables in a driver function are just as bad. State for a driver must be kept elsewhere, such as in a device extension as just described.

Working with the Kernel Stack

On the x86 platform, the kernel stack is only 12 KB in size. On other platforms, the stack size is 16 KB. Therefore, the kernel stack must be considered a precious resource. Overflowing the kernel stack will cause an exception—something to be avoided at all costs in kernel mode. To avoid kernel stack overflowing, follow these guidelines.

- Don't design a driver in such a way that internal routines are deeply nested. Keep the call tree as flat as possible.
- Avoid recursion, but where required, limit the depth of recursion. Drivers are not the place to be calculating Fibonacci series using a recursive algorithm.
- Do not use the kernel stack to build large data structures. Use one of the pool areas instead.

Another characteristic of the kernel stack is that it lives in cached memory. Therefore, it should not be used for DMA operations. DMA buffers should be allocated from nonpaged pool. Chapter 12 describes DMA caching issues in more detail.

Working with the Pool Areas

To allocate memory in the pool area, drivers use the kernel routines **ExAllocatePool** and **ExFreePool.**

These functions allow the following kinds of memory to be allocated:

- **NonPagedPool** is memory available to driver routines running at all IRQL levels, including DISPATCH_LEVEL IRQL.
- **NonPagedPoolMustSucceed** is temporary memory that is crucial to the driver's continuing operation. Use this memory for emergencies only and release it as quickly as possible. In fact, since an exception is generated if the requested memory is unavailable, consider never using this option.
- **NonPagedPoolCacheAligned** is memory that is guaranteed to be aligned on the natural boundary of the CPU data-cache line. A driver might use this kind of memory for a permanent I/O buffer.
- **NonPagedPoolCacheAlignedMustS** is storage for a temporary I/O buffer that is crucial to the operation of the driver. The S at the end of the request name stands for *succeed*. As with the previous Must-Succeed option, this request should probably never be used.
- **PagedPool** is memory available only to driver routines running below DISPATCH_LEVEL IRQL. Normally, this includes the driver's initialization, cleanup, and Dispatch routines and any kernel-mode threads the driver is using.
- **PagedPoolCacheAligned** is I/O buffer memory used by file system drivers.

There are several things to keep in mind when working with the system memory areas. First and foremost, the pools are a precious system resource, and their use should not be extravagant. This is especially true of the Non-Paged area.

Second, a driver must be executing at or below DISPATCH_LEVEL IRQL when allocating or freeing nonpaged memory. A driver must be executing at or below APC_LEVEL IRQL to allocate or free from the paged pool.

Finally, release any memory as soon as it is no longer needed. Otherwise, overall system performance is impacted because of low memory conditions. In particular, be sure to give back pool memory when a driver is unloaded.

System Support for Memory Suballocation

Generally, a driver should avoid constantly allocating and releasing small blocks of pool memory. *Small* is defined as in a request smaller than PAGE_SIZE bytes. Such requests fragment the pool areas and can make it impossible for other kernel-mode code to allocate memory. If such requests are unavoidable in a driver design, consider allocating a single, large chunk of pool and provide private suballocation routines for the driver to use.

In fact, a clever C programmer could write private versions of **malloc** and **free** that operate against a large pool area. A C++ programmer could override the **new** and **delete** operators for such purpose.

Some drivers need to manage a collection of small, fixed-size memory blocks. A SCSI driver, for example, must maintain a supply of SCSI request blocks (SRBs), which are used to send commands to a SCSI device. The kernel provides two different mechanisms that can be used to handle the details of suballocation.

ZONE BUFFERS

A *zone buffer* is just a chunk of driver-allocated pool. Executive routines provide management services of collections of fixed-size blocks in paged or nonpaged memory.

The use of zone buffers requires careful synchronization planning. In particular, if an Interrupt Service, DPC, and/or Dispatch routine all need access to the same zone buffer, an Executive spin lock must be used to guarantee noninterference. If the accessing routines all operate at the same IRQL level, a fast mutex can be used instead. Spin locks are described later in this chapter. Fast mutexes are described in chapter 14.

To set up a zone buffer, a structure of type ZONE_HEADER must be declared. The spin lock or fast mutex object may also need to be declared and initialized. The following steps describe the entire process of managing a zone buffer.

1. Call **ExAllocatePool** to claim space for the zone buffer itself. Then initialize the zone buffer with **ExInitializeZone.** Typically, these steps are performed in the DriverEntry routine.

2. To allocate a block from a zone, call either **ExAllocateFromZone** or **ExInterlockedAllocateFromZone.** The interlocked version of the

function uses a spin lock to synchronize access to the zone buffer. The noninterlocked function leaves synchronization entirely up to the driver code.

3. To release a block back to the zone, use either **ExFreeToZone** or **InterlockedFreeToZone.** Again, the interlocked version of the function synchronizes access to the zone.

4. In the driver's Unload routine, use **ExFreePool** to release the memory used for the entire zone buffer. A driver must ensure that no blocks from the zone are in use when the deallocation occurs.

A zone buffer should be no larger than necessary to keep memory usage to a minimum. A dynamic approach to sizing the zone buffer would be to use the function **MmQuerySystemSize** to discover the total amount of system memory available. Another Executive function, **MmIsThisAnNTAsSystem,** checks whether the current platform is running a server version of Windows 2000 (Server or Advanced Server). Drivers running in server environments could allocate a larger zone buffer size to meet the expected higher I/O demands of the server.

If the request to allocate a block from a zone buffer fails, the driver could use the standard pools to grant the requested block instead. This strategy requires a clever structure to indicate whether an allocation came from the zone or the pool. The appropriate deallocation routine must be called to release the block.

An existing zone buffer can be enlarged by calling **ExExtendZone** or **ExInterlockedExtendZone,** but these routines should be used infrequently. The system does not appear to deallocate memory from extended zones correctly. In fact, the entire zone buffer abstraction is considered obsolete. Windows 2000 provides a more efficient mechanism, which is described in the next section.

LOOKASIDE LISTS

A *lookaside list* is a linked list of fixed-size memory blocks. Unlike zone buffers, lookaside lists can grow and shrink dynamically in response to changing system conditions. Therefore, properly sized lookaside lists are less likely to waste memory than zone buffers.

Compared to zone buffers, the synchronization mechanism used with lookaside lists is also more efficient. If the CPU architecture has an 8-byte compare-exchange instruction, the Executive uses it to serialize access to the list. On platforms without such an instruction, it reverts to using a spin lock in nonpaged pool and a fast mutex for lists in paged pool.

To use a lookaside list, a structure of type NPAGED_LOOKASIDE_LIST or PAGED_LOOKASIDE_LIST (depending on whether the list is nonpaged or paged must be allocated). The following steps describe the process of lookaside list management:

1. Use either the **ExInitializeNPagedLookasideList** or **ExInitialize-PagedLookasideList** function to initialize the list header structure. Normally, the DriverEntry or AddDevice routine performs this task.

2. Call either **ExAllocateNPagedLookasideList** or **ExAllocatePaged-LookasideList** to allocate a block from a lookaside list. These calls are invoked throughout the life of the driver.

3. Call **ExFreeToNPageLookasideList** or **ExFreeToPageLookasideList** to release a block.

4. Use **ExDeleteNPagedLookasideList** or **ExDeletePagedLookasideList** to release any resources associated with the lookaside list. Usually this is a function invoked from the driver's Unload or RemoveDevice routine.

The lookaside list initialize functions simply set up the list headers. They do not actually allocate memory for the list. The initialization functions require that the maximum number of blocks that the list can hold be specified. This is referred to as the *depth of the list*.

When using the allocation functions, the system allocates memory as needed. As blocks are freed, they are chained to the lookaside list up to the maximum allowable depth. After that, any additional blocks freed results in memory being released back to the system. Thus, after a while, the number of available blocks in the lookaside list tend to remain near the depth of the list.

The depth of the lookaside list should be chosen carefully. If too shallow, the system is performing expensive allocation and deallocation operations too often. If too deep, memory is wasted. Statistics are maintained in the list header structure and can help determine a proper value for the depth of the list.

Unicode Strings

All character strings in the Windows 2000 operating system are stored internally as Unicode. The Unicode scheme uses 16 bits to represent each character and makes it easier to port applications and the OS itself to most languages of the world. Unicode is an industry standard (incidentally, the character coding standard for Java). More information can be found at the Web site *http://www.Unicode.org*. Unless otherwise noted, any character strings a driver sends to or receives from Windows 2000 will be Unicode. Note, however, that data transfer between a user's buffer and the device is not necessarily Unicode. Data transfers are considered to be binary and transparent to the I/O subsystem of Windows 2000.

Unicode String Data Types

The Unicode data type is now part of the C-language specification. To use "wide" characters in a program, perform the following:

Table 5.2	*The UNICODE_STRING Data Structure*

UNICODE_STRING, *PUNICODE_STRING

Field	Contents
USHORT Length	Current string length in bytes
USHORT MaximumLength	Maximum string length in bytes
PWSTR Buffer	Pointer to driver-allocated buffer holding the real string data

- Prefix Unicode string constants with the letter L. For example, L"some text" generates Unicode text, while "some text" produces 8-bit ANSI.
- Use the **wchar_t** data type for Unicode characters. The DDK header files provide a typedef, **WCHAR,** for the standard wchar_t, and **PWSTR**, for wchar_t*.
- Use the constant UNICODE_NULL to terminate a Unicode string. A UNICODE_NULL is defined to be 16 bits of zero.

Windows 2000 system routines work with a Unicode structure, UNICODE_STRING, described in Table 5.2. The purpose of this structure is to make it easier to pass around Unicode strings and to help manage them. Although the standard C library provides Unicode string functions to perform common operations (e.g., wcscpy is equivalent to strcpy for wchar_t* data), this environment is not available to kernel-mode driver code.

Incidentally, the DDK also defines an ANSI_STRING structure. It is identical to the UNICODE_STRING structure except that the buffer offset is of type char*. Several Rtl conversion routines require the data type of ANSI_STRING.

Working with Unicode

The kernel provides a number of functions for working with the ANSI and Unicode strings. These functions replace (albeit clumsily) the standard C library routines that work with Unicode. Table 5.3 presents several of these functions. The Windows 2000 DDK provides the authoritative list and usage of the functions and should be reviewed. Some of these functions have restrictions on the IRQL levels from which they can be called, so care must be taken when using them. To be safe, it is best to restrict the use of all Rtl Unicode functions to PASSIVE_LEVEL IRQL.

Working with Unicode can be frustrating primarily because the length in bytes of a Unicode string is twice the content length. C programmers are ingrained with the belief that one character equals one byte, but with Unicode the rule is changed. When working with Unicode, consider the following:

| Table 5.3 | *Common Unicode Manipulation Functions* |

Unicode String Manipulation Functions

Function	Description
RtlInitUnicodeString	Initializes a UNICODE_STRING from a NULL-terminated Unicode string
RtlAnsiStringToUnicodeSize	Calculates number of bytes required to hold a converted ANSI string
RtlAnsiStringToUnicodeString	Converts and ANSI string to Unicode
RtlIntegerToUnicodeString	Converts an integer to Unicode text
RtlAppendUnicodeStringToString	Concatenates two Unicode strings
RtlCopyUnicodeString	Copies a source string to a destination
RtlUpcaseUnicodeString	Converts Unicode string to uppercase
RtlCompareUnicodeString	Compares two Unicode strings
RtlEqualUnicodeString	Tests equality of two Unicode strings

- Remember that the number of characters in a Unicode string is not the same as the number of bytes. Be very careful about any arithmetic that calculates the length of a Unicode string.
- Don't assume anything about the collating sequence of the characters or the relationship of uppercase and lowercase characters.
- Don't assume that a table with 256 entries is large enough to hold the entire character set.

For convenience, this book provides a C++ class wrapper, CUString, for use with the UNICODE_STRING structure. This CUString class encapsulates a UNICODE_STRING structure, providing many constructors and conversion operators that in turn rely on the Rtl Unicode functions of the kernel. A portion of this CUString class declaration is listed below.

```
// Unicode.h
//

#pragma once

class CUString {
public:
    CUString() {Init(); }   // constructor relies on
                            // internal Init function
    CUString(const char* pAnsiString);
    CUString(PCWSTR pWideString);
    ~CUString();            // destructor gives back
                            // buffer allocation
    void Init();  // performs "real" initialization
    void Free (); // performs real destruct
```

```
    // copy constructor (required)
    CUString(const CUString& orig);
    // assignment operator overload (required)
    CUString operator=(const CUString& rop);
    // comparison operator overload
    BOOLEAN operator==(const CUString& rop) const;
    // concatenation operator
    CUString operator+(const CUString& rop) const;
    // cast operator into wchar_t*
    operator PWSTR() const;
    // cast operator into ULONG
    operator ULONG() const;
    // converter: ULONG->CUString
    CUString(ULONG value);
    // buffer access operator
    WCHAR& operator[](int idx);
    USHORT Length() {return uStr.Length/2;}
protected:
    UNICODE_STRING uStr;  // W2K kernel structure for
                          // Unicode string
    enum ALLOC_TYPE {Empty, FromCode, FromPaged};
    ALLOC_TYPE    aType; // where buffer is allocated
};
```

The disk included with this book supplies two files, Unicode.h. and Unicode.cpp, that hold the declaration and implementation of the CUString class. The methods of this class assume that users are at PASSIVE_LEVEL IRQL. Routines that allocate memory do so from the paged pool. The use of the class is intended for convenience, and not for heavy-duty string manipulation. Consider modifying the class implementation to allocate memory from a lookaside list if more intense string manipulation is required by a driver.

Of course, at this point it might seem premature to be introducing portions of driver code. After all, building and loading a driver is not discussed until the next chapter. However, the code included for this chapter supplies a trivial, mock environment to test code such as the CUString class from the Win32 environment. Rtl stub functions rely on either Win32 or C runtime library functions to perform a reasonably faithful emulation of kernel runtime support. A simple Win32 console program is included to demonstrate the use of the CUString class. A portion of the test program is shown below.

```
#include "DDKTestEnv.h"
#include "Unicode.h"
#include "stdio.h"
int main(int argc, char* argv[])
{
    CUString strEmpty;
    CUString strOne("One");
    CUString strTwo(L"Two");

    CUString str2468("2468");
    ULONG ul2468 = str2468;
```

```
CUString strxFF01("xFF01");
ULONG ulxFF01 = strxFF01;
CUString str2244(2244);
CUString strOnePlusTwo = strOne + strTwo;

wprintf(L"strOnePlusTwo: %s\n",
        (PWSTR) strOnePlusTwo);
printf("Conversion of str2468 into ULONG = %d\n",
        ul2468);
printf("Conversion of strxFF01 into ULONG = %x\n",
        ulxFF01);
wprintf(L"Conversion of 2244 into CUString = %s\n",
        (PWSTR) str2244);
wprintf(L"On the fly conversion of 3366 into "
        "CUString = %s\n",
        (PWSTR)(CUString)3366);
printf("Test of buffer access operator []:\n");
for (int i=0; i<strOnePlusTwo.Length(); i++) {
    wprintf(L"%c ", strOnePlusTwo[i]);
    strOnePlusTwo[i] = L'A' + i;
}

wprintf(L"\nAfter replacing buffer, "
        "strOnePlusTwo = %s\n",
        (PWSTR)strOnePlusTwo);
    . . .
```

Two files, DDKTestEnv.h and DDKTestEnv.cpp, supply the declaration and implementation of the emulation environment. This environment was intended to be simple and provide a testbed of some driver logic before entering the real kernel-mode environment.

Interrupt Synchronization

Writing reentrant code that executes at multiple IRQL levels requires attention to proper synchronization. This section examines the issues that arise in this kind of environment.

The Problem

If code executing at two different IRQLs attempts to access the same data structure simultaneously, the structure can become corrupted. Figure 5.1 illustrates the details of this synchronization problem.

To understand the exact problem, consider this sequence of events.

1. Suppose code executing at a low IRQL decides to modify several fields in the **foo** data structure. For this example, the code executes to the point where the field **foo.x** is set to 1.

2. An interrupt occurs and a higher-IRQL piece of code gets control of the processor. This code also modifies **foo,** setting **foo.x** to 10 and **foo.y** to 20.

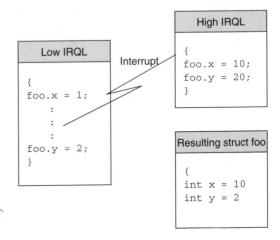

Figure 5.1   *Synchronization problem with interrupting code.*

3. When the higher-IRQL code dismisses its interrupt and control returns to the lower-IRQL routine, the original modification of **foo** completes by setting **foo.y** to 2. The lower-IRQL code is completely unaware that it was interrupted.

4. The **foo** structure is now inconsistent, with 10 in the **x** field and 2 in the **y** field. Neither section of code obtains the desired result.

Of course, similar results occur even when only a single shared value is used with different code threads. When one code path attempts to increment the variable, there may be a brief moment in time when the modified value is held in a CPU register. If this thread is interrupted prior to storing the register back into the variable, the same contention problem arises.

In the following sections, techniques that a driver can use to synchronize the work of multiple code paths is described.

Interrupt Blocking

In the previous example, the lower-IRQL routine could have avoided synchronization problems by preventing itself from being interrupted. To do this, it can temporarily raise the IRQL of the CPU and then lower it back to its original level after completing the modification. This technique is called *interrupt blocking*. Table 5.4 lists the kernel functions that a driver can use to manipulate the IRQL value.

Rules for Blocking Interrupts

When using interrupt blocking, there are certain rules that must be followed.

Table 5.4	*Functions that control the CPU's IRQL level.*

Interrupt Blocking Function

Function	Description
KeRaiseIrql	Changes the CPU IRQL to a specified value, blocking interrupts at or below that IRQL level
KeLowerIrql	Lowers the CPU IRQL value
KeGetCurrentIrql	Returns the IRQL value of the CPU on which this call is made

- Every piece of code touching a protected (shared) data structure must agree on the IRQL level to use for synchronization. The agreement requires that no code path touch the structure (read or write) unless the IRQL has been raised to the chosen level.
- If lower-IRQL level code elevates to the agreed upon IRQL level, it should remain there as briefly as possible. Depending on the blocking level, other hardware interrupts could remain blocked for too long unless this rule is followed.
- While a driver can elevate a code's IRQL level, it should never drop the IRQL level below its original value. Disobeying this rule compromises the entire system interrupt priority mechanism.

Synchronization Using Deferred Procedure Calls

DPCs provide another way to avoid data structure collisions. If all the kernel-mode components using a particular data structure access it only from within a DPC routine, there will be no corruption since DPC routines are always executed serially. The main advantage of using DPCs for synchronization is that they run at a relatively low IRQL.

Another key advantage of DPC routines is that the kernel's DPC Dispatcher automatically handles synchronization in a multi processor (MP) environment. The next section describes what is required to perform manual synchronization among multiple processors.

Synchronizing Multiple CPUs

Modifying the IRQL of one CPU has no effect on other CPUs and multiprocessor systems. Consequently, IRQLs provide only local CPU protection to share data. To prevent corruption of data structures in a multiprocessor environment, Windows 2000 uses synchronization objects called *spin locks*.

How Spin Locks Work

A spin lock is simply a mutual-exclusion object that is associated with a specific group of data structures. When a piece of kernel-mode code wants to touch any of the guarded data structures, it must first request ownership of the associated spin lock. Since only one CPU at a time can own the spin lock, the data structure is safe from contamination. Any CPU requesting an already-owned spin lock will busy-wait until the spin lock becomes available. Figure 5.2 illustrates the process.

A given spin lock is always acquired and released at a specific IRQL level. This has the effect of blocking dangerous interrupts on the local CPU and preventing the synchronization problems described earlier. While a CPU is waiting for a spin lock, all activity at or below the IRQL of the spin lock is blocked on that CPU. Both steps are essential—elevate the IRQL level *and* acquire the spin lock.

Using Spin Locks

There are two major kinds of spin locks provided by the kernel. They are distinguished by the IRQL level at which they are used.

- **Interrupt spin locks.** These synchronize and provide access to driver data structures shared by multiple-driver routines. Interrupt spin locks are acquired at the DIRQL associated with the device.
- **Executive spin locks.** These guard various operating system data structures, and their associated IRQL is DISPATCH_LEVEL.

When a driver uses Interrupt spin locks, operation is straightforward. The function **KeSynchronizeExecution** is described in chapter 8.

Executive spin locks are more complicated to work with. The following steps must be followed when using Executive spin locks:

CPU 1	CPU 2
Raise IRQL	Raise IRQL
Repeat	Repeat
Request Spin Lock	Request Spin Lock
Until ACQUIRED	Until ACQUIRED
foo.x = 1;	foo.x = 10;
foo.y = 2;	foo.y = 20;
Release Spin Lock	Release Spin Lock
Restore IRQL	Restore IRQL

Spin Lock for foo

Resulting struct foo
int x = 10
int y = 20

Figure 5.2   *Spin locks.*

1. Decide what data items must be guarded and how many spin locks should be used. Additional spin locks allow finer granularity of access to the data. However, the possibility of deadlock is present whenever acquisition of more than one spin lock at a time is required.

2. Reserve space for a data structure of type KSPIN_LOCK for each lock. Storage for the spin lock must be in nonpaged pool. Usually, the spin lock is declared in the device or controller extension.

3. Initialize the spin lock once by calling **KeInitializeSpinLock.** This function can be called from any IRQL level, though it is most commonly used from the DriverEntry routine.

4. Call **KeAcquireSpinLock** before touching any resource guarded by a spin lock. This function raises IRQL to DISPATCH_LEVEL, acquires the spin lock, and returns the previous IRQL value. This function must be called at or below DISPATCH_LEVEL IRQL. If the code is already at DISPATCH_LEVEL, a more efficient call is **KeAcquireSpinLockFromDpcLevel.**

5. When access to the resource is complete, use the **KeReleaseSpinLock** function to free the lock. This function is called from DISPATCH_LEVEL IRQL and it restores IRQL to its original value. If the original level was known to be DISPATCH_LEVEL, a more efficient call would be **KeReleaseSpinLockFromDpcLevel,** which releases the lock without changing IRQL.

Some driver support routines (like the interlock lists and queues described in the next section) use Executive spin locks for protection. In these cases, the only requirement is that the spin lock object be initialized. The driver support routines that manage the interlocked object will acquire and release the spin lock on the driver's behalf.

Rules for Using Spin Locks

Spin locks aren't terribly difficult to use, but there are a few rules that should be followed.

- Be sure to release a spin lock as soon as possible because while holding it, other CPU activity may be blocked. The official DDK recommendation is not to hold a spin lock for more than about 25 microseconds.
- Don't cause any hardware or software exceptions while holding the spin lock. This is a guaranteed system crash.
- Don't access any page code or data while holding the spin lock. This may result in a page fault exception.
- Don't try to acquire a spin lock the CPU already owns. This leads to a deadlock situation since the CPU freezes up, waiting for itself to release the spin lock.

- Avoid driver designs that depend on holding multiple spin locks simultaneously. Without careful design, this can lead to a deadly embrace condition. If multiple spin locks must be used, ensure that all code paths agree to acquire them in a fixed order and release them in the exact reverse order.

Linked Lists

Drivers sometimes need to maintain linked list data structures. This section describes the support available for managing singly and doubly linked lists.

Singly Linked Lists

To use singly linked lists, begin by declaring a list head of type **SINGLE_LIST_ENTRY.** This simplistic structure is also the data type of the linked pointer itself. Indeed, the SINGLE_LIST_ENTRY structure has but one offset: **Next.** The list head must be manually initialized, as demonstrated in the following code fragment.

```
typedef struct _DEVICE_EXTENSION {
     :
    SINGLE_LIST_ENTRY listHead;    // Declare head ptr
} DEVICE_EXTENSION, *PDEVICE_EXTENSION;
     :
pDevExt->listHead.Next = NULL;     // init the list
```

To add or remove entries from the front of the list, call **PushEntryList** and **PopEntryList.** Depending on how the list is used, the actual entries can be in either page or nonpaged memory. Remember that the use of these functions may require synchronization.

The Windows 2000 kernel also provides convenient support for singly linked lists guarded by an Executive spin lock. This kind of protection is important when sharing a linked list among driver routines running at or below DISPATCH_LEVEL IRQL. To use one of these lists, set up the list head in the usual way, and then initialize an Executive spin lock that guards the list.

```
typedef struct _DEVICE_EXTENSION {
     :
    SINGLE_LIST_ENTRY listHead;    // head pointer
    KSPIN_LOCK listLock;       // declare list lock
} DEVICE_EXTENSION, *PDEVICE_EXTENSION;
     :
KeInitializeSpinLock(&pDevExt->listLock);
pDevExt->listHead.Next = NULL;
```

Once the list head and spin lock are declared and initialized, the functions **ExInterlockedPushEntryList** and **ExInterlockedPopEntryList** provide convenient, protected access to the list. Code must be running at or below DISPATCH_LEVEL IRQL to use either function. The list entries themselves must reside in nonpaged memory, since the system will be linking and unlinking them from DISPATCH_LEVEL IRQL.

Doubly Linked Lists

To use doubly linked lists, declare a list head of type LIST_ENTRY. This is also the data type of the linked pointer itself. The LIST_ENTRY structure declares two offsets, Flink and Blink, for the forward and back pointers. The list head is initialized with a helper routine, **InitializeListHead,** as demonstrated in the following code fragment.

```
typedef struct _DEVICE_EXTENSION {
    :
LIST_ENTRY listHead;      // head pointer
} DEVICE_EXTENSION, *PDEVICE_EXTENSION;
    :
InitializeListHead( &pDevExt->listHead );
```

To add entries to the list, call **InsertHeadList** or **InsertTailList,** and to pull entries out, call **RemoveHeadList** or **RemoveTailList.** To determine if the list is empty, use **IsListEmpty.** Again, the entries can be paged or nonpaged, but these functions do not perform synchronization.

The Windows 2000 kernel also supports interlocked doubly linked lists. To use these, set up the list head in the usual way, and then initialize an Executive spin lock that guards the list.

```
typedef struct _DEVICE_EXTENSION {
    :
LIST_ENTRY listHead;      // head pointer
KSPIN_LOCK listLock;      // the list's lock
} DEVICE_EXTENSION, *PDEVICE_EXTENSION;
    :
KeInitializeSpinLock( &pDevExt->listLock );
InitializeListHead( &pDevExt->listHead );
```

The spin lock is passed in calls to **ExInterlockedInsertTailList, ExInterlockedInsertHeadList,** and **ExInterlockedRemoveHeadList.** To make these calls, code must be running at or below DISPATCH_LEVEL IRQL. Entries for doubly linked interlock lists have to live in nonpaged memory.

Removing Blocks from a List

When a block is pulled from a list, the pop function returns a pointer to the LIST_ENTRY or SINGLE_LIST_ENTRY structure. Since these structures are merely a part of a bigger structure, a pointer to the containing structure must be obtained. One simple technique would be to ensure that the LIST_ENTRY structure is the first offset of the containing structure. Then, a pointer to the

Table 5.5	CONTAINING_RECORD Macro Arguments

CONTAINING_RECORD Macro

Parameter	Description
Address	Address returned by list "removal" function
Type	Data type of the "containing structure"
Field	Field within "containing structure" where Address argument points
Return value	Pointer to "containing structure"

LIST_ENTRY structure is also a pointer to the containing structure. Otherwise, clever use of the *offsetof* operator is required to dig out a pointer to the containing structure. Fortunately, Windows 2000 provides a macro, CONTAINING_RECORD, to make the process easier. The macro arguments are listed in Table 5.5

The following code fragment demonstrates the use of the CONTAINING_RECORD macro.

```
typedef struct _MYBLOCK {
    ULONG ulSomeThingAtTopOfBlock;
    :
    LIST_ENTRY listEntry;
    :
} MYBLOCK, *PMYBLOCK;
    :
PMYBLOCK pMyBlock;
PLIST_ENTRY pEntry;
    :
pEntry = RemoveHeadList( &pDevExt->listHead );
pMyBlock = CONTAINING_RECORD( pEntry, MYBLOCK, listEntry);
```

Notice that, for whatever reason, the LIST_ENTRY field could not be the first offset within the MYBLOCK structure. Therefore, the address returned by **RemoveHeadList** needed to be converted into a pointer of the containing structure.

Summary

In this chapter some general guidelines for designing and coding a Windows 2000 device driver were covered. The prerequisites to coding the initial Windows 2000 device driver are now in place. In the next chapter, an actual device driver is implemented.

Initialization and Cleanup Routines

CHAPTER OBJECTIVES

*Everything has to start somewhere. In the case of a Windows 2000 kernel-mode driver, the starting point is a function called **DriverEntry**. This chapter shows how to write a DriverEntry routine along with various other pieces of initialization and cleanup code. At the conclusion of this chapter, a minimal driver is produced that can actually load into the system.*

Writing a DriverEntry Routine

Every Windows 2000 kernel-mode or WDM driver, regardless of its purpose, has to expose a routine whose name is **DriverEntry**. This routine initializes various driver data structures and prepares the environment for all the other driver components.

Execution Context

The I/O Manager calls a DriverEntry routine once it loads the driver. As Table 6.1 shows, the DriverEntry routine runs at PASSIVE_LEVEL IRQL, which means it has access to page system resources.

The DriverEntry routine receives a pointer to its own driver object, which it must initialize. It also receives a UNICODE_STRING containing the path to the driver's service key in the Registry. WDM drivers have little use for this registry name. Kernel-mode drivers rely on the string to extract any driver-specific parameters stored in the system registry. The Registry String takes the form HKEY_LOCAL_MACHINE\System\CurrentControlSet\Services\ DriverName.

What a DriverEntry Routine Does

Although the exact details vary based on whether a driver is WDM or kernel-mode, in general the following steps are taken in a DriverEntry routine.

1. DriverEntry locates hardware that it will be controlling. That hardware is *allocated*—it is marked as under the control of this driver.

2. The driver object is initialized by *announcing* other driver entry points. The announcements are accomplished by storing function pointers directly into the driver object.

3. If the driver manages a multiunit or multifunction controller, **IoCreate-Controller** is used to create a controller object. A controller extension is then initialized.

4. **IoCreateDevice** is used to create a device object for each physical or logical device under the control of this driver. A device extension is then initialized.

5. The created device is made visible to the Win32 subsystem by calling **IoCreateSymbolicLink**.

6. The device is connected to an interrupt object. If the ISR requires the use of a DPC object, it is created and initialized in this step.

Table 6.1	*Function Prototype for DriverEntry*
NTSTATUS DriverEntry	**IRQL == PASSIVE_LEVEL**
Parameter	**Description**
IN PDRIVER_OBJECT pDriverObject	Address of driver object for this driver
IN PUNICODE_STRING pRegistryPath	Registry path string for this driver's key
Return value	• STATUS_SUCCESS
	• STATUS_XXX – some error code

7. Steps 4 to 6 are repeated for each physical or logical device controlled by this driver.

8. If successful, DriverEntry should return STATUS_SUCCESS to the I/O Manager.

It is important to understand that steps 1 and 3 to 6 are not performed by a WDM driver's DriverEntry routine. They are deferred to another routine, AddDevice.

If DriverEntry should fail during initialization for any reason, it should release any system resources it may have allocated up to the failure, and return an appropriate NTSTATUS failure code to the I/O Manager.

The following sections describe some of the steps in more detail. The process of finding and allocating hardware is complex and heavily impacted by the device's ability to be autorecognized. Chapter 9 describes this step in more detail. The use of an interrupt object and DPCs is deferred until chapter 8.

Announcing DriverEntry Points

The I/O Manager is able to locate the DriverEntry routine because it has a well-known name. (Actually, the linker announces the address of DriverEntry using a command line switch. Nevertheless, the DDK documentation mandates that this entry point be called *DriverEntry*.) Other driver routines don't have fixed names, so the I/O Manager needs some other way to locate them. The linkage mechanism is the driver object, which contains pointers to other driver functions. A DriverEntry routine is responsible for setting up these function pointers.

These function pointers fall into two categories.

- Functions with explicit slots and names in the driver object.
- IRP dispatch functions that are listed in the driver object's **Major-Function** array. These functions are the subject of chapter 7.

The following code fragment shows how a DriverEntry routine initializes both kinds of function pointers.

```
pDO->DriverStartIo = StartIo;
pDO->DriverUnload = Unload;
//
// Initialize the MajorFunction Dispatch table
//
pDO->MajorFunction[ IRP_ MJ_CREATE ] = DispatchCreate;
pDO->MajorFunction[ IRP_MJ_CLOSE ] = DispatchClose;
:
```

Creating Device Objects

Once hardware is identified and allocated, the next step is to create a device object for each physical or virtual device that is to be exposed to the rest of the system. Most of the work is done by the **IoCreateDevice** function, which takes a description of the device and returns a device object, complete with an attached device extension. **IoCreateDevice** also links the new device object into the list of devices managed by this driver object. Table 6.2 contains a description of this function.

The DeviceType parameter of **IoCreateDevice** is simply a 16-bit value describing the class of device being added. Microsoft reserves the first half of this range for predefined device types. Above 32767, private device types can be defined. Beware, though, that conflict with another vendor's device is always possible. Currently, Microsoft predefines about 30 device types. The predefined device type values are given symbolic names of the form FILE_DEVICE_XXX (e.g., FILE_DEVICE_DVD).

One final point about creating device objects: Although this chapter describes the use of IoCreateDevice from DriverEntry, it is usually called from AddDevice (WDM) and occasionally from a Dispatch routine. In such a case, it is imperative that the driver reset a bit in the **Flags** field of the device object once it is created. This bit is called DO_DEVICE_INITIALIZING and is normally reset upon return from DriverEntry. The bit is reset with code similar to the following:

```
pDevObject->Flags &= ~DO_DEVICE_INITIAILIZING;
```

Do not clear this bit until the device object is actually initialized and ready to process requests.

Table 6.2	*Function Prototype for IoCreateDevice*
NTSTATUS IoCreateDevice	**IRQL == PASSIVE_LEVEL**
Parameter	**Description**
IN PDRIVER_OBJECT pDriverObject	Pointer to driver object
IN ULONG DeviceExtensionSize	Requested size of DEVICE_EXTENSION
IN PUNICODE_STRING pDeviceName	Internal device name (see below)
IN DEVICE_TYPE DeviceType	FILE_DEVICE_XXX (see NTDDK.h)
IN ULONG DeviceCharacteristics	Characteristics of mass-storage device: • FILE_REMOVABLE_MEDIA • FILE_READ_ONLY_DEVICE • Etc.
IN BOOLEAN Exclusive	TRUE if device is not sharable
OUT PDEVICE_OBJECT *pDeviceObject	Variable that receives device object pointer
Return value	• STATUS_SUCCESS –or- • STATUS_XXX – some error code

Choosing a Buffering Strategy

If the **IoCreateDevice** call succeeds, the I/O Manager must be notified of whether buffered I/O or direct I/O will be used with the device. The choice is designated by selecting appropriate bits into the **Flags** field of the new device object.

- **DO_BUFFERED_IO**. The I/O Manager copies data back and forth between user and system-space buffers.
- **DO_DIRECT_IO**. The I/O Manager locks user buffers into physical memory for the duration of an I/O request and builds a descriptor list of the pages in the buffer.

The next chapter explains how user buffers are accessed using both techniques. If neither bit is set in the **Flags** field, the I/O Manager assumes that the driver needs no further help from the I/O Manager when accessing the user's buffer.

Device Names

Devices in Windows 2000 can have more than one name. Internally, the name specified by **IoCreateDevice** is the name by which the device is known to the Windows 2000 Executive itself. This internal name is (almost) completely hidden from Win32 user applications. In order to expose the device to the Win32 subsystem, the Win16 subsystem, or the virtual DOS environment, the new device must be given a symbolic link name in addition to its internal name.

These two types of names live in different parts of the Object Manager's namespace. The Object Manager maintains a directory of names for all resources managed by the operating system. Internal device names are stored beneath the **\Device** section of the directory tree. Symbolic link names appear beneath the **\??** tree. Figure 6.1 illustrates this relationship. When using **IoCreateDevice**, the entire \Device name *must* be supplied. For example, "\\Device\\Minimal0" is a suitable device name string. (The double backslash (\\) is necessary in C so that the character following the first backslash \ will not be considered a special character sequence, like \t.)

Internal and symbolic link names follow different device naming conventions. Internal device names tend to be longer, and they always end in a zero-based number (e.g., *FloppyDisk0* or *FloppyDisk1*). Symbolic link names follow the usual pattern of A through Z for file-system devices, and names ending in a one-based number for other devices (e.g., *LPT1* or *LPT2*).

To create a symbolic link name, use **IoCreateSymbolicLink**. This function takes an existing device name and a new symbolic name (both passed as UNICODE_STRING data types).

Finally, it must be noted that the selection of the device name is not necessarily the option of the driver. In the WDM world, bus drivers, class drivers, and many Plug and Play devices define their own names. Chapter 9 de-

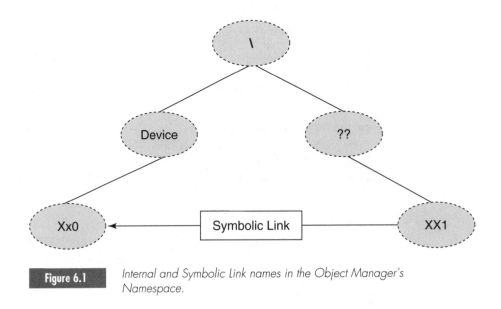

| Figure 6.1 | *Internal and Symbolic Link names in the Object Manager's Namespace.* |

scribes this process more fully. In the meantime, non-WDM drivers must supply their own unique names for each device added.

Code Example: Driver Initialization

The following example shows how a basic kernel-mode device driver initializes itself. The code for this example is in chapter 6 directory on the disk that accompanies this book.

This first minimal driver must be manually loaded. It does not touch any hardware, but instead creates an internal device name (MINIMAL0) and a symbolic link name (MIN1). It consists of a single source module, Driver.cpp. A header file, Driver.h, declares driver-specific information about our non-hardware device, such as the DEVICE_EXTENSION.

DRIVERENTRY

In our first non-WDM driver example, the DriverEntry routine is small and straightforward. The responsibilities include

1. Announcing other DriverEntry points. For the Minimal driver, the only other routine to announce is the driver's Unload function.

2. Creating the logical devices that will be managed by the Minimal driver. For initial testing purposes, only a single device will be created.

```
//++
// Function: DriverEntry
//
// Description:
//        Initializes the driver, locating and claiming
//        hardware resources. Creates the kernel objects
//        needed to process I/O requests.
//
// Arguments:
//        pDriverObject - Passed from I/O Manager
//        pRegistryPath - UNICODE_STRING pointer to
//                                registry info (service key)
//                                for this driver
//
// Return value:
//        NTSTATUS signaling success or failure
//-
NTSTATUS DriverEntry (
                IN PDRIVER_OBJECT pDriverObject,
                IN PUNICODE_STRING pRegistryPath  ) {
    ULONG ulDeviceNumber = 0;
    NTSTATUS status;

    // If this driver controlled real hardware,
    // code would be placed here to locate it.
    // Using IoReportResourceUsage, the ports,
    // IRQs, and DMA channels would be "marked"
    // as "in use" and under the control of this driver.
    // This minimal driver has no HW, so...

    // Announce other driver entry points
    pDriverObject->DriverUnload = DriverUnload;
    // Over time, the MajorFunction array will be filled

    // For each physical or logical device detected
    // that will be under this Driver's control,
    // a new Device object must be created.
    status =
        CreateDevice(pDriverObject, ulDeviceNumber);
    // This call would be repeated until
    // all devices are created. E.g.,
    // ulDeviceNumber++;
    // status =
    // CreateDevice(pDriverObject, ulDeviceNumber);

    return status;
}
```

CREATEDEVICE

The work of actually creating the device object is delegated to a module-private (static) routine called **CreateDevice.** Although this routine doesn't do much, modularizing this work is appropriate as this driver evolves into a full WDM driver. Its responsibilities include

1. Choosing and forming an internal device name. This driver hard-codes the name passed into the function.

2. Creating the internal device object. The size of the DEVICE_EXTENSION is specified in the call to IoCreateDevice.

3. Initializing the DEVICE_EXTENSION. In the case of this Minimal driver, the DEVICE_EXTENSION holds a back pointer to the device object and names for the device and symbolic link.

4. Forming a symbolic link name and linking the name created.

The CreateDevice routine relies on the C++ class, CUString, discussed in the last chapter. The use of CUString makes it simple to convert numbers into Unicode strings and append them onto device names.

```
//++
// Function: CreateDevice
//
// Description:
//          Adds a new device
//
// Arguments:
//          pDriverObject - Passed from I/O Manager
//          ulDeviceNumber - Logical device number (zero-based)
//
// Return value:
//          None
//--
NTSTATUS CreateDevice (
      IN PDRIVER_OBJECT      pDriverObject,
      IN ULONG               ulDeviceNumber ) {

 NTSTATUS status;
 PDEVICE_OBJECT pDevObj;
 PDEVICE_EXTENSION pDevExt;

 // Form the internal Device Name
 CUString devName("\\Device\\MINIMAL"); // for "minimal" device
 devName += CUString(ulDeviceNumber);

 // Now create the device
 status =
        IoCreateDevice( pDriverObject,
                        sizeof(DEVICE_EXTENSION),
                        &(UNICODE_STRING)devName,
                        FILE_DEVICE_UNKNOWN,
                        0, TRUE,
                        &pDevObj );
 if (!NT_SUCCESS(status))
        return status;

 // Initialize the Device Extension
 pDevExt = (PDEVICE_EXTENSION)pDevObj->DeviceExtension;
```

```
pDevExt->pDevice = pDevObj;      // back pointer
pDevExt->DeviceNumber = ulDeviceNumber;
pDevExt->ustrDeviceName = devName;

// Form the symbolic link name
CUString symLinkName("\\??\\MIN");
symLinkName += CUString(ulDeviceNumber+1);      // 1 based
pDevExt->ustrSymLinkName = symLinkName;

// Now create the link name
status =
      IoCreateSymbolicLink( &(UNICODE_STRING)symLinkName,
                            &(UNICODE_STRING)devName );
if (!NT_SUCCESS(status)) {
      // if it fails now, must delete Device object
      IoDeleteDevice( pDevObj );
      return status;
}

// Made it
return STATUS_SUCCESS;
}
```

Writing Reinitialize Routines

Intermediate-level drivers loading at system boot time may need to delay their initialization until one or more lower-level drivers have finished loading. If the loading of the drivers is under central control, the load sequence can be fixed by setting various Registry entries at installation. But if the drivers are supplied by different vendors, the load order may be indeterminate. In the latter case, the intermediate driver must register and implement a Reinitialize routine.

Execution Context

If the DriverEntry routine discovers that it can't finish its initialization because system bootstrapping hasn't yet gone far enough, it can announce a Reinitialize routine by calling **IoRegisterDriverReinitialization**. The I/O Manager calls the Reinitialize routine at some later point during the bootstrap. As described in Table 6.3, the Reinitialize routine runs at PASSIVE_ LEVEL IRQL, which means it has access to paged system resources. Reinitialize routines are useful only for drivers that load automatically at system boot.

What a Reinitialize Routine Does

The Reinitialize routine can perform any driver initialization that the Driver-Entry routine was unable to complete. If the Reinitialize routine discovers that

Table 6.3	*Function Prototype for Reinitialize Routine*
VOID Reinitialize	**IRQL == PASSIVE_LEVEL**
Parameter	**Description**
IN PDRIVER_OBJECT pDriverObject	Pointer to driver object
IN PVOID Context	Context block specified at registration
IN ULONG Count	Zero-based count of reinitialization calls
Return value	(void)

the environment still isn't suitable, it can call **IoRegisterDriverReinitialization** again to reregister itself.

Writing an Unload Routine

By default, once the driver is loaded, it remains in the system until a reboot occurs. To make a driver unloadable, an Unload routine is necessary. The Unload routine is announced during DriverEntry. The I/O Manager then calls this routine whenever the driver is manually or automatically unloaded.

Execution Context

The I/O Manager calls a driver's Unload routine just before removing the driver from memory. Table 6.4 shows that the Unload routine runs at PASSIVE_LEVEL IRQL, which means it has access to paged system resources.

What an Unload Routine Does

Although the exact details vary from driver to driver, in general the following steps are performed in an Unload routine.

1. For some kinds of hardware, the state of the device should be saved in the Registry. That way, the device can be restored to its last known state

Table 6.4	*Function Prototype for Unload Routine*
VOID Unload	**IRQL == PASSIVE_LEVEL**
Parameter	**Description**
IN PDRIVER_OBJECT pDriverObject	Pointer to driver object for this driver
Return value	(void)

the next time DriverEntry executes. For example, an audio card driver might save the current volume setting of the card.

2. If interrupts have been enabled for the device, the Unload routine must disable them and disconnect from its interrupt object. It is crucial that the device not generate any interrupt requests once the interrupt object is deleted.

3. Hardware belonging to the driver must be deallocated.

4. The symbolic link name must be removed from the Win32 namespace. This is accomplished using **IoDeleteSymbolicLink**.

5. The device object itself must be removed using **IoDeleteDevice**.

6. If managing multiunit controllers, repeat steps 4 and 5 for each device attached to the controller. Then remove the controller object itself, using **IoDeleteController.**

7. Repeat steps 4 through 6 for all controllers and devices that belong to the driver.

8. Deallocate any pool memory held by the driver.

It is important to note that for WDM drivers, the responsibilities of Unload are performed in the RemoveDevice routine.

One final note: A driver's Unload routine is not called at system shutdown time. Any special work required during system shutdown must be performed inside of a separate shutdown routine.

Code Example: Driver Unload

In the Minimal driver, an Unload routine is supplied that undoes the work of DriverEntry. Its work is straightforward, as it must delete each symbolic link and device object that has been created. To perform this work, the Unload routine relies on the fact that the driver object points to a linked list of device objects controlled by the driver.

The first device controlled by a driver is pointed to by the field **DeviceObject** within the driver object. Each device points to the next via the field **NextDevice**. When examining the Unload routine, remember that the Minimal DEVICE_EXTENSION structure maintains a back pointer to the parent device object.

```
//++
// Function:   DriverUnload
//
// Description:
//          Stops & Deletes devices controlled by this driver.
//          Stops interrupt processing (if any)
//          Releases kernel resources consumed by driver
//
// Arguments:
```

```
//         pDriverObject - Passed from I/O Manager
//
// Return value:
//         None
//-

VOID DriverUnload (
        IN PDRIVER_OBJECT    pDriverObject ) {

    PDEVICE_OBJECT pNextObj;

    // Loop through each device controlled by Driver
    pNextObj = pDriverObject->DeviceObject;
    while (pNextObj != NULL) {
        // Dig out the Device Extension from the
        // Device Object
        PDEVICE_EXTENSION pDevExt = (PDEVICE_EXTENSION)
            pNextObj->DeviceExtension;
        // This will yield the symbolic link name
        UNICODE_STRING pLinkName =
            pDevExt->ustrSymLinkName;
        // ... which can now be deleted
        IoDeleteSymbolicLink(&pLinkName);
        // a little trickery...
        // we need to delete the device object, BUT
        // the Device object is pointed to by pNextObj
        // If we delete the device object first,
        // we can't traverse to the next Device in the list
        // Rather than create another pointer, we can
        // use the DeviceExtension's back pointer
        // to the device.
        // So, first update the next pointer...
        pNextObj = pNextObj->NextDevice;
        // then delete the device using the Extension
        IoDeleteDevice( pDevExt->pDevice );
    }
    // Finally, hardware that was allocated in DriverEntry
    // would be released here using
    // IoReportResourceUsage
}
```

Writing Shutdown Routines

If a driver has special processing to do before the operating system disappears, a driver should supply a Shutdown routine.

Execution Context

The I/O Manager calls a Shutdown routine during a system shutdown. As described in Table 6.5, the Shutdown routine runs at PASSIVE_LEVEL IRQL, which means it has access to paged system resources.

Table 6.5	*Function Prototype for Shutdown Routine*
NTSTATUS Shutdown	**IRQL == PASSIVE_LEVEL**
Parameter	**Description**
IN PRDRIVE_OBJECT pDriverObject	Pointer to driver object for this driver
IN PIRP pIrp	Pointer to shutdown IRP
Return value	• STATUS_SUCCESS –or- • STATUS_XXX – some error code

What a Shutdown Routine Does

The main purpose of the Shutdown routine is to put the device into a quiescent state and perhaps store some device information into the system Registry. Again, saving the current volume settings from a sound card is a good example of something a Shutdown routine might do.

Unlike the driver's Unload routine, Shutdown routines don't have to worry about releasing driver resources because the operating system is about to disappear anyway.

Enabling Shutdown Notification

There is no direct field in the Driver object for announcing the Shutdown routine. Instead, the event of system shutdown is sent as a separate I/O request to a driver. It is handled with an entry inside of the driver's **Major-Function** code array.

Additionally, the I/O Manager must be notified that a driver is interested in receiving shutdown notifications. This is done by making a call to **IoRegisterShutdownNotification**. The following code fragment shows how to enable shutdown notifications in a driver.

```
NTSTATUS DriverEntry (
    IN PDRIVER_OBJECT pDriverObject,
    IN PUNICODE_STRING pRegistryPath ) {
    :
    pDriverObject->MajorFunction[ IRP_MJ_SHUTDOWN ] =
            Shutdown;
    IoRegisterShutdownNotification( pDriverObject );
    :
}
```

Testing the Driver

Even though the Minimal driver is far from being useful, its operation can be verified in several ways. In particular, it can be tested to ensure that it

- Compiles and links successfully
- Loads and unloads without crashing the system
- Creates device objects and Win32 symbolic links
- Releases any resources when it unloads

While these goals may not seem very ambitious, they are an important milestone in beginning the construction of the rest of a truly useful driver.

Testing Procedure

While a description of the production-level installation of the device driver must be left until chapter 16, a manual installation of the Minimal driver can be performed now. The disk accompanying this book includes a useful tool that makes this job much easier.

Visual C++ Device Driver AppWizard

In the Tools folder of the accompanying disk, there is a file called DDApp-Wiz.awx. This file is the result of building a custom AppWizard project for Visual C++. When properly installed, it allows the creation of the new project that sets up the Visual C++ environment for Windows 2000 device driver development. For example, it modifies the linker settings to specify the -driver switch. It supplies the correct list of DDK libraries to the linker. It specifies the required load address of 0x10000. In short, it makes the construction of the Windows 2000 device driver project about as simple as starting an MFC application.

To install this AppWizard, it is necessary to copy DDAppWiz.awx into the appropriate Visual Studio directory. The exact location varies based on the installation directory chosen for Visual Studio. Typically, the correct target directory for the AppWizard file is \Program Files\Microsoft Visual Studio\Common\MSDev98\Template. The correct directory can be confirmed by examining a file called Readme.txt in the target. Once the file is correctly copied, selecting File, then New, and then Project should reveal a new option for Windows 2000 device driver development.

Indeed, a Developer Studio Project and Workspace environment is supplied in the chapter 6 folder of the disk. The Minimal.dsw workspace can be opened directly and the build attempted. The example code listed in this chapter is already included in this project.

The Windows 2000 DDK

The Windows 2000 Device Driver Kit must be installed on a development system in order to build device drivers. As mentioned in chapter 1, the DDK is available for download from the *Microsoft.com* site. By default, it installs into a folder named NTDDK. If another folder name is chosen during installation of the DDK, the Project settings supplied by the device driver AppWizard must be modified.

The DDK allows for two different build environments, checked and free. The checked build environment is analogous to the Debug build environment of Visual C++, while the free build environment is analogous to the Release setting. As such, two different sets of libraries are supplied with the DDK, Libfre and Libchk. For the initial build of the Minimal project, it is suggested that a checked build be performed. This is easily done by selecting the Debug project target.

Results of the Driver Build

Once a driver is successfully built, a file ending with a .SYS extension is created. In the case of the Minimal driver, the file is called Minimal.SYS. This file must be copied to the appropriate Windows directory before it can be loaded. The target directory is typically \WINNT\System32\Drivers. The WINNT portion of the name varies based on the name selected during the Windows 2000 installation.

The project settings supplied by the AppWizard include a post-build step, which copies the driver to the appropriate directory. It is important to keep the results of each build in sync with the Drivers directory.

Installing a Kernel-Mode Driver Manually

Merely copying the driver file to its target directory is not enough to complete the installation of the new device driver. For non-WDM drivers, appropriate entries must be made into the system Registry before the driver can be loaded.

A list of available device drivers is kept in the Registry path HKEY_LOCAL_MACHINE\System\CurrentControlSet\Services. Each driver is listed with a separate subkey whose name must be the same as the Driver.SYS file, without the .SYS extension.

For each driver subkey, three Registry DWORD values must be supplied: **ErrorControl**, **Start**, and **Type**. These entries describe when the driver is loaded (e.g., boot or on-demand), how it reports errors (e.g., MsgBox), and a very generic description of the type of driver (kernel-mode or file system). For the Minimal driver, it is suggested that the values be set as follows:

    ErrorControl = 1

    Start = 3

    Type = 1

Optionally, a **DisplayName** value can be set, which is the name shown in the Computer Management Console window when using its Device Manager.

A file, Minimal.reg, sets the subkey name and values automatically. Simply double-click the filename from Windows Explorer. A reboot of Windows 2000 is necessary after adding a new device driver using this method. Once the Registry entries have been established, however, the driver can be replaced at will without need of further reboots.

Loading the Driver

Once the driver is known to the system, it may or may not start automatically when the system boots. The **Start** value in the driver's Registry key specifies this behavior. A **Start** value of 3 specifies demand-loading for a driver. With versions of NT prior to Windows 2000, the Control Panel could be used to start and stop on-demand drivers. With the advance of WDM drivers, Windows 2000 has delegated this task to the Computer Management Console—which can be activated from Control Panel.

The dynamic loading of device drivers is largely handled by a system component known as the Service Control Manager (SCM). The SCM provides many services for software components that run under Windows 2000. For example, it starts, stops, and controls *services*. A service is a process that runs outside the context of a logged-on user. It is analogous to a Unix daemon.

A Control Panel applet supplied with NT 4 was a simple front-end for the SCM. In Windows 2000 it has been replaced with a Device Manager group of the Computer Management Console plug-in (part of the Microsoft Management Console (MMC) initiative). The Computer Management tool provides useful information for loaded device drivers and a (somewhat) hidden mechanism to manually load and unload kernel-mode drivers such as Minimal.

The CD included with this book includes a simple tool, DriverControl.exe in the CD's Tools folder. This utility registers a legacy driver with the SCM. It must be used before the Computer Management Console can recognize the new driver. Simply type the name of the driver (e.g., Minimal) into the Driver Name box and click Start.

Windows 2000 Computer Management Console

Once the Minimal driver has been successfully built and copied to the Drivers directory, the new Computer Management Console can be used to verify the presence of the driver. To use the standard tool, click Start, Settings, then Control Panel, and then choose the Computer Management option. A familiar navigation pane is displayed on the left that includes a list of System Tools. One of these tools is the Device Manager. Expanding its group allows the display of the list of devices currently installed for the system. To see devices that are not Plug and Play compatible, right-click the Devices group, choose View, and select *Show hidden devices*. The Minimal driver should appear in the non-WDM drivers of the right pane. See Figure 6.2 for a display showing the DisplayName for the Minimal driver.

By double-clicking the appropriate DisplayName and then selecting the Driver tab, the Minimal driver can be started and stopped. See Figure 6.3.

Additionally, the System Information group beneath the System Tools group can be used to display information about the Minimal driver. Expand System Information, then select Drivers.

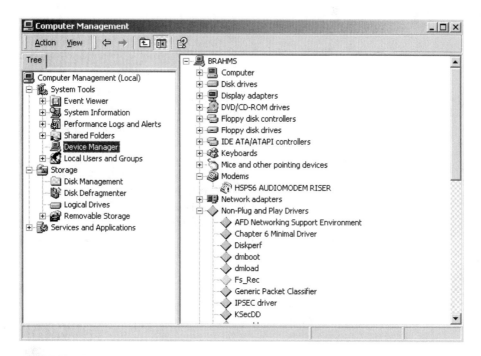

Figure 6.2   *Computer Management Console.*

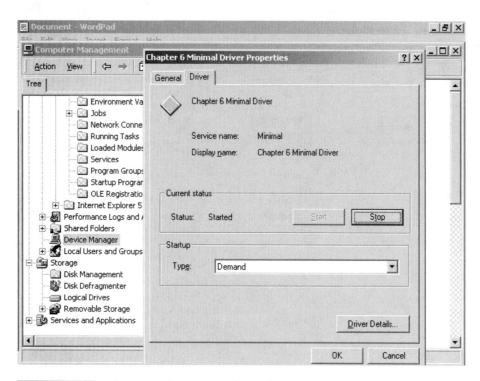

Figure 6.3   *Starting and stopping a device driver.*

The WINOBJ Utility

WINOBJ is a utility that is supplied with the Win32 Platform SDK (*not* with the DDK). This tool allows the user to view the internal namespace of the Windows 2000 Object Manager. For device driver authors, WINOBJ is useful because it displays the contents of the *Drivers, Devices,* and *??* directories.

WINOBJ has not been a well-supported utility by Microsoft. It still contains many quirks that have been present for many versions of Windows NT. A much-improved version of WINOBJ is supplied at the site *http://www.sysinternals.com*. The improved version of WINOBJ, available at the site, works well with Windows 2000. The site also contains many useful utilities for device driver authors. A sample screen of WINOBJ with two Minimal devices (MIN1 and MIN2) is shown in Figure 6.4.

Using WINOBJ, a properly installed version of the Minimal driver should reveal the name *Minimal0* under the Device directory, the name *Min1* under the *??* directory, and the driver name *Minimal* under the Driver

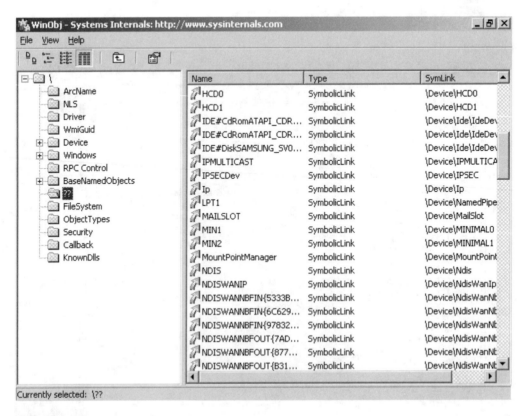

Figure 6.4   *WINOBJ from www.sysinternals.com.*

directory. When the driver is stopped, the names *Minimal0* and *Min1* should disappear. Do not forget to refresh the view of these directories.

Summary

This completes the implementation of an initial Windows 2000 device driver. Granted, this Minimal driver is kernel-mode only. Converting it to a WDM driver must wait until chapter 9. Nevertheless, tools to build and install a driver are now ready to go. Additionally, the beginning structure of the kernel-mode device driver is forming.

The next chapter discusses the Dispatch routines necessary to make the driver useful. Read, Write, and I/O Control functions are implemented. Coding shown in the next chapter builds upon the minimal driver built in this chapter.

Driver Dispatch Routines

CHAPTER OBJECTIVES

Getting a driver to load is the first step, but ultimately the job of a driver is to respond to I/O requests—from user-mode applications or from other parts of the system. Windows 2000 drivers process these requests by implementing Dispatch routines. The I/O Manager in response to a request calls these routines. This chapter describes the basic Dispatch routines and explains the overall process of handling I/O requests.

Announcing Driver Dispatch Routines

Before a driver can process I/O requests, it must announce what kinds of operations it supports. This section describes the I/O Manager's dispatching mechanism and explains how to enable receipt of appropriate I/O function codes. It also presents guidelines for deciding which function codes should be supported for different device types.

I/O Request Dispatching Mechanism

Windows 2000 I/O operations are packet-driven. When an I/O request is initiated, the I/O Manager first builds an IRP work-order to keep track of the request. Among other things, it stores a function code in the **MajorField** field of the IRP's I/O stack location to uniquely identify the type of request.

The **MajorField** code is used by the I/O Manager to index the Driver object's **MajorFunction** table. The table contains a function pointer to a Dispatch routine specific to the I/O request. If a driver does not support the requested operation, the **MajorFunction** table entry points to an entry within the I/O Manager, **_IopInvalidDeviceRequest,** which returns an error to the original caller. Thus, it is the responsibility of the driver author to provide Dispatch routines for each I/O function code that it supports. Figure 7.1 illustrates this process.

Enabling Specific Function Codes

To enable specific I/O function codes, a driver must first "announce" the Dispatch routine that responds to such a request. The announcement mechanism is simply the work performed by DriverEntry that stores the Dispatch routine

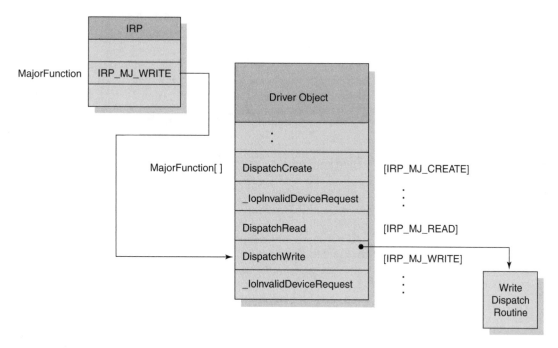

Figure 7.1   *Dispatch routine selection.*

function address into the appropriate slot of the **MajorFunction** table of the driver object. The I/O function code is the index used for the table. The following code fragment illustrates the process of announcement.

```
NTSTATUS DriverEntry( IN PDRIVER_OBJECT pDO,
                      IN PUNICODE_STRING pRegPath ) {
        :
    pDO->MajorFunction[ IRP_MJ_CREATE ] = DispCreate;
    pDO->MajorFunction[ IRP_MJ_CLOSE ] = DispClose;
    pDO->MajorFunction[ IRP_MJ_CLEANUP ] = DispCleanup;
    pDO->MajorFunction[ IRP_MJ_READ ]= DispRead;
    pDO->MajorFunction[ IRP_MJ_WRITE ] = DispWrite;
        :
    return STATUS_SUCCESS;
}
```

Notice that each I/O function code (table index) is identified by a unique symbol of the form IRP_MJ_XXX, defined by the NTDDK.h (and WDM.h) include file. Of course, these symbolic constants should always be used in lieu of hard-coded constants.

The announcement technique also allows for a single routine to be used to handle multiple request types. DriverEntry would place the common Dispatch routine address in multiple table slots. Since the IRP workorder contains the requested code, the common function could dispatch internally as appropriate.

Finally, it should be noted that function codes drivers do not support should be left untouched by DriverEntry. The I/O Manager fills the entire MajorFunction table of the Driver object with pointers to _IopInvalidDeviceRequest *before* calling DriverEntry.

Deciding Which Function Codes to Support

All drivers must support the function code IRP_MJ_CREATE since this code is generated in response to the Win32 **CreateFile** call. Without support for this code, Win32 applications would have no way to obtain a handle to the device. Similarly, the IRP_MJ_CLOSE must also be supported to handle the Win32 **CloseHandle** call. Incidentally, the CloseHandle call is made automatically by the system for all handles left open at the time of application termination.

The other function codes that a driver should support depend on the nature of the device it controls. Table 7.1 associates I/O function codes with the Win32 calls that generate them. When writing layered drivers, the higher driver must support a superset of the lower driver(s) since the user request dispatches through the higher driver first.

Table 7.1	*IRP Function Codes*

IRP MajorFunction Codes

Function Code	Description
IRP_MJ_CREATE	Request for a handle
	• **CreateFile**
IRP_MJ_CLEANUP	Cancel pending IRPs on handle close
	• **CloseHandle**
IRP_MJ_CLOSE	Close the handle
	• **CloseHandle**
IRP_MJ_READ	Get data from device
	• **ReadFile**
IRP_MJ_WRITE	Send data to device
	• **WriteFile**
IRP_MJ_DEVICE_CONTROL	Control operation
	• **DeviceIoControl**
IRP_MJ_INTERNAL_DEVICE_CONTROL	Control operation available only to kernel-mode clients (no Win32 call)
IRP_MJ_QUERY_INFORMATION	Get length of file
	• **GetFileSize**
IRP_MJ_SET_INFORMATION	Set length of file
	• **SetFileSize**
IRP_MJ_FLUSH_BUFFERS	Write or discard buffers
	• **FlushFileBuffers**
	• **FlushConsoleInputBuffer**
	• **PurgeComm**
IRP_MJ_SHUTDOWN	System shutting down
	• **InitiateSystemShutdown**

Writing Driver Dispatch Routines

Depending on the complexity of the device operation and the kind of I/O request, driver Dispatch routines range from trivial to quite difficult to implement. This section explains how to code these routines.

Execution Context

All Dispatch routines share the same function signature. (A function signature includes the number and type of parameters, and its calling convention.) Table 7.2 shows the prototype for all Dispatch routines. Like the driver's initialization and unload routines, Dispatch routines run at PASSIVE_LEVEL IRQL, which means they can access paged system resources.

The I/O Manager invokes Dispatch routines in response to user-mode or kernel-mode requests. Before calling, the I/O Manager builds and fills the IRP with valid data. This includes the pointer to the user's buffer. The user buffer is validated by the I/O Manager to ensure that each page address spanned by the buffer is readable or writeable within the context of the requestor. If the request is for Buffered I/O, the I/O Manager first allocates a nonpaged pool buffer and, if a write request, copies data from the user buffer into the pool. If the request is for Direct I/O, the I/O Manager faults the entire user buffer into physical memory and locks it down.

A Dispatch routine can usually track the state of an I/O request using only the IRP. If a Dispatch routine uses any data structures outside the IRP, the driver must ensure that proper synchronization steps are taken. This would mean using a spin lock to coordinate with other driver routines running at DISPATCH_LEVEL or below IRQL, and **KeSynchronizeExecution** to synchronize with Interrupt Service code.

The IRP is shared data, albeit serially, with the I/O Manager. In particular, the I/O Manager uses fields of the **Parameters** union to complete the I/O request. For example, after a Buffered I/O request, it needs to copy data from the nonpaged pool into the user buffer. It must then deallocate the pool buffer. A field within the **Parameters** union points to this buffer. Therefore, changing the value of this buffer pointer would lead to disastrous results.

In general, if a Dispatch routine needs to modify an IRP field, it should make working copies on the stack or in the device extension.

Table 7.2	*Function Prototype for Dispatch Routines*
NTSTATUS Dispatch	**IRQL==PASSIVE_LEVEL**
Parameter	**Description**
IN PDEVICE_OBJECT pDevObject	Pointer to target device for this request
IN PRIP pIrp	Pointer to IRP describing this request
Return value	• STATUS_SUCCESS – request complete
	• STATUS_PENDING – request pending
	• STATUS_XXX – appropriate error code

What Dispatch Routines Do

The exact behavior of a Dispatch routine will depend on the function it supports. However, the general responsibilities of these routines include the following.

1. Call **IoGetCurrentIrpStackLocation** to get a pointer to the IRP stack location belonging to this driver.

2. Perform any additional parameter validation specific to this request and device.

3. For an intermediate-level driver, consideration must be given to the limitations of the underlying physical device (for example, its maximum transfer size). The Dispatch routine may need to split the caller's request into multiple requests for the lower-level driver.

4. Continue processing the IRP until the request is complete or an error condition prevents further processing.

Exiting the Dispatch Routine

When a Dispatch routine processes an IRP, there are only three possible outcomes.

- The request's parameters do not pass the driver's validation tests and the request is rejected.
- The request can be handled entirely within the Dispatch routine without need for any device operation. An example of such a request would be a Read of zero bytes.
- The device must be started in order to complete the request.

Each of these possible outcomes is described in more detail in the following sections.

SIGNALING AN ERROR

If a Dispatch routine uncovers a problem with the IRP, it needs to reject the request and notify the caller. The following steps describe how to reject an IRP.

1. Store an appropriate error code in the **Status** field of the IRP's **IoStatus** block and clear the **Information** field.

2. Call **IoCompleteRequest** to release the IRP with no priority increment. (Priority increment is discussed in a later section.)

3. The Dispatch routine should return the same error code placed in the **Status** field of the IRP.

The code fragment below shows how a Dispatch routine rejects an I/O request.

```
NTSTATUS DispatchWrite(  IN PDEVICE_OBJECT pDO,
                         IN PIRP pIrp ) {
    :
    // If the request is not supported by this device…
    // report it and reject the request
    pIrp->IoStatus.Status = STATUS_NOT_SUPPORTED;
    // report that no bytes were transferred
    pIrp->IoStatus.Information = 0;
    // Mark the IRP as "complete", no priority increment
    IoCompleteRequest( pIrp, IO_NO_INCREMENT);
    return STATUS_NOT_SUPPORTED;
}
```

Note that after marking the IRP as complete, the I/O Manager is free to release the IRP memory storage from nonpaged pool. As such, it would be incorrect to

```
return pIrp->IoStatus.Status;
```

since the memory pointed to by pIrp has already been released.

COMPLETING A REQUEST

Some I/O requests can be handled without performing any actual device operations. Opening a handle to a device or returning information stored in the device object are examples of these kinds of requests. To complete such a request in the Dispatch routine, do the following:

1. Put a successful completion code in the **Status** field of the IRP's **IoStatus** block, and set the **Information** field to some appropriate value.
2. Call **IoCompleteRequest** to release the IRP with no priority increment.
3. Exit the Dispatch routine with a value of STATUS_SUCCESS.

The code fragment below shows how a Dispatch routine completes a request.

```
NTSTATUS DispatchClose(  IN PDEVICE_OBJECT pDO,
                         IN PIRP pIrp ) {
    :
    pIrp->IoStatus.Status = STATUS_SUCCESS;
    // Indicate that zero bytes of data were transferred
    pIrp->IoStatus.Information = 0;
    // "Mark" the IRP as complete - no further processing
    IoCompleteRequest( pIrp, IO_NO_INCREMENT );
    return STATUS_SUCCESS;
}
```

SCHEDULING A DEVICE OPERATION

The last action a Dispatch routine might take is the most likely—that it will need to interact with the actual device to fulfill the request. Examples include a data transfer, a control function, or an informational query. In this case, the Dispatch routine must queue the IRP for ultimate processing by the driver's Start I/O routine and then promptly return to the I/O Manager stating that the request is pending. To schedule (queue) a device operation, do the following:

1. Call **IoMarkIrpPending** to inform the I/O Manager that the request is still in progress.

2. Call **IoStartPacket** to queue the IRP for the Start I/O routine. A driver can also provide its own custom queuing mechanism in lieu of using the I/O Manager's routine.

3. Exit the Dispatch routine with a value of STATUS_PENDING. This allows the original requestor to continue its other operations in parallel with the device's operation.

The following code fragment shows how a Dispatch routine schedules a device operation.

```
NTSTATUS DispatchWrite(  IN PDEVICE_OBJECT pDO,
                         IN PIRP pIrp ) {
    :
    // Mark the IRP as "in progress"
    IoMarkIrpPending( pIrp );
    // Now queue (schedule) the IRP for eventual passage
    // to the driver's Start I/O routine.
    // Third parameter allows insertion into the queue
    //            other than at the tail
    // Fourth parameter allows specification of a
    //            Cancel routine
    IoStartPacket( pDO, pIrp, 0, NULL );
    return STATUS_PENDING;
}
```

It is a little-known fact that the I/O Manager automatically completes any IRP that isn't marked pending as soon as the Dispatch routine returns. Unfortunately, this automatic mechanism does not call I/O Completion routines attached to the IRP by higher-level drivers. Consequently, it is important that a driver either calls **IoCompleteRequest** or **IoMarkIrpPending** to explicitly set the status of the IRP.

Processing Read and Write Requests

The most basic of I/O requests is to exchange data between a user buffer and a device. The I/O Manager presents a traditional read/write abstraction to requestors for such data transfers. The requests are presented to a driver in the form of an IRP with major function code of either IRP_MJ_READ or IRP_MJ_WRITE. Another field within the IRP specifies the address of the requestor's buffer. Whether the buffer address is a direct virtual address or an intermediate nonpaged pool buffer allocated and maintained by the I/O Manager is determined by the device object's **Flags** field. Regardless, it is the responsibility of the read and write Dispatch routines to transfer data between the buffer and the actual device for the requested number of bytes.

User Buffer Access

As discussed in chapter 6, a driver can specify DO_DIRECT_IO or DO_BUFFERED_IO on a per-device basis (via the **Flags** field of the device object.) The exact behavior of the I/O Manager as well as the subsequent responsibilities of the Dispatch routine is discussed in the following sections.

BUFFERED I/O

At the start of either a read or write operation, the I/O Manager validates that all virtual memory pages spanned by the user's buffer are valid. For buffered I/O, it then allocates a nonpaged pool buffer of a size sufficient to hold the user's request. The address of this temporary buffer is place in the IRP field **AssociatedIrp.SystemBuffer**. This address remains valid for the duration of the transfer (i.e., until the IRP is marked as complete).

For read operations, the I/O Manager remembers the address of the original user buffer in the **UserBuffer** field of the IRP. It then uses this retained address upon completion of the request to copy data from the nonpaged pool into user memory.

For write operations, the I/O Manager copies the user buffer into the nonpaged buffer before invoking the write Dispatch routine. It then sets the **UserBuffer** field of the IRP to NULL, since there is no additional need to retain this state.

DIRECT I/O

At the start of the operation, the I/O Manager validates the page table entries spanned by the user's buffer. It then builds a data structure known as a *Memory Descriptor List* (MDL) and stores the address of the MDL in the IRP's **MdlAddress** field. Both the **AssociatedIrp.SystemBuffer** and **UserBuffer** fields are set to NULL.

For DMA operations, the MDL structure is used directly with an adapter object to perform the data transfer. Chapter 12 will discuss this process in detail. For programmed I/O devices, the MDL can be used with the function **MmGetSystemAddressForMdl** to get a system-address view of the user buffer. Using this technique, the user's buffer is locked down into physical memory (i.e., forced to be nonpagable) and is made accessible to driver code via an address above 0x80000000. (User-mode code must still access the same physical memory with its original address below 0x7FFFFFFF.) When the I/O request is ultimately completed, the user buffer is unlocked and unmapped from system address space.

NEITHER METHOD

There are two bits within the **Flags** field of the device object which specify either DO_BUFFERED_IO or DO_DIRECT_IO. If neither bit is set for a device, the I/O Manager performs neither action specified above. Instead, it simply places the user-space address of the requestor's buffer into the IRP's **UserBuffer** field. The **AssociatedIrp.SystemBuffer** and **MdlAddress** fields are set to NULL.

A simple user-mode address is not terribly useful. Most routines within a driver cannot be assured that at the time of their execution the original requestor's page tables are mapped. Thus, the user buffer address is usually worthless. There is one exception: At the time a Dispatch routine of a highest-level driver is invoked, execution occurs using the original requestor's thread. As such, the user-space address is mapped and valid. An intermediate driver or any DPC or Interrupt Service Routine (ISR) can never rely upon a user-space buffer being valid.

Code Example: A Loopback Device

An interesting (albeit simplistic) example to consider is a loopback device. The driver processes write requests by reserving a paged pool buffer and copying user data into this temporary buffer. The buffer is retained until such time as a read request is issued. The data returned by the read request is the contents of the temporary buffer, which is then released. The example demonstrates the implementation of read and write Dispatch routines as well as user buffer access.

```
NTSTATUS DispatchWrite(  IN PDEVICE_OBJECT pDO
                         IN PIRP pIrp ) {
    NTSTATUS status = STATUS_SUCCESS;
    PDEVICE_EXTENSION pDE;
    PVOID userBuffer;
    ULONG xferSize;
    // The stack location contains the user buffer info
    PIO_STACK_LOCATION pIrpStack;
    pIrpStack = IoGetCurrentIrpStackLocation( pIrp );
    // The example assumes the device is using BUFFERED_IO
    userBuffer = pIrp->AssociatedIrp.SystemBuffer;
    xferSize = pIrpStack->Parameters.Write.Length;
    // The temporary buffer pointer is kept
    // in the DEVICE_EXTENSION (obtained from Device obj)
    pDE = (PDEVICE_EXTENSION) pDO -> DeviceExtension;
```

```
        // If there is already a buffer, free it...
        if (pDE->deviceBuffer != NULL) {
            ExFreePool( pDE->deviceBuffer );
            PDE->deviceBuffer = NULL;
            xferSize = 0;
        }
        pDE->deviceBuffer =
            ExAllocatePool(PagedPool, xferSize);
        if (pDE->deviceBuffer == NULL) {
            // buffer didn't allocate???
            status = STATUS_INSUFFICIENT_RESOURCES;
            xferSize = 0;
        } else {
            // copy the buffer
            pDE->deviceBufferSize = xferSize;
            RtlCopyMemory( pDE->deviceBuffer, userBuffer,
                            xferSize );
        }
        // Now complete the IRP - no device operation needed
        pIrp->IoStatus.Status = status;
        pIrp->IoStatus.Information = xferSize;
        IoCompleteRequest( pIrp, IO_NO_INCREMENT );
        return status;
    }
NTSTATUS DispatchRead(   IN PDEVICE_OBJECT pDO,
                         IN PIRP pIrp ) {
    NTSTATUS status = STATUS_SUCCESS;
    PDEVICE_EXTENSION pDE;
    PVOID userBuffer;
    ULONG xferSize;
    // The stack location contains the user buffer info
    PIO_STACK_LOCATION pIrpStack;
    pIrpStck = IoGetCurrentIrpStackLocation( pIrp );
    userBuffer = pIrp->AssociatedIrp.SystemBuffer;
    xferSize = pIrpStack->Parameters.Read.Length;
    // The temporary buffer pointer is kept
    // in the DEVICE_EXTENSION (obtained from Device obj)
    pDE = (PDEVICE_EXTENSION) pDO -> DeviceExtension;
    // Don't transfer more than the user's request
    xferSize = (xferSize < pDE->deviceBufferSize) ?
            xferSize : pDE->deviceBufferSize;
    // Now copy the temporary buffer into user space
    RtlCopyMemory(userBuffer, pDE->deviceBuffer,
                                xferSize);
    // Free the temporary paged pool buffer
    ExFreePool( pDE->deviceBuffer );
    pDE->deviceBuffer = NULL;
    pDE->deviceBufferSize = 0;
    // and complete the I/O request...
    pIrp->IoStatus.Status = status;
```

```
        pIrp->IoStatus.Information = xferSize;
        IoCompleteRequest( pIrp, IO_NO_INCREMENT );
        return status;
}
```

This code example shows only the Dispatch routines for read and write. While they do very little, create and close Dispatch routines must be provided to make this a usable driver. A complete working version of this loopback driver, including a Win32 console test program, is included on the accompanying disk for chapter 7. The driver requires manual installation, as was demonstrated in the last chapter.

Extending the Dispatch Interface

Much of the I/O Manager operation supports a standard Read/Write abstraction. The requestor supplies a buffer and transfer length, and data is transferred from or to the device. Not all devices or their operations always fit this abstraction. For example, a disk format or repartition are requests that are not well-suited to a normal Read or Write operation. Such kinds of requests are handled with one of two extensible I/O function request codes. These codes allow any number of driver-specific operations, without the restrictions of the Read/Write abstraction.

- **IRP_MJ_DEVICE_CONTROL** allows for extended requests from user-mode clients through the Win32 **DeviceIoControl** call. The I/O Manager constructs an IRP with this **MajorFunction** code and an **IoControlCode** value (subcode) as specified by the caller of **DeviceIoControl**.
- **IRP_MJ_INTERNAL_DEVICE_CONTROL** allows for extended requests from kernel-mode code. No access to these operations is provided for user-mode requests. This facility is primarily used by other drivers in a layered stack to communicate special requests. Otherwise, the internal version of the device control operation is identical to the standard version. An **IoControlCode** value is placed into the IRP by the requestor.

As should be apparent, the implementation of either of these Dispatch routines requires a secondary dispatch based on the value of **IoControlCode** in the IRP. This value is also known as the **IOCTL** device control code. Since the secondary dispatch mechanism is completely contained within the driver's private routine(s), the interpretation of the **IOCTL** value is driver-specific. The remainder of this section describes the details of the device control interface.

Defining Private IOCTL Values

The IOCTL values passed to a driver follow a specific structure. Figure 7.2 illustrates the fields of this 32-bit structure. The DDK includes a macro, CTL_CODE, that offers a convenient mechanism to generate IOCTL values. Table 7.3 describes the arguments to this macro.

IOCTL Argument-Passing Methods

The extended functions defined with an IOCTL value within a driver often require an input or output buffer. For example, a driver might report performance data using an IOCTL value. The data reported would be transferred through a buffer supplied by the user. Indeed, the Win32 **DeviceIoControl** function defines parameters for two buffers, one for input, one for output. The buffer transfer mechanism provided by the I/O Manager is defined within the IOCTOL value itself. It can be either buffered or direct I/O. As described previously, with buffered I/O, the I/O Manager copies the user buffer (into or out of) nonpaged system memory, where driver code can then conveniently operate. With direct I/O, the driver is given direct access to the user buffer.

Interestingly, the driver's overall strategy for buffer handling (defined during DriverEntry) is not enforced for IOCTL transfers. Instead, the buffer transfer mechanism is defined with each IOCTL value specification and is a field within the IOCTL structure. This provides maximum flexibility when performing **DeviceIoControl** operations.

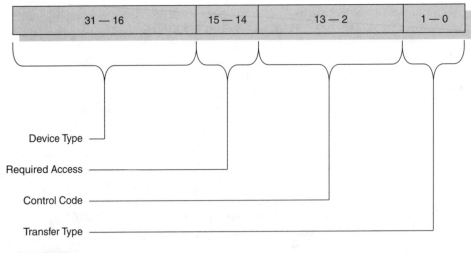

Figure 7.2   *Layout of the IOCTL code structure.*

Table 7.3	*The CTL_CODE Macro Arguments*

CTL_CODE Macro

Parameter	Description
DeviceType	FILE_DEVICE_XXX value supplied to IoCreateDevice
	• 0x0000 to 0x7FFF – reserved for Microsoft
	• 0x8000 to 0xFFFF – customer defined
ControlCode	Driver-defined IOCTL code
	• 0x000 to 0x7FF – reserved for Microsoft (public)
	• 0x800 to 0xFFF – customer (private) defined
TransferType	Buffer passing mechanism for this control code
	• METHOD_BUFFERED
	• METHOD_IN_DIRECT
	• METHOD_OUT_DIRECT
	• METHOD_NEITHER
RequiredAccess	Requestor access requirement
	• FILE_ANY_ACCESS
	• FILE_READ_DATA
	• FILE_WRITE_DATA
	• FILE_READ_DATA | FILE_WRITE_DATA

The **TransferType** field of the IOCTL field is two-bits wide and defines one of the following:

- **METHOD_BUFFERED.** The I/O Manager copies the user buffer to and from an intermediate nonpaged pool buffer on behalf of the driver.
- **METHOD_IN_DIRECT.** The I/O Manager provides a list of pages that encompass the user buffer. The driver uses this list to provide direct I/O (using DMA or programmed I/O) from the device into user space (i.e., like a Read operation).
- **METHOD_OUT_DIRECT.** The I/O Manager provides a list of pages that encompass the user buffer. The driver uses this list to provide direct I/O from user space into the device (i.e., like a Write operation).
- **METHOD_NEITHER.** The I/O Manager does not assist with the buffer transfer. The user's original buffer address (presumably from paged memory) is provided to the driver.

Since the **TransferType** field is a part of the IOCTL code itself, the public codes defined by Microsoft specify the I/O transfer mechanism. For private IOCTL values (driver defined), any appropriate transfer mechanism can be defined. For small, slower transfer, buffered I/O is appropriate. For faster, larger transfers, direct I/O is most suitable.

Writing IOCTL Header Files

Since both the driver project itself and all the clients of the driver need symbolic definitions for the IOCTL codes, it is customary for the driver author to provide a separate header file with device control-code definitions. This header file should also contain any structure definitions that describe the buffer contents of specific control operations. A Win32 program needs to include WINIOCTL.h before including the driver's IOCTL header. A driver project needs to include DEVIOCTL.h before including the driver-specific IOCTL header. These files define the CTL_CODE macro, among other things. The following is an example of an IOCTL header file:

```
#define IOCTL_MISSLEDEVICE_AIM CTL_CODE(     \
                    FILE_DEVICE_UNKNOWN,
                    0x801,                   \
                    METHOD_BUFFERED,         \
                    FILE_ACCESS_ANY )
// Structures used by IOCTL_MISSLEDEVICE_AIM
typedef struct _AIM_IN_BUFFER {
    ULONG Longitude;
    ULONG Latitude;
} AIM_IN_BUFFER, *PAIM_IN_BUFFER;
typedef struct _AIM_OUT_BUFFER {
    ULONG ExtendedStatus;
} AIM_OUT_BUFFER, *PAIM_OUT_BUFFER;
#define IOCTL_MISSLEDEVICE_LAUNCH CTL_CODE( \
                    FILE_DEVICE_UNKNOWN,    \
                    0x802,                  \
                    METHOD_NEITHER,         \
                    FILE_ACCESS_ANY )
```

Processing IOCTL Requests

Once a driver has announced Dispatch routines for either IRP_MJ_DEVICE_CONTROL or IRP_MJ_INTERNAL_DEVICE_CONTROL function codes, the I/O Manager starts passing IRPs directly to driver code. The interpretation of the IOCTL Device Control code is strictly the responsibility of the driver. Not even the various fields of the IOCTL code itself are verified by the I/O Manager prior to invocation of the driver's Dispatch routine. Any random number passed by the requestor as an IOCTL code finds its way to the driver.

Therefore, the typical structure of a device control Dispatch routine is a large switch statement. The following is an example of such a routine:

```
NTSTATUS DispatchIoControl(    IN PDEVICE_OBJECT pDO,
                               IN PIRP pIrp ) {
    NTSTATUS status = STATUS_SUCCESS;
    PDEVICE_EXTENSION pDE;
    PVOID userBuffer;
    ULONG inSize;
    ULONG outSize;
    ULONG controlCode;    // will be the IOCTL request
    // The stack location contains the user buffer info
    PIO_STACK_LOCATION pIrpStack;
    pIrpStack = IoGetCurrentIrpStackLocation( pIrp );
    // Dig out the IOCTL request
    controlCode = pIrpStack->
        Parameters.DeviceIoControl.IoControlCode;
    // and the requested transfer sizes
    inSize = pIrpStack->
        Parameters.DeviceIoControl.InputBufferLength;
    OutSize = pIrpStack->
        Parameters.DeivceIoControl.OutputBufferLength;
    //
    // Now perform the secondary dispatch
    switch (controlCode) {
    case IOCTL_MISSLEDEVICEAIM:
        // Always validate parameters for each case...
        if (inSize < sizeof(AIM_IN_BUFFER) ||
            (outSize < sizeof(AIM_OUT_BUFFER) ) {
            status = STATUS_INVALID_BUFFER_SIZE;
            break;
        }
        // Valid IRP values - start the device
        IoMarkIrpPending( pIrp );
        IoStartPacket( pDO, pIrp, 0, NULL);
        return STATUS_PENDING;
    case IOCTL_DEVICE_LAUNCH:
        if (inSize > 0 || outSize > 0) {
            // Is it really an error to pass buffers
            // to a function that doesn't use them?
            // Maybe not, but the caller is now forced
            // to re-think the purpose of the call.
            status = STATUS_INVALID_PARAMETER;
            break;
        }
        // Same kind of processing - start the device
        // :
        return STATUS_PENDING;
    default:
        // Driver received unrecognized control code
        status = STATUS_INVALID_DEVICE_REQUEST;
        break;
    }
    // Valid control code cases returned above.
```

```
      // Execution here means an error occurred.
      // Fail the IRP request...pIrp->IoStatus.Status = status;
      pIrp->IoStatus.Information = 0;   // no data xfered
      IoCompleteRequest( pIrp, IO_NO_INCREMENT )
      return status;
}
```

Managing IOCTL Buffers

IOCTL requests can specify both an input and an output buffer in the same call. As a result, they present a read-after-write abstraction to the caller. IOCTL requests differ in user buffer access in two ways.

- The buffer transfer mechanism is specified with the IOCTL control-code definition, independent of the overall device object strategy.
- There are two buffers involved, one for input, one for output.

The following sections describe how the different buffer strategies work with IOCTL control codes.

METHOD_BUFFERED

The I/O Manager allocates a single temporary buffer from nonpaged pool, large enough to hold the larger of the caller's input or output buffer. The address of this pool buffer is placed in the IRP's **AssociatedIrp.SystemBuffer** field. It then copies the requestor's input buffer into the pool buffer and sets the **UserBuffer** field of the IRP to the user-space output buffer address.

Upon completion of the IOCTL request, the I/O Manager copies the contents of the system buffer into the requestor's user-space buffer. Notice that only a single internal buffer is presented to the driver code, even though the user has specified independent input and output buffers. The driver code must take care to extract all necessary information from the requestor's input *before* performing writes into the output buffer.

METHOD_IN_DIRECT

The I/O Manager checks the accessibility of the requester's input buffer and locks it into physical memory. It then builds an MDL for the input buffer and stores a pointer to the MDL in the **MdlAddress** field of the IRP.

It also allocates a temporary output buffer from nonpaged pool and stores the address of this buffer in the IRP's **AssociatedIrp.SystemBuffer** field. The IRP's **UserBuffer** field is set to the original caller's output buffer address. When the IOCTL IRP is completed, the contents of the system buffer are copied into the caller's original output buffer.

METHOD_OUT_DIRECT

The I/O Manager checks the accessibility of the caller's output buffer and locks it down in physical memory. It then builds an MDL for the output buffer and stores a pointer to the MDL in the **MdlAddress** field of the IRP.

The I/O Manager also allocates a temporary input buffer from non-paged pool and stores its address in the IRP's **AssociatedIrp.SystemBuffer** field. It copies the contents of the caller's original input buffer into the system buffer and sets the IRP's **UserBuffer** field to NULL.

METHOD_NEITHER

The I/O Manager puts the address of the caller's input buffer in the **Parameters.DeviceIoControl.Type3InputBuffer** field of the IRP's current I/O stack location. It stores the address of the output buffer in the IRP's **UserBuffer** field. Both of these are user-space addresses.

Testing Driver Dispatch Routines

Even though a driver may be far from complete when only the DriverEntry, Unload, and Dispatch routines are present, significant code paths can be tested at this point. In particular, all of the following can be verified with a simple Win32 console program:

- Opens and closes a handle to the device.
- Supports Win32 I/O function calls that return successfully, even if zero byte transfers are specified.
- Manages requests from multiple callers.

While the successful completion of these tests is hardly earth-shattering, it does form a tried-and-true recipe for driver authoring: Build a driver framework that is proven *before* adding hardware interaction.

Testing Procedure

The following procedure checks all the code paths through a driver's Dispatch routines:

1. Write IRP_MJ_CREATE and IRP_MJ_CLOSE Dispatch routines for the driver.

2. Test the driver with a simple Win32 console program that gets a handle to the device under test and then closes the handle.

3. Write other Dispatch routines but ensure that all call **IoCompeteRequest** rather than starting any device operations.

4. Enhance the Win32 test program to make **ReadFile**, **WriteFile**, and

DeviceIoControl calls that exercise each driver's Dispatch routine. Alternatively, the test program can request zero-byte transfers.

5. If a device is sharable, run several copies of the test program at once to be sure the driver works with multiple open handles.

6. If a driver supports multiple physical devices, repeat the test with each device unit.

Sample Test Program

This is an example of a Win32 console test program that can be used to verify code paths through a driver's Dispatch routines.

```
#include <windows.h>
#include <stdio.h>

void main() {
    HANDLE hDevice;
    BOOL status;
    hDevice = CreateFile( "\\\\.\\LBK1" … );
    :
    status = ReadFile( hDevice, … );
    :
    status = WriteFile( hDevice, … );
    :
    status = DeviceIoControl( hDevice, … );
    :
    status = CloseHandle( hDevice );
}
```

Summary

Dispatch routines form the basic interface between a requestor and a driver. This chapter presented the framework for these functions and discussed the details for accessing the user's buffers and other parameters. Read, Write, and DeviceIoControl requests can now be presented to the driver.

The next chapter begins the interface with the real device. The path from starting the device to register data transfer to interrupt handling is discussed.

Interrupt-Driven I/O

CHAPTER OBJECTIVES

Some devices transfer data through registers, requiring continual CPU interaction. Such devices usually move small amounts of data at relatively infrequent intervals. For example, the mouse and keyboard transfer just a few bytes sporadically. Such devices remain idle for minutes (or hours) at a time and so are given the ability to interrupt the processor whenever data is available. This chapter explains how to write the data transfer routines for drivers of this kind of hardware.

How Programmed I/O Works

This section describes the events that occur during a programmed I/O operation as well as the actions that a driver must take in response to these events.

What Happens During Programmed I/O

In a programmed I/O operation, the CPU transfers each unit of data to or from the device in response to an interrupt. The following sequence of events occurs.

1. An IRP request (typically an IRP_MJ_READ or IRP_MJ_WRITE) determines that device interaction is required to complete the request. The Dispatch routine queues the IRP for eventual delivery to the driver's Start I/O routine.

2. The Start I/O routine performs any necessary preprocessing and setup based on the IRP's function code. It then starts the device, typically by writing or reading the first word of device data.

3. Eventually, the device generates an interrupt, which the kernel passes to the driver's Interrupt Service Routine (ISR).

4. If there is additional data for the driver to download, the ISR starts the next transfer. Steps 3 and 4 repeat until the entire data transfer specified in the request is complete.

5. When the entire transfer is complete, the ISR queues a request to fire the driver's DpcForIsr routine. As described in chapter 3, DPC routines run at a lower IRQL level than the ISR.

6. The I/O Manager's DPC dispatcher eventually runs the DpcForIsr routine scheduled by the ISR. The DpcForIsr routine marks the IRP as complete and informs the I/O Manager that another waiting IRP can now be presented to the Start I/O routine, repeating the entire cycle.

Synchronizing Driver Routines

As is apparent from the programmed I/O process just described, there are at least four separate code paths executing at three different IRQL levels.

- The original I/O request is handled by a Dispatch routine running at PASSIVE_LEVEL IRQL.
- The driver's Start I/O routine runs at DISPATCH_LEVEL IRQL.
- The driver's ISR runs at the device's DIRQL level.
- The driver's DpcForIsr routine runs at DISPATCH_LEVEL IRQL.

If any of these code paths share registers or memory areas, synchronization is required. Without such protection, an interrupt might arrive while a lower-level IRQL routine is using the shared resource, and an inconsistent state could result. The solution to this problem is to place code that touches shared resources in a SynchCritSection routine. Table 8.1 shows the prototype for one of these routines.

This technique for synchronization requires that *the* code which touches the shared resource be placed in an appropriate SynchCritSection routine.

Table 8.1	*Function Prototype for a SynchCritSection Routine*
BOOLEAN SynchCritSection	**IRQL == DIRQL**
Parameter	**Description**
IN PVOID pContext	Context passed to KeSynchronizeExecution
Return value	● TRUE—success ● FALSE—something failed

When the shared resource is required, a code path invokes **KeSynchronize-Execution** (see Table 8.2), which takes the function address of the SynchCrit-Section as an argument. This kernel function raises the IRQL level of the calling code path to the DIRQL level of the device's interrupt object, acquires the object's spin lock, and then calls the supplied SynchCritSection routine.

While the SynchCritSection is running, it cannot be interrupted by any code running at DIRQL or below (which includes the device's ISR) and is thus guaranteed temporary exclusive access to the resource. When the SynchCritSection routine returns, **KeSynchronizeExecution** releases the spin lock, drops IRQL back to its original level, and then returns to the caller.

Notice that the call to **KeSynchronizeExecution** receives a void* argument, pContext. This single argument is passed to the subsequent call to the SynchCritSection routine. It allows passing of instance data to the callback routine and is typically a pointer to the device or controller extension.

Driver Initialization and Cleanup

Programmed I/O device drivers must perform extra initialization during DriverEntry (or AddDevice for WDM drivers). Similarly, the driver's Unload routine must be extended to remove the additional resources allocated.

Table 8.2	*Function Prototype for KeSynchronizeExecution*
BOOLEAN KeSynchronizeExecution	**IRQL < DIRQL**
Parameter	**Description**
IN PKINTERRUPT pInterruptObj	Pointer to interrupt object
IN PKSYNCHRONIZE_ROUTINE pRoutine	SynchCritSection callback routine
IN PVOID pContext	Argument passed to SynchCritSection
Return value	Value returned by SynchCritSection

Initializing the Start I/O Entry Point

If a driver has a Start I/O routine, it must be announced during DriverEntry. This is done by storing the address of the Start I/O routine into the **Driver-StartIo** field of the driver object, as in the following code fragment.

```
NTSTATUS DriverEntry( IN PDRIVER_OBJECT pDriverObject,
                      IN PUNICODE_STRING pRegistryPath ) {
    :
    // Export other driver entry points…
    //
    pDriverObject->DriverStartIo = StartIo;
    pDriverObject->DriverUnload = DriverUnload;

    pDriverObject->MajorFunction[ IRP_MJ_CREATE ] =
            DispatchOpenClose;
    :
}
```

An unitialized **DriverStartIo** field within the driver object results in an access violation (and blue screen crash) when the Dispatch routines invoke **IoStart-Packet**.

Initializing a DpcForIsr Routine

The I/O Manager provides a simplified version of the DPC mechanism for use with standard interrupt processing. One special DPC object may be associated with each device object, DpcForIsr. To utilize this mechanism, a driver must call **IoInitializeDpcRequest** to associate the DpcForIsr routine with the Device object (typically from DriverEntry or AddDevice). During the actual interrupt service (ISR), the driver schedules the DPC by invoking **IoRequestDpc**.

Of course, this simplified mechanism is quite restrictive. Some drivers require multiple DPCs for different circumstances. A subsequent chapter explains the process of creating custom DPCs for multiple purposes.

Connecting to an Interrupt Source

All interrupts are initially handled by the kernel of Windows 2000. As explained in chapter 1, this is done so that portability to multiple platforms can be easily achieved. The kernel dispatches interrupts to a driver's ISR by creation of and then connection to an interrupt object. These steps are accomplished by the I/O Manger's **IoConnectInterrupt** function, described in Table 8.3. The driver's ISR address is passed (along with nine other input parameters) to this function so that the kernel associates a specific hardware interrupt with it.

IoConnectInterrupt returns a pointer to an interrupt object (via the first argument). This pointer should be saved in the Device or Controller Extension since it will be needed to ultimately disconnect from the interrupt source or to execute any SynchCritSection routines.

Table 8.3	*Function Prototype for IoConnectInterrupt*
NTSTATUS IoConnectInterrupt	**IRQL == PASSIVE_LEVEL**
Parameter	**Description**
OUT PKINTERRUPT *pInterruptObject	Address of pointer to receive pointer to interrupt object
IN PKSERVICE_ROUTINE ServiceRoutine	ISR that handles the interrupt
IN PVOID pServiceContext	Context argument passed to ISR; usually the device extension
IN PKSPIN_LOCK pSpinLock	Initialized spin lock (see below)
IN ULONG Vector	Translated interrupt vector value
IN KIRQL Irql	DIRQL value for device
IN KIRQL SynchronizeIrql	Usually same as DIRQL (see below)
IN KINTERRUPT_MODE InterruptMode	• LevelSensitive • Latched
IN BOOLEAN ShareVector	If TRUE, interrupt vector is sharable
IN KAFFINITY ProcessorEnableMask	Set of CPUs which can take interrupt
IN BOOLEAN FloatingSave	If TRUE, save the state of the FPU during an interrupt
Return Value	• STATUS_SUCCESS • STATUS_INVALID_PARAMETER • STATUS_INSUFFICIENT_RESOURCES

The use of interrupt objects requires care in several areas. First, if an ISR handles more than one interrupt vector, or if a driver has more than one ISR, a spin lock must be supplied to prevent collisions over the ISR's ServiceContext.

Second, if the ISR manages more than one interrupt vector, or a driver has more than one ISR, ensure that the value specified for SynchronizeIrql is the highest DIRQL value of any of the vectors used.

Finally, a driver's Interrupt Service routine must be ready to run as soon as **IoConnectInterrupt** is called. Clearly, interrupts at the IRQL specified may preempt any additional initialization attempted by a driver, and the ISR must be able to handle these interrupts correctly. In general, the following sequence should be used:

1. Call **IoInitializeDpcRequest** to initialize the device object's DPC and perform any initialization needed to make the DpcForIsr routine execute properly.

2. Disable interrupts from the device by setting appropriate bits and the device's control registers.

3. Perform any driver initialization required by the ISR in order for it to run properly.

4. Call **IoConnectInterrupt** to attach the ISR to an interrupt source and store the address of the Interrupt object in the Device Extension.

5. Use a SyncCritSection routine to put the device into a known initial state and to enable device interrupts.

Disconnecting from an Interrupt Source

If a driver is capable of being unloaded, it needs to detach its Interrupt Service routine from the kernel's list of interrupt handlers before the driver is removed from memory. If the device generates an interrupt after the driver is unloaded, the kernel will try to call the address in nonpaged pool where the ISR used to live. This results in a system crash.

Disconnecting from an interrupt is a two-step procedure. First, use **KeSyncrhonizeExecution** and a SynchCritSection routine to disable the device and prevent it from generating any further interrupts. Second, remove the ISR from the kernel's list of handlers by passing the device's interrupt object to **IoDisconnectInterrupt.**

Writing a Start I/O Routine

The remainder of this chapter discusses the development of a programmed I/O driver for a parallel port. For simplicity, this driver ignores many of the details that would have to be considered if writing a commercial driver.

Execution Context

The I/O manager calls the driver's Start I/O routine (described in Table 8.4) either when a Dispatch routine calls **IoStartPacket** (if the device was idle), or when some other part of the driver calls **IoStartNextPacket**. In either case, Start I/O runs at DISPATCH_LEVEL IRQL, so it must not do anything that causes a page fault.

What the Start I/O Routine Does

A driver's Start I/O routine is responsible for doing any function code-specific processing needed by the current IRP and then starting the actual device operation. In general terms, a Start I/O routine will do the following:

Table 8.4	Function Prototype for a Start I/O Routine
VOID StartIo	**IRQL == DISPATCH_LEVEL**
Parameter	**Description**
IN PDEVICE_OBJECT pDevObj	Target device for this request
IN PIRP pIrp	IRP describing this request
Return value	Void

1. Call **IoGetCurrentStackLocation** to get a pointer to the IRP's stack location.
2. If a device supports more than one IRP_MJ_XXX function code, examine the I/O stack location's **MajorFunction** field to determine the operation.
3. Make working copies of the system buffer pointer and byte counts stored in the IRP. The Device Extension is the best place to keep these items.
4. Set a flag in the Device Extension, indicating that an interrupt is expected.
5. Begin the actual device operation.

To guarantee proper synchronization, any of these steps that access data shared with the ISR should be performed inside the SynchCritSection routine rather than in Start I/O itself.

Writing an Interrupt Service Routine (ISR)

Once the device operation begins, the actual data transfer is driven by the arrival of hardware interrupts. When an interrupt arrives, the driver's Interrupt Service routine acknowledges the request and either transfers the next piece of data or invokes a DPC routine.

Execution Context

When the kernel receives a device interrupt, it uses its collection of interrupt objects to locate an ISR willing to service the event. It does this by running through all the interrupt objects attached to the DIRQL of the interrupt and calling ISRs until one of them claims the interrupt.

The kernel interrupt dispatcher calls an ISR at the synchronization IRQL specified in the call to **IoConnectInterrupt.** Usually this is the DIRQL level of the device. The kernel dispatcher also acquires and releases the device spin lock.

Running at such a high IRQL, there are several things an ISR isn't allowed to do. In addition to the usual warning about page faults, an ISR shouldn't try to allocate or free various system resources (like memory). If system support routines must be called from an ISR, check for restrictions on the level of which they can be run. Such calls might require delegation to a DPC routine.

As shown in Table 8.5, the kernel passes a pointer to whatever context information was identified in the original call to **IoConnectInterrupt.** Most often, this is a pointer to the Device or Controller Extension.

What the Interrupt Service Routine Does

The Interrupt Service routine is the real workhorse in a programmed I/O driver. In general, one of these routines does the following:

1. Determine if the interrupt belongs to this driver. If not, immediately return a value of FALSE.

2. Perform any operations needed by the device to acknowledge the interrupt.

3. Determine if any more data remains to be transferred. If so, start the next device operation. This eventually results in another interrupt.

4. If all the data has been transferred (or if a device error occurred), queue up a DPC request by calling **IoRequestDpc.**

5. Return a value of TRUE.

Always code an ISR for speed. Any work that isn't absolutely essential should go in a DPC routine. It is especially important that an ISR determine whether or not it will handle an interrupt immediately. There may be a number of other ISRs waiting in line for a given interrupt, and nonessential preprocessing blocks their proper operation.

Table 8.5	*Function Prototype for an Interrupt Service Routine*
BOOLEAN ISR	**IRQL == DIRQL**
Parameter	**Description**
IN PKINTERRUPT pInterruptObj	Interrupt object generating interrupt
IN PVOID pServiceContext	Context area passed to **IoConnectInterrupt**
Return value	• TRUE – interrupt was serviced by ISR • FALSE – interrupt not serviced

Writing a DpcForIsr Routine

A driver's DpcForIsr routine is responsible for determining a final status for the current request, completing the IRP, and starting the next one.

Execution Context

In response to the ISR's call to **IoRequestDpc**, a driver's DpcForIsr routine (described in Table 8.6) is added to the DPC dispatch queue. When the CPU's IRQL value drops below DISPATCH_LEVEL, the DPC dispatcher calls the DpcForIsr routine. A DpcForIsr routine runs at DISPATCH_LEVEL IRQL, which means it has no access to pagable addresses.

The I/O Manager ignores multiple calls to **IoRequestDpc** for a given device until the DpcForIsr routine executes. This is normal behavior for all DPC objects. If a driver design is such that it might issue overlapping DPC requests for the same device, then the driver must perform custom queuing of the DPC requests.

What the DpcForIsr Routine Does

Since most of the work happens during interrupt processing, the DpcForIsr routine in a programmed I/O driver doesn't have a lot to do. In particular, this routine should

1. Set the IRP's I/O status block. Put an appropriate STATUS_XXX code in the **Status** field and the actual number of bytes transferred in the **Information** field.

2. Call **IoCompleteRequest** to complete the IRP with an appropriate priority boost. Once called, the IRP must not be touched again.

3. Call **IoStartNextPacket** to send the next IRP to Start I/O.

Table 8.6	Function Prototype for a DpcForIsr Routine
VOID DpcForIsr	**IRQL == DISPATCH_LEVEL**
Parameter	**Description**
IN PKDPC pDpc	DPC object for this call
IN PDEVICE_OBJECT pDevObj	Target device for I/O request
IN PIRP pIrp	IRP describing this request
IN PVOID pContext	Context passed by IoRequestDpc
Return value	Void

Priority Increments

The Windows 2000 thread scheduler uses a priority boosting strategy to keep the CPU and I/O devices as busy as possible. As can be seen from the boost values listed in Table 8.7, priority increments are weighted in favor of threads working with interactive devices like the mouse and keyboard.

As part of this strategy, a driver should compensate any thread that waits for an actual device operation by giving a priority boost. Choose an appropriate increment from the table and specify it as an argument to **IoCompleteRequest.**

Some Hardware: The Parallel Port

Before walking through an example of a programmed I/O driver, it is helpful to look at some actual hardware. This serves the dual purpose of showing what kinds of devices tend to perform programmed I/O and providing a hardware example for the minimal driver to control.

How the Parallel Port Works

The parallel interface found on most PCs is based on an ancient standard from the Centronics Company. Although its original purpose was to commu-

Table 8.7	*Priority Increment Values*

Priority Increment Values		
Symbol	**Boost**	**Use when completing**
IO_NO_INCREMENT	0	No device I/O
IO_CD_ROM_INCREMENT	1	CDROM I/O
IO_DISK_INCREMENT	1	Disk I/O
IO_PARALLEL_INCREMENT	1	Parallel port I/O
IO_VIDEO_INCREMENT	1	Video output
IO_MAILSLOT_INCREMENT	2	Mailslot I/O
IO_NAMED_PIPE_INCREMENT	2	Named pipe I/O
IO_NETWORK_INCREMENT	2	Network I/O
IO_SERIAL_INCREMENT	2	Serial port I/O
IO_MOUSE_INCREMENT	6	Pointing device input
IO_KEYBOARD_INCREMENT	6	Keyboard input
IO_SOUND_INCREMENT	8	Sound board I/O

nicate with printers, clever people have found many ways of attaching everything from disks to optical scanners to the parallel port. The DB-25 connector on this port carries a number of signals, the most important ones being

- **RESET.** The CPU sends a pulse down this line when it wants to initialize the printer.
- **DATA.** The CPU uses these eight lines to send one byte of data to the printer. On systems with extended parallel interfaces, these lines can also be used for input.
- **STROBE#.** The CPU pulses this line to let the printer know that valid information is available on the data lines. (The sharp character signifies an inverted signal. A valid pulse is sent by transitioning the line from a logical 1 to 0.)
- **BUSY.** The printer uses this line to let the CPU know that it can't accept any data.
- **ACK#.** The printer sends a single pulse down this line when it is no longer busy.
- **Errors.** The printer can use several lines to indicate a variety of not-ready and error conditions to the CPU.

The following sequence of events occurs during a data transfer from the CPU to a printer attached to the parallel port:

1. The CPU places a byte on the eight data lines and lets the data settle for at least half a microsecond.
2. The CPU grounds the STROBE# line for at least half a microsecond and then raises it again. This is the signal to the printer that it should latch the byte on the data lines.
3. In response to the new data, the printer raises the BUSY line and starts to process the byte. This usually means moving the byte to an internal buffer.
4. After it processes the character (which may take microseconds or seconds, depending on how full the printer's buffer is), the printer lowers the BUSY line and pulses the ACK# line.

As is apparent from this description, the parallel port offers a very low-level interface to the outside world. Most of the signaling protocol involved in a data transfer has to be implemented by the CPU itself. A driver for a legacy parallel port must be designed for this primitive operation.

Device Registers

The software interface to the parallel port is through a set of three registers, described in Table 8.8. Since the parallel port is one of the things detected by autoconfiguration (even on an ISA system), the driver is able to use the Configuration Manager to find the base address of the data register.

Table 8.8	Parallel Port Register Usage

Parallel Port Registers

Offset	Register	Access	Description
0	Data	R/W	Data bits
1	Status	R	Port status
	Bits 0-1		Reserved
	Bit 2		0—Interrupt requested
	Bit 3		0—Error occurred
	Bit 4		1—Printer selected
	Bit 5		1—Out of paper
	Bit 6		0—Acknowledge
	Bit 7		0—Printer busy
2	Control	R/W	Commands to port
	Bit 0		1—Strobe data
	Bit 1		1—Auto linefeed
	Bit 2		0—Reset printer
	Bit 3		1—Select printer
	Bit 4		1—Enable interrupts
	Bit 5		1—Read data from port
	Bits 6-7		Reserved; must be 1

Interrupt Behavior

Traditionally, the parallel port designated as LPT1 is assigned IRQ 7, and LPT2 is assigned IRQ 5. A device connected to a parallel port generates an interrupt by momentarily forcing the ACK# to zero. Real printers force an interrupt for any of the following reasons:

- The printer has finished initializing.
- The printer has processed one character and is now ready for another.
- Power to the printer has been switched off.
- The printer has gone offline or has run out of paper.

Driving real printers requires considerable experimentation with the real device. In fact, it is not the purpose of the driver example in this chapter to drive a real peripheral device. Instead, the example is intended to demonstrate the use of interrupts and programmed I/O in a generic way.

Table 8.9		*Parallel Port Loopback Connector*			
Parallel Port Loopback Connector					
Signal Out	**DB-25 Pin**	**Connects To**	**Signal In**	**To Write**	**To Read**
Strobe#	1	13	Select	Control-0	Status-4
Data 0	2	15	Error	Data-0	Status-3
Autofeed	14	12	Paper Out	Control-1	Status-5
Reset	16	10	Acknowledge	Control-2	Status-6
Select	17	11	Busy	Control-3	Status-7

A Loopback Connector for the Parallel Port

For the purposes of this example driver, it is suggested that a special loop-back cable be created or purchased for the parallel port. The loopback connector precludes the need to connect to a real printer, and therefore eliminates the need to adjust the example code to the idiosyncrasies of different printers.

The example code assumes a parallel port loopback connector wired according to the TouchStone® CheckIt specification. The loopback connector wiring is shown in Table 8.9.

The loopback connector can be purchased directly from Touchstone or can be self-made from a simple DB-25 connector.

Code Example: Parallel Port Loopback Driver

This example shows how to write a basic programmed I/O driver for the parallel port. The code for this example is in the *Chap8* directory on the disk that accompanies this book. Several code fragments follow.

Purpose of Driver

The purpose of this driver is to allow a test program to output nibbles (4-bit quantities) to the parallel port with the loopback connector attached. The data returned by the connector is stored in a temporary pool buffer within the driver. Thus, subsequent reads to the device should return the same nibble data that was output. Just to keep things interesting, the driver returns the nibble data shifted left by four bits.

Since the loopback connector is wired in a non-straightforward manner, the driver code must assemble the nibble data from various data and status bits.

Driver.H

The main header file for this driver builds on the two seen in previous chapters. Changes were made to the DEVICE_EXTENSION structure to support the parallel port hardware and driver-specific functionality.

```
typedef struct _DEVICE_EXTENSION {
    PDEVICE_OBJECT pDevice;
    ULONG DeviceNumber;
    CUString ustrDeviceName;    // internal name
    CUString ustrSymLinkName;   // external name
    PUCHAR deviceBuffer;        // temporary pool buffer
    ULONG deviceBufferSize;
    ULONG xferCount;            // current transfer count
    ULONG maxXferCount;         // requested xfer count
    ULONG portBase;             // I/O register address
    ULONG Irq;                  // Irq for parallel port
    PKINTERRUPT pIntObj; // the interrupt object
} DEVICE_EXTENSION, *PDEVICE_EXTENSION;
```

Additionally, macros were added to the file for convenience in reading the parallel port device registers.

```
#define PPORT_REG_LENGTH 4
#define DATA_REG    0
#define STATUS_REG 1
#define CONTROL_REG        2

//
// Define access macros for registers. Each macro takes
// a pointer to a Device Extension as an argument
//
#define ReadStatus( pDevExt )                             \
(READ_PORT_UCHAR( (PUCHAR)                                \
  pDevExt->portBase + STATUS_REG ))

#define ReadControl( pDevExt )                            \
(READ_PORT_UCHAR( (PUCHAR)                                \
  pDevExt->PortBase + CONTROL_REG ))

#define WriteControl( pDevExt, bData )                    \
(WRITE_PORT_UCHAR( (PUCHAR)                               \
  pDevExt->portBase + CONTROL_REG, bData ))

#define WriteData( pDevExt, bData )                       \
(WRITE_PORT_UCHAR( (PUCHAR)                               \
  pDevExt->portBase + DATA_REG, bData ))
```

Driver.cpp

The basis for the code in this module is the same as from the last chapter. Noteworthy changes follow.

CREATEDEVICE

This code excerpt demonstrates a necessary technique for device detection prior to Plug and Play. A device resource is claimed directly and forcibly through use of a helper function, ClaimResources. This function accepts as arguments the I/O port base address and IRQ level. The port address and IRQL are converted to system-wide port and interrupt numbers through use of an obsolete function, **HalGetInterruptVector**. This function and overall technique is replaced in the next chapter.

```
// Since this driver controls real hardware,
// the hardware controlled must be "discovered."
// Chapter 9 will discuss auto-detection,
// but for now we will hard-code the hardware
// resource for the common printer port.
// We use IoReportResourceForDetection to mark
// PORTs and IRQs as "in use."
// This call will fail if another driver
// (such as the standard parallel driver(s))
// already control the hardware
status =
    ClaimHardware(pDriverObject,
                  pDevObj,
                  0x378,     // fixed port address
                  PPORT_REG_LENGTH,
                  0x7);              // fixed irq

if (!NT_SUCCESS(status)) {
    // if it fails now, must delete Device object
    IoDeleteDevice( pDevObj );
    return status;
}

// We need a DpcForIsr registration
IoInitializeDpcRequest(
    pDevObj,
    DpcForIsr );

// Create & connect to an Interrupt object
// To make interrupts real, we must translate irq into
// a HAL irq and vector (with processor affinity)
KIRQL kIrql;
KAFFINITY kAffinity;
ULONG kVector =
  HalGetInterruptVector(Internal, 0, pDevExt->Irq, 0,
                        &kIrql, &kAffinity);

status =
    IoConnectInterrupt(
        &pDevExt->pIntObj,    // the Interrupt object
        Isr,             // our ISR
        pDevExt,         // Service Context
```

```
                NULL,                    // no spin lock
                kVector,                 // vector
                kIrql,         // DIRQL
                kIrql,         // DIRQL
                LevelSensitive, // Latched or Level
                TRUE,                    // Shared?
                -1,                      // processors in an MP set
                FALSE );                 // save FP registers?
if (!NT_SUCCESS(status)) {
    // if it fails now, must delete Device object
    IoDeleteDevice( pDevObj );
    return status;
}
```

DISPATCHWRITE

This function was cut down considerably since its main purpose is no longer
to perform the I/O transfer. Instead, it simply queues the IRP for the Start I/O
routine.

```
// Start the I/O
IoMarkIrpPending( pIrp );
IoStartPacket( pDevObj, pIrp, 0, NULL);
return STATUS_PENDING;
```

DISPATCHREAD

This function was not touched since it returns the device's pool buffer contents (now containing nibble data) to the user buffer.

STARTIO

This new routine is called by the I/O Manager each time an IRP is dequeued.
The routine completes the work initiated by DispatchWrite. It transmits the
first character from the user's output buffer by a call to a helper function,
TransmitByte. The helper function constructs the output nibble and sends it
to the physical device.

```
VOID StartIo(
    IN PDEVICE_OBJECT pDevObj,
    IN PIRP pIrp
    ) {
    PIO_STACK_LOCATION  pIrpStack =
        IoGetCurrentIrpStackLocation( pIrp );

PDEVICE_EXTENSION pDevExt = (PDEVICE_EXTENSION)
    pDevObj->DeviceExtension;
PUCHAR userBuffer;
ULONG xferSize;

switch( pIrpStack->MajorFunction ) {
```

```
// Use a SynchCritSection routine to
    // start the write operation...
    case IRP_MJ_WRITE:
            // Set up counts and byte pointer
            pDevExt->maxXferCount =
                pIrpStack->Parameters.Write.Length;
            pDevExt->xferCount = 0;

            // Since we processing a new Write request,
            // free up any old buffer
            if (pDevExt->deviceBuffer != NULL) {
                ExFreePool(pDevExt->deviceBuffer);
                pDevExt->deviceBuffer = NULL;
                pDevExt->deviceBufferSize = 0;
            }
            // Determine the length of the request
            xferSize =
                pIrpStack->Parameters.Write.Length;
            // Obtain user buffer pointer
            userBuffer = (PUCHAR)
                pIrp->AssociatedIrp.SystemBuffer;

            // Allocate the new buffer
            pDevExt->deviceBuffer = (PUCHAR)
                ExAllocatePool( PagedPool, xferSize );
            if (pDevExt->deviceBuffer == NULL) {
                // buffer didn't allocate???
                // fail the IRP
                pIrp->IoStatus.Status =
                    STATUS_INSUFFICIENT_RESOURCES;
                pIrp->IoStatus.Information = 0;
                IoCompleteRequest( pIrp,
                        IO_NO_INCREMENT );
                IoStartNextPacket( pDevObj, FALSE );
            }
            pDevExt->deviceBufferSize = xferSize;
            //
            // Try to send the first byte of data.
            //
            TransmitByte( pDevExt );
            break;
```

ISR

The interrupt service routine for this driver is quite simple. It relies on a Dpc-ForIsr routine to mark a completed IRP when the last byte of the user's output buffer has been sent to the printer port.

```
BOOLEAN Isr (
            IN PKINTERRUPT pIntObj,
            IN PVOID pServiceContext            ) {
```

```
    PDEVICE_EXTENSION pDevExt = (PDEVICE_EXTENSION)
        pServiceContext;
    PDEVICE_OBJECT pDevObj = pDevExt->pDevice;
    PIRP pIrp = pDevObj->CurrentIrp;

    UCHAR status = ReadStatus( pDevExt );
    if (!(status & STS_NOT_IRQ))
        return FALSE;

    // its our interrupt, deal with it
    // transmit another character
    if (!TransmitByte( pDevExt ))
        // if no more bytes, complete the request
        IoRequestDpc( pDevObj, pIrp, (PVOID)pDevExt );
    return TRUE;
}
```

DPCFORISR

The final interesting routine for this driver completes an I/O request when so ordered by the ISR.

```
VOID
DpcForIsr(
    IN PKDPC pDpc,
    IN PDEVICE_OBJECT pDevObj,
    IN PIRP pIrp,
    IN PVOID pContext
    )
{
    PDEVICE_EXTENSION pDevExt = (PDEVICE_EXTENSION)
        pContext;

    pIrp->IoStatus.Information =
            pDevExt->xferCount;

    // This loopback device always works
    pIrp->IoStatus.Status =
            STATUS_SUCCESS;

    //
    // If we're being called directly from Start I/O,
    // don't give the user any priority boost.
    //
    if( pDpc == NULL )
        IoCompleteRequest( pIrp, IO_NO_INCREMENT );
    else
        IoCompleteRequest( pIrp, IO_PARALLEL_INCREMENT );

    //
    // This one's done. Begin working on the next
    IoStartNextPacket( pDevObj, FALSE );
}
```

Testing the Parallel Port Loopback Driver

At this point, a real driver is working, touching real hardware. A tester routine is included with this driver to demonstrate correct functionality and use. It verifies that the driver

- Sends IRPs from its Dispatch routine to its Start I/O routine.
- Responds to device interrupts.
- Transfers data successfully.
- Completes requests.
- Manages requests from multiple callers.

On the other hand, this driver is far from complete. It assumes that all data transfer requests complete without error. Simply removing the parallel port loopback connector before starting the test demonstrates this problem—a hung system. Subsequent chapters correct this problem as well as explain and demonstrate the correct way to locate hardware.

Testing Procedure

When testing programmed to I/O device drivers, it is advisable to follow a fixed procedure.

1. Write a minimal Start I/O routine that simply completes each IRP as soon as it arrives. This allows the test of the linkage between the driver's Dispatch and Start I/O routines.

2. Write the real Start I/O routine, the ISR, and the DpcForIsr routine. If the driver supports both read and write operations, implement and test each path separately.

3. Exercise all the data transfer paths through the driver with a simple Win32 program that makes **ReadFile**, **WriteFile**, and **DeviceIoControl** calls.

4. Stress test the driver with a program that generates large numbers of I/O requests as quickly as possible. Run this test on a busy system.

5. If the device is sharable, run several copies of the test program at once to be sure the driver works with multiple open handles.

6. If the driver supports multiple physical devices, repeat the test with each device unit.

7. If possible, repeat steps 4 to 6 on a multiprocessor system to verify SMP synchronization.

Summary

At this point, the basic components of the working driver are in place. The Start I/O routine is initiating each request and the ISR is servicing interrupts. The DpcForIsr routine is correctly completing IRPs below the DIRQL level of the device.

In the next chapter, the detection of Plug and Play devices is covered.

Hardware Initialization

CHAPTER OBJECTIVES

At the end of the last chapter, the sample parallel loopback driver was unrealistic in one critical area: the configuration of the parallel hardware was presumed. Hard-coded driver logic assumed that port hardware could be found at a fixed I/O address with a fixed IRQ level. Clearly, real driver code cannot be presumptuous. This chapter covers the subject of driver and device initialization.

First, in sections 9.1 and 9.2 the challenges of initialization are discussed from a historical perspective. The role of the Windows 2000 Registry in tracking installed devices is covered.

Next, the current Plug and Play architecture of Windows 2000 is discussed, including the use of layered drivers used in this implementation. The specifics of new IRP Dispatch functions are shown.

Finally, the driver presented in the last chapter is "corrected" to use the Plug and Play architecture. The parallel port hardware is automatically detected and its real configuration is used.

The Plug and Play Architecture: A Brief History

It is apparent that the revolution of the PC within the industry occurred because everyone could afford and use computers. Yet more than a decade went by during which naive users were expected to understand the hardware details of each device inserted into their systems. Knowledge of I/O port, interrupt level, and DMA channel usage of every existing device within a system was prerequisite when installing a new device.

Further, the design of operating systems assumed a very static hardware configuration. The installation or removal of a device required, at a minimum, a full reboot of the OS.

With the advent of Windows 95 (and some hardware prerequisites), a concerted effort to automate the configuration of new and removed devices was implemented. This attempt greatly enhanced the acceptance of and migration to Windows 95, which in turn accelerated the migration to 32-bit OS PC environments such as NT. With Windows 2000, Microsoft has enhanced and implemented a complete Plug and Play architecture for the I/O subsystem.

Goals of Plug and Play

The overall goal of the Plug and Play (PnP) architecture is to provide automated support for the installation and removal of system devices. To support this overall goal, several features are necessary.

- Automatic detection of installed and removed hardware. The device and the bus in which it inserts must notify controlling software that a particular device configuration has changed.
- Devices must allow for software configuration. The port, IRQ, and DMA resources used by a device must be capable of assignment by controlling software. (In other words, configuration of a board can no longer come from DIP switches or jumpers.)
- Necessary drivers for new hardware must be automatically loaded as needed by the operating system.
- When devices and their interfacing buses permit, the system should support *hot plugging* of the device. That is, it should be possible to insert or remove the device into or from a "live" system without disturbing operation.

While necessary, these goals are aggressive and invasive, and they require support from all levels of hardware and software.

Components of Plug and Play

The Windows 2000 operating system implements PnP with numerous software components. These components are depicted in Figure 9.1.

PLUG AND PLAY MANAGER

The PnP Manager consists of two parts, kernel-mode and user-mode. The kernel-mode part interacts with hardware and other kernel-mode components to manage proper detection and configuration of hardware. The user-mode part interacts with user interface components to allow interactive programs to query and alter the configuration of installed PnP software.

POWER MANAGER

The Power Manager facilitates the management of power to devices. Depending upon its nature, it may be possible to temporarily remove power from a device that is not being used over a prolonged period of time. This component recognizes and routes power events to appropriate drivers.

REGISTRY

The Windows 2000 Registry maintains a database of installed hardware and software of PnP devices. The contents of the Registry assist drivers and other components in identifying and locating the resources used by a device.

INF FILES

Each device must be fully described by a file used during installation of the controlling driver. Each device/driver combination must supply a properly formatted INF file.

PLUG AND PLAY DRIVERS

Drivers for PnP devices fall into two categories, WDM and NT drivers. NT PnP drivers are legacy drivers that rely upon some aspects of the PnP architecture but do not otherwise fully conform to the WDM model. For example, they might rely upon the services of the PnP Manager to obtain configuration information, but do respond to PnP IRP messages. WDM drivers are, by definition, fully PnP compliant.

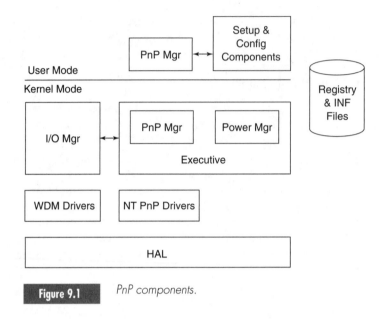

| Figure 9.1 | *PnP components.* |

The Role of the Registry for Legacy Drivers

In recent history, it was common for hardware to remain dormant until software somehow magically became aware of its existence and began to stimulate it. The techniques used by drivers and the NT operating system fell into one of three categories:

- A driver would maintain a list of potential hardware resources (i.e., port address, DMA channels, and interrupt levels) for each device that it might encounter. By probing each potential resource during DriverEntry, a driver would create an appropriate Device object (**IoCreateDevice**).
- A driver would rely upon an installation program to specify (either by probing or by user specification) the resources and devices that the driver would manage. This list of devices and associated resources would then be conveniently stored in the system registry.
- The NT operating system, as part of a preboot process, would probe for conventional devices and resources. For example, COM serial ports are routinely present at 0x3F8 or 0x2F8 (et. al.) and are therefore probed during the boot process. The discovery of devices was reported and maintained within the system Registry.

As system designers recognized the need for a more orderly hardware configuration process, new buses and protocols were specified that automatically reported the presence (or removal) of hardware. Generally, any bus type other than ISA supports some form of autodetection.

As an intermediate step to take advantage of autodetecting buses and hardware, earlier versions of NT augmented the preboot process to include autodetected hardware within the system Registry. Thus, an initializing driver (DriverEntry) would have the ability to see the list of autodetected hardware that was present during the boot process and create appropriate devices.

Regardless of which technique the OS or driver utilized, it was still imperative to force the loading of a driver *manually*. That is, appropriate entries within the system registry allowed a driver to load (either at system boot or later), which in turn would control discovered devices. Indeed, the examples given in previous chapters rely upon a manual installation of the driver. Because a driver would first load and then begin to control devices, the technique is sometimes referred to as *driver-centric*.

With the advent of Windows 95, and subsequently Windows 98 and Windows 2000, the model has been reversed. Devices that announce themselves, either during boot or by subsequent insertion (hot plug), force the loading of an appropriate registered driver. The new technique is said to be *device-centric*.

While the original Windows 95 driver model supported Plug and Play, it differed significantly from the NT driver model. Microsoft, recognizing the need for a compatible driver environment, extended the NT model to support Plug and Play and incorporated this technique in Windows 2000 and Windows 98. The new common model is designated the *Windows Driver Model* (WDM).

Detecting Devices with Plug and Play

The WDM model is an extension of the NT driver model. DriverEntry still serves as the driver's initial entry point, but its responsibilities are reduced. In particular, the role of DriverEntry is limited to the announcement of other driver functions. Specifically, DriverEntry does not create device objects for hardware it is capable of controlling.

A new driver function, AddDevice, is announced within (interestingly) the Driver Extension. The prototype for the AddDevice function is shown in Table 9.1 and is announced with code typical of the following:

```
NTSTATUS DriverEntry( IN PDRIVER_OBJECT pDriverObject,
                      IN PUNICODE_STRING pRegistryPath ) {
    :
    // Export other driver entry points…
    // for example…
    pDriverObject->DriverUnload = DriverUnload;

    pDriverObject->DriverExtension->AddDevice =
     AddDevice;
    :
}
```

Table 9.1	*Function Prototype for an AddDevice Routine*
NTSTATUS AddDevice	**IRQL == PASSIVE_LEVEL**
Parameter	**Description**
IN PDRIVER_OBJECT pDriverObject	Pointer to driver object
IN PDEVICE_OBJECT pdo	Pointer to physical device object
Return value	Success or failure code

The prime responsibility of the AddDevice function is to create a device object using **IoCreateDevice** in the same manner described in chapter 6.

The Role of Driver Layers in Plug and Play

The WDM model of drivers is built upon structured layers of Physical Device Objects (PDOs) and Functional Device Objects (FDOs). Generally, a PDO exists for each physical piece of hardware attached to a bus and assumes the responsibility for low-level device control common to multiple functions realized by the hardware. An FDO exists for each logical or abstract function presented to higher-level software.

As an example, consider a physical disk drive and driver. It can be represented by a PDO that implements bus adapter functions (e.g., adapting an IDE disk bus to a PCI bus). Once the PDO for the disk bus adapter is realized, an FDO assumes responsibility for the functional operations of the disk itself. The FDO may choose to handle a particular disk I/O request directly (e.g., reading a disk sector). It may choose to pass down other requests to its physical device partner (e.g., a power down request).

In reality, the role of a PDO can quickly become complicated and recursive. For example, a USB host adapter starts life as a physical device of the bus it adapts (e.g., PCI). The host adapter then takes on the role of a new bus driver, enumerating each USB device it discovers as its collection of PDOs. Each PDO then controls its FDO.

The technique is further complicated by allowing FDOs to be surrounded by *filter device objects*. These upper- and lower-level filter objects may exist in any number to modify or enhance the way that I/O Requests are handled by the resulting stack of device objects.

In order to distinguish between those FDOs which implement hardware buses and those that do not, the terms *bus FDO* and *nonbus FDO* are used within the DDK. A bus FDO implements the bus driver's responsibility of enumerating the devices attached to a bus. The bus FDO then creates a PDO for each attached device.

It is also worth noting that there is only a conceptual difference between a nonbus FDO and a filter device object. From the PnP Manager's perspective, all Device objects position themselves within the device stack, and the fact that some devices choose to consider themselves more than a filter is inconsequential.

The arrangement of a device stack is shown in Figure 9.2. The distinction between a bus FDO and a nonbus FDO is depicted in Figure 9.3.

Understanding the device stack is important in order to describe *when* the AddDevice function is called for a specific device. The overall algorithm used by Windows 2000 to load drivers and invoke the driver's AddDevice function is described by the following:

1. During the installation of the operating system, Windows 2000 discovers and enumerates all buses in the system registry. The topology and interconnect of the buses is also discovered and registered.

2. During the boot process, a bus driver for each known bus is loaded. Typically, Microsoft supplies all bus drivers but specialized drivers can also be supplied for proprietary buses.

3. One of the prime responsibilities of a bus driver is to enumerate all devices attached to the bus. A PDO is created for each device found.

4. For each device discovered, a *class* of device is located within the system registry that defines lower and upper filters, if any, as well as the driver for the FDO.

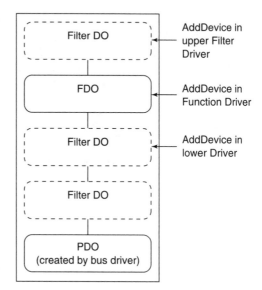

Figure 9.2   *The device stack.*

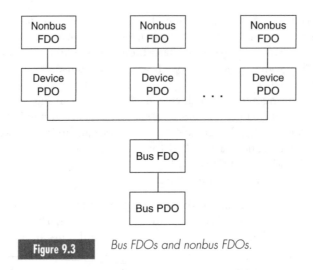

Figure 9.3   *Bus FDOs and nonbus FDOs.*

5. If the filter or FDO driver is not yet loaded, the system performs the load and invokes DriverEntry.

6. AddDevice is called for each FDO, which in turn invokes **IoCreateDevice** and **IoAttachDeviceToDeviceStack**, building the device stack.

The function **IoAttachDeviceToDeviceStack** is made from AddDevice to place the FDO at the (current) top of the device stack. Its prototype is shown in Table 9.2.

For convenience, it is advisable to maintain a relationship of the device stack elements within the Device extension structures of each PDO, FDO, and filter drivers. This is best done by reserving space for a pLowerDevice and pUpperDevice pointer within each Device extension. Unfortunately, while the pLowerDevice pointer initialization is straightforward, the upward pointer can only be initialized safely if the lower device type (filter or function) is known. This is because the return value from **IoAttachDeviceTo-**

PDEVICE_OBJECT **IoAttachDeviceToDeviceStack**	**IRQL == PASSIVE_LEVEL**
Parameter	**Description**
IN PDEVICE_OBJECT pThisDevice	Pointer to new top of stack device object
IN PDEVICE_OBJECT pdo	Pointer to PDO for this stack
Return value	Pointer to previous "top of stack" device

Table 9.2   *Prototype for IoAttachDeviceToDeviceStack*

DeviceStack is simply a DEVICE_OBJECT. The extension, extracted from the returned Device object, needs to be explicitly cast so that the pUpperDevice offset is accurate. In a generalized device stack, no driver could be certain, a priori, of its lower device type. Fortunately, the upward pointer is generally unnecessary, so only the lower pointer is routinely maintained.

The final task of the AddDevice function is to create a symbolic link name, if any, for the newly created and enabled device. This technique is exactly as described in chapter 6. A completed AddDevice function might be

```
//++
// Function:        AddDevice
//
// Description:
//   Called by the PNP Manager when a new device is
//   detected on a bus. The responsibilities include
//   creating an FDO, device name, and symbolic link.
//
// Arguments:
//   pDriverObject - Passed from PNP Manager
//   pdo           - pointer to Physcial Device Object
//                   passed from PNP Manager
//
// Return value:
//   NTSTATUS signaling success or failure
//--
NTSTATUS AddDevice (
          IN PDRIVER_OBJECT pDriverObject,
          IN PDEVICE_OBJECT pdo   ) {
  NTSTATUS status;
  PDEVICE_OBJECT pfdo;
  PDEVICE_EXTENSION pDevExt;

  // Form the internal Device Name
  CUString devName("\\Device\\MINPNP"); // for "minimal" dev
  UlDeviceNumber++;
  devName += CUString(ulDeviceNumber);

  // Now create the device
  status =
      IoCreateDevice( pDriverObject,
                      sizeof(DEVICE_EXTENSION),
                      &(UNICODE_STRING)devName,
                      FILE_DEVICE_UNKNOWN,
                      0, TRUE,
                      &pfdo );
  if (!NT_SUCCESS(status))
     return status;

  // Initialize the Device Extension
  pDevExt = (PDEVICE_EXTENSION)pfdo->DeviceExtension;
```

```
pDevExt->pDevice = pfdo;        // back pointer
pDevExt->DeviceNumber = ulDeviceNumber;
pDevExt->ustrDeviceName = devName;

// Pile this new fdo on top of the existing lower stack
pDevExt->pLowerDevice =         // downward pointer
    IoAttachDeviceToDeviceStack( pfdo, pdo);

// This is where the upper pointer would be initialized.
// Notice how the cast of the lower device's extension
// must be known in order to find the offset pUpperDevice.
// PLOWER_DEVEXT pLowerDevExt = (PLOWER_DEVEXT)
//         pDevExt->pLowerDevice->DeviceExtension;
// pLowerDevExt->pUpperDevice = pfdo;

// Form the symbolic link name
CUString symLinkName("\\??\\MPNP");
symLinkName += CUString(ulDeviceNumber+1); // 1 based
pDevExt->ustrSymLinkName = symLinkName;

// Now create the link name
status =
    IoCreateSymbolicLink( &(UNICODE_STRING)symLinkName,
                          &(UNICODE_STRING)devName );
if (!NT_SUCCESS(status)) {
    // if it fails now, must delete Device object
    IoDeleteDevice( pfdo );
    return status;
}

// Made it
return STATUS_SUCCESS;
}
```

The device stack (multilayered) approach to Plug and Play drivers is more flexible during the hardware discovery process and better models the actual implementation of hardware (i.e., devices "layer" on a bus).

The New WDM IRP Dispatch Functions

The AddDevice function, called by the PnP Manager, merely initializes the device (and its extension) object. It is apparent from the AddDevice code that hardware is not yet touched. In fact, two general responsibilities remain for a driver.

- Reserve and configure hardware resource requirements for the device
- Initialize the hardware to prepare it for use

Both tasks are performed by a driver upon receipt of a special IRP function (and subfunction) code that is new for WDM drivers: IRP_MJ_PNP. PnP IRP codes are sent by the PnP Manager when a variety of events occur, including

- Device initialization (perhaps due to insertion)
- Device shutdown (perhaps due to removal)
- Configuration queries

As described in chapter 6, IRP major function codes, such as Read and Write requests, are handled by an indexed table of Dispatch routines. Since an entire category of IRP_MJ_PNP messages are routed through this single Dispatch routine, it is the responsibility of this handler to perform a secondary dispatch using the minor subcode contained within the IRP. For PnP, the minor subcodes take the symbolic form IRP_MN_XXX, where XXX is a specific Plug and Play action requested by the PnP Manager.

An example of the initialization of the major function dispatch is shown below.

```
...
pDriverObject->MajorFunction[IRP_MJ_PNP] =
            DispPnP;
```

The code to perform the secondary dispatch based upon the minor subcode of the IRP is shown below.

```
NTSTATUS DispPnp(        IN PDEVICE_OBJECT pDO,
                         IN PIRP pIrp ) {
    // Obtain current IRP stack location
    PIO_STACK_LOCATION pIrpStack;
    pIrpStack = IoGetCurrentIrpStackLocation( pIrp );

    switch (pIrpStack->MinorFunction) {
    case IRP_MN_START_DEVICE:
        ...
    case IRP_MN_STOP_DEVICE:
        ...
    default:
        // if not supported here, just pass it down
        return PassDownPnP(pDO, pIrp);
    }

    // all paths from the switch statement will "return"
    // the results of the handler invoked
}
```

Required Plug and Play IRPs

In order to be WDM compliant, drivers *must* support specific PnP IRPs, depending upon the type of device object—nonbus FDO, bus FDO, and PDO. Table 9.3 lists the subcodes that must be supported for all device object types.

| Table 9.3 | PnP IRP Minor Codes Supported by All WDM Drivers |

PnP IRP Minor Code	**Meaning**
IRP_MN_START_DEVICE	(Re)Initialize device with specified resources
IRP_MN_QUERY_STOP_DEVICE	May device be stopped now for possible resource reassignment?
IRP_MN_STOP_DEVICE	Stop device, await potential restart or removal
IRP_MN_CANCEL_STOP_DEVICE	Notifies that previous QUERY_STOP will not be enacted
IRP_MN_QUERY_REMOVE_DEVICE	May device be safely removed now?
IRP_MN_REMOVE_DEVICE	Undoes work of AddDevice
IRP_MN_CANCEL_REMOVE_DEVICE	Notifies that previous QUERY_REMOVE will not be enacted
IRP_MN_SURPRISE_REMOVAL	Notifies that device has been removed without prior warning

From an examination of Table 9.3, it should be apparent that PnP devices exist in one of many states and, indeed, the DDK provides a state diagram depicting transitions based on PnP IRPs processed by a driver. The states can be divided into two categories: the states traversed by a device while it is being inserted (i.e., the prestart states) and the states encountered after the device is started. A state diagram for the prestart states is shown in Figure 9.4. The only responsibility of a driver during these state transitions is to correctly implement DriverEntry and AddDevice.

Once a device has entered the "Started" state, PnP IRPs direct all subsequent transitions. The possibilities are depicted in Figure 9.5. Drivers maintain post-start state within the device extension.

PDO Plug and Play IRPs

In addition to the PnP IRPs that must be handled by all WDM drivers, PDOs typically implement handlers for other minor subcodes of IRPs, as shown in Table 9.4. These IRP requests permit a driver to implement additional features such as device eject and reassignment of hardware resources. The closer a driver is to the hardware (i.e., the physical device or PDO), the more likely it is that a driver should support one or more of these codes.

Passing Down Plug and Play Requests

All PnP requests are initiated by the PnP Manager. The PnP Manager always routes these requests to the highest driver in a device stack.

Regardless of which PnP minor codes are handled by a driver, those that are not must be passed down the device stack to lower drivers, which may implement their own handler. Indeed, it is typical for a functional driver

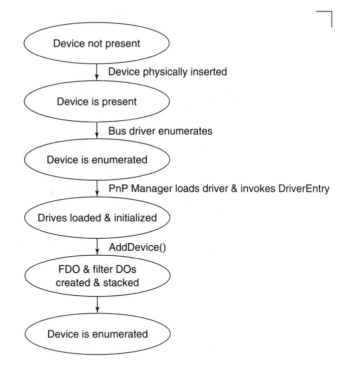

Figure 9.4 *Prestart device states.*

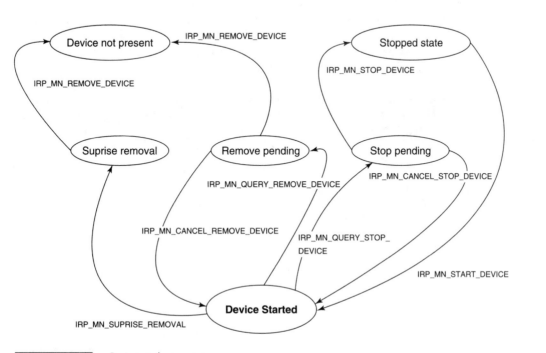

Figure 9.5 *Post-start device states.*

Table 9.4	*PnP IRP Minor Codes Supported by PDO Drivers*

PnP IRP Minor Code	Meaning
IRP_MN_QUERY_CAPABILITIES	What features does device support? (e.g., lock, eject, surprise removal)
IRP_MN_QUERY_DEVICE_RELATIONS	Request for information about related device objects (FDOs, PDOs, or filter DOs)
IRP_MN_ QUERY_INTERFACE	Request for support of a specific interface
IRP_MN_ EJECT	Request to eject device from slot
IRP_MN_ SET_LOCK	Request to lock device

(controlling an FDO) to rely upon the physical driver (controlling a PDO) to implement many PnP requests. In turn, the physical driver relies upon the bus driver (i.e., a bus FDO) to implement many PnP requests.

Passing a PnP request down the device stack is necessary for several reasons. Some drivers within the stack must "add value" to the request, and no one driver may assume that the complete response can be compiled from that level. In other cases, many levels of the stack benefit from a PnP notification. For example, a stopped device notice is critical to all layers.

To pass down a PnP request, a driver taking action on the request must mark the IRP as complete (described in chapter 7) by setting the IoStatus.Status and IoStatus.Information fields of the IRP as appropriate. It then invokes **IoCopyCurrentStackLocationToNext** and **IoCallDriver** on the lower device. The lower device is known from the AddDevice call to **IoAttachDeviceToDeviceStack**, the result of which was saved in the device extension. An example of this technique is shown below.

```
...
IoCopyCurrentStackLocationToNext(pIrp);
PDEVICE_EXTENSION pDevExt = (PDEVICE_EXTENSION)
    pDO->DeviceExtension;
IoCallDriver(pDevExt->pLowerDevice, pIrp);
...
```

If a driver has no need to await the completion of lower drivers handling the passed down request, a more efficient mechanism for skipping the current IRP stack location can be utilized. The function **IoSkipCurrentIrpStackLocation** simply removes the current IRP stack location from participation in the IRP processing. Indeed, this is the suggested mechanism for handling PnP requests that are not handled by a driver and merely passed to the next lower driver:

```
NTSTATUS PassDownPnP( IN PDEVICE_OBJECT pDO,
                        IN PIRP pIrp ) {
    IoSkipCurrentIrpStackLocation( pIrp );
    PDEVICE_EXTENSION pDevExt = (PDEVICE_EXTENSION)
        pDO->DeviceExtension;
    return IoCallDriver(pDevExt->pLowerDevice, pIrp);
}
```

Sometimes a driver passes down a PnP request before it can complete its own work on the request. For example, in response to a start request, IRP_MN_START_DEVICE, a driver typically needs to wait until lower-level drivers have started before starting its own hardware. The bus and any lower-level hardware initializes before individual devices start. Thus, a higher-level driver must first pass down the request and then await lower-level processing before continuing. This is best handled with a completion routine tied to the IRP by the higher-level driver.

I/O Completion Routines

An I/O Completion routine is an I/O Manager callback that lets a driver layer recapture an IRP after a lower-level driver has completed it. I/O Completion routines are registered by a higher-level driver with **IoSetCompletionRoutine** described in Table 9.5. When a lower-level driver ultimately calls **IoCompleteRequest**, the I/O Completion routine executes as the IRP bubbles its way back to the top of the driver hierarchy.

Except for the driver on the bottom, each driver in the hierarchy can attach its own I/O Completion routine to an IRP. The I/O Completion routines execute in the driver-stacking order, from bottom to top.

Table 9.5	*Function Prototype for IoSetCompletionRoutine*
VOID IoSetCompletionRoutine	**IRQL <= DISPATCH_LEVEL**
Parameter	**Description**
IN PIRP pIrp	Pointer to IRP being tracked
IN PIO_COMPLETION_ROUTINE CompletionRoutine	Function to receive control when IRP completes
IN PVOID pContext	Argument ultimately passed to completion routine
IN BOOLEAN bInvokeOnSuccess	Call completion routine if IRP succeeds
IN BOOLEAN bInvokeOnError	Call completion routine if IRP fails
IN BOOLEAN bInvokeOnCancel	Call completion routine if IRP cancels
Return value	- void -

The three Boolean arguments passed to **IoSetCompletionRoutine** determine when and if the Completion routine ultimately runs. As an IRP returns "up the device stack," the field **IoStatus.Status** is used in conjunction with the three arguments to determine whether or not to invoke the registered routine.

The prototype for an I/O Completion routine is described in Table 9.6. An example of the use of an I/O Completion routine to regain control of a PnP IRP after handling by a lower-level driver follows:

```
...
IoCopyCurrentStackLocationToNext(pIrp);

// Register the presence of a completion routine.
// The completion routine is called when the IRP
//   is "completed" by the lower level.
IoSetCompletionRoutine( pIrp, OnIoComplete, NULL,
                             TRUE, TRUE, TRUE);

PDEVICE_EXTENSION pDevExt = (PDEVICE_EXTENSION)
      pDO->DeviceExtension;
IoCallDriver(pDevExt->pLowerDevice, pIrp);
...

NTSTATUS OnIoComplete( PDEVICE_OBJECT pDO, PIRP pIrp,
                       PVOID pContext) {
      // Perform post processing for IRP request here
      // At what IRQL level does this code run?
      // (see text below for explanation)
      ...
      return pIrp->IoStatus.Status;
}
```

Unfortunately, it is difficult to predict at what IRQL level a completion routine executes. If the lower-level driver calls **IoCompleteRequest** from

Table 9.6	*Function Prototype for an I/O Completion Routine*
NTSTATUS OnIoCompletion	**IRQL == ??? (see text)**
Parameter	**Description**
IN PDEVICE_OBJECT pDevObj	Pointer to Device object
IN PIRP pIrp	Pointer to IRP just completed
IN PVOID pContext	Argument passed from **IoSetCompletionRoutine**
Return value	• STATUS_MORE_PROCESSING_REQUIRED
	• STATUS_SUCCESS

PASSIVE_LEVEL IRQL, then higher-level I/O Completion routines execute at PASSIVE_LEVEL. If the lower-level driver completes the IRP request from DISPATCH_LEVEL (for example, from a DPC routine), then the higher-level Completion routines execute at DISPATCH_LEVEL.

Since PnP IRP requests sent by the PnP Manager execute at PASSIVE_LEVEL, no special design is necessary to ensure that a returned (completed from a lower level) PnP IRP continues to execute at PASSIVE_LEVEL. Code executing at DISPATCH_LEVEL is restricted in the kernel calls it may use and, as described in chapter 3, must ensure it does not reference paged memory. To ensure that PnP handlers execute at PASSIVE_LEVEL, a kernel Event object is used.

A kernel Event object is a synchronization mechanism that is analogous to a flag. A thread of execution patiently waits for the Event flag to be raised (set) without consuming CPU resource. Once the Event flag is raised, the blocked (waiting) thread is scheduled for resumed operation. A full description of the use of kernel Events is contained in chapter 14.

For now, however, it is sufficient to note that the Event flag could be used as a signal between an I/O Completion routine and a PASSIVE_LEVEL thread within a higher-level driver. To use a kernel event, storage must be reserved by the programmer in nonpaged memory. The full technique is shown below.

```
...
IoCopyCurrentStackLocationToNext(pIrp);

// Reserve space for a kernel Event object
KEVENT event;
// And initialize it, flag DOWN
KeInitializeEvent( &event, NotificationEvent, FALSE);

// Register the presence of a completion routine.
// Pass the Event object to the Completion routine.
IoSetCompletionRoutine( pIrp, OnIoComplete,
                        (PVOID)&event,
                        TRUE, TRUE, TRUE);

// Call the lower level(s)
PDEVICE_EXTENSION pDevExt = (PDEVICE_EXTENSION)
    pDO->DeviceExtension;
IoCallDriver(pDevExt->pLowerDevice, pIrp);

// Wait for lower level(s) to complete
KeWaitForSingleObject( &event, Executive, KernelMode,
                       FALSE, NULL);

// Perform post-processing functions here...
// On return from Wait, PASSIVE_LEVEL IRQL guaranteed
...
```

| Table 9.7 | *PnP IRP Minor Codes Supported by Bus Drivers* |

PnP IRP Minor Code	**Meaning**
IRP_MN_QUERY_RESOURCES	Requests boot configuration resources
IRP_MN_ QUERY_RESOURCE_REQUIREMENTS	Requests resource information for a device
IRP_MN_QUERY_ID	Request for device instance ID
IRP_MN_ QUERY_DEVICE_TEXT	Request for device description and/or location
IRP_MN_QUERY_BUS_INFORMATION	Request parent bus instance and ID
IRP_MN_ READ_CONFIG	Request to read configuration space of bus slot occupied by device
IRP_MN_ WRITE_CONFIG	Request to write configuration space

```
NTSTATUS OnIoComplete( PDEVICE_OBJECT pDO, PIRP pIrp,
                       PVOID pContext) {
    // cast the pContext arg into what it really is:
    //    an Event pointer.
    PEVENT pEvent = (PEVENT) pContext;

    // Raise the Event flag to signal waiting thread
    KeSetEvent(pEvent, 0, FALSE);

    // Hold off further higher level processing
    // until this level completes:
    return STATUS_MORE_PROCESSING_REQUIRED;
}
```

Bus Driver Plug and Play Requests

In the unusual circumstance where a bus driver or filter must be written, it should be noted that some PnP IRP requests must be handled by such a driver. These minor code handlers are additional requirements above and beyond those already listed and are described in Table 9.7.

Device Enumeration

As briefly described earlier in this chapter, the PnP Configuration Manager is responsible for *enumerating* the hardware discovered on a system. Starting at system boot, or as devices are inserted or removed, a bus driver is responsible for identifying and listing (i.e., *enumerating*) attached hardware. The hardware resources assigned to a device are supplied to the driver when the PnP Start Message subcode (IRP_MN_START_DEVICE) is sent.

The technique used to assign unique hardware resources to a device is bus- and driver-dependent. For example, it is possible that two devices installed in a system have conflicting resource requirements at boot time. Both devices might default to the same I/O port address. The PnP Configuration Manager is responsible for sorting out any such conflicts. Further, an individual driver (FDO) might choose not to utilize a resource at all. For example, printer drivers do not always use an interrupt line even though the hardware allows it. An unused printer IRQL can be safely assigned to other devices. In other words, the assignment of hardware resources is a dynamic and iterative process involving the bus and device hardware, the PnP Manager, and the device driver.

Hardware Resource Descriptors

When a driver receives the PnP subcode IRP_MN_START_DEVICE, two fields within the IRP stack list the assigned hardware resources: **Parameters.StartDevice.AllocatedResourcesTranslated** and **Parameters.StartDevice.AllocatedResources**.

The structure used to describe these resources is of the type CM_RESOURCE_LIST, which is a *counted array*. The first offset within the structure, **Count**, signifies the number of array elements which follow. Each array element is of the type CM_FULL_RESOURCE_DESCRIPTOR. The array element contains a bus type and number (e.g., ISA bus 0) as well as a CM_PARTIAL_RESOURCE_LIST, which is another counted array. Each element of the inner array is of the type CM_PARTIAL_RESOUCE_DESCRIPTOR, which finally (and thankfully) describes the resources assigned to the device. Figure 9.6 depicts this four-level structure.

The structure of interest is within the fourth level and is a union, **u**. The four significant united types are **Port**, **Interrupt**, **Memory**, and **Dma**. The fields of each of these types are copied into the device extension and are used by an FDO driver for the duration. For example, when the time comes to perform an actual DMA operation, the **Channel** and **Port** offsets of the Dma structure are required.

Example code that would retrieve the ith element within the PARTIAL_RESOUCE_LIST follows.

```
PCM_RESOURCE_LIST pResourceList;
PCM_FULL_RESOURCE_DESCRIPTOR pFullDescriptor;
PCM_PARTIAL_RESOURCE_LIST pPartialList;
PCM_PARTIAL_RESOURCE_DESCRIPTOR pPartialDescriptor;
int i;

pResourceList =
    &Parameters.StartDevice.AllocatedResourcesTranslated;
pFullDescriptor =
    pResourceList->List;
```

```
┌──────────────────────┐
│ CM_RESOURCE_LIST     │
├──────────────────────┤
│       Count          │
├──────────────────────┤
│       List[ ]        │   ┌────────────────────────────────┐
│                      │   │ CM_FULL_RESOURCE_DESCRIPTOR    │
│                      │   ├────────────────────────────────┤
│                      │   │       InterfaceType            │
│                      │   ├────────────────────────────────┤
│                      │   │       BusNumber                │
│                      │   ├────────────────────────────────┤
│                      │   │     PartialResourceList        │   ┌──────────────────────────────┐
│                      │   │                                │   │ CM_PARTIAL_RESOURCE_LIST     │
│                      │   │              •                 │   ├──────────────────────────────┤
│                      │   │              •                 │   │          Version             │
│                      │   │              •                 │   ├──────────────────────────────┤
│                      │   │                                │   │          Revision            │
│                      │   │                                │   ├──────────────────────────────┤
│                      │   │                                │   │          Count               │
│                      │   │                                │   ├──────────────────────────────┤
│                      │   │                                │   │     PartialDescriptors[]     │   ┌────────────────────────────────────┐
│                      │   │                                │   │                              │   │ CM_PARTIAL_RESOURCE_DESCRIPTOR     │
│                      │   │                                │   │                              │   ├────────────────────────────────────┤
│                      │   │                                │   │                              │   │            Type                    │
│                      │   │                                │   │                              │   ├────────────────────────────────────┤
│                      │   │                                │   │                              │   │        ShareDisposition            │
│                      │   │                                │   │                              │   ├────────────────────────────────────┤
│                      │   │                                │   │                              │   │            Flags                   │
│                      │   │                                │   │                              │   ├────────────────────────────────────┤
│                      │   │                                │   │                              │   │           union u                  │
│                      │   │                                │   │                              │   ├────────────────────────────────────┤
│                      │   │                                │   │                              │   │              •                     │
│                      │   │                                │   │                              │   │              •                     │
│                      │   │                                │   │                              │   │              •                     │
└──────────────────────┘   └────────────────────────────────┘   └──────────────────────────────┘   └────────────────────────────────────┘
```

Figure 9.6   *Resource list data structures.*

```
pPartialList =
     pFullDescriptor->PartialResourceList;
for (i=0; i<pPartialList->Count; i++) {
    pPartialDescriptor =
         &pPartialList->PartialDescriptors[i];
    switch (pPartialDescriptor->Type) {
    case Interrupt:
        pDevExt->IRQL =
             pPartialDescriptor->u.Interrupt.Level;
        pDevExt->Vector =
             pPartialDescriptor->u.Interrupt.Vector;
        pDevExt->Affinity =
             pPartialDescriptor->u.Interrupt.Affinity;
        IoConnectInterrupt(...);
        break;
    case Dma:
        pDevExt->Channel =
             pPartialDescriptor->u.Dma.Channel;
        pDevExt->Port =
             pPartialDescriptor->u.Dma.Port;
        break;
```

```
case Port:
    pDevExt->PortBase =
        pPartialDescriptor->u.Port.Start;
    pDevExt->PortLength =
        pPartialDescriptor->u.Port.Length;
    ...
case Memory:
    ...
    MmMapIoSpace(...);
...
}
```

Using Hardware Resources Within the Driver

There are two sets of hardware resources supplied by the fields of the IRP when the IRP_MN_START_DEVICE subcode is received—raw and translated—and they serve different purposes throughout the life of the driver. (The **Parameters.StartDevice.AllocatedResources** field describes raw resources.)

Raw resources describe bus-relative addresses (ports, IRQLs, and DMA channels) that formerly would have been passed to routines such as HalTranslateBusAddress. Such functions are now obsolete since a PnP driver receives the translated resource list at the same time it receives the raw list. There should be a one-to-one correspondence between each raw resource and its translated counterpart.

Since the HAL macros (READ_PORT_XXX, WRITE_PORT_XXX, etc.) assume translated resources, there is little value (other than trace purposes) to keep track of raw resources.

Finally, it should be noted that devices are *presented* with their resource list. A driver that wishes to minimize the resources it consumes must implement a PnP handler for the IRP_MN_FILTER_RESOURCE_REQUIREMENTS subcode. The PnP Configuration Manager submits this request (opportunity) to a device stack *after* devices start. The PnP Manager supplies the current list of device resources and allows a driver to modify (usually by deletion) the set of resources it consumes. In this way, a printer driver, for example, could announce that the IRQL resource will not be serviced.

Device Interfaces

In chapter 7, a primitive mechanism for extending the Dispatch interface is described. It relies upon a single user-mode call, DeviceIoControl, which allows specification of a control code that is generally device-specific. The remaining arguments of the Win32 API call specify separate input and output buffers. Of course, the structure and meaning of the buffers is code-dependent and relies upon a specification outside the scope of the I/O Manager or any other system component.

Interface Definition

With the introduction of Plug and Play for Windows 2000, Microsoft allows device drivers to extend a generic *interface* to user-mode code. An interface is a *specification,* or contract, between caller and implementer that is nothing more than a group of (hopefully) related function calls (methods). A single driver can support many interfaces, and interfaces can be reimplemented by many drivers. Thus, the functionality of a driver (using interfaces) is merely the mix and match conglomeration of the interfaces it implements.

An interface should be *immutable.* Once formally published (or distributed), an interface should not be changed. Once multiple drivers implement the same interface, it realistically cannot be changed. This includes additions as well as deletions. The immutability requirement allows client code to be certain that if a driver supports an interface, its meaning is completely unambiguous.

Interfaces are identified by a unique number, or interface type (ID). To avoid inter-vendor collisions, the ID space is somewhat large, consisting of 128 bits. Microsoft has chosen to conform to the Open Software Foundation (OSF) Distributed Computing Environment (DCE) specification for the generation of these Universally Unique Identifiers (UUID). To generate a statistically unique UUID, Microsoft supplies two tools, GUIDGEN (Windows based) and UUIDGEN (console based).

Although a direct call interface is available only for kernel-mode code, user-mode code can also benefit. The interfaces supported by a driver can be enumerated by an application, and if recognized, offer a level of assurance as to driver functionality.

Interface Construction

Once a suitable ID is generated, the interface is constructed with a structure that includes a function pointer for each method of the specification. All device interfaces are based on the following structure:

```
typedef VOID (*PINTERFACE_REFERENCE)(PVOID pContext);
typedef VOID (*PINTERFACE_DEREFERENCE)(PVOID pContext);

typedef struct _INTERFACE {
    USHORT Size;
    USHORT Version;
    PVOID Context;
    PINTERFACE_REFERENCE InterfaceReference;
    PINTERFACE_DEREFERENCE InterfaceDereference;
    // interface-specific entries go here
} INTERFACE, *PINTERFACE;
```

If using C++, it is acceptable to define the new interface using inheritance (structs support inheritance as well as classes in C++). For example, to define an interface used to launch a missile,

```
typedef struct _COORDINATES {
    LONG latitude;
    LONG longitude;
}  COORDINATES, *PCOORDINATES;

typedef BOOLEAN
    (*PLAUNCH_INTERFACE_LAUNCH)(COORDINATES coords);
typedef BOOLEAN    (*PLAUNCH_INTERFACE_DESTROY)(VOID);

// Derive the new struct from the generic struct
typedef struct _LAUNCH_INTERFACE : INTERFACE {
    // only need to define interface-specific entries

    PLAUNCH_INTERFACE_LAUNCH Launch;

    // the next function cancels a missile launch
    // we wouldn't want this function to be optional
    PLAUNCH_INTERFACE_DESTROY Destroy;

} LAUNCH_INTERFACE, *PLAUNCH_INTERFACE;
```

Interface Reference Counting

Notice that the custom functions of the interface are provided as function pointers within the struct. Also, the base interface includes two standard functions, InterfaceReference and InterfaceDereference. These functions provide a counting mechanism that determine the lifetime of the interface. Each "user" or client of an interface must increment the interface's reference count by invoking InterfaceReference. As each user finishes its use of the interface, the reference count is decremented with InterfaceDereference. Typically, Interface-Reference is used whenever one function passes an interface to another function. Each function is independently responsible for decrementing the count when the function ultimately completes. This usage is analogous to COM's AddRef and Release functionality.

As to whether an interface would actually care to know if it is being "used" or not largely depends on the nature of the interface. An interface that allocates significant resources could use the interface count to determine when to deallocate its usage.

Registering and Enabling an Interface

Once constructed, an interface is registered by a device driver during its AddDevice routine using IoRegisterDeviceInterface. The prototype for this function is shown in Table 9.8.

Table 9.8	Function Prototype for IoRegisterDeviceInterface
NTSTATUS IoRegisterDeviceInterface	**IRQL == PASSIVE_LEVEL**
Parameter	**Description**
IN PDEVICE_OBJECT pdo	Pointer to physical device object
IN CONST GUID *pInterfaceClassGuid	Pointer to Interface ID
IN PUNICODE_STRING refString	Additional modifying string to differentiate conflicting Interface Ids (optional)
OUT PUNICODE_STRING symbolicLinkName	Name for referring to interface by driver and user-mode code
Return value	• STATUS_SUCCESS • STATUS_INVALID_DEVICE_REQUEST

The symbolic link name generated by the system after the very first call to IoRegisterDeviceInterface is persisted in the system registry. Future calls return the original name. Drivers should save the created symbolic link name in the device extension. The symbolic link name is also the name by which user-mode code can refer to the device.

Once registered, a driver must still enable the interface, typically during receipt of the PnP subcode IRP_MN_START_DEVICE. To enable or disable an interface, the function IoSetDeviceInterfaceState is used and is described in Table 9.9.

Once registered and enabled, the interface is available to kernel-mode code via a PnP subcode request, IRP_MN_QUERY_INTERFACE. The IRP of the request contains a field, **Parameters.QueryInterface.Interface** that

Table 9.9	Function Prototype for IoSetDeviceInterfaceState
NTSTATUS IoSetDeviceInterfaceState	**IRQL == PASSIVE_LEVEL**
Parameter	**Description**
IN PUNICODE_STRING symbolicLinkName	Reference name returned by previous call to IoRegisterDeviceInterface
IN BOOLEAN bEnableInterface	TRUE – Enable the interface FALSE – Disable the interface
Return value	• STATUS_SUCCESS • STATUS_OBJECT_NAME_NOT_FOUND

points to a caller-allocated structure of the size dictated by the interface specification. The implementing driver is responsible for filling in the function pointers (or data, for that matter) that actually implement the interface. By convention, a driver should increment the reference count on the interface when initialized in this manner.

Code Example: A Simple Plug and Play Driver

A complete, albeit simple, Plug and Play driver for the parallel port is included on the CD which accompanies this book and on the companion Web site, *www.W2KDriverBook.com.*

Summary

The conversion of a legacy driver into a simple WDM driver is relatively straightforward, as demonstrated with the previous example. Nevertheless, the number of details requiring mastery and understanding is formidable. It pays to have a base understanding of Windows 2000 drivers *before* attempting to add Plug and Play support.

The next chapter deals with the "full blown" WDM and PnP models, examining and demonstrating power management and hot plug issues.

Power Management

CHAPTER OBJECTIVES

The WDM model is ideal for enumerating and arbitrating discovered hardware. Additionally, the model supports the frugal management of power to those devices.

Devices that consume power only when used are hardly a new concept. After all, household appliances normally remain off until used. Yet within legacy computers, every device consumes power even during significant idle periods. The fact that a device might be burning just a few watts or less encourages the thought that the waste is unworthy of concern.

The need to manage power to installed devices is obvious in mobile and portable environments where the source of energy is limited. Even in desktop and server environments, however, the reduction of unnecessary power expenditure lowers heat production, increases component reliability, and lowers electric consumption and cost.

This chapter starts by describing the goals of and problems associated with power management. Then the mechanics of power management with a device driver is presented. This involves gracefully powering down a device through various levels of power consumption and reversing the process when new device requests arrive.

Finally, an example driver with power management handling incorporated is presented.

Hot Plug Devices

In order to manage power within a computer system, three major categories require cooperative design.

- System and bus hardware
- Devices
- Operating system and device driver software

Windows 2000 and Windows 98 support the WDM driver model, which incorporates sophisticated power management for bus and device hardware. Since the remainder of this chapter discusses the software support for power management, it is appropriate to first review the hardware requirements for the feature.

Bus Considerations

First and foremost, before a device can be powered down, the bus into which it plugs must electrically provide for such a state. For example, many bus drivers require power to guarantee an on-bus or off-bus state. Without power to the electrical bus-driver chip itself, the driver and its effect on the rest of the bus is indeterminate. Clearly, the hardware bus specification must allow for powered down bus drivers in order to support robust power management.

In some cases, the bus design must meet physical constraints. Especially in mobile systems, devices are routinely inserted and ejected. If the device installation and removal is allowed on a "hot" system, the physical bus characteristics must be carefully designed. Besides the obvious requirement that each device be physically separate (i.e., one device cannot scrape another as it is inserted or removed) there is the less obvious concern for which bus signals will "break" first. Typically, the ground pins for such buses are physically longer than the power pins, ensuring that ground *makes first* and *breaks last* during insertion and removal.

Such trivia aside, all modern buses support power management and incorporate necessary electrical and physical specifications to meet the stated requirements of the bus. PCI, PCMCIA (PC Card), USB, and IEEE 1394 are all designed for the feature. All but PCI allow "hot plug" of devices.

Device Considerations

Besides meeting the requirements for a given bus, individual devices can allow for remarkably clever management of power. For example, a modem card might allow for power down of the UART and bus circuitry, while still powering a ring detection circuit that triggers an awaken sequence.

Indeed, when considering the possible segregation of power to a device's subsections, it becomes clear a device can have multiple states for describing its power condition. Between the extremes of "completely on" and "completely off," a device can implement decreasing power states corresponding to decreasing capability. The transition from state to state can be directed by system or user request, or simply after an extended idle time.

OnNow Initiative

In an attempt to standardize (read: *abstract*) the various approaches to power management, Microsoft developed the OnNow Initiative. This specification builds on the capabilities of the hardware, providing a common platform for the various Microsoft operating systems to exploit.

The OnNow initiative abstracts the power management capabilities of the system (mainboard) and devices. While individual devices may incorporate many clever powering schemes, the OnNow model describes distinct power states that a device or system can occupy at any given time.

Power States

A system exists in one of six power states, designated S0 through S5. The meanings are described in Table 10.1. The overall state of the system largely restricts the maximum power state of individual devices.

Devices, meanwhile, occupy one of four power states, D0 through D3. The meanings are described in Table 10.2. Device power state primarily determines whether or not the hardware is capable of retaining its internal context at the designated Dx level.

Table 10.1	*System Power States Defined by OnNow*
System Power State	**Meaning**
S0	CPU fully on
	Devices may occupy any power state
S1	CPU halted; RAM refreshed
S2	CPU without power; RAM refreshed
S3	CPU without power; RAM in slow refresh mode
	Power supply output reduced
S4	System off; RAM saved to disk
S5	System off and shutdown; full reboot necessary to restore operation

Table 10.2	*Device Power States Defined by OnNow*
Device Power State	**Meaning**
D0	Device fully on
D1	Device in low-power mode
	Device context probably retained
D2	Device in low-power mode
	Device context probably not valid
D3	Device is without power; context lost

A confusing terminology point arises from the power state designations. As the system or device moves to a lower power state, its power state designation *increases*. For example, a device that moves from fully on to fully off has its power state *increase* from D0 to D3. The problem is compounded by the fact that the header file defining the enumeration of the states (wdm.h) specifies *increasing* enumeration values for the *decreasing* power-consuming states. For example, D0, enumerated symbolically as PowerDeviceD0, has the ordinal value 1. PowerDeviceD3 has the ordinal value 4. Thus, ordinal comparisons of power states are confusing. For example, a test of *newState < oldState* is a check to see if the new state consumes more power than the old state.

To further confuse the issue, PowerDeviceMaxium is defined to be the maximum power consumption state of a device. As currently defined within <wdm.h>, its ordinal value is 5.

Power Policies

Devices of the same class share a common power *policy*. The policy is owned by a single driver, typically a high-level driver common to all device stacks of the class (e.g., a class driver). The policy owner makes power decisions for the entire class of devices and is responsible for communicating with the operating system to confirm or reject power state changes.

Once the policy owner decides on a power state change, it issues IRP requests to individual devices or stacks to enact the decision. Such an IRP might pass between many drivers (down to the bus driver, up to the PDO, back to filters and FDO) before the entire request is realized.

Regardless of which driver assumes the role of policy owner, each device stack driver is responsible for acting on individual power requests. This means that each FDO is responsible for the device-specific power manipulation, while the PDO bus drivers take responsibility for manipulating power to the bus slot.

Power State Matrix

The system power states (S0-S5) dictate a maximum power state for devices (D0-D3). Since this maximum power state varies from system to system and device to device, a dynamic configuration occurs each time a driver is loaded. The results of this configuration are maintained within a device structure, DEVICE_CAPABILITIES, primarily within an array substructure, DEVICE_POWER_STATE (offset: DeviceState). Each element of the array corresponds to a system power state, Sx, and contains the maximum device power state, Dx, that is allowed.

On a given system, the collection of all DeviceState arrays forms a *power state matrix* that governs device power state transitions as the system power state changes.

The DeviceState array is filled using the following algorithm:

1. After a WDM AddDevice function is called, the PnP Manager issues a request, IRP_MN_QUERY_CAPABILITIES, to each created device stack.

2. The FDO (and any intervening filters) forward the request to the bus driver (PDO).

3. Using whatever means the bus allows, the bus driver fills in the DeviceState array. It also fills in "wake" fields that specify the minimum system and device states at which a device can still issue a wake event. (DeviceWake and SystemWake)

4. The IRP is returned to the higher levels. The FDO is permitted to degrade the bus determinations (e.g., stating that at S1, the device cannot support D1) and then complete the IRP.

The primary consumer of the power state matrix is a policy owner, which issues a PnP request, IRP_MN_SET_POWER, to a device stack to alter a device's power state. A policy owner should not violate the constraints of the power matrix and, therefore, must issue its own PnP request, IRP_MN_QUERY_CAPABILITIES, to obtain the relevant array entries.

Power State Changes

When a system power state change is requested, all power policy owners are notified with an IRP_MN_SET_POWER PnP request. The policy owner invokes the PnP Manager call PoRequestPowerIrp, described in Table 10.3, to construct a new PnP IRP request. The new IRP is sent to the device stack specified by the target FDO (or PDO).

An FDO, upon receiving the request to change power states, alters its power state using whatever device-specific means are available to it. It then issues the PnP Manager call PoSetPowerState to acknowledge accomplishment of the state change request. PoSetPowerState is described in Table 10.4.

| **Table 10.3** | Function Prototype for PoRequestPowerIrp |

NTSTATUS PoRequestPowerIrp	IRQL <= DISPATCH_LEVEL
Parameter	**Description**
IN PDEVICE_OBJECT pDeviceObject	Pointer to target FDO or PDO
IN UCHAR MinorFunction	• IRP_MN_QUERY_POWER
	• IRP_MN_SET_POWER
	• IRP_MN_WAIT_WAKE
IN POWER_STATE PowerState	New device or system power state request
IN PREQUEST_POWER_COMPLETE CompletionRoutine	Function called when new IRP has completed
IN PVOID pContext	Argument passed to Completion routine
OUT PIRP *pIrp	Optional pointer to newly allocated IRP
Return value	• STATUS_PENDING
	• STATUS_INSUFFICIENT_RESOURCES
	• STATUS_INVALID_PARAMETER_2

The power state change request must also be forwarded to lower-level devices in the stack, especially to the bus driver. If the device power state is being increased (i.e., moving to a lower consumption state), the device should act first on the request, then forward the request to the bus driver. If the device power state is being lowered (i.e., moving toward the "fully on" condition), the device should forward the request first to the bus driver, await

| **Table 10.4** | Function Prototype for PoSetPowerState |

POWER_STATE PoSet PowerState	IRQL <= DISPATCH_LEVEL
Parameter	**Description**
IN PDEVICE_OBJECT pDeviceObject	Pointer to target FDO or PDO
IN POWER_STATE_TYPE Type	Must be DevicePowerState for FDOs
IN POWER_STATE PowerState	New device power state being entered
	PowerDeviceDn (n = 0 to 3)
Return value	Previous power state (Windows 2000 only)

Table 10.5	*Function Prototype for PoStartNextPowerIrp*
VOID PoStartNextPowerIrp	**IRQL <= DISPATCH_LEVEL**
Parameter	**Description**
IN PRIP pIrp	Pointer to current IRP
Return value	- void -

completion, and then act on the request. The order of acting vs. forwarding varies because the bus needs to power up a slot before the device can act. Conversely, the device must enter a quiescent state before the slot is powered down.

Forwarding a PnP Power Request IRP to lower-layer drivers is different from forwarding other PnP IRPs. Two special functions, PoStartNextPowerIrp and PoCallDriver, are provided for this purpose. PoStartNextPowerIrp, described in Table 10.5, alerts the requestor that the current device stack level has completed work on the power IRP and is ready for another. This function must be called from every device driver within the device stack. PoCallDriver, described in Table 10.6, then forwards the current IRP to the lower-level driver.

The action of forwarding Power IRPs when increasing or decreasing power states is shown in Figure 10.1. An example of handling PnP Power IRP requests is shown below (along with the requisite Completion routine when awaiting lower levels to complete first).

Table 10.6	*Function Prototype for PoCallDriver*
NTSTATUS PoCallDriver	**IRQL <= PASSIVE_LEVEL** **(in some cases, DISPATCH_LEVEL** **is OK)**
Parameter	**Description**
IN PDEVICE_OBJECT pDevObj	Pointer to next lower-level device object (i.e., next recipient)
IN OUT PRIP pIrp	Pointer to current IRP
Return value	• STATUS_SUCCESS
	• STATUS_PENDING

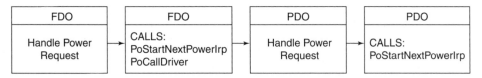

When reducing power consumption

When increasing power consumption

Figure 10.1   *Forwarding Power IRP requests.*

```
NTSTATUS OnPowerIrp(PDEVICE_OBJECT pDevObj, PIRP pIrp) {
    NTSTATUS status;
    PIO_STACK_LOCATION stack =
        IoGetCurrentIrpStackLocation( pIrp );
    PDEVICE_EXTENSION pDevExt = (PDEVICE_EXTENSION)
        pDevObj -> DeviceExtension;
    ULONG subCode = stack->MinorFunction;
    switch (subCode) {
    ...
    case IRP_MN_SET_POWER:
        POWER_STATE_TYPE type =
            stack->Parameters.Power.Type;
        if (type != DevicePowerState)
            // System power state change notification
            // Driver can prepare for eventual device
            //   power change - sent later
            ForwardPowerIrp(pDevObj, pIrp);
        DEVICE_POWER_STATE newState =
            stack->Parameters.Power.State;
        if (newState < pDevExt->currentPowerState) {
            // Request to raise power - tell PDO first.
            // Set a completion routine so that we can
            // regain control after lower-level finishes
            IoCopyCurrentIrpStackLocationToNext( pIrp );
            IoSetCompletionRoutine( pIrp, PowerUpFinish,
                NULL, TRUE, TRUE, TRUE);
            PoCallDriver( pDevExt->LowerDriver, pIrp );
                Return STATUS_PENDING;

        } else {
                // request to reduce power - do it first.
```

```
        // Perform device-specific power-up ops.
        // Tell Power Mgr device has changed state
        PoSetPowerState( pDevObj, type, newState);
        // Tell Power Mgr OK to send this level
        //   another Power IRP
        PoStartNextPowerIrp( pIrp );
        // And pass the Power IRP down…
        return
        PoCallDriver( pDevExt->LowerDriver, pIrp );
        }
        break;
        ...
NTSTATUS PowerUpFinish( PDEVICE_OBJECT pDevObj,
                        PIRP pIrp, PVOID pContext) {
    PIO_STACK_LOCATION stack =
        IoGetCurrentIrpStackLocation( pIrp );
    PDEVICE_EXTENSION pDevExt = (PDEVICE_EXTENSION)
        pDevObj -> DeviceExtension;
    DEVICE_POWER_STATE newState =
        stack->Parameters.Power.State;

    // Perform device-specific power-up now that the bus
    //     has supplied the device with power

    // Inform the Power Mgr of the state change
    PoSetPowerState( pDevObj, DevicePowerState, newState);
    // And signal an OK for more Power IRPs
    PoStartNextPowerIrp( pIrp );
    return STATUS_SUCCESS;
}
```

Wake Requests

To understand the Windows 2000 architecture for handling wake requests, it is important to first understand the hardware operation. A device that is *armed* for wake detection appears to have the capability to force a sleeping system back to life. In fact, since the device is a slave of the bus, it really has only the capability to signal its intent to the bus. It is the bus hardware that in turn forces the system out of its sleep.

The significance of this is that the software that drives the hardware is ultimately centered at the bus driver. The arming process starts at the top of the device stack, but the actual waiting occurs at the bottom bus driver. Thus, the overall process for the wake process is

1. A power policy owner (usually a bus driver) initiates a request to arm or disarm the wake mechanism for a device using PoRequestPowerIrp, subcode IRP_MN_WAIT_WAKE. (A callback routine, fired when the IRP eventually finishes, is set.)

2. A driver of wake-capable hardware handles requests to arm and disarm the trigger mechanism.

3. Wake-aware drivers pass down the arm/disarm request to lower-level drivers. The request will pend (perhaps for hours) at the bus driver.

4. The system enters sleep mode.

5. The wake hardware (obviously without suspended software support) tickles the bus and awakens the system CPU.

6. The bus driver (now executing) completes the original IRP_MN_WAIT_WAKE IRP.

7. Any higher-level driver with a registered I/O Completion routine will be notified as the IRP works its way back up the device stack. A function driver might need to reset the wake trigger mechanism.

8. The original creator of the arming request is notified that the (multi-hour) process is complete. Presumably, the creator re-arms the wake trigger mechanism for the next (multihour) cycle.

This process is depicted in Figure 10.2.

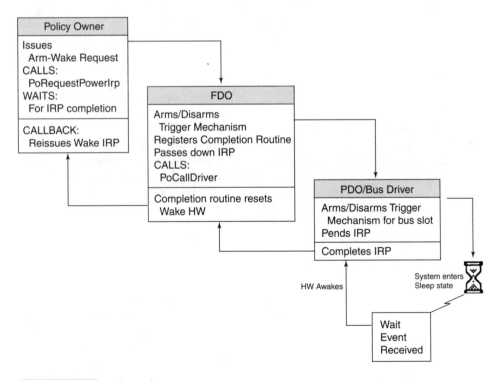

Figure 10.2 *The wake process.*

Table 10.7	*Function Prototype for IoCancelIrp*
BOOLEAN IoCancelIrp	**IRQL <= DISPATCH_LEVEL**
Parameter	**Description**
IN PRIP pIrp	Pointer to IRP to cancel
Return value	• TRUE – IRP cancellation succeeded
	• FALSE – IRP could not be canceled

There are several noteworthy points concerning the process. First, a device stack is allowed, at most, one outstanding WAIT_WAKE IRP at a time. Therefore, a single pointer within the FDO device extension is appropriate to hold the WAIT_WAKE IRP pointer if established.

Second, the policy owner that issues the arm or disarm request must do so only when the device is at full power, state D0. Additionally, neither the device nor the system may be in a power state transition at the time the arm or disarm request is made. This last rule appears a bit restrictive in that it might make sense to decide to arm the wake device just before the device enters a reduced power mode. Instead, the decision to arm must be made *a priori*, with the device stack left enabled for a potential sleep-wake cycle.

Canceling the Wake-Armed IRP

Once issued, an IRP_MN_WAKE_WAIT IRP remains outstanding indefinitely. The bus driver holds this request in a pended state, long before the system even enters the sleep state.

To disarm the wake capability, the IRP must be canceled by the original requestor, the power policy owner. To cancel the request, the policy owner invokes the I/O Manager function IoCancelIrp, described in Table 10.7.

A typical need to cancel the power IRP occurs when an armed device is stopped or ejected from the system.

Power Management Issues

As part of the OnNow initiative, Microsoft, working with hardware system developers, established the Advanced Configuration and Power Interface (ACPI) BIOS. ACPI replaces the outdated Advanced Power Management (APM) BIOS interface for power management. Proper operation of Windows 2000 power management features depend upon BIOS support of ACPI. When installed on non-ACPI-compliant platforms, Windows 2000 degrades to the capability extended by APM-compliant BIOS.

To fully exercise WDM driver power management code, a system with ACPI BIOS enabled must be used. Further, Windows 2000 should be installed with ACPI enabled (typically a BIOS setup screen option).

While APM-only support is suitable for gross-level power management, the full blown ACPI feature set is required to gain the full range of device power management supported by Windows 2000. APM support is sufficient for battery management in mobile devices.

Idle Management

Since the most obvious form of power savings that occurs is the power down of idle devices (i.e., devices that remain unused for an extended period of time), Windows 2000 provides a convenient mechanism for device drivers to request a power IRP IRP_MN_SET_POWER after a specified timeout period. The Power Manager function PoRegisterDeviceForIdleDetection, described in Table 10.8, provides this functionality.

The return value from PoRegisterDeviceForIdleDetection is a pointer to an idle counter that is incremented each second. When and if the counter reaches the timeout value specified (argument two or three), the Power Manager sends an IRP_MN_SET_POWER request of the power state specified in argument four.

The timer/counter must be manually reset by driver code, as appropriate, by calling PoSetDeviceBusy, described in Table 10.9. Of course, setting too short a timeout interval burdens a driver with frequent calls to PoSetDeviceBusy, so conservative timeout values would seem appropriate.

Table 10.8   *Function Prototype for PoRegisterDeviceForIdleDetection*

PULONG PoRegisterDevice ForIdleDetection	IRQL < DISPATCH_LEVEL
Parameter	**Description**
IN PDEVICE_OBJECT pDevObj	Pointer to device object to receive power IRP
IN ULONG ConservationIdleTime	Timeout value (seconds) when system is running with scarce power (battery-driven)
IN ULONG PerformanceIdleTime	Timeout value (seconds) when system is running with abundant power (docked)
IN DEVICE_POWER_STATE State	Power state requested when timeout exceeded
Return value	• Pointer to "idle counter"
	• NULL – Idle timeout could not be enabled

Table 10.9	*Function Prototype for PoSetDeviceBusy*
VOID PoSetDeviceBusy	**IRQL < DISPATCH_LEVEL**
Parameter	**Description**
IN PULONG pIdleCounter	Pointer to "idle counter"
Return value	- void -

User Interface for Power Management

The suggested user interface for Power Management is the Control Panel applet of Windows 2000, Power Options. To extend the Power Options applet with a driver-customized property sheet requires the use of Microsoft's COM object model and registration of the property sheet. An example of providing such an extension is provided on the companion Web site of this book, *www.W2KdriverBook.com*

Some knowledge of ATL (Active Template Library) is required to understand the example.

Summary

Power Management within the Windows 2000 WDM model is somewhat complex. The nature of power management with multiple device power states contributes to the complexity. Partly, the child-parent, device-bus relationship is also to blame. And of course, the handling of wake requests from otherwise sleeping devices adds more code to the driver.

Nevertheless, a properly written power-managed WDM driver contributes greatly to the elegant operation of the overall system. Power consumption, heat, and reliability benefit from the incorporation of this feature.

The next chapter deals with the handling of a practical device problem: timeouts. What if a hardware request does not complete within a reasonable period of time?

Timers

CHAPTER OBJECTIVES

Software developers have known about it from the beginning. Hardware does not always behave the way it should. For example, error conditions may prevent a device from generating an interrupt when one is expected. Even worse, some devices don't use interrupts to signal interesting state changes. Handling these situations requires some kind of timer or polling mechanism, and this chapter describes just such a process.

Handling Device Timeouts

A driver can never assume that an expected device interrupt will arrive. The device might be offline; it might be waiting for some kind of operator intervention; or, perhaps it's just broken. This section explains how to use I/O Timer routines to detect unresponsive devices.

How I/O Timer Routines Work

An I/O Timer routine is a (somewhat) optional piece of driver code that an AddDevice routine attaches to a specific Device object. After the timer is started, the I/O Manager begins calling the I/O Timer routine once every second. These calls continue until the timer is explicitly stopped. Table 11.1 lists the functions available for working with I/O timers.

Table 11.2 shows the prototype for the I/O Timer routine itself. When this callback executes, it receives a pointer to the associated Device object and the context argument that was specified in the call to **IoInitializeTimer**. As always, the address of the Device Extension is a good choice for context.

How to Catch Device Timeout Conditions

In general terms, a driver that wants to catch device timeouts should do the following:

1. In AddDevice, call **IoInitializeTimer** to associate an I/O Timer routine with a specific device.

2. When a handle is associated with the device (e.g., when a user-mode program calls CreateFile), the driver's Dispatch routine for IRP_MJ_CREATE calls **IoStartTimer**. As long as the device handle remains open, the device receives I/O Timer calls.

3. If the driver needs a longer timeout than one second (and it probably does), a separate counter value must be maintained. This counter is initialized in the Start I/O routine to the maximum number of seconds the driver is willing to wait for an interrupt.

4. The ISR resets or cancels the timer, depending on whether additional device interrupts are expected.

5. Each time the driver's I/O Timer routine is called, the timer counter is decremented and checked. If the counter reaches zero before an interrupt arrives, the I/O Timer routine stops the device, clears the timeout counter, and processes the request as a timed-out operation.

6. When the user-mode program calls CloseHandle, the Dispatch routine for IRP_MJ_CLOSE calls **IoStopTimer**, which disables I/O timer callbacks for the device.

Notice that the Start I/O and I/O Timer routines (running at DISPATCH_LEVEL IRQL), and the ISR (running at DIRQL) all have access to the timeout counter in the Device Extension. These independent code paths must syn-

Table 11.1	*I/O Timer Routines*	
Function	**Purpose**	**IRQL**
IoInitializeTimer	Attach a timer to a device	PASSIVE_LEVEL
IoStartTimer	Start receiving callbacks	<= DISPATCH_LEVEL
IoStopTimer	Stop receiving callbacks	<= DISPATCH_LEVEL

Table 11.2	*Function Prototype for IoTimer Callback*
VOID IoTimer	**IRQL == DISPATCH_LEVEL**
Parameter	**Description**
IN PDEVICE_OBJECT pDeviceObject	Pointer to device object whose timer just fired
IN PVOID pContext	Context argument passed with **IoInitializeTimer**
Return value	- void -

chronize their access to the timeout counter. The code example that appears later in this chapter demonstrates such synchronization.

Of course, a driver can choose to use **IoStartTimer** and **IoStopTimer** outside of Dispatch routines. Since the timer callback interval is one second, disregarding unneeded callbacks does not incur significant overhead. For example, a driver could call **IoStartTimer** in AddDevice and just let the callback routine continually fire.

Once it is determined that a device operation has timed out, a driver may do any of the following:

- Retry the device operation a fixed number of times before failing the IRP that generated it.
- Fail the IRP by calling **IoCompleteRequest** with an appropriate final status value. Do not use STATUS_IO_TIMEOUT as the final status for the failed IRP. This status code maps onto the ERROR_ SEM_TIMEOUT Win32 error message, signifying a semaphore timeout.
- Log a timeout error for the device in the system event log. This can help system administrators track down failing hardware.

Code Example: Catching Device Timeouts

This example shows the addition of timeout support to the simple parallel port driver developed in previous chapters.

Device Extension Additions

The Device Extension is modified to include the timeout counter. A counter value of −1 signifies that timeouts are to be ignored.

```
typedef struct _DEVICE_EXTENSION {
    . . .
    LONG timeRemaining; // timeout counter - seconds
    . . .
} DEVICE_EXTENSION, *PDEVICE_EXTENSION;
```

AddDevice Additions

AddDevice is changed to initialize the I/O Timer for the device. The counter value does not need to be initialized until the timer is actually started.

```
NTSTATUS AddDevice(IN PDRIVER_OBJECT pDriverObject,
                   IN PDEVICE_OBJECT pdo) {
    PDEVICE_EXTENSION pDevExt = (PDEVICE_EXTENSION)
        pDevObj->DeviceExtension;
. . .
// Near the end of the function, after IoCreateDevice
//   has been called…
//
// Create the I/O Timer
    IoInitializeTimer( pdo, IoTimer, pDevExt);
    . . .
}
```

Create Dispatch Routine Changes

When the device is "opened" from user-mode (via the Win32 **CreateFile** call), the I/O Timer is started. It continues to tick so long as the handle remains open. Since the time is ticking, the timeout counter must be initialized to show that at present the ticks should be ignored.

```
NTSTATUS DispatchCreate( IN PDEVICE_OBJECT pDevObj,
                         IN PIRP pIrp ) {
    PDEVICE_EXTENSION pDevExt = (PDEVICE_EXTENSION)
        pDevObj->DeviceExtension;
    . . .
    // Near the end of the function, the timeout
    //   counter is initialized and the I/O Timer
    //   is started.
    pDevExt->timeRemaining = -1;
    IoStartTimer( pDevObj );
    . . .
}
```

StartIo Changes

Each time the physical device is started and an interrupt becomes expected, the maximum number of seconds to wait for the interrupt must be set into the timeout counter. An operational counter must be synchronized with all code paths to ensure it does not become corrupted. The ISR and I/O Timer callback routines, running as interrupting code paths, also read and write the counter.

The use of InterlockedExchange assures that the 32-bit timeout counter is stored atomically.

```
VOID StartIo( IN PDEVICE_OBJECT pDevObj,
              IN PIRP pIrp ) {
    PDEVICE_EXTENSION pDevExt = (PDEVICE_EXTENSION)
        pDevObj->DeviceExtension;
    ...
    // Before physically starting the device, the
    // timeout counter must be set. Remember to
    // account for all forms of device latency,
    // including device power/spin-up, etc.
    InterlockedExchange( pDevExt->timeRemaining,
                         INTERRUPT_TIMEOUT );
    //
    // Now start the device:
    CallTransmitBytes( pDevObj, pIrp );
    ...
}
```

ISR Changes

The Interupt Service Routine is modified so that each time an expected interrupt arrives, the I/O Timeout wait period is either canceled or reset. If the ISR starts another device operation, a fresh timeout period is established. If there are no more pending transfer operations, the timeout is canceled (set to –1).

```
BOOLEAN Isr( IN PKINTERRUPT pInterruptObj,
             IN PVOID pServiceContext ) {
    PDEVICE_EXTENSION pDevExt = (PDEVICE_EXTENSION)
        pServiceContext;
    ...
    // If there are more bytes to send,
    //    reset the timeout counter to a fresh start
    if (TransmitBytes( pDevExt )
        InterlockedExchange(&pDevExt->timeRemaining,
                            INTERRUPT_TIMEOUT );
    // If no more bytes to send, clear the timeout
    else
        InterlockedExchange(&pDevExt->timeRemaining,
                            -1 );
    ...
```

I/O Timer Callback Routine

Finally, the Timer Callback routine itself is presented. If the routine detects that the timeout has expired, it uses the driver's DprForIsr routine to fail the IRP.

```
VOID IoTimer( IN PDEVICE_OBJECT pDevObj,
              IN PVOID pContext ) {
    PDEVICE_EXTENSION pDevExt = (PDEVICE_EXTENSION)
        pContext;
    // Check the timeout value
    if (InterlockedCompareExchange(
        &pDevExt->timeRemaining, -1, -1) < 0)
        return;           // timer not active

    // Since the timer is active, decrement it
    if (InterlockedDecrement(&devExt->timeRemaining)
            == 0) {
        // timeout has expired - fail the IRP
        InterlockedExchange(&pDevExt->timeRemaining,
                        -1 );
        DpcForIsr( NULL, pDevObj,
                pDevObj->CurrentIrp, pDevExt );
    }
    return;
}
```

There is a small window of interest between the check to see if the timer is active and the decrementing of the timer. Between the two calls, the ISR could execute, setting the (formerly) active timer counter to –1. When the IoTimer routine regains control, it decrements the –1 to –2. The code accounts for this window by comparing the timeRemaining value to any negative value.

Managing Devices without Interrupts

Some devices don't generate interrupts with every significant state change. Even when the device does generate interrupts, a case can be made to drive an infrequently used, relatively slow device with a polled technique. Printer drivers are a common example of this technique. Since the printer device buffer is large in comparison to the physical print rate, a device driver has a considerable window in which it can occasionally check for the need to refill the buffer.

Working with Polled Devices

Once a device is started, it is generally unacceptable for driver code to hang in a tight loop waiting for the device to finish. In a multiprocessing and multitasking operating system such as Windows 2000, there are always useful chores that can or must occur in parallel with the device's operation.

By Microsoft edict, a driver is not allowed to stall in a tight polling loop for more than 50 microseconds. With today's extraordinary processor speeds,

50 microseconds is an eternity—a period in which hundreds of instructions could have executed.

When polling is required, drivers can utilize one of four techniques based on the amount of required poll time and the context in which the stall occurs.

- Driver code running at PASSIVE_LEVEL IRQL can call **KeDelayExecutionThread**, described in Table 11.3, to suspend a thread's execution for a specified interval. The thread is removed from the "ready to run" queue of threads and thus does not interfere with other "good to go" threads.

  This technique is available only to kernel-mode threads started by other driver code or during the device's initialization or cleanup code.

- Driver code can "busy wait" the processor using **KeStallExecutionProcessor**, described in Table 11.4. The function call is equivalent to code hanging in a tight countdown loop, except that the time stalled is processor speed-independent. Threads should not stall the processor for more than 50 microseconds.

- Synchronization objects, such as kernel events and mutexes, can be utilized. The "stalling" code then waits on the synchronization object to enter the signaled state—an act for which another nonstalled code path must take responsibility.

- A driver can utilize CustomTimerDpc routines to gain the benefit of I/O Timer functionality with controllable timing granularity.

If a device needs to be polled repeatedly, and the delay interval between each polling operation is more than 50 microseconds, the driver design should incorporate system threads (discussed in Chapter 14).

Table 11.3	*Function Prototype for KeDelayExecution Thread*
NSTATUS **KeDelayExecutionThread**	**IRQL == PASSIVE_LEVEL**
Parameter	**Description**
IN KPROCESSOR_MODE waitMode	• KernelMode • UserMode
IN BOOLEAN bAlertable	TRUE – if wait is canceled upon receipt of Async Procedure Call FALSE – in kernel mode
IN PLARGE_INTEGER interval	Wait interval in 100 nanosecond units
Return value	Success or failure code

Table 11.4	Function Prototype for KeStallExecutionProcessor
VOID KeStallExecutionProcessor	**IRQL == Any Level**
Parameter	**Description**
IN ULONG interval	Wait interval in microseconds
Return value	- void -

How CustomTimerDpc Routines Work

A CustomTimerDpc routine is just a DPC routine that is associated with a kernel Timer object. The CustomTimerDpc routine runs after the timer's timeout value expires. The Kernel automatically queues the DPC routine for execution. When the Kernel's DPC dispatcher pulls the request from the queue, the Custom-TimerDpc routine finally executes. Of course, there could be some delay between the moment the Timer object expires and the actual execution of the DPC routine.

Kernel Timer objects can be programmed to fire once or repeatedly. Thus, CustomTimerDpc routines can be scheduled to run at regular intervals. Like all other DPC routines, a CustomTimerDpc runs at DISPATCH_LEVEL IRQL. Table 11.5 shows the prototype for one of these routines. Notice the CustomTimerDpc routine always receives two reserved arguments from the system. The contents of these two system arguments are undefined. With CustomTimerDpc routines, there is a single context argument that is permanently associated with the DPC object.

CustomTimerDpc routines differ from I/O Timer routines in several ways.

- Unlike I/O Timer routines, a CustomTimerDpc is not associated with any particular Device object. There can be one CustomTimerDpc for

Table 11.5	Function Prototype for a CustomTimerDpc Routine
VOID CustomTimerDpc	**IRQL == Any Level**
Parameter	**Description**
IN PKDPC pDpc	DPC object generating the request
IN PVOID pContext	Context passed when DPC initialized
IN PVOID SystemArg1	Reserved
IN PVOID SystemArg2	Reserved
Return value	- void -

many device objects or many CustomTimerDpc's for one device
object.

- The minimum resolution of an I/O Timer is one second; the expiration time of a CustomTimerDpc is specified in units of 100 nanoseconds. In reality, the resolution is limited to about 10 milliseconds.
- The I/O Timer always uses a one-second interval. The expiration interval for a CustomTimerDpc can be specified differently with each
  firing.
- The storage for an I/O Timer object is automatically part of the Device object. To use a CustomTimerDpc, both a KDPC and a KTIMER
  object must be manually declared in nonpaged storage.

How to Set Up a CustomTimerDpc Routine

Working with CustomTimerDpc routines is very straightforward. A driver simply needs to follow these steps.

1. Allocate nonpaged storage (usually in a device or controller extension)
   for both a KDPC and a KTIMER object.

2. AddDevice calls **KeInitializeDpc** (Table 11.6) to associate a DPC routine and a context item with the DPC object. This context item is passed
   to the CustomTimerDpc routine when it fires. The address of the device
   or controller extension is a good choice for the context item.

3. AddDevice also calls **KeInitializeTimer** (Table 11.7) just once to set up
   the timer object.

4. To start a one-shot timer, call **KeSetTimer** (Table 11.8); to set up a repeating timer, use **KeSetTimerEx** instead. If these functions are used

Table 11.6	*Function Prototype for KeInitializeDpc*
VOID KeInitializeDpc	**IRQL == PASSIVE_LEVEL**
Parameter	**Description**
IN PKDPC pDpc	Pointer to a DPC object for which the caller provides the storage
IN PKDEFERRED_ROUTINE DeferredRoutine	Specifies the entry point for a routine to be called when the DPC object is removed from the DPC queue
IN PVOID pContext	Pointer to a caller-supplied context to be passed to the **DeferredRoutine** when it is called
Return value	- void -

Table 11.7	Function Prototype for KeInitializeTimer
VOID **KeInitializeTimer**	**IRQL == PASSIVE_LEVEL**
Parameter	**Description**
IN PKTIMER Timer	Pointer to a timer object for which the caller provides the storage
Return value	- void -

on a timer object that is currently active, the previous request is canceled and the new expiration time replaces the old one.

To keep a timer from firing, call **KeCancelTimer** (Table 11.9) before the Timer object expires. This also cancels a repeating Timer. To find out whether a Timer has already expired, call **KeReadStateTimer** (Table 11.10).

To initialize the DPC and timer objects, code must be executing at PASSIVE_LEVEL IRQL. To set, cancel, or read the state of the timer, code must be running at or below DISPATCH_LEVEL IRQL. In general, the function **KeInsertQueueDpc** should be avoided with the DPC object used for CustomTimerDpc routine. It can lead to race conditions within the driver.

How to Specify Expiration Times

Internally, Windows 2000 maintains the current system time by counting the number of 100-nanosecond intervals since January 1, 1601. This being a very

Table 11.8	Function Prototype for KeSetTimer
BOOLEAN KeSetTimer	**IRQL <= DISPATCH_LEVEL**
Parameter	**Description**
IN PKTIMER Timer	Pointer to timer object to set
IN LARGE_INTEGER DueTime	Specifies the absolute or relative time at which the timer is to expire
IN PKDPC Dpc	Pointer to a DPC object that was initialized by **KeInitializeDpc**
Return value	• TRUE – Timer was armed before call • FALSE – Timer is freshly armed

Table 11.9	*Function Prototype for KeCancelTimer*
BOOLEAN **KeCancelTimer**	**IRQL <= DISPATCH_LEVEL**
Parameter	**Description**
IN PKTIMER Timer	Pointer to timer object to cancel
Return value	• TRUE – Timer was armed before call • FALSE – Timer was not armed

big number, 64 bits are required to hold it in a structure tagged LARGE_
INTEGER. Table 11.11 lists the functions drivers can use to work with time
values.

When using **KeSetTimer** to on a timer object, the expiration time can
be specified in one of two ways.

- A positive LARGE_INTEGER value represents an absolute system
  time at which the timer will expire. Absolute times correspond to
  some exact moment in the future, like December 28, 2020 at 6:42
  PM.
- A negative LARGE_INTEGER value represents the length of an interval measured from the current moment, like "10 seconds from now."
  Clearly, relative time intervals are more useful within driver work.

This fragment of code shows how to set a Timer object to expire after
an interval of 75 microseconds. It assumes that **pDevExt** holds a pointer to a
device extension, and that the Extension contains initialized Timer and DPC
objects.

```
LARGE_INTEGER timeDue;

timeDue = RtlConvertLongToLargeInteger( -75 * 10 );
KeSetTimer( &pDevExt->Timer, timeDue, &pDevExt->DPC );
```

Table 11.10	*Function Prototype for KeReadStateTimer*
BOOLEAN **KeReadStateTimer**	**IRQL <= DISPATCH_LEVEL**
Parameter	**Description**
IN PKTIMER Timer	Pointer to the timer object to query
Return value	• TRUE – Timer has expired • FALSE – Timer still armed

Table 11.11	*Functions That Operate on System Time Values*
Time Functions	
Function	**Description**
KeQuerySystemTime	Return 64-bit absolute system time
RtlTimeToTimeFields	Break 64-bit time into date and time fields
RtlTimeFieldsToTime	Convert date and time into 64-bit system time
KeQueryTickCount	Return number of clock interrupts since boot
KeQueryTimeIncrement	Return number of 100-nanosecond units added to system time for each clock interrupt
RtlConvertLongToLargeInteger	Create a signed LARGE_INTEGER
RtlConvertUlongToLargeInteger	Create a positive LARGE_INTEGER
RtlLargeIntegerXxx	Perform various arithmetic and logical operations on LARGE_INTEGERs

Since the value passed to **KeSetTimer** is negative, the system interprets it as a relative time value. Scaling the number by 10 is necessary because the basic unit of system time for the call is 100 nanoseconds, one-tenth of a microsecond.

Other Uses for CustomTimerDpc Routines

In the next section, an example of a driver that performs data transfers using the CustomTimerDpc is presented. Typically, this technique is used to manage devices that do not generate interrupts. However, a CustomTimerDpc can also be used in specialized device timeout situations.

Code Example: A Timer-Based Driver

This modified version of the parallel port driver disables interrupts and uses a CustomTimerDpc routine to transfer data at fixed intervals. The code for this example is included on the companion CD and on the companion Web site, *www.W2KDriverBook.com*.

Device Extension Additions

The Device Extension is modified to include the DPC and Timer objects, plus a polling interval value, stored in microseconds.

```
typedef struct _DEVICE_EXTENSION {
    ...
```

```
    KDPC pollingDPC;        // reserve custom DPC object
    KTIMER pollingTimer;    // and the Timer object
    LARGE_INTEGER pollingInterval; // timeout counter
                                   // in us
    ...
} DEVICE_EXTENSION, *PDEVICE_EXTENSION;

// Define the interval between polls of device in us
// 100 us
#define POLLING_INTERVAL 100
```

AddDevice Modifications

AddDevice is changed in that **IoConnectInterrupt** is no longer called for this polling driver. The polling timer and DPC are initialized.

```
NTSTATUS AddDevice(IN PDRIVER_OBJECT pDriverObject,
                   IN PDEVICE_OBJECT pdo) {
    PDEVICE_EXTENSION pDevExt = (PDEVICE_EXTENSION)
        pDevObj->DeviceExtension;
...
// Near the end of the function, after IoCreateDevice
//    has been called…
//
// Calculate the polling interval in microseconds
//    and keep as relative time (negative value)
    pDevExt->pollingInterval =
        RtlConvertLongToLargeInteger(
            POLLING_INTERVAL * -10 );
//
// Prepare the polling timer and DPC
    KeInitializeTimer( &pDevExt->pollingTimer );
// Notice that the DPC routine receives the fdo
    KeInitializeDpc( &pDevExt->pollingDPC,
              PollingTimerDpc,
              (PVOID) pfdo );
...
}
```

TransmitBytes Changes

Each time a transfer is started using the TransmitBytes routine, the timer is initialized so that the polling timer DPC runs when the polling interval expires. Too large a polling interval does not keep the printer busy; too small an interval needlessly wastes CPU time.

```
BOOLEAN TransmitBytes( IN PDEVICE_EXTENSION pDevExt) {
    // Do all the work necessary to transfer bytes
    // to the physical device, as usual
    ...
    // Then start the polling timer
```

```
KeSetTimer( &pDevExt->pollingTimer,
            pDevExt->pollingInterval,
            &pDevExt->pollingDPC );
return TRUE;
}
```

PollingTimerDpc Routine

Finally, the DPC routine itself is presented. The DPC routine executes each
time the timer object expires. The DPC has the responsibility for checking on
the device—if more room is available in the printer buffer, more data is sent.
If the IRP's requested transfer is complete (or if the transfer encountered an
error from the device), the IRP is completed.

```
VOID PollingTimerDpc( IN PKDPC pDpc,
                      IN PVOID pContext,
                      IN PVOID SysArg1,
                      IN PVOID SysArg2 ) {
    PDEVICE_OBJECT pDevObj = (PDEVICE_OBJECT)
        pContext;
    PDEVICE_EXTENSION pDevExt = (PDEVICE_EXTENSION)
        pDevObj->DeviceExtension;

    // Try to send more data
    if (!TransmitBytes( pDevExt ) ) {
        // Transfer complete (normal or error)
        // Complete the IRP appropriately
        PIRP pIrp = pDevObj->CurrentIrp;
        pIrp->IoStatus.Information =
            pDevExt->xferCount;
        // Figure out what the final status should be
        pIrp->IoStatus.Status = STATUS_SUCCESS;
        // Based on HW error status bit, change Status
        ...

        // Now complete the IRP
        IoCompleteRequest( pIrp, IO_PARALLEL_INCREMENT
);

        // And request another IRP
        IoStartNextPacket( pDevObj, FALSE );
}
```

Summary

This chapter presented two distinct methods of dealing with time within a
driver. Typically, a driver needs to keep track of time either to ensure the device is working normally or to poll for further device interaction.

The I/O Timer mechanism is simple but crude, generating callbacks at fixed one-second intervals.

CustomTimerDpc routines are used primarily for efficient polling of devices in lieu of device interrupts.

The next chapter deals with DMA operations within the device and its associated driver.

DMA Drivers

CHAPTER OBJECTIVES

*N*ot all devices can depend on the CPU to move data between memory and the peripherals. While this technique is fine for slower hardware, fast devices that transfer large amounts of data incur too much overhead. Such devices are usually capable of directly accessing system memory and transferring data without the CPU's intervention. This chapter explains how to write drivers for these kinds of devices.

How DMA Works under Windows 2000

Just as the Windows 2000 operating system abstracts all other pieces of system hardware, DMA operations also follow a strict abstract model. Drivers that perform DMA within the framework of this abstraction can ignore many

214

of the hardware-specific aspects of the system platform. This section presents the major features of the Windows 2000 DMA framework.

Hiding DMA Hardware Variations with Adapter Objects

The purpose of using DMA is to minimize the CPU's involvement in data transfer operations. To do this, DMA devices use an auxiliary processor, called a *DMA controller*, to move data between memory and a peripheral device. This allows the CPU to continue doing other useful work in parallel with the I/O operation.

Although the exact details vary, most DMA controllers have a very similar architecture. In its simplest form, this consists of an address register for the starting address of the DMA buffer and a count register for the number of bytes or words to transfer. When these registers are properly programmed and the device started, the DMA controller begins moving data on its own. With each transfer, it increments the memory address register and decrements the count register. When the count register reaches zero, the DMA controller generates an interrupt, and the device is ready for another transfer.

Unfortunately, the needs of real-world hardware design complicate the simple picture. Consider the DMA implementation on ISA-based machines, described in chapter 2. These systems use a pair of Intel 8237 controller chips cascaded to provide four primary and three secondary DMA data channels. The primary channels (identified as zero through three) can perform single-byte transfers, while the secondary channels (five through seven) always transfer two bytes at a time. Since the 8237 uses a 16-bit transfer counter, the primary and secondary channels can handle only 64 KB and 128 KB per operation, respectively. Due to limitations of the ISA architecture, the DMA buffer must be located in the first 16 megabytes of physical memory.

Contrast this with the DMA architecture used by EISA systems. The Intel 82357 EISA I/O controller extends ISA capabilities by supporting one-, two-, and four-byte transfers on any DMA channel, as well as allowing DMA buffers to be located anywhere in the 32-bit address space. In addition, EISA introduces three new DMA bus-cycle formats (known as types A, B, and C) to give peripheral designers the ability to work with faster devices.

Even on the same ISA or EISA bus, different devices can use different DMA techniques. For example, slave DMA devices compete for shareable system DMA hardware on the motherboard, while bus masters avoid bottlenecks by using their own built-in DMA controllers.

The problem with all this variety is that it tends to make DMA drivers very platform-dependent. To avoid this trap, Windows 2000 drivers don't manipulate DMA hardware directly. Instead, they work with an abstract representation of the hardware in the form of an Adapter object. Chapter 4 briefly introduced these objects and said they help with orderly sharing of system DMA resources. It turns out that Adapter objects also simplify the task of writing platform-independent drivers by hiding many of the details of setting up the DMA hardware. The rest of this section explains more about what Adapter objects do and how to use them in a driver.

The Scatter/Gather Problem

Although virtual memory simplifies the lives of application developers, it introduces two major complications for DMA-based drivers. The first problem is that the buffer address passed to the I/O Manager is a *virtual* address. Since the DMA controller works with *physical* addresses, DMA drivers need some way to determine the physical pages making up a virtual buffer. The next section explains how Memory Descriptor Lists perform this translation.

The other problem (illustrated in Figure 12.1) is that a process doesn't necessarily occupy consecutive pages of physical memory, and what appears to be a contiguous buffer in virtual space is probably scattered throughout physical memory. The Windows 2000 Virtual Memory Manager uses the platform's address translation hardware (represented by a generic page table in the diagram) to give the process the illusion of a single, unbroken virtual address space. Unfortunately, the DMA controller doesn't participate in this illusion.

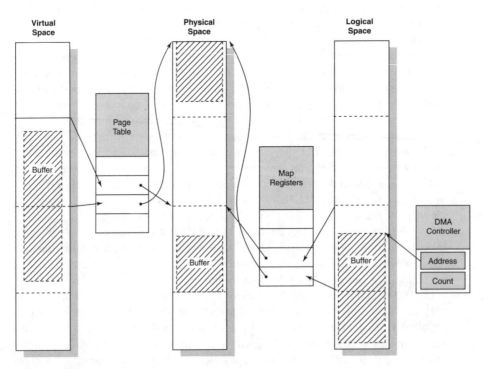

Figure 12.1   *Address spaces involved in DMA operations.*

Since most DMA controllers can only generate sequential physical addresses, buffers that span virtual page boundaries present a serious challenge. Consider what happens if a DMA controller starts at the top of a multipage buffer and simply increments its way through successive pages of physical memory. It's unlikely that any page after the first actually corresponds to one of the caller's virtual buffer pages. In fact, the pages touched by the DMA controller probably won't even belong to the process issuing the I/O request.

All virtual memory systems have to deal with the problem of scattering and gathering physical buffer pages during a DMA operation. Support for scatter/gather capabilities can come either from system DMA hardware or from hardware built into a smart bus master device. Once again, Windows 2000 tries to simplify the process by presenting drivers with a unified, abstract view of whatever scatter/gather hardware happens to exist on the system. This model consists of a contiguous range of addresses, called *logical space,* used by the DMA hardware and a set of *mapping registers* to translate logical space addresses into physical space addresses.

Referring to Figure 12.1, each mapping register corresponds to one page of DMA logical space, and a group of consecutively numbered registers represents a contiguous range of logical addresses. To perform a DMA transfer, a driver first allocates enough contiguous mapping registers to account for all the pages in the caller's buffer. It then loads consecutive mapping registers with the physical addresses of the caller's buffer pages. This has the effect of mapping the physically noncontiguous user buffer into a contiguous area of logical space. Finally, the driver loads the DMA controller with the starting address of the buffer in *logical* space and starts the device. While the operation is in progress, the DMA controller generates sequential, logical addresses that the scatter/gather hardware maps to appropriate physical page references.

While the conceptual model of mapping registers is nothing more than page tables for DMA devices, the actual implementation depends on the platform, the bus, and the I/O device. To minimize the driver's awareness of these details, Windows 2000 includes the mapping registers with the Adapter object and provides a set of routines for their management.

Memory Descriptor Lists

As described, loading physical addresses into mapping registers is an important part of setting up a DMA transfer. To make this process easier, the I/O Manager uses a structure called a *Memory Descriptor List* (MDL). An MDL keeps track of physical pages associated with a virtual buffer. The buffer described by an MDL can be in either user- or system-address space.

Direct I/O operations require the use of MDLs. If a Device object has the DO_DIRECT_IO bit set in its **Flags** field, the I/O Manager automatically builds an MDL describing the caller's buffer each time an I/O request is sent to the device. It stores the address of this MDL in the IRP's **MdlAddress** field, and a driver uses it to prepare the DMA hardware for a transfer.

As seen in Figure 12.2, the MDL consists of a header describing the virtual buffer followed by an array that lists the physical pages associated with the buffer. Given a virtual address within the buffer, the MDL data describes the corresponding physical page. Some of the fields in the header help clarify the use of an MDL.

StartVa and ByteOffset. The **StartVa** field contains the address of the buffer described by the MDL, rounded down to the nearest virtual page boundary. Since the buffer doesn't necessarily start on a page boundary, the **ByteOffset** field specifies the distance from this page boundary to the actual beginning of the buffer. Keep in mind that if the buffer is in user space, a driver can use the **StartVa** field to calculate indexes into the MDL, but *not* as an actual address pointer.

MappedSystemVa. If the buffer described by the MDL is in user space and its contents must be accessed, the buffer must first be mapped into system space with **MmGetSystemAddressForMdl**. This field of the MDL is used to hold the system-space address where the user-space buffer has been mapped.

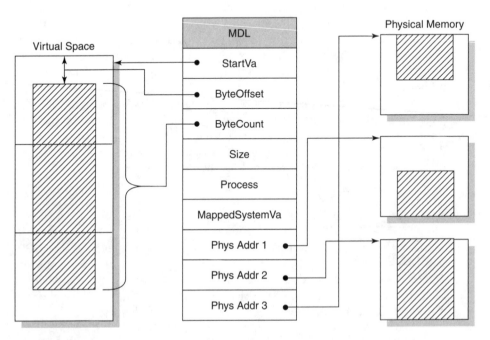

Figure 12.2   *Structure of a Memory Descriptor List (MDL).*

ByteCount and Size. These fields contain the number of bytes in the buffer described by the MDL and the size of the MDL itself, respectively.

Process. If the buffer lives in user space, the **Process** field points to the process object that owns the buffer. The I/O Manager uses this information when it cleans up the I/O operation.

Keep in mind that MDLs are opaque data objects defined by the Virtual Memory Manager. Their actual contents may vary from platform to platform, and they might also change in future versions of the operating system. Consequently, access to an MDL should be performed using system support functions. Any other approach could lead to future (if not present) disaster. Table 12.1 lists the common MDL functions that a driver is most likely to use. Some of the functions in this table are implemented as macros.

MDLs give drivers a convenient, platform-independent way of describing buffers located either in user- or system-address space. For drivers that perform DMA operations, MDLs are important because they make it easier to set up an Adapter object's mapping registers. Later parts of this chapter show the use of MDLs to set up DMA transfers.

Maintaining Cache Coherency

The final consideration is the impact of various caches on DMA operations. During a DMA transfer, data may be cached in various places, and if everything isn't coordinated properly, a device or CPU might end up with stale data. Figure 12.3 demonstrates the concern.

Table 12.1	*Functions That Operate on Memory Descriptor Lists*
MDL Access Functions	
Function	**Description**
IoAllocateMdl	Allocates an empty MDL
IoFreeMdl	Releases MDL allocation by IoAllocateMdl
MmBuildMdlForNonPagedPool	Builds MDL for an existing nonpaged pool buffer
MmGetSystemAddressForMdl	Returns a nonpaged system space address for the buffer described by an MDL
IoBuildPartialMdl	Builds an MDL describing part of a buffer
MmGetMdlByteCount	Returns count of bytes in buffer described by MDL
MmGetMdlByteOffset	Returns page-offset of buffer described by MDL
MmGetMdlVirtualAddress	Returns starting VA of buffer described by MDL

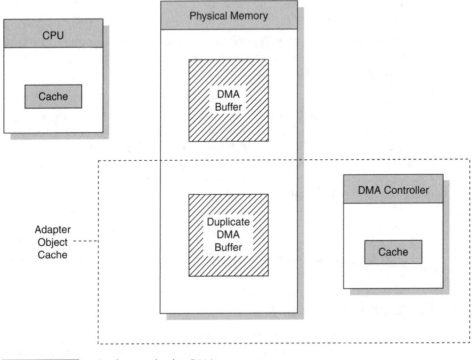

Figure 12.3 *Caches involved in DMA processing.*

CPU DATA CACHE

Modern CPUs support both on-chip and external caches for holding copies of recently used data. When the CPU wants something from physical memory, it first looks for the data in the cache. If the CPU finds what it wants, it doesn't have to make the long, slow trip down the system memory bus. For write operations, data moves from the CPU to the cache, where (depending on the cache and policy) it may stay for a while before making its way out to main memory.

The problem is that on some architectures, the CPU's cache controller and the DMA hardware are unaware of each other. This lack of awareness can lead to incoherent views of memory. For instance, if the CPU cache is holding part of the buffer, and that buffer is overwritten in physical memory by a DMA input, the CPU cache will contain stale data. Similarly, if modified data hasn't been flushed from the CPU cache when a DMA output begins, the DMA controller will be sending stale data from physical memory out to the device.

One way of handling this problem is to make sure that any portion of the DMA buffer residing in the CPU's data cache is flushed before a DMA operation begins. A driver can do this by calling **KeFlushIoBuffers** and giving it the MDL describing the DMA buffer. This function flushes any pages in the MDL from the data cache of every processor on the system.

Of course, the casual use of **KeFlushIoBuffers** can seriously impact system performance. Since many platforms automatically maintain cache coherency between CPU and DMA hardware, the call to **KeFlushIoBuffers** is not always necessary. On such systems, the call is defined to be a *no-op*. To ensure platform independence, drivers should always include the call.

ADAPTER OBJECT CACHE

The Adapter object is another place where data may be cached during a DMA transfer. Unlike the CPU cache, which is always a real piece of hardware, the Adapter object cache is an abstraction representing platform-dependent hardware or software. It might be an actual cache in a system DMA controller or a software buffer maintained by the I/O Manager. In fact, for some combinations of hardware, there might not even be a cache, but a driver still needs to use the Adapter object in order to guarantee portability.

Another benefit of using the Adapter object is that problems presented by certain buses are transparently handled for the driver. For example, the DMA controller for an ISA bus can access only the first 16 megabytes of physical memory. If any pages of a user buffer are outside this range, the I/O Manager allocates another buffer in low memory when the driver sets up the DMA mapping registers of the Adapter object. For output operation, the I/O Manager also copies the contents of the user buffer pages into this Adapter object buffer.

The Adapter object cache must be explicitly flushed after an input operation, or to notify the I/O Manager that it can release the memory in the adapter buffer. The function that performs the flush and release is **FlushAdapterBuffers**, a method of the Adapter object.

Packet-Based and Common Buffer DMA

The Windows 2000 DMA model divides drivers into two categories, based on the location of the DMA buffer itself: *packet-based DMA* and *common buffer DMA*.

In packet-based DMA, data moves directly between the device and the locked-down pages of a user-space buffer. This is the type of DMA associated with direct I/O operations. The significant point is that each new I/O request will probably use a different set of physical pages for its buffer. This impacts the kind of setup and cleanup steps the driver has to take for each I/O.

In common buffer DMA, the device uses a single nonpaged buffer from system space and all DMA transfers occur through this buffer.

Packet-based and common buffer DMA are not mutually exclusive categories. Some complex devices perform both kinds of DMA. One example is the Adaptec Ultra160 family of SCSI host adapters. It uses packet-based DMA to transfer data between SCSI devices and user buffers. The same controller exchanges command and status information with its driver using a set of mailboxes kept in a common buffer area.

Although all DMA drivers have similar characteristics, certain implementation details depend on whether packet-based or common buffer DMA is utilized. Later sections of this chapter present the specifics of writing each kind of driver.

Limitations of the Windows 2000 DMA Architecture

While the use of the Windows 2000 DMA abstraction simplifies driver construction, it does impose some restrictions. For one, the model is somewhat biased toward slave DMA devices. A driver is burdened with additional work to force the Adapter object model to fit a master DMA device.

More significantly, the Windows 2000 DMA model does not support device-to-device data transfers. Since modern buses such as PCI promote the concept of peer-to-peer relationships between devices, it is unfortunate that the Adapter model does not extend to nonsystem-hosted DMA.

Working with Adapter Objects

Although the specific details vary with the nature of the device and the architecture of the driver, DMA drivers generally have to perform several kinds of operations on Adapter objects.

- Locate the Adapter object associated with the specific device.
- Acquire and release ownership of Adapter objects and their mapping registers.
- Load the Adapter object's mapping registers at the start of a transfer.
- Flush the Adapter object's cache after a transfer completes.

The following sections discuss these topics in general terms. Later sections of this chapter add more detail.

Finding the Right Adapter Object

All DMA drivers need to locate an Adapter object before they can perform any I/O operations. To find the right one, a driver's initialization code needs to call the **IoGetDmaAdapter** function described in Table 12.2.

Given a description of some DMA hardware, **IoGetDmaAdapter** returns a pointer to a structure of function pointers that manipulate the corresponding Adapter object. It also reports a count of the maximum number of mapping registers available for a single transfer. The driver needs to save

Table 12.2	*Function Prototype for IoGetDmaAdapter*
PDMA_ADAPTER **IoGetDmaAdapter**	**IRQL == PASSIVE_LEVEL**
Parameter	**Description**
IN PDEVICE_OBJECT pdo	Points to the physical device object for the device
IN PDEVICE_DESCRIPTION pDeviceDescription	Points to a DEVICE_DESCRIPTION structure
IN OUT PULONG NumberOfMapRegisters	Input: number of map registers requested. Output: maximum number of map registers that the driver can allocate for any DMA transfer operation.
Return value	Pointer to DMA_ADAPTER

both these items in nonpaged storage (usually the Device or Controller Extension) for later use.

By returning a structure of function pointers, the Adapter object is truly an encapsulated object—it can only be manipulated through its interface.

The main input to **IoGetDmaAdapter** is the DEVICE_DESCRIPTION block listed in Table 12.3. Unused entries of this input structure must be zero. Some fields of this structure deserve comment.

ScatterGather. For bus master devices, this field signifies that the hardware supports transfer of data to and from noncontiguous ranges of physical memory. For slave devices, this field indicates that the device can be paused between page transfers, allowing the I/O Manager to repoint the DMA channel's address register to a new page of physical memory.

DemandMode. DMA demand mode is a transfer protocol that allows a device to hold off the (slave) DMA controller. In normal mode (DemandMode==FALSE), the DMA controller does not allow the device to delay its request to transfer another block of data.

Autoinitialization. DMA autoinitialization mode allows system DMA channels to restart themselves after a completed transfer. Specified address and count values are automatically reset into the DMA hardware and another operation is "good to go."

IgnoreCount. Some DMA hardware maintains an improper count of bytes transferred. This can occur because the hardware counts words instead of bytes. If this field is set to TRUE, the HAL manually maintains the transfer count on behalf of the device.

Table 12.3	The DEVICE_DESCRIPTION Structure for IoGetDmaAdapter

DEVICE_DESCRIPTION, *PDEVICE_DESCRIPTION

Field	Contents
ULONG Version	• DEVICE_DESCRIPTION_VERSION • DEVICE_DESCRIPTION_VERSION1
BOOLEAN Master	TRUE – Bus master device FALSE – Slave device
BOOLEAN ScatterGather	TRUE – Device supports scatter/gather
BOOLEAN DemandMode	Slave device uses demand mode
BOOLEAN AutoInitialize	Slave device uses autoinitialize mode
BOOLEAN Dma32BitAddresses	DMA addressing uses 32 bits
BOOLEAN IgnoreCount	TRUE – Device's transfer count not maintained accurately
BOOLEAN Reserved1	Must be FALSE
BOOLEAN Dma64BitAddresses	DMA addressing uses 64 bits
ULONG BusNumber	System-assigned bus number (unused by WDM drivers)
ULONG DmaChannel	Slave device DMA channel number
INTERFACE_TYPE InterfaceType	• Internal • Isa • Eisa • MicroChannel • PCIBus
DMA_WIDTH DmaWidth	• Width8Bits • Width16Bits • Width32Bits
DMA_SPEED DmaSpeed	• Compatible • TypeA • TypeB • TypeC
ULONG MaximumLength	Largest transfer size (in bytes) device can perform
ULONG DmaPort	Microchannel-type bus port number (obsolete)

Acquiring and Releasing the Adapter Object

There is no guarantee that the DMA resources needed for a device transfer will be free when a driver's Start I/O routine runs. For example, a slave device DMA channel may already be in use by another device, or there may not be enough mapping registers to handle the request. Consequently, all packet-based DMA drivers and drivers for common buffer slave devices have to request ownership of the Adapter object before starting a data transfer.

Since the Start I/O routine runs at DISPATCH_LEVEL IRQL, there is no way it can stop and wait for the Adapter object. Instead, it calls the **Allocate-AdapterChannel** method of the Adapter object (see Table 12.4) and then returns control to the I/O Manager.

When the requested DMA resources become available, the I/O Manager notifies the driver by calling its Adapter Control routine. It's important to keep in mind that this is an asynchronous callback. It may happen as soon as Start I/O calls **AllocateAdapterChannel**, or it may not occur until some other driver releases the Adapter resources.

Notice that the caller of **AllocateAdapterChannel** must be at DISPATCH_LEVEL IRQL. Since the function is normally called from the Start I/O routine, this poses no problem. However, if it is called from another driver routine from PASSIVE_LEVEL, make sure to use **KeRaiseIrql** and **KeLowerIrql** before and after the call to **AllocateAdapterChannel**.

Table 12.4	Function Prototype for AllocateAdapterChannel
NTSTATUS **AllocateAdapterChannel**	**IRQL == DISPATCH_LEVEL**
Parameter	**Description**
IN PDMA_ADAPTER pDmaAdapter	Points to the DMA_ADAPTER structure returned by IoGetDmaAdapter
IN PDEVICE_OBJECT pDeviceObject	Points to the target DMA device object
IN ULONG NumberOfMapRegisters	Specifies the number of map registers to be used in the transfer
IN PDRIVER_CONTROL ExecutionRoutine	Points to a driver-supplied AdapterControl routine to be called as soon the system DMA controller or bus master adapter is available
IN PVOID pContext	Points to the driver-determined context to be passed to the AdapterControl routine
Return value	STATUS_SUCCESS or STATUS_INSUFFICIENT_RESOURCES

The Adapter Control routine in a DMA driver is responsible for calling **MapTransfer** to set up the DMA hardware and starting the actual device operation. Table 12.5 contains a prototype of the Adapter Control callback.

The MapRegisterBase argument is an opaque value that identifies the mapping registers assigned to the I/O request. It is really a kind of handle to a specific group of registers. This handle is used to set up the DMA hardware for the transfer. Normally, this handle value is saved in the Device or Controller extension because it is needed in later parts of the DMA operation.

The pIrp argument passed to the Adapter Control callback is valid only when **AllocateAdapterChannel** is called from the Start I/O routine. If it is called from some other context, the pIrp pointer will be NULL. In such a case, another mechanism must be used to pass the IRP (and its associated MDL address) to the Adapter Control routine. The context pointer argument can possibly be used for this purpose.

After it programs the DMA controller and starts the data transfer, the Adapter Control routine gives control back to the I/O Manager. Drivers of slave devices should return a value of KeepObject from this function so that the Adapter object remains the exclusive property of this request. Bus master drivers return DeallocateObjectKeepRegisters.

When the DpcForIsr routine in a DMA driver completes an I/O request, it needs to release any Adapter resources it owns. Drivers of DMA devices do this by calling **FreeAdapterChannel**.

Setting Up the DMA Hardware

All packet-based drivers, as well as common buffer drivers for slave devices, have to program the DMA hardware at the beginning of each data transfer. Using the abstract DMA model of Windows 2000, this means loading the Adapter object's mapping registers with physical page addresses taken from

Table 12.5	*Function Prototype for an Adapter Control Routine*
IO_ALLOCATION_ACTION AdapterControl	**IRQL == DISPATCH_LEVEL**
Parameter	**Description**
IN_PDEVICE_OBJECT pDeviceObject	Target device for DMA operation
IN PIRP pIrp	IRP describing this operation
IN PVOID MapRegisterBase	Handle to a group of mapping registers
IN PVOID pContext	Driver-determined context
Return value	• DeallocateObjectKeepRegisters • KeepObject

the MDL. This setup work is done by the **MapTransfer** method of the Adapter object, described in Table 12.6.

MapTransfer uses the CurrentVa and Length arguments to figure out what physical page addresses to put into the mapping registers. These values must fall somewhere within the range of addresses described by the MDL.

Keep in mind that **MapTransfer** may actually move the contents of the DMA output buffer from one place to another in memory. For example, on an ISA machine, if the pages in the MDL are outside the 16-megabyte DMA limit, calling this function results in data being copied to a buffer in low physical memory. Similarly, if the DMA input buffer is out of range, **MapTransfer** allocates a buffer in low memory for the transfer. On buses that support 32-bit DMA addresses, no copying or duplicate buffers are required.

Drivers of bus master devices also need to call **MapTransfer**. In this case, however, the function behaves differently, since it doesn't know how to program the bus master's control registers. Instead, **MapTransfer** simply returns address and length values that the driver again loads into the device's registers. For bus masters with built-in scatter/gather support, this same mechanism allows the driver to create a scatter/gather list for the device. Later sections of this chapter explain how this works.

Flushing the Adapter Object Cache

At the end of a data transfer, all packet-based DMA drivers and drivers for common buffer slave devices have to call **FlushAdapterBuffers**, a method of the Adapter object (see Table 12.7). For devices using the system DMA

Table 12.6	Function Prototype for MapTransfer
PHYSICAL_ADDRESS **MapTransfer**	**IRQL <= DISPATCH_LEVEL**
Parameter	**Description**
IN PDMA_ADAPTER pDmaAdapter	Points to the DMA adapter object returned by IoGetDmaAdapter
IN PMDL pMdl	Memory Descriptor List for DMA buffer
IN PVOID MapRegisterBase	Handle to a group of mapping registers
IN PVOID CurrentVA	Virtual address of buffer within the MDL
IN OUT PULONG Length	• IN – count of bytes to be mapped • OUT – actual count of bytes mapped
IN BOOLEAN bWriteToDevice	• TRUE – send data to device • FALSE – read data from device
Return value	DMA logical address of the mapped region

Table 12.7	Function Prototype for FlushAdapterBuffers
BOOLEAN FlushAdapterBuffers	**IRQL <= DISPATCH_LEVEL**
Parameter	**Description**
IN PDMA_ADAPTER pDmaAdapter	Points to the DMA adapter object returned by IoGetDmaAdapter
IN PMDL pMdl	MDL describing the buffer
IN PVOID MapRegisterBase	Handle passed to AdapterControl
IN PVOID CurrentVA	Starting virtual address of buffer
IN ULONG Length	Length of the buffer
IN BOOLEAN WriteToDevice	• TRUE – operation was an output • FALSE – operation was an input
Return value	• TRUE – Adapter buffers flushed • FALSE – an error occurred

controller, this function flushes any hardware caches associated with the Adapter object.

In the case of ISA devices doing packet-based DMA, this call releases any low memory used for auxiliary buffers. For input operations, it also copies data back to the physical pages of the caller's input buffer. Refer back to the section on cache coherency for a discussion of this process.

Writing a Packet-Based Slave DMA Driver

In packet-based slave DMA, the device transfers data to or from the locked down pages of the caller's buffer using a shared DMA controller on the mainboard. The system is also responsible for providing scatter/gather support.

How Packet-Based Slave DMA Works

Although the specifics depend on the nature of the device, most packet-based slave DMA drivers conform to a very similar pattern. The following subsections describe the routines of these drivers.

IRP_MN_START_DEVICE HANDLER

Along with its usual duties, this PnP handler performs the following DMA preparation tasks:

1. Locates the DMA channel used by the device. The DMA resources would normally be sent with the requesting IRP in the stack's Parameters.StartDevice.AllocatedResourcesTranslated field.

2. The DEVICE_DESCRIPTION structure is built. **IoGetDmaAdapter** is invoked to identify the Adapter object associated with the device.

3. The DMA_OBJECT pointer returned from **IoGetDmaAdapter** is saved in the Device Extension.

4. The DO_DIRECT_IO bit in the **Flags** field of the Device object is set, causing the I/O Manager to lock user buffers in memory and create MDLs for them.

START I/O ROUTINE

Unlike its counterpart in a programmed I/O driver, the DMA Start I/O routine doesn't actually start the device. Instead, it requests ownership of the Adapter object and leaves the remainder of the work to the Adapter Control callback routine. Specifically, the Start I/O routine does the following:

1. It calls **KeFlushIoBuffers** to flush data from the CPU cache out to main memory (RAM).

2. Start I/O decides how many mapping registers to request. Initially, it calculates the number of registers needed to cover the entire user buffer. If this number turns out to be more mapping registers than the Adapter object has available, it will ask for the maximum available.

3. Based on the number of mapping registers and the size of the user buffer, Start I/O calculates the number of bytes to transfer in the first device operation. This may be the entire buffer or it may be only the first portion of a split transfer.

4. Next, Start I/O calls **MmGetMdlVirtualAddress** to recover the virtual address of the user buffer from the MDL. It stores this address in the Device Extension. Subsequent parts of the driver use this address as an offset in the MDL to set up the actual DMA transfer.

5. Start I/O then calls **AllocateAdapterChannel** to request ownership of the Adapter object. If this function succeeds, the rest of the setup work is performed by the Adapter Control routine, so Start I/O simply returns control to the I/O Manager.

6. If **AllocateAdapterChannel** returns an error, Start I/O fails the requesting IRP, calls **IoCompleteRequest**, and starts processing the next IRP.

ADAPTER CONTROL ROUTINE

The I/O Manager calls back the Adapter Control routine when the necessary Adapter resources become available. Its job is to initialize the DMA controller for the transfer and start the device itself. In essence, it is the second half of Start I/O that occurs with the Adapter object in hand. This routine does the following:

1. It stores the value of the MapRegisterBase argument it receives in the Device Extension for subsequent use.

2. The Adapter Control routine then calls **MapTransfer** to load the Adapter object's mapping registers. To make this call, it uses the buffer's virtual address and the transfer size calculated by the Start I/O routine.

3. Next, it sends appropriate commands to the device to begin the transfer operation.

4. Finally, the Adapter Control routine returns the value KeepObject to retain ownership of the Adapter object.

At this point, the transfer is in progress, and other code is executing in parallel until an interrupt arrives from the device.

INTERRUPT SERVICE ROUTINE

Compared to a programmed I/O driver, the ISR in a packet-based DMA driver is not very complicated. Unless hardware limitations force the driver to split a large transfer request across several device operations, there is only a single interrupt service when the whole transfer completes. When this interrupt arrives, the ISR does the following:

1. It issues commands as necessary to acknowledge the device and prevent it from generating additional interrupts.

2. The ISR then stores device status (and any relevant error information) in the Device Extension.

3. It calls **IoRequestDpc** to continue processing the request in the driver's DpcForIsr routine.

4. The ISR returns the value of TRUE to indicate that it serviced the interrupt.

DpcForIsr ROUTINE

The DpcForIsr routine is triggered by the ISR at the end of each partial data transfer operation. Its job is to start the next partial transfer (if there is one) or to complete the current request. Specifically, the DpcForIsr routine in a packet-based DMA driver does the following:

1. It calls **FlushAdapterBuffers,** a method of the Adapter object, to force any remaining data from the Adapter object's cache.

2. The DpcForIsr routine checks the Device Extension to see if there were any errors during the operation. If so, it completes the request with an appropriate status code and length, and starts the next request.

3. Otherwise, it decrements the count of bytes remaining by the size of the last transfer. If the whole buffer has been processed, it completes the current request and starts the next.

4. If more data remains, the DpcForIsr routine increments the user-buffer address pointer (stored in the Device Extension) by the size of the last operation. It then calculates the number of bytes transferred in the next device operation, calls **MapTransfer** to reset the mapping registers, and starts the device.

If the DpcForIsr routine started another partial transfer, the I/O Manager will return control to the driver when the device generates an interrupt.

Splitting DMA Transfers

When a packet-based DMA driver receives a buffer, it may not be able to transfer all the data in a single device operation. It could be that the Adapter object doesn't have enough mapping registers to handle the whole request at once, or there could be limitations on the device itself. In any event, the driver has to be prepared to split the request across multiple data transfer operations.

There are two solutions to this problem. One is to have the driver reject any requests that it can't handle in a single I/O. With this approach, any user of the driver is responsible for breaking the request into chunks small enough to process. Of course, the driver will have to provide some mechanism for letting its clients know the maximum allowable buffer size (an IOCTL, for example). For this approach, it might make sense to write a higher-level driver that sits on top of the DMA device driver and splits the requests. This has the advantage of shielding application programs from the details of splitting the request.

Another approach is to write a single, monolithic driver that accepts requests of any size and splits them into several I/O operations. This is the strategy used by the sample driver in the next section of this chapter.

This second method requires maintenance of a pointer that tracks position within the user buffer as successive chunks of data are transferred. There may also be a need to maintain a count of the number of bytes left to process. The following sections explain how to initialize and update these data items during an I/O request.

FIRST TRANSFER

The Start I/O routine normally sets things up for the first transfer. Initially, it tries to grab enough mapping registers to do everything in one I/O. If the Adapter object doesn't have enough mapping registers for this to work, Start

I/O asks for as many as it can get and sets up the current transfer accordingly. The following code fragment shows how this is done:

```
pDevExt->transferVA = (PUCHAR)
    MmGetMdlVirtualAddress( pIrp->MdlAddress );

pDevExt->bytesRemaining =
    MmGetMdlByteCount( pIrp->MdlAddress );

pDevExt->transferSize =
    pDevExt->bytesRemaining;

mapRegsNeeded = ADDRESS_AND_SIZE_TO_SPAN_PAGES(
                    pDevExt->transferVA,
                    pDevExt->transferSize );

if ( mapRegsNeeded > pDevExt->mapRegsAvailable ) {
    mapRegsNeeded = pDevExt->mapRegsAvailable;
    pDevExt->transferSize =
        mapRegsNeeded * PAGE_SIZE -
            MmGetMdlByteOffset( pIrp->MdlAddress );
}

// Note the use of the Adapter object - the DmaAdapter
// pointer returned by IoGetDmaAdapter contains
// function pointers for Adapter operations.
pDevExt->pDmaAdapter->DmaOperations->
    AllocateAdapterChannel(pDevExt->pDmaAdapter,
                            pDevObj,
                            mapRegsNeeded,
                            AdapterControl,
                            pDevExt );
```

ADDITIONAL TRANSFERS

After each interrupt, the DpcForIsr checks to see if there is any data left to process. If there is, it calculates the number of mapping registers needed to transfer all the remaining bytes in a single I/O operation. If there are not enough mapping registers available, it sets up another partial transfer. The following code fragment illustrates the procedure:

```
pDevExt->bytesRemaining -= pDevExt->transferSize;
if (pDevExt->bytesRemaining > 0) {
    pDevExt->transferVA += pDevExt->transferSize;
    pDevExt->transferSize = pDevExt->bytesRemaining;
    mapRegsNeeded = ADDRESS_AND_SIZE_TO_SPAN_PAGES(
                        pDevExt->transferVA,
                        pDevExt->transferSize );
    if (mapRegsNeeded > pDevExt->mapRegsAvailable ) {
        mapRegsNeeded = pDevExt->mapRegsAvailable;
```

```
                pDevExt->transferSize =
                    mapRegsNeeded * PAGE_SIZE -
                    BYTE_OFFSET( pDevExt->transferVA );
    }
    pDevExt->pDmaAdapter->DmaOperations->
        MapTransfer( pDevExt->pDmaAdapter,
                     pMdl,
                     pDevExt->mapRegisterBase,
                     pDevExt->transferVA,
                     transferSize,
                     pDevExt->bWriting );
    }
```

Code Example: A Packet-Based Slave DMA Driver

This example is a skeleton of a packet-based driver for a generic slave
DMA device. Although it doesn't actually manage a specific kind of hardware, it may help in understanding how these drivers work. The complete code for this example is included on the CD that accompanies this book
and on the companion website www.W2KDriverBook.com.

DRIVER.H

This excerpt from the driver-specific header file shows the changes that need
to be made to the Device Extension structure.

```
typedef struct _DEVICE_EXTENSION {
...
PDMA_ADAPTER pDmaAdapter;
ULONG mapRegisterCount;
ULONG dmaChannel;

// This is the "handle" assigned to the map registers
// when the AdapterControl routine is called back
PVOID mapRegisterBase;

ULONG bytesRequested;
ULONG bytesRemaining;
ULONG transferSize;
PUCHAR transferVA;

// This flag is TRUE if writing, FALSE if reading
BOOLEAN bWriting;
...
} DEVICE_EXTENSION, *PDEVICE_EXTENSION;

#define MAX_DMA_LENGTH 4096
```

GetDmaInfo Routine

The GetDmaInfo helper routine is responsible for making the call to **IoGet-DmaAdapter**. Primarily, this is an example of setting up the DEVICE_DESCRIPTION structure.

```
NTSTATUS GetDmaInfo( IN INTERFACE_TYPE busType,
                     IN PDEVICE_OBJECT pDevObj ) {
    PDEVICE_EXTENSION pDevExt = (PDEVICE_EXTENSION)
        pDevObj->DeviceExtension;

    DEVICE_DESCRIPTION dd;

    // Zero out the entire structure
    RtlZeroMemory( &dd, sizeof(dd) );

    dd.Version = DEVICE_DESCRIPTION_VERSION1;
    dd.Master = FALSE;   // this is a slave device
    dd.ScatterGather = FALSE;
    dd.DemandMode = FALSE;
    dd.AutoInitialize = FALSE;
    dd.Dma32BitAddresses = FALSE;

    dd.InterfaceType = busType;        // as passed in

    dd.DmaChannel = pDevExt->dmaChannel;
    dd.MaximumLength = MAX_DMA_LENGTH;
    dd.DmaWidth = Width16Bits;
    dd.DmaSpeed = Compatible;

    // Compute the maximum number of mapping regs
    // this device could possibly need. Since the
    // transfer may not be paged aligned, add one
    // to allow the max xfer size to span a page.
    pDevExt->mapRegisterCount =
        (MAX_DMA_LENGTH / PAGE_SIZE) + 1;

    pDevExt->pDmaAdapter =
        IoGetDmaAdapter( pDevObj,
                         &dd,
                         &pDevExt->mapRegisterCount);

    // If the Adapter object can't be assigned, fail
    if (pDevExt->pDmaAdapter == NULL)
        return STATUS_INSUFFICIENT_RESOURCES;
    else
        return STATUS_SUCCESS;
}
```

Start I/O Changes

Start I/O no longer starts the device. Instead, it sets up the DMA operation and defers to the Adapter Control routine, called back when the Adapter Channel can be allocated. Nevertheless, the DMA setup is significant work.

```
VOID StartIo( IN PDEVICE_OBJECT pDevObj,
                IN PIRP pIrp ) {
PIO_STACK_LOCATION pStack =
    IoGetCurrentIrpStackLocation( pIrp );

PDEVICE_EXTENSION pDevExt = (PDEVICE_EXTENSION)
    pDevObj->DeviceExtension;

// The IRP holds the MDL structure, already set up by
//  the I/O Manager because DO_DIRECT_IO flag is set
PMDL pMdl = pIrp->MdlAddress;

ULONG mapRegsNeeded;
NTSTATUS status;

pDevExt->bWriting = FALSE;       // assume read operation

switch ( pStack->MajorFunction ) {
case IRP_MJ_WRITE:
    pDevExt->bWriting = TRUE;  // bad assumption
case IRP_MJ_READ:
    pDevExt->bytesRequested =
        MmGetMdlByteCount( pMdl );
    pDevExt->transferVA = (PUCHAR)
        MmGetMdlVirtualAddress( pMdl );
    pDevExt->bytesRemaining =
    pDevExt->transferSize =
        pDevExt->bytesRequested;

    mapRegsNeeded =
        ADDRESS_AND_SIZE_TO_SPAN_PAGES(
            pDevExt->transferVA,
            pDevExt->transferSize );

    if (mapRegsNeeded > pDevExt->mapRegisterCount) {
        mapRegsNeeded = pDevExt->mapRegisterCount;
        pDevExt->transferSize =
            mapRegsNeeded * PAGE_SIZE -
            MmGetMdlByteOffset( pMdl );
}

    status = pDevExt->pDmaAdapter->DmaOperations->
        AllocateAdapterChannel(
            pDevExt->pDmaAdapter,
            pDevObj,
            mapRegsNeeded,
```

```
                         AdapterControl,
                         pDevExt );

        if (!NT_SUCCESS( status )) {
            // fail the IRP & don't continue with it
            pIrp->IoStatus.Status = status;
            // Show no bytes transferred
            pIrp->IoStatus.Information = 0;
            IoCompleteRequest( pIrp, IO_NO_INCREMENT );
            IoStartNextPacket( pDevObj, FALSE);
        }
        break;  // nice job - AdapterControl takes it
                //                    from here on

    default:
        // Shouldn't be here - ditch this strange IRP
        pIrp->IoStatus.Status = STATUS_NOT_SUPPORTED;
        pIrp->IoStatus.Information = 0;
        IoCompleteRequest( pIrp, IO_NO_INCREMENT );
        IoStartNextPacket( pDevObj, FALSE );
    }
}
```

AdapterControl Routine

This callback routine completes the work started with Start I/O. It programs
the DMA hardware and starts the device itself. It is called by the I/O Manager
after the Adapter object is assigned to the device and sufficient mapping registers are available to handle the request.

```
IO_ALLOCATION_ACTION AdapterControl(
                        IN PDEVICE_OBJECT pDevObj,
                        IN PIRP pIrp,
                        IN PVOID MapRegisterBase,
                        IN PVOID pContext ) {
PDEVICE_EXTENSION pDevExt = (PDEVICE_EXTENSION)
                                    pContext;

// Save the handle to the mapping register set
pDevExt->mapRegisterBase = MapRegisterBase;

// Flush the CPU cache(s),
//     if necessary on this platform...
KeFlushIoBuffers( pIrp->MdlAddress,
                !pDevExt->bWriting,        // inverted
                TRUE );              // yes DMA

pDevExt->pDmaAdapter->DmaOperations->
    MapTransfer( pDevExt->pDmaAdapter,
                pIrp->MdlAddress,
                MapRegisterBase,
                pDevExt->transferVA,
```

```
                    &pDevExt->transferSize,
                    pDevExt->bWriting );

// Start the device
StartTransfer( pDevExt );

return KeepObject;
}
```

DpcForIsr Routine

The Interrupt Service Routine for a DMA device is usually straightforward. An interrupt is generated at the end of each partial transfer, or when a transfer error occurs. As usual, the ISR schedules a DPC, using **IoRequestDpc**. The DPC fires the registered routine, DpcForIsr.

DpcForIsr sets up the next partial transfer. If the entire transfer has completed, it marks the IRP for completion and starts the next.

```
VOID DpcForIsr(IN PKDPC pDpc,
               IN PDEVICE_OBJECT pDevObj,
               IN PIRP pIrp,
               IN PVOID pContext ) {
PDEVICE_EXTENSION pDevExt = (PDEVICE_EXTENSION)
     pContext;
ULONG mapRegsNeeded;
PMDL pMdl = pIrp->MdlAddress;

// Flush the Apapter buffer to system RAM or device.
pDevExt->pDmaAdapter->DmaOperations->
FlushAdapterBuffers( pDevExt->pDmaAdapter,
                     pMdl,
                     pDevExt->mapRegisterBase,
                     pDevExt->transferVA,
                     pDevExt->transferSize,
                     pDevExt->bWriting );

// If the device is reporting errors, fail the IRP
if (DEVICE_FAIL( pDevExt )) {
    // An error occurred, the DMA channel is now free
    pDevExt->pDmaAdapter->DmaOperations->
         FreeAdapterChannel( pDevExt->pDmaAdapter );
    pIrp->IoStatus.Status = STATUS_DEVICE_DATA_ERROR;
    pIrp->IoStatus.Information =
         pDevExt->bytesRequested -
         pDevExt->bytesRemaining;
    IoCompleteRequest( pIrp, IO_NO_INCRMENT );
    IoStartNextPacket( pDevObj, FALSE);
}

// Device had no errors, see if another partial needed
pDevExt->bytesRemaining -= pDevExt->transferSize;
if (pDevExt->bytesRemaining > 0) {
```

```
        // Another partial transfer needed
        // Update the transferVA and try to finish it
        pDevExt->transferVA += pDevExt->transferSize;
        pDevExt->transferSize = pDevExt->bytesRemaining;
        mapRegsNeeded =
                ADDRESS_AND_SIZE_TO_SPAN_PAGES(
                    pDevExt->transferVA,
                    pDevExt->transferSize );
        // If it still doesn't fit in one swipe,
        //      cut back the expectation
        if (mapRegsNeeded > pDevExt->mapRegisterCount) {
            mapRegsNeeded = pDevExt->mapRegisterCount;
            pDevExt->transferSize =
                mapRegsNeeded * PAGE_SIZE -
                BYTE_OFFSET( pDevExt->transferVA );
        }

        // Now set up the mapping registers for another
        pDevExt->pDmaAdapter->DmaOperations->
            MapTransfer( pDevExt->pDmaAdapter,
                         pMdl,
                         pDevExt->mapRegisterBase,
                         pDevExt->transferVA,
                         &pDevExt->transferSize,
                         pDevExt->bWriting );

        // And start the device
        StartTransfer( pDevExt );
    } else {
        // Entire transfer has now completed -
        // Free the DMA channel for another device
        pDevExt->pDmaAdapter->DmaOperations->
            FreeAdapterChannel( pDevExt->pDmaAdapter );
        // And complete the IRP in glory
        pIrp->IoStatus.Status = STATUS_SUCCESS;
        pIrp->IoStatus.Information =
            pDevExt->bytesRequested;

        // Choose a priority boost appropriate for device
        IoCompleteRequest( pIrp, IO_DISK_INCREMENT );
        IoStartNextPacket( pDevObj, FALSE );
    }
}
```

Writing a Packet-Based Bus Master DMA Driver

In packet-based bus master DMA, the device transfers data to or from the locked down pages of the caller's buffer, using DMA hardware that is part of the device itself. Depending on the capabilities of the device, it might be providing its own scatter/gather support as well.

The architecture of a packet-based bus master driver is almost identical to that of a driver for a slave device. The only difference is the way the driver sets up the bus master hardware. The following sections describe these differences.

Setting Up Bus Master Hardware

A bus master device is more complicated to program because Windows 2000 doesn't know how to program the device's onboard DMA controller. The most the I/O Manager can do is provide the driver with two pieces of information.

- An address in DMA logical space, where a contiguous segment of the buffer begins
- A count indicating the number of bytes in that segment

It then becomes the driver's responsibility to load this information into the address and length registers of the device and start the transfer.

The function that performs this work is familiar—**MapTransfer**. If the DEVICE_DESCRIPTION supplied in the call to **IoGetDmaAdapter** described a bus mastering device, then **MapTransfer** returns a physical address that can be used to program the device's DMA address register. The physical address corresponds to the MDL and CurrentVa arguments of the call.

There is little chance that the user buffer, if it spans more than a page, resides in contiguous physical RAM. Therefore, **MapTransfer** returns the physical *starting* address and the length of the "first" block that can be transferred contiguously. In all likelihood, the length returned by **MapTransfer** is the length of a page—no part of the user buffer is likely to be contiguous. Should two or more pages of the user buffer *happen* to be contiguous, then **MapTransfer** correctly reports such a length.

After the device transfers what it can from the contiguous buffer, it must be reprogrammed to transfer the next part of the buffer from another contiguous block. Figure 12.4 shows how this process needs to work, with the somewhat optimistic case of some pages of the user buffer actually residing in contiguous memory.

Supporting bus master devices requires some changes to the driver's AdapterControl and DpcForIsr routines. The following sections contain fragments of these routines. Compare them with the corresponding routines in the packet-based slave DMA driver in the previous section of this chapter.

AdapterControl ROUTINE

Being optimistic, the AdapterControl routine asks **MapTransfer** to map the entire buffer at the start of the first transfer. **MapTransfer** reports to the driver how much contiguous memory is actually available in the first segment of the buffer.

```
PHYSICAL_ADDRESS DmaAddress;

PMDL pMdl = pIrp->MdlAddress;
```

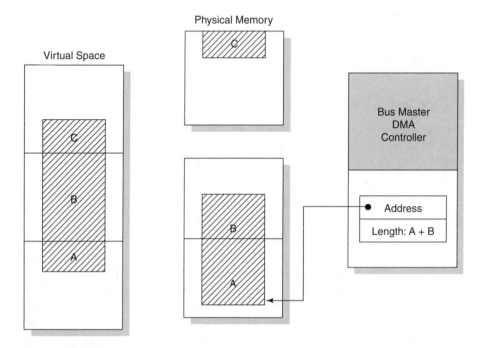

Figure 12.4 *MapTransfer points to contiguous buffer segments.*

```
pDevExt->transferVA = (PUCHAR)
    MmGetMdlVirtualAddress( pMdl );

PDevExt->transferSize =
pDevExt->bytesRemaining =
    MmGetMdlByteCount( pMdl );

DmaAddress =
    pDevExt->pDmaAdapter->DmaOperations->
        MapTransfer( pDevExt->pDmaAdapter,
                     pMdl,
                     pDevExt->mapRegisterBase,
                     pDevExt->transferVA,
                     &pDevExt->transferSize,
                     pDevExt->bWriting );

// transferSize has been reset to the maximum
//    contiguous length for the first segment

// WriteDmaAddress is a device-specific routine that
//    programs the device's DMA address register
WriteDmaAddress( pDevExt, DmaAddress.LowPart );
// Similarly, WriteDmaCount is device-specific
```

```
WriteDmaCount( pDevExt, pDevExt->transferSize );

// Now the device is started
StartDevice( pDevExt );

// must return indicating bus master at work
return DeallocateObjectKeepRegisters;
```

DpcForIsr ROUTINE

After each partial transfer, the DpcForIsr routine increments the CurrentVa
pointer by the previously returned Length value. It then calls **MapTransfer**
again with this updated pointer and asks to map all the bytes remaining in
the buffer. **MapTransfer** returns another logical address and a new Length
value indicating the size of the next contiguous buffer segment. This process
continues until the whole buffer has been processed.

```
PHYSICAL_ADDRESS DmaAddress;

PMDL pMdl = pIrp->MdlAddress;

// Clear out the adapter object buffer (if any)
pDevExt->pDmaAdapter->DmaOperations->
    FlushAdapterBuffers( pDevExt->pDmaAdapter,
                         pMdl,
                         pDevExt->mapRegisterBase,
                         pDevExt->transferVA,
                         pDevExt->transferSize,
                         pDevExt->bWriting );

pDevExt->bytesRemaining -= pDevExt->transferSize;
if (pDevExt->bytesRemaining > 0) {
    pDevExt->transferVA += pDevExt->transferSize;
    pDevExt->transferSize = pDevExt->bytesRemaining;
    DmaAddress =
        pDevExt->pDmaAdapter->DmaOperations->
            MapTransfer( pDevExt->pDmaAdapter,
                         pMdl,
                         pDevExt->mapRegisterBase,
                         pDevExt->transferVA,
                         &pDevExt->transferSize,
                         pDevExt->bWriting );

    WriteDmaAddress( pDevExt, DmaAddress.LowPart );
    WriteDmaCount( pDevExt, pDevExt->transferSize );
    // Now the device is re-started
    StartDevice( pDevExt );
}
```

Hardware with Scatter/Gather Support

Some bus master devices contain multiple pairs of address and length registers, each one describing a single contiguous buffer segment. This allows the device to perform I/O using buffers that are scattered throughout DMA address space. These multiple address and count registers are often referred to as a *scatter/gather list*, but they can be considered devices with their own built-in mapping registers. Yet another way to consider scatter/gather is as a device with its own private page table hardware. Figure 12.5 shows a bus master device with scatter/gather hardware.

   Before each transfer, the driver loads as many pairs of the address and count registers as there are segments in the buffer. When the device is started, it walks through the scatter/gather list entries in sequence, reading or writing each segment of the buffer and then moving on to the next. When all the list entries have been processed, the device generates an interrupt.

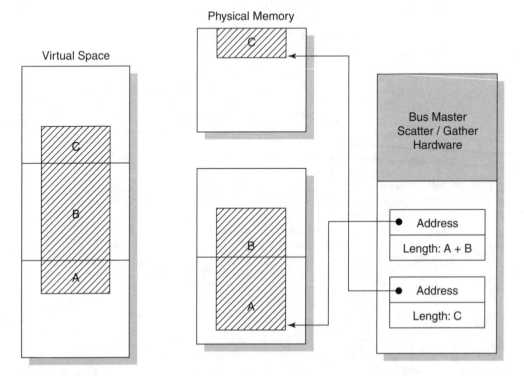

Figure 12.5   *Bus master device with scatter/gather hardware.*

Building Scatter/Gather Lists with MapTransfer

Once again, **MapTransfer** is used to find contiguous segments of the DMA buffer. In this case, however, the driver calls it several times before each data transfer operation—once for each entry in the hardware scatter/gather list. These fragments of an AdapterControl and DpcForIsr routine demonstrate the process.

AdapterControl Routine

Before the first transfer operation, the AdapterControl routine loads the hardware scatter/gather list and starts the device. The remainder of the buffer is handled by the ISR and DpcForIsr routines.

For scatter/gather devices, the state of each address/counter pair may need to be persisted somewhere, perhaps in the device extension. An array or linked list would be appropriate structures.

```
PHYSICAL_ADDRESS DmaAddress;
ULONG bytesLeftInBuffer;
ULONG segmentSize;
ULONG mapRegisterIndex;
PUCHAR segmentVA;
PMDL pMdl = pIrp->MdlAddress;

pDevExt->transferVA =
    MmGetMdlVirtualAddress( pMdl );
pDevExt->bytesRemaining =
    MmGetMdlByteCount( pMdl );
pDevExt->transferSize = 0;

bytesLeftInBuffer = pDevExt->bytesRemaining;
segmentVA = pDevExt->transferVA;
mapRegisterIndex = 0;

while (mapRegisterIndex < pDevExt->mapRegisterCount &&
        bytesLeftInBuffer > 0) {
    // Try for the whole enchilada
    segmentSize = bytesLeftInBuffer;
    DmaAddress =
        pDevExt->pDmaAdapter->DmaOperations->
            MapTransfer( pDevExt->pDmaAdapter,
                         pMdl,
                         pDevExt->mapRegisterBase,
                         segmentVA, &segmentSize,
                         pDevExt->bWriting );
    // WriteMapRegister is a device-specific method.
    // It programs one pair of scatter/gather regs.
    WriteMapRegister( pDevExt, mapRegisterIndex,
                      DmaAddress.LowPart,
                      segmentSize );
```

```
        mapRegisterIndex++;

        // Move on the next scatter/gather pair
        pDevExt->transferSize += segmentSize;
        segmentVA += segmentSize;
        bytesLeftInBuffer -= segmentSize;
    }

    // Now start the device
    StartDevice( pDevExt );
    // And indicate that scatter/gather regs are in use
    return DeallocateObjectKeepRegisters;
```

DpcForIsr ROUTINE

After each transfer is finished, the ISR issues a DPC request. The DpcForIsr
routine flushes the previous request, and if there are more bytes left to transfer, it rebuilds the scatter/gather list.

```
PHYSICAL_ADDRESS DmaAddress;
ULONG bytesLeftInBuffer;
ULONG segmentSize;
ULONG mapRegisterIndex;
PUCHAR segmentVA;
PMDL pMdl = pIrp->MdlAddress;

// Clear out the adapter object buffer (if any)
pDevExt->pDmaAdapter->DmaOperations->
    FlushAdapterBuffers( pDevExt->pDmaAdapter,
                         pMdl,
                         pDevExt->mapRegisterBase,
                         pDevExt->transferVA,
                         pDevExt->transferSize,
                         pDevExt->bWriting );

pDevExt->bytesRemaining -= pDevExt->transferSize;
if (pDevExt->bytesRemaining > 0) {
    pDevExt->transferVA += pDevExt->transferSize;
    pDevExt->transferSize = 0;
    bytesLeftInBuffer = pDevExt->bytesRemaining;
    segmentVA = pDevExt->transferVA;

    mapRegisterIndex = 0;

    while (mapRegisterIndex <
            pDevExt->mapRegisterCount &&
            bytesLeftInBuffer > 0) {
        segmentSize = bytesLeftInBuffer;
        DmaAddress =
            pDevExt->pDmaAdapter->DmaOperations->
```

```
                    MapTransfer(pDevExt->pDmaAdapter,
                        pMdl,
                        pDevExt->mapRegisterBase,
                        segmentVA,
                        &segmentSize,
                        pDevExt->bWriting );

            WriteMapRegister( pDevExt, mapRegisterIndex,
                        DmaAddress.LowPart,
                        segmentSize );
            mapRegisterIndex++;

            // Move on the next scatter/gather pair
            pDevExt->transferSize += segmentSize;
            segmentVA += segmentSize;
            bytesLeftInBuffer -= segmentSize;
        }
        // Then re-start the device
        StartDevice( pDevExt );
    } else {
        // Last device operation completed transfer
        // Free up the mapping registers:
        pDevExt->pDmaAdapter->DmaOperations->
            FreeMapRegisters(...);
        // And complete the IRP
        IoCompleteRequest(...);
        IoStartNextPacket(...);
    }
}
```

Writing a Common Buffer Slave DMA Driver

In common buffer slave DMA, the device transfers data to or from a contiguous buffer in nonpaged pool, using a system DMA channel. Although originally intended for devices that use the system DMA controller's autoinitialize mode, common buffers can also improve throughput for some types of ISA-based slave devices.

Allocating a Common Buffer

Memory for a common buffer must be physically contiguous and visible in the DMA logical space of a specific device. To guarantee that both these conditions are met, the function **AllocateCommonBuffer**, a method of the Adapter object, is used. It is described in Table 12.8.

The CacheEnabled argument for this function is normally set to FALSE. Using noncached memory for the common buffer eliminates the need to call

Table 12.8	*Function Prototype for AllocateCommonBuffer*
PVOID AllocateCommonBuffer	**IRQL == PASSIVE_LEVEL**
Parameter	**Description**
IN PDMA_ADAPTER pDmaAdapter	Points to the DMA_ADAPTER structure returned by IoGetDmaAdapter
IN ULONG Length	Requested size of buffer in bytes
OUT PPHYSICAL_ADDRESS LogicalAdress	Address of the common buffer in the DMA controller's logical space
IN BOOLEAN CacheEnabled	• TRUE – memory is cacheable • FALSE – memory is not cached
Return value	• Non-NULL – VA of common buffer • FALSE – error

KeFlushIoBuffers. On some platforms, this can significantly improve the performance of both the driver and the system.

Besides allocating the common buffer, **AllocateCommonBuffer** also allocates map registers (if required) and sets up a translation for the device, loading map registers as necessary. Thus, the buffer is available for immediate and continuous use. The buffer remains usable until **FreeCommonBuffer** is explicitly invoked, typically in the handler routine for IRP_MN_STOP_DEVICE.

Using Common Buffer Slave DMA to Maintain Throughput

Common buffer slave DMA is useful if the driver can't afford to set up mapping registers for each data transfer that it performs. The overhead of setting up mapping registers using **MapTransfer** can be significant, especially for ISA buses. There is always the possibility that **MapTransfer** will be forced to copy the transfer buffer into the lowest 16 MB of RAM—clearly an expensive proposition. Since common buffers are guaranteed to be accessible by their associated DMA devices, there is never a need to move data from one place to another.

For example, drivers of some ISA-based tape drives need to maintain very high throughput if they want to keep the tape streaming. They may not be able to do this if the buffer copy must occur during a call to **MapTransfer**. To prevent this, the driver can use a ring of common buffers for the actual DMA operation. Other, less time-critical portions of the driver move data between these common buffers and the actual user buffers.

Consider the operation of the driver for a hypothetical ISA output device. To maintain a high DMA data rate, it uses a series of common buffers that are shared between the driver's Dispatch and DpcForIsr routines.

The Dispatch routine copies user-output data into an available common buffer and attaches the buffer to a queue of pending DMA requests. Once a DMA is in progress, the DpcForIsr removes buffers from the queue and processes them as fast as it can. Figure 12.6 shows the organization of this driver, and the various driver routines are described in the sections that follow.

AddDevice ROUTINE

Besides creating the device object, this routine should set the DO_BUFFERED_IO bit in the **Flags** field. Even though DMA is used for the actual device transfer, the user buffers are initially copied into system space.

IRP_MN_START_DEVICE HANDLER

Besides the usual responsibilities of initializing the physical device, the handler must now perform the following:

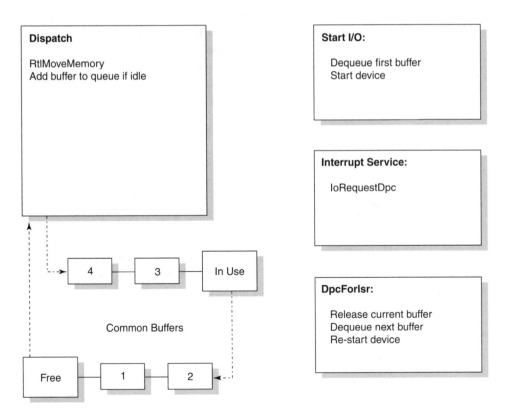

Figure 12.6   *Using common buffers to improve I/O throughput.*

1. Two queues should be initialized in the device extension. One holds a list of free common buffers. The other is for work requests in progress.

2. Two spin locks should be created to guard each queue. The spin lock for the work list also protects a flag in the device extension called DmaInProgress.

3. **IoGetDmaAdapter** is used to find the adapter object associated with the device. Using the count of mapping registers returned by this function is helpful to determine the size of the common buffers.

4. Individual common buffers should be allocated, using **AllocateCommonBuffer** once for each buffer. Initially they should be placed in the free list of the device extension.

5. Finally, the Start handler initializes a semaphore object and sets its initial count to the number of common buffers it has just created.

DISPATCH ROUTINE

The Dispatch routine of this driver is somewhat uncommon. The Dispatch routine is responsible for queuing and starting each request. This is what the Dispatch routine does to process an output request:

1. It calls **KeWaitForSingleObject** to wait for the Semaphore object associated with the driver's list of free buffers. The thread issuing the call will suspend until there is at least one buffer in the queue. (Chapter 14 explains the details of Semaphore use.)

2. The Dispatch routine removes an available common buffer from the free list and uses **RtlMoveMemory** to fill it with data from the user's buffer.

3. It prevents the I/O Manager from completing the request by calling **IoMarkIrpPending**.

4. Next, it acquires the spin lock associated with the queue of active requests. As a side-effect, acquiring the spin lock raises IRQL up to DISPATCH_LEVEL. After it owns the spin lock, the Dispatch routine adds the new request to the list of buffers to be output.

5. Still holding the spin lock, the Dispatch routine checks an internal DmaInProgress flag to see if other parts of the driver are already performing an output operation. If the flag is TRUE, it simply releases the spin lock. If the flag is FALSE, the Dispatch routine sets it to TRUE and starts the device. It then releases the spin lock.

6. Finally, it returns a value of STATUS_PENDING.

At this point, the work request for this buffer has been either started or queued. The next phase of the transfer occurs within the Start I/O routine.

START I/O ROUTINE

If the device is idle, the Start I/O function is called to start it. It performs the following tasks:

1. It removes the first request from the work queue and saves its address in the Device Extension as the current request.
2. It programs the device's DMA registers to point to the dequeued buffer.
3. The device is started and DMA transfer begins.

INTERRUPT SERVICE ROUTINE

As with packet-based DMA, the ISR in a common buffer driver for a slave device merely saves hardware status in the Device Extension. It then calls **IoRequestDpc** to request the DpcForIsr routine.

DpcForIsr ROUTINE

In this driver, the DpcForIsr routine sets up each additional work request after the first.

1. It calls **FlushAdapterBuffers** to flush any data from the system DMA controller's hardware cache.
2. It attempts to dequeue the next I/O request from the work queue. If there is another request, the driver makes it the new current request and restarts the device. Otherwise, it clears the DmaInProgress flag in the Device Extension.
3. Next, it moves the just-completed work buffer back in the free queue. **KeReleaseSemaphore** is used to signal an increase in the number of available free buffers.
4. Finally, the IRP is marked as complete.

Each completed DMA operation causes another interrupt that brings the driver back through the DpcForIsr routine. This loop continues until all the requests in the work queue have been processed.

IRP_MN_STOP_DEVICE HANDLER

When the device is stopped, the driver should ensure that the device will no longer attempt use of the common buffer. Once the device is quiescent, the Stop handler calls **FreeCommonBuffer** to release the memory associated with the ring of buffers.

Writing a Common Buffer Bus Master DMA Driver

In common-buffer bus master DMA, the device transfers data to or from a contiguous nonpaged pool buffer, using a DMA controller that is part of the device itself. Frequently, this kind of hardware treats the common buffer as a mailbox for exchanging control and status messages with the driver.

How Common-Buffer Bus Master DMA Works

The exact operation of a common-buffer bus master driver will depend on the physical device. The description that follows is based on the typical architecture. It assumes the device uses one mailbox for commands and another to return status information. Figure 12.7 illustrates this arrangement.

IRP_MN_START_DEVICE HANDLER

This handler must now perform the following tasks:

1. Invoke **IoGetDmaAdapter** to locate the Adapter object associated with the device.

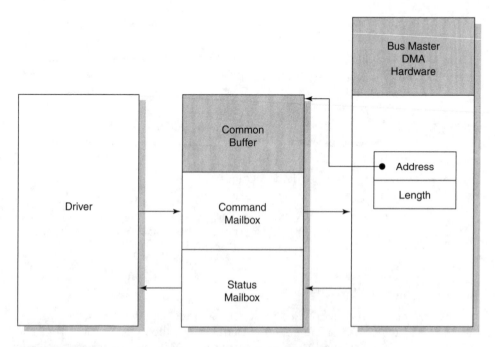

Figure 12.7   *Common buffer implementation of message exchange.*

2. Use **AllocateCommonBuffer** to get a block of contiguous, nonpaged memory that both the driver and the device can access.

3. Store the virtual address of the common buffer in the Device Extension for subsequent use.

START I/O ROUTINE

To send a command to the device, the Start I/O routine performs the following:

1. Builds a command structure in the common buffer, using the virtual address stored in the Device Extension.

2. If needed (CacheEnabled parameter set to TRUE), **KeFlushIoBuffers** is invoked to force data from the CPU's cache out to physical memory.

3. Finally, Start I/O sets a bit in the device control register to notify the device that there is a command waiting for it. In essence, this is equivalent to starting the device.

In response to the notification bit being set, the device begins processing the command in the common buffer.

INTERRUPT SERVICE ROUTINE

When the device has finished processing the command in the common buffer, it puts a message in the status mailbox and generates an interrupt. In response to this interrupt, the driver's Interrupt Service Routine does the following:

1. Copies the contents of the status mailbox into various fields of the Device Extension.

2. If necessary, the ISR sets another bit in the device control register to acknowledge that it has read the status message.

3. Calls **IoRequestDpc** to continue processing the request at a lower IRQL.

IRP_MN_STOP_DEVICE HANDLER

When the device is stopped, a driver should quiet the device. The Stop handler calls **FreeCommonBuffer** to release the memory associated with the buffer.

Summary

Without a doubt, drivers for DMA devices are more complicated than drivers for programmed I/O hardware. In return for this added complexity, the system achieves greater throughput by overlapping CPU activity with data transfers. The I/O Manager tries to simplify the process by providing a generic framework in which to perform DMA. This chapter has presented the details of the Windows 2000 abstract DMA model and discussed the various styles of DMA.

The next chapter begins the discussion of how devices report and log their operational status to the operating system.

Windows Management and Instrumentation

CHAPTER OBJECTIVES

*D*evice drivers can be written to report their performance and reliability statistics. For example, it is useful for a network driver to track the number of corrupted packets received. Devices that start to perform erratically should be identified before they fail completely.

Overall device and driver performance rates are vital pieces of information to analyze and improve system performance. Tracking and reporting such instrumentation data begins at the driver level.

Another separate but common requirement is that devices and drivers need a mechanism for dynamic configuration. Traditionally, drivers use Control Panel applets and private IOCTLs to provide this facility.

The WDM driver model includes the capability for standardizing the collection, storage, and reporting of instrumentation data—the Windows Management and Instrumentation (WMI) interface. Drivers that choose to participate in the WMI scheme can collect performance and reliability data in a standardized way for applications to obtain.

The facility also provides a standardized way that clients can use to set a driver state for the purpose of device configuration. A driver can export specialized methods that client applications can invoke (almost) directly.

This chapter starts by describing the relationship of WMI to industry standards for similar functionality. The steps necessary to incorporate WMI into a driver are then presented along with an example of a WMI-enabled driver. Finally, the chapter covers the conventional mechanism of sending event messages to the Windows 2000 event log.

WMI: The Industry Picture

The need for system instrumentation and configuration is not unique to device drivers, Windows 2000, or Microsoft. The Open Software Foundation (OSF) includes a task group, the Desktop Management Taskforce (DMTF), that has published an initiative for unified system management compatible with Internet standards, Web-Based Enterprise Management (WBEM).

WBEM defines an interface for the purpose of unified management and instrumentation: the Common Information Model (CIM). CIM is designed to encapsulate and accommodate other industry initiatives such as the Simple Network Management Protocol (SNMP) and the Desktop Management Interface (DMI).

CIM is a very general-purpose way of describing properties, methods, and events that clients can use to efficiently obtain system-supplied data. WMI is Microsoft's implementation of WBEM. Therefore, it is based on CIM and extends itself to components within Windows 2000 to provide a functional environment for management and instrumentation.

CIM defines a new language (actually an extension of C) called MOF (Managed Object Format). MOF is loosely based on the Interface Definition Language (IDL) familiar to users of Remote Procedure Calls (RPCs) and Microsoft COM (Component Object Model).

A diagram that describes the relationship between WBEM and WMI is shown in Figure 13.1.

Acronym overload aside, MOF is the language by which the provider and the consumer can precisely communicate and exchange data. For example, a data definition within the MOF file to describe the total packet count transferred by a driver might appear as follows:

```
[read, WmiDataId(1),
    Description("Total Packet Count")]
    uint64 PacketsTransferred;
```

A client application, having been built with knowledge of the MOF contents, is now aware that the packet count is available from the provider as a 64-bit unsigned integer.

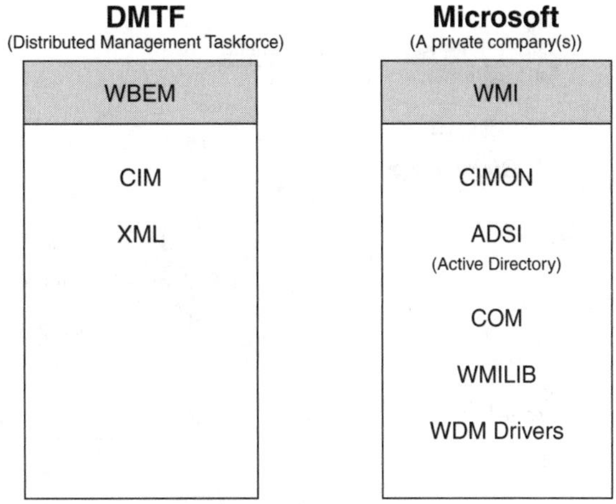

DMTF (Distributed Management Taskforce)	Microsoft (A private company(s))
WBEM	**WMI**
CIM XML	CIMON ADSI (Active Directory) COM WMILIB WDM Drivers

Figure 13.1   *WBEM and WMI relationship.*

The advantage of conformance with industry standards for system management and instrumentation is obvious: heterogeneous system integration. With sufficient industry acceptance and conformance, Microsoft-based, Linux, and mainframe systems can cooperate in a peer-to-peer configuration, management, and reporting environment.

The WMI Architecture

The WMI architecture consists of five layers:

- A source of WMI data (e.g., a device driver) designated the *data provider*
- A central repository of WMI data that implements a CIM-compliant data store, based on the CIM object model (CIMOM)
- A WMI provider (e.g., the WDM WMI provider) that provides the necessary linkage between a WMI data source and the data store
- A consumer (or client) of the WMI data
- A protocol (e.g., COM) that presents the data store to a consumer

The WMI provider for WDM consists of two parts:

- A user-mode Win32 DLL that provides linkage between a user-mode client
- A set of kernel-mode services that invoke and respond to driver code. An IRP, IRP_MJ_SYSTEM_CONTROL, is the mechanism by which these services make requests of the driver for WMI data.

A diagram of the WMI architecture is shown in Figure 13.2.

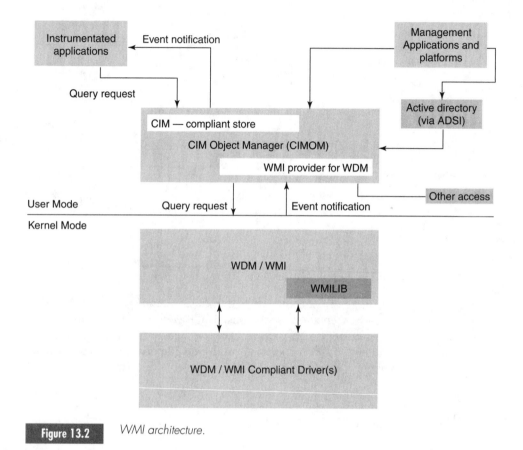

WMI architecture.

Providing WMI Support in a WDM Driver

In order to supply WMI data, a driver must perform the following steps:

1. Provide a MOF description of the data, methods, and events that will be provided and generated by the driver.

2. Compile the MOF source file (.MOF) using the **mofcomp.exe** tool provided with the DDK. This tool produces a platform-independent binary file (.BMF) for the next step.

3. Include the compiled MOF data within the resource section of the driver binary.

4. Provide an IRP_MJ_SYSTEM_CONTROL dispatch routine within the driver code. When received, the minor subcode field of the IRP specifies the exact kind of WMI request.

5. Register as a provider of WMI data using **IoWmiRegistrationControl**.

6. Process the IRP_MJ_SYSTEM_CONTROL IRP with minor subcode IRM_MN_REGINFO. The IRP for such a request contains an *action code* (in Parameters.WMI.DataPath) that is either WMIREGISTER or WMIUP-DATE. The action code forms a third dispatch level for such an IRP. (Major, minor, and action code form the three dispatch levels.)

7. Process the action code WMIREGISTER by providing information about the data and event blocks defined within the MOF description.

8. Process the action code WMIUPDATE by invoking helper functions declared with WMILIB.h.

Each of these eight steps is described in more detail below.

MOF Syntax

MOF syntax follows the standard structure of RPC interface definitions described by the Interface Definition Language (IDL). The basic form is

```
[ATTRIUBUTES and QUALIFIERS]
ENTITY TYPE and NAME
{
    [DATA ITEM QUALIFIERS] DATA TYPE and NAME;
    . . .
};
```

The definitions can be nested, much as a structure is defined within a structure. The entity type can consist of such keywords as *class*, *string*, or *boolean*. The basic MOF description starts with a *class* name, which is case insensitive and must be unique within the entire WMI namespace. Classes can inherit the definitions of a base class, just as in C++.

```
[ // Class qualifiers ]
class HiResCamera : Camera
{
// Data definitions added by HiResCamera

};
```

A derived class name is uniquely qualified by its base class name and thus the name "HiResCamera" need only be unique beneath the base class of Camera.

Class qualifiers are listed in Table 13.1 and three of these attributes are required for a WMI-compliant driver: *Provider*, *WMI*, and *Guid*.

Each data definition constitutes an *item* within the class, complete with its own set of item qualifiers, listed in Table 13.2. The list of MOF-legal data types is described in Table 13.3.

The MOF syntax requires two items within a class definition: *Instance-Name* and *Active*. These two items are managed internally by WMI and,

Table 13.1	Class Qualifiers for WMI MOF Definition
Class Qualifier	**Description**
Dynamic	Data for the MOF block is supplied at runtime on a per-instance basis of the class.
Static	Data for the MOF block is included as part of the WMI database.
Provider("WmiProv")	Required. Indicates that the provider of this class is WMI-compliant.
WMI	Required. Indicates WMI class.
Description("text")	Documentation or comment which can be made available to clients of the class.
Guid("guid")	The unique 128-bit number identifying the class.
Locale("MS\lcid")	The locale (language) ID for which the Description text is supplied.
WmiExpense(cost)	The collection cost in CPU cycles for data described and collected by the class.

therefore, should not be considered data that is part of the driver itself. The data types of *InstanceName* and *Active* are string and boolean, respectively.

Example MOF Class Definition

The following is a simple example of a completed MOF class definition:

```
[WMI, guid("12345678-1234-5678-9ABC-123456789ABC"),
    Dynamic, Provider("WMIProv"),
    WmiExpense(1),
    Locale("MS\\0x409"),
    Description("Example class")]

class W2KDriverBook_Missile {

// Required item definitions - unused by driver
    [key, read] string InstanceName;
    [read] boolean Active;

// Property: Total Launches
    [read,
    WmiDataId(1),
    WmiScale(0),
    Description("Total Missile Launches")]
    uint32 TotalLaunches;
```

Table 13.2	*MOF Data Item Qualifiers*

Data Item Qualifier	Description
key	This data item uniquely identifies class instance.
read	WMI client can read the item.
write	WMI client can write the item.
BitMap	List of string names representing "bit names" corresponding to bit positions within BitValues. The string list is enclosed within braces ({,}) immediately after the BitMap keyword.
BitValues	Bit positions corresponding to the names specified by BitMap. The bit list is enclosed within braces immediately after the BitValues keyword.
ValueMap	List of string names representing the enumerated values within Values. The string list is enclosed within braces immediately after the ValueMap keyword.
Values	List of values corresponding to the names specified by ValueMap. The value list is enclosed within braces immediately after the Values keyword.
WmiDataId(ItemId)	Required. Specifies the location of the data item within the MOF data block. The first item has ID of 1, the fourth has ID of 4.
WmiSizeIs("ItemName")	Specifies another "ItemName" that indicates the number of elements for this array item (valid only for array data items).
WmiScale(ScaleFactor)	Specifies the magnitude (base 10) for the report of this data item. For example, with ScaleFactor = 3, a data item of value 7 would indicate 7000.
WmiTimeStamp	Indicates the 64-bit item value is a 100 nanosecond tick count since 01/01/1601.
WmiComplexity("Level")	A comment potentially used by clients in deciding whether to expose this item. Possible values are "Novice," "Advanced," "Expert," "Wizard."
WmiVolatility(Interval)	Specifies the interval in milliseconds for the frequency of updates to the item.
WmiEventTrigger("ItemName")	For an event block, specifies another ItemName that defines the value at which this event item triggers.
WmiEventRate("ItemName")	For an event block, specifies another ItemName that defines the frequency at which this event item fires.

Table 13.3	MOF Data Types	
Data Type	**Description**	**sizeof**
string	Counted Unicode string	12
boolean	TRUE or FALSE (zero or nonzero)	1
sint8	Signed 8-bit integer	1
uint8	Unsigned 8-bit integer	1
sint16	Signed 16-bit integer	2
uint16	Unsigned 16-bit integer	2
sint32	Signed 32-bit integer	4
uint32	Unsigned 32-bit integer	4
sint64	Signed 64-bit integer	8
uint64	Unsigned 64-bit integer	8
datetime	Unicode string holding date & time: "yyyymmddhhmmss:$\mu\mu\mu\mu\mu\mu$±utc" where $\mu\mu\mu\mu\mu\mu$ = microseconds utc = GMT (UTC) minute offset	50

```
//The number of silos in the SiloStatus array
    [read,
    WmiDataId(2) ]
    uint32 SiloCount;

//SiloStatus Array
    [read,
    WmiDataId(3),
    WmiSizeIs("SiloCount") ]
    uint8 SiloStatus[];
};
```

Compiling the MOF Source

To compile the MOF source, the tool **mofcomp.EXE**, located in the **system32** directory, is used. Two switches are needed for WDM driver development.

- `-B:filename.bmf`
- `-WMI`

The −B switch instructs the MOF compiler to place the binary results into the specified filename, which is then inserted into the driver's resource area. The −WMI switch forces a second pass on the MOF input to validate compliance with WMI. For the example MOF file listed above, the command line

```
mofcomp -B:Example.bmf -WMI Example.MOF
```

successfully compiles the definitions.

Once the binary MOF (.bmf) file is created, the driver must include a source *resource* file (.RC) into the project (makefile) with the following line:

```
MofResource MOFDATA Example.bmf
```

When the driver loads into system memory, its resource section is placed into RAM and is accessible to the driver. The resource name, specified by the .bmf filename, is announced in response to the WMI IRP request WMIREGISTER.

Handling WMI IRP Requests

The first step a driver must take to handle WMI requests is to register itself with the I/O Manager as a WMI participant. This is performed with the **IoWMIRegistrationControl** function, described in Table 13.4. Initially, a driver should perform the Action of WMIREG_ACTION_REGISTER, presumably during the **AddDevice** routine. Similarly, during **RemoveDevice**, the Action WMIREG_ACTION_DEREGISTER is performed.

Once registered for WMI action, a driver must respond to the IRP Dispatch function for the major code IRP_MJ_SYSTEM_CONTROL. This IRP request supplies one of several minor subcodes, listed in Table 13.5. The IRP stack's Parameters' union contains a **WMI** structure, defined in Table 13.6. This WMI structure supplies data for the request (input and output).

Table 13.4	*IoWMIRegistrationControl Function Prototype*
NTSTATUS **IoWMIRegistrationControl**	**IRQL == PASSIVE_LEVEL**
Parameter	**Description**
IN PDEVICE_OBJECT pDeviceObject	Pointer to Device object
IN ULONG Action	• WMIREG_ACTION_REGISTER • WMIREG_ACTION_DEREGISTER • WMIREG_ACTION_REREGISTER • WMIREG_ACTION_UPDATE_GUIDS • WMIREG_ACTION_BLOCK_IRPS
Return value	Success or failure code

| **Table 13.5** | *IRP_MJ_SYSTEM_CONTROL Minor Functions* |

IRP_MJ_SYSTEM_CONTROL

Minor Function Subcodes	Description
IRP_MN_QUERY_ALL_DATA	Request for all instances of a data block
IRP_MN_QUERY_SINGLE_INSTANCE	Request for a specific instance
IRP_MN_CHANGE_SINGLE_INSTANCE	Request to modify all data of a specific instance
IRP_MN_CHANGE_SINGLE_ITEM	Request to modify one datum
IRP_MN_ENABLE_EVENTS	Informs driver that a data consumer has requested event notification
IRP_MN_DISABLE_EVENTS	Data consumer no longer wishes notification of events
IRP_MN_ENABLE_COLLECTION	Request to begin collection of "expensive" instrument data
IRP_MN_DISABLE_COLLECTION	Request to stop collecting
IRP_MN_REGINFO	Query or modify a driver's registration information
IRP_MN_EXECUTE_METHOD	Invokes a method defined in the MOF data block

Classes and Instances

A data block described as a *class* within the MOF syntax declares a *class data block*. No instances of the class exist (i.e., no data space is reserved) until such time as the driver *registers* the data block, typically performed within the DpWmiQueryReginfo function, described below.

While typically only one instance of a class is appropriate, some circumstances suggest the existence of an array of instances to best model the data

| **Table 13.6** | *Parameters. WMI Structure Definition* |

struct WMI

Field	Description
ProviderId	Pointer to target Device object
DataPath	GUID of MOF data block
BufferSize	Size of the Buffer
Buffer	Buffer whose contents are minor function code specific

being collected. For example, suppose the Missile driver collects data for each of the three engines powering the rocket. The fuel used by one engine may be separate data from that used by another. If each missile engine is described by a separate instance of a MOF Missile_Engine class, each query or update of data requires an additional *instance index* to fully qualify the request.

Of course, the fuel level of each engine could also be kept as an array of values within a single instance. Thus, the decision to use multiple instances of data blocks is dictated by whether or not *all* the entries within the block should be stacked, one per instance.

WMILIB

Responding to WMI IRP requests is facilitated by a kernel-mode DLL, WMILIB. The heart of this library support is a routine, **WmiSystemControl**, described in Table 13.7. The function receives as input a data structure of type WMILIB_CONTEXT, described in Table 13.8, which is primarily a list of function pointers that get, set, or otherwise control MOF items. The functions are provided by the driver, and if not supplied, should be set to NULL.

The GuidList member of the WMILIB_CONTEXT structure is an array of structures of type WMIGUIDREGINFO, one array element for each MOF data block *class* exposed by the driver. The WMIGUIDREGINFO structure is described in Table 13.9.

WmiSystemControl returns a disposition status that describes how the IRP was handled.

Table 13.7	*WmiSystemControl Function Prototype*
NTSTATUS WmiSystemControl	**IRQL == PASSIVE_LEVEL**
Parameter	**Description**
IN PWMILIB_CONTEXT WmiLibInfo	Pointer to WMILIB_CONTEXT structure, provided and initialized by driver
IN PDEVICE_OBJECT pDeviceObject	Driver's Device Object
IN PIRP pIrp	Pointer to IRP of request
OUT PSYSCTL_IRP_DISPOSITION pIrpDisposition	• IrpProcessed • IrpNotCompleted • IrpNotWmi • IrpForward
Return value	Success or failure code

Table 13.8	WMILIB_CONTEXT Structure Definition

struct WMILIB_CONTEXT

Field	Description
ULONG GuidCount	Number of MOF data blocks registered by driver
PWMIGUIDREGINFO GuidList	Array of GUIDs and instance counts
PWMI_QUERY_REGINFO QueryWmiRegInfo	Function pointer to driver-supplied routine, DpWmiQueryReginfo
PWMI_QUERY_DATABLOCK QueryWmiDataBlock	Function pointer to driver-supplied routine, DpWmiQueryDataBlock
PWMI_SET_DATABLOCK SetWmiDataBlock	Function pointer to driver-supplied routine, DpWmiSetDataBlock (may be NULL)
PWMI_SET_DATAITEM SetWmiDataItem	Function pointer to driver-supplied routine, DpWmiSetDataItem (may be NULL)
PWMI_EXECUTE_METHOD ExecuteWmiMethod	Function pointer to driver-supplied routine, DpWmiExecuteMethod (may be NULL)
PWMI_FUNCTION_CONTROL WmiFunctionControl	Function pointer to driver-supplied routine, DpWmiFunctionControl (may be NULL)

On the surface, **WmiSystemControl** does little more than dispatch the minor subcode of IRP_MJ_SYSTEM_CONTROL to the appropriate driver-supplied DpWmiXxx routine. The real advantage of WMILIB is that it handles the complete WMI protocol, leaving the driver with only the necessary task of MOF data-specific handling.

Table 13.9	WMIGUIDREGINFO Structure Definition

struct WMIGUIDREGINFO

Field	Description
LPCGUID Guid	Pointer to GUID that identifies block
ULONG InstanceCount	Number of instances to create
ULONG Flags	Characteristics of block:
	• WMIREG_FLAG_INSTANCE_PDO
	• WMIREG_FLAG_EVENT_ONLY_GUID
	• WMIREG_FLAG_EXPENSIVE
	• WMIREG_FLAG_REMOVE_GUID

Each dispatch function pointed to by an entry within WMILIB_CONTEXT is a unique function signature (prototype) with various responsibilities. These DpWmi functions are described in further detail below.

With the exception of **DpWmiQueryReginfo**, each of these routines completes its normal work by invoking **WmiCompleteRequest**, described in Table 13.10. This WMILIB function marks the IRP as "complete" and finishes the WMI protocol sequence.

DpWmiQueryReginfo

The DpWmiQueryReginfo function, supplied by the driver, is described in Table 13.11. It is invoked by WMILIB when the requesting IRP contains the minor subcode IRP_MN_REGINFO with action code (Parameters.WMI.DataPath) equal to WMIREGISTER or WMIUPDATE. The prime purpose of this driver routine is to register one or more instances of data class.

The implementation of this function should include code to implement the driver's strategy for the naming of data block instances. The RegFlags parameter includes a bit, WMIREG_FLAG_INSTANCE_BASENAME, which allows WMI to automatically append an instance counter number to the base name specified by InstanceName. Otherwise, the driver can implement its own naming strategy. It is noteworthy that these instance names are persistent (sticky) across boots of the OS. The names are registered in the CIMOM store.

Yet another driver strategy is to use the PDO name for the instance base name. To utilize this strategy, a driver sets the RegFlags' bit WMI_FLAG_INSTANCE_PDO.

Table 13.10	WmiCompleteRequest Function Prototype
NTSTATUS WmiCompleteRequest	**IRQL <= DISPATCH_LEVEL**
Parameter	**Description**
IN PDEVICE_OBJECT pDeviceObject	Pointer to driver's device object
IN PIRP pIrp	Pointer to IRP of request
IN NTSTATUS Status	Final status to return in IRP
IN ULONG BufferUsed	If buffer was too small for request, this value holds what was required; otherwise, holds bytes used.
IN CCHAR PriorityBoost	Same as IoCompleteRequest PriorityBoost, usually a fixed value

Table 13.11	*DpWmiQueryRegInfo Function Prototype*
NTSTATUS DpWmiQueryReginfo	**IRQL == PASSIVE_LEVEL**
Parameter	**Description**
IN PDEVICE_OBJECT pDeviceObject	Pointer to driver's device object
OUT PULONG pRegFlags	Registration flags set by driver for all registered MOF data blocks
OUT PUNICODE_STRING InstanceName	When RegFlags has bit WMIREG_FLAG_INSTANCE_ BASENAME set, InstanceName is used as base with instance counter appended. WMI frees this string with a call to **ExFreePool**.
OUT PUNICODE_STRING *pRegistryPath	Same string passed to driver's DriverEntry
OUT PUNICODE_STRING MofResourceName	String containing name of MOF .bmf file
OUT PDEVICE_OBJECT *pPDO	PDO to use for generation of physical device instance names (only if RegFlags WMIREG_FLAG_ INSTANCE_PDO set)
Return value	STATUS_SUCCESS

DpWmiQueryDataBlock

The DpWmiQueryDataBlock function is described in Table 13.12. It is invoked by WMILIB when the requesting IRP contains the minor subcode IRP_MN_QUERY_DATA_BLOCK or IRP_MN_QUERY_ALL_DATA. The purpose of this driver routine is to return the instance(s) data requested.

DpWmiSetDataBlock

The DpWmiSetDataBlock function is described in Table 13.13. It is invoked by WMILIB when the requesting IRP contains the minor subcode IRP_MN_CHANGE_SINGLE_INSTANCE. The purpose of this driver routine is to modify the specified instance data. As defined, only one instance can be changed at one time, but when multiple instances exist, the InstanceIndex value of zero remains undefined.

DpWmiSetDataItem

The DpWmiSetDataItem function is described in Table 13.14. It is invoked by WMILIB when the requesting IRP contains the minor subcode IRP_MN_ CHANGE_SINGLE_ITEM. The purpose of this driver routine is to modify the specified data item within the specified instance data.

Table 13.12	*DpWmiQueryDataBlock Function Prototype*

NTSTATUS DpWmiQueryDataBlock	IRQL == PASSIVE_LEVEL
Parameter	**Description**
IN PDEVICE_OBJECT pDeviceObject	Pointer to driver's device object
IN PIRP pIrp	Pointer to IRP of WMI request
IN ULONG GuidIndex	Index into WMILIB_CONTEXT structure's GuidList, identifying data block
IN ULONG InstanceIndex	Specific data instance being queried (0 if all instances being queried)
IN ULONG InstanceCount	Number of instances being queried
IN OUT PULONG InstanceLengthArray	Array of ULONGs specifying length of each instance being returned
IN ULONG BufferAvail	Size of Buffer
OUT PUCHAR Buffer	Buffer to receive instance data
Return value	• STATUS_SUCCESS • STATUS_BUFFER_TOO_SMALL • STATUS_WMI_GUID_NOT_FOUND • STATUS_WMI_INSTANCE_NOT_ FOUND

Table 13.13	*DpWmiSetDataBlock Function Prototype*

NTSTATUS DpWmiSetDataBlock	IRQL == PASSIVE_LEVEL
Parameter	**Description**
IN PDEVICE_OBJECT pDeviceObject	Pointer to driver's device object
IN PIRP pIrp	Pointer to IRP of WMI request
IN ULONG GuidIndex	Index into WMILIB_CONTEXT structure's GuidList, identifying data block to modify
IN ULONG InstanceIndex	Specific data instance being modified
IN ULONG BufferSize	Size of Buffer
IN PUCHAR Buffer	Buffer supplying new instance data
Return value	• STATUS_SUCCESS • STATUS_PENDING • STATUS_WMI_READ_ONLY • STATUS_WMI_SET_FAILURE • STATUS_WMI_GUID_NOT_FOUND • STATUS_WMI_INSTANCE_NOT_ FOUND

Table 13.14	*DpWmiSetDataItem Function Prototype*
NTSTATUS DpWmiSetDataItem	**IRQL == PASSIVE_LEVEL**
Parameter	**Description**
IN PDEVICE_OBJECT pDeviceObject	Pointer to driver's device object
IN PIRP pIrp	Pointer to IRP of WMI request
IN ULONG GuidIndex	Index into WMILIB_CONTEXT structure's GuidList, identifying data block
IN ULONG InstanceIndex	Specific data instance being modified
IN ULONG DataItemId	ID of data item being modified
IN ULONG BufferSize	Size of Buffer
IN PUCHAR Buffer	Buffer supplying new instance data
Return value	● STATUS_SUCCESS ● STATUS_PENDING ● STATUS_WMI_READ_ONLY ● STATUS_WMI_SET_FAILURE ● STATUS_WMI_GUID_NOT_FOUND ● STATUS_WMI_INSTANCE_NOT_ FOUND ● STATUS_WMI_ITEM_ID_NOT_FOUND

DpWmiExecuteMethod

The DpWmiExecuteMethod function is described in Table 13.15. It is invoked by WMILIB when the requesting IRP contains the minor subcode IRP_MN_EXECUTE_METHOD. The purpose of this driver routine is to dispatch execution to the specified method.

In many ways, this is a "direct call" interface from WMI clients into driver code. The interface is *marshaled* by the **DpWmiExecuteMethod** routine, which has the ability to validate and convert parameters before presentation to the requested method. Separately, the output buffer can be marshaled before it is returned to the client. The passing of addresses within the input or output buffer is problematic and should probably be avoided.

DpWmiFunctionControl

The DpWmiFunctionControl function is described in Table 13.16. It is invoked by WMILIB when the requesting IRP contains the minor subcode IRP_MN_ENABLE_COLLECTION, IRP_MN_DISABLE_COLLECTION, IRP_MN_ ENABLE_EVENTS, or IRP_MN_DISABLE_EVENTS. The purpose of this driver routine is to start or stop the collection of data (i.e., data that is marked as "expensive" with the bit WMIREG_FLAG_EXPENSIVE at registration) or to start or stop the generation of events.

Table 13.15   *DpWmiExecuteMethod Function Prototype*

NTSTATUS DpWmiExecuteMethod	IRQL == PASSIVE_LEVEL
Parameter	**Description**
IN PDEVICE_OBJECT pDeviceObject	Pointer to driver's device object
IN PIRP pIrp	Pointer to IRP of WMI request
IN ULONG GuidIndex	Index into WMILIB_CONTEXT structure's GuidList, identifying data block
IN ULONG InstanceIndex	Specific instance with method to execute
IN ULONG MethodId	ID of method to execute
IN ULONG InBufferSize	Number of bytes passed in Buffer to method
IN ULONG OutBufferSize	Size of Buffer
IN OUT PUCHAR Buffer	Input and output buffer for executing method
Return value	• STATUS_SUCCESS • STATUS_BUFFER_TOO_SMALL • STATUS_INVALID_DEVICE_REQUEST • STATUS_WMI_INSTANCE_NOT_ FOUND • STATUS_WMI_ITEM_ID_NOT_FOUND

Table 13.16   *DpWmiFunctionControl Function Prototype*

NTSTATUS DpWmiFunctionControl	IRQL == PASSIVE_LEVEL
Parameter	**Description**
IN PDEVICE_OBJECT pDeviceObject	Pointer to driver's device object
IN PIRP pIrp	Pointer to IRP of WMI request
IN ULONG GuidIndex data block	Index into WMILIB_CONTEXT structure's GuidList, identifying
IN WMIENABLEDISABLECONTROL Function	• WmiEventControl: control event generation • WmiDataBlockControl: control collection
IN BOOLEAN bEnable	• TRUE – Enable event or collection • FALSE – Disable event or collection
Return value	• STATUS_SUCCESS • STATUS_WMI_GUID_NOT_FOUND • STATUS_INVALID_DEVICE_REQUEST

WMI Summary

Clearly, the implementation of WMI can be involved. At this point in the evolution of WBEM and WMI, the payback is minimal. The addition of WMI support to a driver is a plan for the future. The ultimate acceptance of WMI (and WBEM in general) remains to be seen.

A WDM driver is not required to support WMI. It can use the conventional method of logging system events for notification messages, which is described in the next section. For data collection (instrumentation), the registry or custom IOCTLs can be utilized.

Conventional Driver Event Logging

The original Windows NT architecture includes a mechanism that allows software components to keep a record of noteworthy events. This event-logging capability can help monitor the behavior of software that is under development or in production.

How Event Logging Works

The developers of Windows NT had several goals for the event-logging architecture. The first was to provide subsystems with the unified framework for recording information. This framework includes a simple yet flexible standard for the binary format of event-logging entries.

Another goal was to give system administrators an easy and consistent way to view these messages. As part of this goal, viewer utilities must be able to display event messages in the currently selected national language. Figure 13.3 shows the event-logging architecture.

The overall process for the generation and display of event messages is described by the following:

1. All event messages take the form of packets in Windows 2000. When a kernel-mode driver wants to log an event, it first calls the I/O Manager to allocate a message packet from nonpaged pool.

2. The driver fills this packet with various pieces of descriptive information. One of the key items is a 32-bit message code number that identifies the text to be displayed for this packet. Once the packet is ready, the driver returns it to the I/O Manager.

3. The I/O Manager takes the message packet and sends it to the system event-logging thread. This thread accumulates packets and periodically writes them to the proper event-log file.

4. The Event Viewer utility reads binary packets from the log files. To translate a packet's 32-bit message code into text, the Viewer goes to

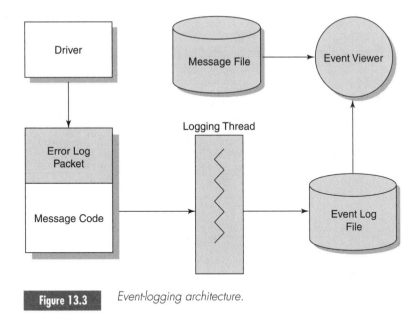

Figure 13.3   *Event-logging architecture.*

the Registry. There it finds the path names of one or more message files associated with the packet. These message files contain the actual message text (possibly in multiple languages), which the Viewer displays.

Working with Messages

As just described, a driver does not include the actual text for its messages in an event-log entry. Instead, it identifies messages using code numbers. The text associated with these code numbers takes the form of a message resource stored somewhere on disk. This section describes how these message code numbers work and explains how to generate custom message resources.

The code number identifying a specific message is a 32-bit value consisting of several fields. Figure 13.4 shows the layout of a message code.

The Severity field of a message code is a 2-bit field which signifies success (0), warning (2), error (3), or informational (1) status. The I/O Manager provides a number of standard messages that a driver can use. The header file, **NTIOLOGC.h**, defines symbolic names for these message codes, all of which begin with IO_ERR_. The file can be browsed for a complete list of standard messages.

To use standard messages, a driver must be included in the list of event-logging system components within the Registry. The actual text file for these shared messages must also be supplied (**IOLOGMSG.dll**). The procedure for performing this registration is described later in this chapter.

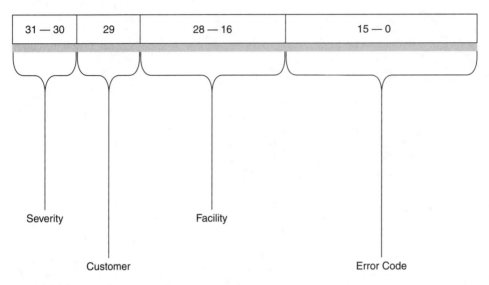

31 — 30	29	28 — 16	15 — 0

Severity

Customer

Facility

Error Code

Figure 13.4   *Layout of a message-code number.*

A driver can also supply custom message text. To do this, the following steps should be followed:

1. Write a message definition file that associates the message code with a specific text string.

2. Compile this file using the message compiler (MC) utility.

3. Incorporate the message resources generated by MC into the driver.

4. Register the driver as an event-logging system component and identify the driver executable as the file containing the text for these private messages.

Writing Message Definition Files

To use the MC utility, a definition file describing all the driver messages must be written. This definition file is divided into two major sections.

Header section. Keywords in the header define names for values that are used in the actual message definitions. Table 13.17 contains the keywords that can be used in the header section of a message definition file.

Message section. This portion of the message definition file contains the actual text of the messages. Each message begins with the keywords listed in Table 13.18.

| Table 13.17 | *Keywords Used in Header Section of Message Definition File* |

Header section keywords

Keyword	Description
MessageIdTypedef = *DataType*	Typecast applied to all message codes
SeverityNames = (*name=number[:name]*)	Up to four severity values used in the message section
FacilityNames = (*name=number[:name]*)	Facility names used in the message section
LanguageNames = (*name=number:filename*)	Language names used in the message section

The message text itself begins after the last keyword. The text of a message can occupy several lines. A message is ended with a line containing only a single period character.

The message compiler ignores any white space or carriage returns in a message definition. Various escape sequences (listed in Table 13.19) can be included in the body of the message.

The %1–%99 escape codes represent Unicode strings (embedded in the event log packet) that are inserted in the message when the Event Viewer displays it. If a kernel-mode driver associates an event packet with its device object, %1 will automatically contain the OS name of the device; if the driver associates the packet with its driver object, %1 is blank. In either case, the first real insertion string is %2, the second %3, and so on.

A Simple Example

Here is the message definition file for a simple example.

| Table 13.18 | *Keywords Used in Message Section of Message Definition File* |

Message section keywords

Keyword	Description
MessageID = *[number	+number]*	16-bit value assigned to this message
Severity = *Severity name*	Severity level of the message
Facility = *Facility name*	Facility generating the message
SymbolicName = *SymbolicName*	Name of message code in generated header file
Language = *LanguageName*	Language ID associated with the message

Table 13.19	*Escape Codes Used Within Message Text*

Message formatting escape codes	
If you use...	**THEN it is replaced with...**
%b	A single space character
%t	A single tab character
%r%n	Carriage return and linefeed
%1–%99	An insertion string

HEADER SECTION

The first part of the message definition file contains header information.

```
MessageIdTypedef = NTSTATUS
SeverityNames = (
   Success        = 0x0:STATUS_SEVERITY_SUCCESS
   Informational  = 0x1:STATUS_SEVERITY_INFORMATIONAL
   Warning        = 0x2:STATUS_SEVERITY_WARNING
   Error          = 0x3:STATUS_SEVERITY_ERROR
)

FacilityNames = (
   System      = 0x0
   RpcRuntime  = 0x2:FACILITY_RPC_RUNTIME
   RpcStubs    = 0x3:FACILITY_RPC_STUBS
   Io          = 0x4:FACILITY_IO_ERROR_CODE
   MyDriver    = 0x7:FACILITY_MY_ERROR_CODE
)
```

MESSAGE SECTION

This section contains message text and identifiers. It defines the actual text to be associated with a message code number.

```
MessageId=0x0001
Facility=MyDriver
Severity=Informational
SymbolicName=MSG_LOGGING_ENABLED
Language=English
Event logging enabled for MyDriver.
.

MessageId=+1
Facility=MyDriver
Severity=Informational
SymbolicName=MSG_DRIVER_STARTING
```

```
Language=English
MyDriver has successfully initialized.
.
```

Compiling a Message Definition File

Once written, the message definition file must be compiled using the MC tool supplied with the Platform SDK and the DDK. Table 13.20 shows the syntax of the MC command.

After a successful message definition file is compiled, the following files are generated:

- **filename.RC**. This is a resource control script that identifies all the languages used in the message definition file. For each language, it also identifies the binary message file containing the message text.
- **filename.H**. This header file contains #define statements for all the message code numbers in the MC input file. The compiler also puts inline commentary in the header, including the text of the corresponding message.
- **MSGnnnnn.BIN**. This binary file holds all the text for messages for one language. MC generates separate files for each national language used in the message definition file.

Table 13.20	Syntax of the MC Command

MC [-?cdosvw] [-herx argument] [-uU] filename.MC	
Parameter	**Description**
-c	Set Customer bit in all message codes.
-d	Use decimal definitions of facility and severity codes in header.
-o	Generate OLE2 header file.
-s	Insert symbolic name as first line of each message.
-v	Generate verbose output.
-h *pathname*	Location of generated header file. (Default is current directory.)
-e *extension*	One-character to three-character extension for header file.
-r *pathname*	Location of generated RC and binary message files.
-x *pathname*	Location of generated debug file.
-u	Input file is Unicode.
-U	Message text in binary; output binary file should be Unicode.
filename	Name of the message definition file to compile.

Adding Message Resources to a Driver

In most cases, the output from the MC compilation is included in the driver executable itself. Simply including the name of the .RC script file within the driver project (makefile) is sufficient.

Registering a Driver as an Event Source

The system Registry serves as the linkage between an *event source* and the message files needed to translate any message codes appearing in its log entries. To register a driver as an event source, the following changes must be made to the Registry under **HKEY_LOCAL_MACHINE\System\Current-ControlSet\Services\EventLog\System**:

1. Add the name of the driver's executable (without the .SYS extension) to a REG_MULTI_SZ value called **Sources**.

2. Add a key with the same name as the driver.

3. In this new key, create a REG_EXPAND_SZ value named **EventMes-sageFile**. It should contain the full path names of the message files used by the driver, separated with semicolons (;). If standard messages from **NTIOLOGC.h** are used, IOLOGMSGodll must also appear in the list.

4. In the same key, create a REG_DWORD value named **Types-Supported**. A value of 0x7 indicates that all message types may be generated.

Generating Log Entries

Code to actually generate a message is relatively straightforward. It involves allocating an event message packet, filling it, and sending it to the system logging thread.

It is common practice to trigger the verbosity of driver event generation based on a driver-specific registry value. For example, under the **Parameters** subkey of the driver's service key, a value called **EventLogLevel** might determine the number and extent of actual messages generated. Thus, during debugging or during a production incident, full event logging could be enabled.

Allocating an Error-Log Packet

When a driver uncovers an event that needs reporting, it must prepare an error-log packet. There are three sections to an error-log packet.

- A standard header
- An array of driver-defined ULONGs (referred to as *dump data*)
- One or more NULL-terminated Unicode insertion strings. These strings are not the counted UNICODE_STRING data structures used elsewhere.

Both the dump-data and insertion strings are variable in length and are optional. Figure 13.5 shows the structure of an error-log packet.

Before an error-log packet can be allocated, its size must be determined. Sufficient space must be allocated for any dump-data and insertion strings. The size of the packet can be calculated using a variation of the following piece of code:

```
PacketSize =
    sizeof( IO_ERROR_LOG_PACKET ) +
    (sizeof( ULONG ) * (DumpDataCount-1)) +
    sizeof( InsertionStrings );
```

The requested size of the packet cannot exceed ERROR_LOG_MAXI-MUM_SIZE.

The **IoAllocateErrorLogEntry**, described in Table 13.21, is used to allocate the packet. As seen, the packet can be associated either with the Driver object or with a specific Device object. The choice determines how the Event Viewer utility displays the message. Initialization and shutdown messages are typically Driver-level messages, while problems involving specific IRPs or hardware should be associated with a Device object.

Notice that the use of **IoAllocateErrorLogEntry** requires a thread context at or below DISPATCH_LEVEL IRQL. Therefore, if an ISR needs to log an error (a common occurrence), a CustomDpc routine must be used to perform the actual work.

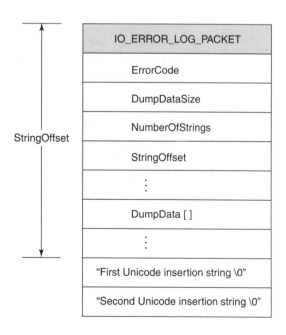

Figure 13.5   *Layout of an error-log packet.*

Table 13.21	*IoAllocateErrorLogEntry Function Prototype*
PVOID **IoAllocateErrorLogEntry**	**IRQL <= DISPATCH_LEVEL**
Parameter	**Description**
IN PVOID IoObject	• Address of a Device object generating an error • Address of a Driver object reporting an error
IN UCHAR EntrySize	Size in bytes of packet to be allocated
Return value	• PIO_ERROR_LOG_PACKET: success • NULL: allocation failure

Logging the Error

Once the packet is allocated, all the relevant fields must be filled. In addition to the fields listed in Table 13.22, any driver-specific data and strings must be added.

When the packet is ready, use **IoWriteErrorLogEntry** to send it to the system logging thread. The packet is no longer owned by the driver once this

Table 13.22	*Layout of an IO_ERROR_LOG_PACKET*
IO_ERROR_LOG_PACKET, *PIO_ERROR_LOG_PACKET	
Field	**Description**
UCHAR MajorFunctionCode	IRP_MJ_XXX code of current IRP
UCHAR RetryCount	Zero-based count of consecutive retries
USHORT DumpDataSize	Bytes of driver-specific data
USHORT NumberOfStrings	Number of insertion strings
USHORT StringOffset	Byte offset of first insertion string
USHORT EventCategory	Event category from driver's message file
NTSTATUS ErrorCode	IO_ERR_XXX (see **NTIOLOGC.H**)
ULONG UniqueErrorValue	Indicates where in the driver the error occurred
NTSTATUS FinalStatus	STATUS_XXX value from the IRP
ULONG SequenceNumber	Driver-assigned number for current IRP
ULONG IoControlCode	IOCTL_XXX if this is a DeviceIoControl request
LARGE_INTEGER DeviceOffset	Device offset where error occurred, or zero
ULONG DumpData [1]	Driver-specific data if DumpDataSize is zero

function is called, so the driver must not be touched again. As with packet al-location, this function can only be used at or below DISPATCH_LEVEL IRQL.

Summary

The incorporation of WMI and event logging into a driver is tedious, but it is inconceivable that a production driver can be supplied without some system reporting mechanism. The ability to trace back through events after a failure report is essential to discover true faults.

Code examples are included on the CD that accompanies this book and on the book's Web site: *www.W2kDriveBook.com*; they demonstrate the use of WMI and event logging.

The next chapter deals with system threads and their appropriate use.

System Threads

CHAPTER OBJECTIVES

*T*he work that must be performed within a driver cannot always be done in response to a request—at least, not at the very
moment of the request. Some work must be performed asynchronous to a caller, perhaps at a different priority to other driver activity. Windows 2000 allows the creation of separate threads of
execution, each following a code path that is independent of others. The threads perform units of work at their own pace, triggered by appropriate events.

This chapter explains the process of creating a kernel-mode thread. It also explains the synchronization techniques provided by the kernel between different threads.

Definition and Use of System Threads

A thread is a *unit of execution*. Each thread maintains an independent program counter and hardware context that includes a private set of CPU registers. Each thread maintains a *priority* value that determines when it gains

control of the system processor(s). In general, the higher a thread's priority, the more likely it is to receive control.

Threads can operate in user mode or kernel mode. A system thread is one that runs exclusively in kernel mode. It has no user-mode context and cannot access user address space. Just like a Win32 thread, a system thread executes at or below APC_LEVEL IRQL and it competes for use of the CPU based on its scheduling priority.

When To Use Threads

There are several reasons to use threads in a driver. One example is working with hardware that has the following characteristics:

- The device is slow and infrequently accessed.
- It takes a long time (more than 50 microseconds) for the device to make a state transition, and the driver must wait for the transition to occur.
- The device needs to make several state transitions in order to complete a single operation.
- The device does not generate interrupts for some state transitions, and the driver must poll the device for an extended period.

Such a device could be managed using a CustomTimerDpc routine. Depending on the amount of device activity, however, this approach could saturate the DPC queues and slow down other drivers. Threads, on the other hand, run at PASSIVE_LEVEL and do not interfere with DPC routines.

Fortunately, most modern hardware is designed to operate in a way that allows good system performance. (Granted, there are many contradictions to this statement.) Legacy hardware, however, is legendary in forcing drivers to poll (and retry) for state transitions, thus burdening the driver with considerable and messy design. The most notable examples are floppy disks and other devices attached to floppy controllers.

Another need for threads occurs with devices that take excessive time to initialize. The driver must monitor the initialization process, polling the state transitions throughout. A separate thread is needed because the Service Control Manager gives drivers only about 30 seconds to execute their DriverEntry routine. Otherwise, the Service Control Manager forcibly unloads the driver. The only solution is to put the long-running device start-up code in a separate thread and return promptly from the DriverEntry routine with STATUS_SUCCESS.

Finally, there may be some operations that can be performed only at PASSIVE_LEVEL IRQL. For example, if a driver has to access the registry on a regular basis, or perform file operations, a multi-thread design should be considered.

Creating and Terminating System Threads

To create a system thread, a driver uses **PsCreateSystemThread**, described in Table 14.1. Since this function can only be called at PASSIVE_LEVEL IRQL, threads are usually created in the DriverEntry or AddDevice routines.

When a driver unloads, it must ensure that any system thread it may have created has terminated. System threads must terminate themselves, using **PsTerminateSystemThread**, described in Table 14.2. Unlike Win32 user-mode threads, there is no way to forcibly terminate a system thread. This means that some kind of signaling mechanism needs to be set up to let a thread know it should exit. As discussed later in this chapter, Event objects provide a convenient mechanism for this.

Managing Thread Priority

In general, system threads running in a driver should have priorities near the low end of the real-time range. The following code fragment demonstrates this:

```
VOID ThreadStartRoutine( PVOID pContext ) {
    ...
    KeSetPriorityThread(
                    KeGetCurrentThread(),
                    LOW_REALTIME_PRIORITY );
    ...
}
```

Table 14.1	*PsCreateSystemThread Function Prototype*
NTSTATUS PsCreateSystemThread	**IRQL == PASSIVE_LEVEL**
Parameter	**Description**
OUT PHANDLE ThreadHandle	Handle of new thread
IN ULONG DesiredAccess	0 for a driver-created thread
IN POBJECT_ATTRIBUTES Attrib	NULL for a driver-created thread
IN HANDLE ProcessHandle	NULL for a driver-created thread
OUT PCLIENT_ID ClientId	NULL for a driver-created thread
IN PKSTART_ROUTINE StartAddr	Entry point for thread
IN PVOID Context	Argument passed to thread routine
Return value	• STATUS_SUCCESS: thread was created • STATUS_XXX: an error code

Table 14.2	*PsTerminateSystemThread Function Prototype*
NTSTATUS **PsTerminateSystemThread**	**IRQL == PASSIVE_LEVEL**
Parameter	**Description**
IN NTSTATUS ExitStatus	Exit code signifying reason for termination
Return value	• STATUS_SUCCESS: thread was killed

Be aware that real-time threads have no quantum timeout value. This means that the CPU is relinquished only when the thread voluntarily enters a wait state, or when preempted by a thread of higher priority. Therefore, drivers cannot depend upon round-robin scheduling.

System Worker Threads

For occasional, quick operations at PASSIVE_LEVEL IRQL, creating and terminating a separate thread may not be very efficient. The alternative is to have one of the kernel's *system worker threads* perform the task. These threads use a callback mechanism to do work on behalf of any driver.

It is not difficult to use system worker threads. First, allocate storage for a WORK_QUEUE_ITEM structure. The system will use this block to keep track of the work request. Next, call **ExInitializeWorkItem** to associate a callback function in the driver with the WORK_QUEUE_ITEM.

Later, when a system thread is needed to execute the callback function, call **ExQueueWorkItem** to insert the request block into one of the system work queues. The request can be executed either by a worker thread with a real-time priority or by one with a variable priority.

Keep in mind that all drivers are sharing the same group of system worker threads. Requests that take a very long time to complete may delay the execution of requests from other drivers. Tasks involving lengthy operations or long time delays should utilize a private driver thread rather than the system work queues.

Thread Synchronization

Like user-mode threads in a Win32 application, system threads may need to suspend their execution until some other condition has been satisfied. This section describes the basic synchronization techniques available to system threads.

Time Synchronization

The simplest kind of synchronization involves stopping a thread's execution until a specific time interval elapses. Although Timer objects, described later in this chapter, can be used, the kernel provides a convenient function, KeDelayExecutionThread (illustrated in Table 14.3) that is easier to use.

General Synchronization

System threads can synchronize their activities in more general ways by waiting for *dispatcher objects*. Thread synchronization depends on the fact that a dispatcher object is always in either the *signaled* or *nonsignaled* state. When a thread asks to wait for a nonsignaled dispatcher object, the thread's execution stops until the object becomes signaled. (Waiting for a dispatcher object that is already Signaled is a no-op.) There are two different functions that can be used to wait for a dispatcher object.

KeWaitForSingleObject

This function, described in Table 14.4, puts the calling thread into a wait state until a specific dispatcher object is set to the signaled state.

Optionally, a timeout value may be specified that causes the thread to awaken even if the dispatcher object is nonsignaled. If the timeout argument is NULL, **KeWaitForSingleObject** waits indefinitely.

KeWaitForMultipleObjects

This function, described in Table 14.5, puts the calling thread into a wait state until any or all of a group of dispatcher objects are set to the signaled state. Again, a timeout value for the wait may be specified.

Be aware that there are limits on how many objects the thread can wait for at one time. Each thread has a built-in array of Wait blocks that it uses for

Table 14.3	*KeDelayExecutionThread Function Prototype*
NTSTATUS **KeDelayExecutionThread**	**IRQL == PASSIVE_LEVEL**
Parameter	**Description**
IN KPROCESSOR_MODE WaitMode	KernelMode for drivers
IN BOOLEAN bAlertable	FALSE for drivers
IN PLARGE_INTEGER Interval	Absolute or relative due time
Return value	STATUS_SUCCESS: wait completed

Table 14.4	*KeWaitForSingleObject Function Prototype*

NTSTATUS KeWaitForSingleObject

Parameter	Description
IN PVOID Object	Pointer to an initialized dispatcher object
IN KWAIT_REASON Reason	Executive for drivers
IN KPROCESSOR_MODE WaitMode	KernelMode for drivers
IN BOOLEAN Alertable	False for drivers
IN PLARGE_INTEGER Timeout	• Absolute or relative timeout value • NULL for an infinite wait
Return value	• STATUS_SUCCESS • STATUS_ALERTED • STATUS TIMEOUT

concurrent wait operations. The thread can use this array to wait for up to THREAD_WAIT_OBJECTS number of objects. If the number THREAD_WAIT_OBJECTS is insufficient, a driver-supplied array of Wait blocks must be included in the call to **KeWaitForMultipleObjects**. Regardless, the number of objects waited upon cannot exceed MAXIMUM_WAIT_OBJECTS.

Table 14.5	*KeWaitForMultipleObjects Function Prototype*

NTSTATUS KeWaitForMultipleObjects

Parameter	Description
IN ULONG Count	Number of objects to wait for
IN PVOID Object [ ]	Array of pointers to dispatcher objects
IN WAIT_TYPE WaitType	• WaitAll: wait until all are signaled • WaitAny: wait until one is signaled
IN KWAIT_REASON Reason	Executive for drivers
IN KPROCESSOR_MODE WaitMode	KernelMode for drivers
IN BOOLEAN Alertable	FALSE for drivers
IN PLARGE_INTEGER Timeout	• Absolute or relative timeout value • NULL for an infinite wait
IN PKWAIT_BLOCK WaitBlocks [ ]	Array of wait blocks for this operation
Return value	• STATUS_SUCCESS • STATUS_ALERTED • STATUS_TIMEOUT

The **KeWaitForXxx** functions may be called from either PASSIVE_ LEVEL or DISPATCH_LEVEL IRQL. However, from DISPATCH_LEVEL IRQL, a zero timeout value *must* be specified. At DISPATCH_LEVEL IRQL, the calls are effectively used as a polling mechanism for Signaled objects.

Using Dispatcher Objects

Except for Thread objects themselves, the driver must allocate storage for any dispatcher objects that are used. The objects must be permanently resident and are, therefore, usually allocated within the Device or Controller Extension. In any case, they must be in nonpaged memory.

Also, the dispatch object must be initialized once with the proper **KeInitializeXxx** function before it is used. Since the initialization functions can only be called at PASSIVE_LEVEL IRQL, dispatcher objects are usually prepared in the DriverEntry or AddDevice routine.

The following sections describe each category of dispatcher objects in greater detail.

Event Objects

An event is a dispatcher object that must be explicitly set to the signaled or nonsignaled state. An event is analogous to a binary flag, allowing one thread to signal other threads of a specific occurrence by raising (set to signaled) the flag. This behavior can be seen in Figure 14.1, where thread A awakens B, C, and D by setting an event object.

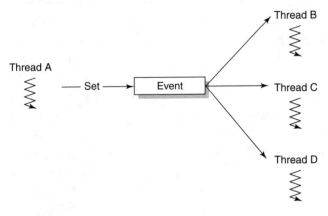

Figure 14.1   *Event objects synchronize system threads.*

These objects actually come in two different flavors: notification events and synchronization events. The type is chosen when the object is initialized. These two types of events exhibit different behavior when put into the signaled state. As long as a notification event remains signaled, all threads waiting for the event come out of their wait state. A notification event must be explicitly reset to put it into the nonsignaled state. These events exhibit behavior like user-mode (Win32) manual-reset events.

When a synchronization event is placed into the signaled state, it remains set only long enough for one call to **KeWaitForXxx**. It then resets itself to the nonsignaled state automatically. In other words, the gate stays open until exactly one thread passes through, and then it shuts. This is equivalent to a user-mode auto-reset event.

To use an event, storage is first allocated for an item of type KEVENT, and then functions listed in Table 14.6 are called.

Notice that either of two functions put an event object into the nonsignaled state. The difference is that **KeResetEvent** returns the state of the event before it became nonsignaled, and **KeClearEvent** does not. **KeClearEvent** is somewhat faster, so it should be used unless the previous state must be determined.

The sample driver at the end of this chapter provides an example of using events. It has a worker thread that needs to pause until an interrupt arrives, so the thread waits for an event object. The driver's DpcForIsr routine sets the event into the signaled state, waking up the worker thread.

| Table 14.6 | *Functions that Operate on Event Objects* |

How to use event objects		
If you want to	**THEN call**	**IRQL**
Create an event	KeInitializeEvent	PASSIVE_LEVEL
Create a named event	IoCreateSynchronizationEvent IoCreateNotificationEvent	PASSIVE_LEVEL
Modify event state	KeSetEvent KeClearEvent KeResetEvent	<= DISPATCH LEVEL
Wait for a timer	KeWaitForSingleObject KeWaitForMultipleObjects	PASSIVE_LEVEL
Interrogate an event	KeReadStateEvent	<= DISPATCH_LEVEL

Sharing Events Between Drivers

It is difficult for two unrelated drivers to share an Event object created with **KeInitializeEvent**. The event object is referenced only by pointer, and without some kind of explicit agreement (for example, an internal IOCTL), there is no simple way to pass a pointer from one driver to another. Even then, there is the issue of ensuring that the driver creating the Event stays loaded while another driver uses the object.

The **IoCreateSynchronizationEvent** and **IoCreateNotificationEvent** functions allow the creation of named Event objects. As long as two drivers use the same Event name, they can each obtain pointers to the same Event object. Both functions behave like the Win32 **CreateEvent** system call. In other words, the first driver to make a call with a specific Event name causes the Event object to be created. Subsequent calls attempting to create a duplicate Event object simply return a handle to the existing Event object.

There are two notable behaviors of the **IoCreateXxxEvent** functions. First, memory for the KEVENT object is not allocated by the driver. Storage is supplied by the system. When the last user of the Event releases it, the system deletes the object automatically.

Second, the **IoCreateXxxEvent** calls return a *handle* to the event object, not a memory pointer. To use the Event object in calls to the **KeXxx** functions listed in Table 14.6, a pointer is required. To convert a handle into an object pointer, the following steps must be performed:

1. Call **ObReferenceObjectByHandle**. This function obtains a pointer to the Event object itself and increments the object's pointer reference count.

2. When the handle itself is no longer needed (and it is usually not needed at all), call **ZwClose** to release it. This function decrements the object's handle reference count.

3. When the Event object is no longer needed, call **ObDereferenceObject** to decrement the Event object's pointer reference count and possibly delete the Event object.

These functions can be called only from PASSIVE_LEVEL IRQL, which limits where a driver can use them.

Mutex Objects

A Mutex (short for mutual exclusion) is a dispatcher object that can be owned by only one thread at a time. The object becomes nonsignaled when a thread owns it and signaled when it is available (unowned). Mutexes provide an easy mechanism for coordinating mutually exclusive access to some shared resource, usually memory.

Figure 14.2 shows threads B, C, and D waiting for a Mutex owned by thread A. When A releases the Mutex, one of the waiting threads wakes up and becomes its new owner.

To use a Mutex, nonpaged storage for an item of type KMUTEX must be reserved. Functions listed in Table 14.7 can then be used. Be aware that when a Mutex is initialized, it is always set to the signaled state.

If a thread calls **KeWaitForXxx** on a Mutex it already owns, the thread never waits. Instead, the Mutex increments an internal counter to record the fact that this thread is making recursive ownership requests. When the thread wants to free the Mutex, it has to call **KeReleaseMutex** as many times as it requested ownership. Only then will the Mutex go into the signaled state. This is the same behavior exhibited by Win32 Mutex objects.

It is also crucial that a driver release any Mutexes it might be holding before it makes a transition back into user mode. The kernel will bug-check if any driver threads attempt to return control to the I/O Manager while owning a Mutex. For example, a DriverEntry or Dispatch routine is not allowed to acquire a Mutex that would later be released by some other Dispatch routine or by a system thread.

Semaphore Objects

A Semaphore is a dispatcher object that maintains a count. The object remains signaled as long as its count is greater than zero, and nonsignaled when the count is 0. In other words, a Semaphore is a counting Mutex.

Figure 14.3 shows the operation of the Semaphore. Threads B, C, and D are all waiting for a Semaphore whose current count is 0. When thread A calls **KeReleaseSemaphore** twice, the count increments to 2, and two of the

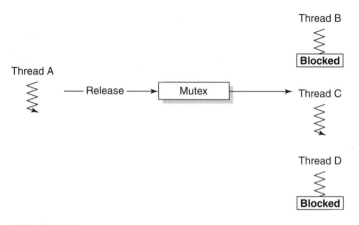

Figure 14.2   *Mutex objects synchronize system threads.*

Table 14.7	*Functions that Operate on Mutex Objects*

How to use mutex objects

If you want to...	THEN call...	IRQL
Create a Mutex	KeIntializeMutex	PASSIVE_LEVEL
Request Mutex ownership	KeWaitForSingleObject KeWaitForMultipleObjects	PASSIVE_LEVEL
Give up Mutex ownership	KeReleaseMutex	PASSIVE_LEVEL
Interrogate Mutex	KeReadStateMutex	<= DISPATCH_LEVEL

waiting threads are allowed to resume execution. Waking up two threads also causes the Semaphore to decrement back to zero.

Again, the sample driver at the end of this chapter provides a good example. Its Dispatch routine increments a Semaphore each time it adds an IRP to an internal work queue. As a worker thread removes IRPs from the queue, it decrements the Semaphore and finally goes into a wait state when the queue is empty.

To use the Semaphore, storage must be allocated for an item of type KSEMAPHORE. Then the functions listed in Table 14.8 can be used.

Timer Objects

A Timer is a dispatcher object with a timeout value. When a Timer is started, it goes into the nonsignaled state until its timeout value expires. At that point, it becomes signaled. In chapter 10, a Timer object is used to force a Custom-

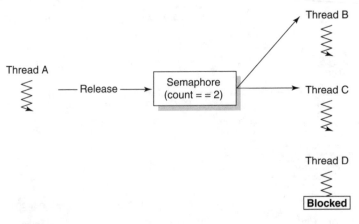

Figure 14.3	*Semaphore objects synchronize system threads.*

Table 14.8	Functions that Operate on Semaphore Objects	

How to use semaphore objects

If you want to...	THEN call...	IRQL
Create a semaphore	KeIntializeSemaphore	PASSIVE_LEVEL
Decrement semaphore	KeWaitForSingleObject KeWaitForMultipleObjects	PASSIVE_LEVEL
Increment semaphore	KeReleaseSemaphore	<= DISPATCH_LEVEL
Interrogate semaphore	KeReadStateSemaphore	Any

TimerDpc routine to execute. Since they are just kernel dispatcher objects, they can also be used in calls to **KeWaitForXxx**.

Figure 14.4 illustrates the operation of the Timer object. Thread A starts the Timer and then calls **KeWaitForSingleObject**. The thread blocks until the Timer expires. At that point, the timer goes into the signaled state and the thread wakes up.

Timer objects actually come in two different flavors: Notification Timers and Synchronization Timers. The type is chosen when the object is initialized. Although both types of Timers go into the signaled state when their timeout value expires, the period that the object remains signaled differs.

When a Notification Timer times out, it remains in the signaled state until it is explicitly reset. While the Timer is signaled, all threads waiting for the Timer are awakened.

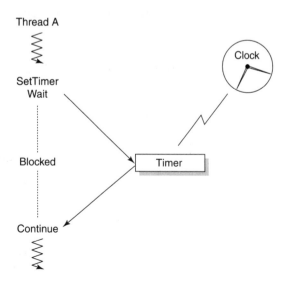

Figure 14.4	Timer objects synchronize system threads.

When a Synchronization Timer expires, it remains in the Signaled state only long enough to satisfy a single **KeWaitForXxx** request. At that point, the Timer becomes nonsignaled automatically.

To use a Timer, storage must be allocated for an item of type KTIMER and then the functions listed in Table 14.9 can be used.

Thread Objects

System threads are also dispatcher objects, which means they have a signaled state. When a system thread terminates, its Thread object changes from the nonsignaled to the signaled state. This allows a driver to synchronize its cleanup operations by waiting for the Thread object.

Notably, when **PsCreateSystemThread** is called, it returns a *handle* to the Thread object. To use a Thread object in a call to **KeWaitForXxx**, a *pointer* to the object is required rather than a handle. To convert a handle into an object pointer, the following steps must be performed:

1. Call **ObReferenceObjectByHandle**. This function provides a pointer to the Thread object itself and increments the object's pointer reference count.

2. When the handle itself is no longer needed (and it is usually not needed at all), call **ZwClose** to release it. This decrements the object's handle reference count.

3. After the thread terminates, call **ObDereferenceObject** to decrement the Thread object's pointer reference count and possibly delete the Thread object.

These functions can be called only from PASSIVE_LEVEL IRQL, which limits the places in a driver where they can be used.

Table 14.9	*Functions that Operate on Timer Objects*	
How to use timer objects		
If you want to...	**THEN call...**	**IRQL**
Create a Timer	KeIntializeTimerX	PASSIVE_LEVEL
Start a one-shot Timer	KeSetTimer	<= DISPATCH_LEVEL
Start a repeating Timer	KeSetTimerEx	<= DISPATCH_LEVEL
Stop a Timer	KeCancelTimer	<= DISPATCH_LEVEL
Wait for a Timer	KeWaitForSingleObject KeWaitForMultipleObjects	PASSIVE_LEVEL
Interrogate a Timer	KeReadTimerState	<= DISPATCH_LEVEL

Variations on the Mutex

The Windows 2000 Executive supports two variations on Mutex objects. The following sections describe them briefly. In general, using these objects instead of kernel Mutexes can result in better driver performance. See the NT DDK documentation for more complete information.

FAST MUTEXES

A Fast Mutex is a synchronization object that acts like a kernel Mutex, except that it does not allow recursive ownership requests. By removing this feature, the Fast Mutex does not have to do as much work, and its speed improves.

The Fast Mutex itself is an object of type FAST_MUTEX that is associated with one or more data items needing protection. Any code touching the data items must acquire ownership of the corresponding FAST_MUTEX first. Use the functions listed in Table 14.10 to work with Fast Mutexes. Notice that these objects have their own functions for requesting ownership. The **Ke-WaitForXxx** functions cannot be used to acquire Fast Mutexes.

EXECUTIVE RESOURCES

Another synchronization object that behaves very much like a kernel Mutex is an Executive resource. The main difference is the resource can either be owned exclusively by a single thread, or shared by multiple threads for read access. Since it is common (in the real world) for multiple readers to request simultaneous access to a resource, Executive Resource objects provide better throughput than standard kernel Mutexes.

The Executive Resource itself is just an object of type ERESOURCE that is associated with one or more data items needing protection. Any code planning to touch the data items has to acquire ownership of the corresponding ERESOURCE first. Table 14.11 lists the functions that work with Executive Resources. Notice that these objects have their own functions for requesting ownership. The **KeWaitForXxx** functions cannot be used to acquire Executive Resources.

Table 14.10	Functions that Operate on Fast Mutexes	
How to use Fast Mutexes		
If you want to...	**THEN call...**	**IRQL**
Create a Fast Mutex	ExInitializeFastMutex	<= DISPATCH_LEVEL
Request Fast Mutex ownership	ExAcquireFastMutex	< DISPATCH_LEVEL
Give up Fast Mutex ownership	ExReleaseFastMutex	< DISPATCH_LEVEL

Table 14.11	Functions that Operate on Executive Resources	
How to use Executive resources		
If you want to...	**THEN call...**	**IRQL**
Create	ExInitializeResourceLite	<= DISPATCH_LEVEL
Acquire	ExAcquireResourceExclusiveLite	< DISPATCH_LEVEL
	ExAcquireResourceSharedLite	< DISPATCH_LEVEL
	ExTryToAcquireResourceExclusiveLite	< DISPATCH_LEVEL
	ExConvertExclusiveToSharedLite	< DISPATCH_LEVEL
Release	ExReleaseResourceforThreadLite	<= DISPATCH_LEVEL
Interrogate	ExIsResourceAcquiredSharedLite	<=DISPATCH_LEVEL
	ExIsResourceAcquiredExclusiveLite	<= DISPATCH_LEVEL
Delete	ExDeleteResourceLite	<=DISPATCH_LEVEL

Synchronization Deadlocks

Deadlock situations can occur whenever multiple threads compete for simultaneous ownership of multiple resources. Figure 14.5 shows the simplest form of this problem:

1. Thread A acquires resource X.

2. Thread B acquires resource Y.

3. Thread A requests ownership of resource Y and goes into a wait state until B releases Y.

4. Thread B then requests ownership of resource X. This causes B to go into a wait state until A releases X. The result is a deadlock, or deadly embrace.

A deadlock can occur using Events, Mutexes, or Semaphores. Even Thread objects can deadlock waiting for each other to terminate. There are two general approaches to solving deadlock problems.

- Use the Timeout arguments of the **KeWaitForXxx** functions to limit the time of the wait. While this technique may help detect a deadlock, it does not really correct the underlying problem.
- Force all the threads using a given set of resources to acquire them in the same order. In the previous example, if A and B had both gone after resource X first and then Y second, there would have been no deadlock.

Mutex objects provide some protection against the deadlocks through the use of level numbers. When a Mutex is initialized, a level number is as-

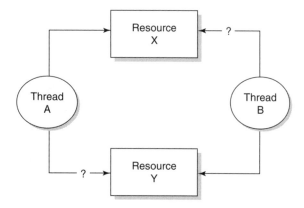

Figure 14.5 *Deadlock scenario.*

signed. Later, when a thread attempts to acquire the Mutex, the kernel will not grant ownership if that thread is holding any Mutex with a lower level number. By enforcing this policy, the kernel avoids deadlocks involving multiple Mutexes.

Code Example: A Thread-Based Driver

This section presents a modified version for the packet-based slave DMA driver introduced in Chapter 12. What is different about this driver is that it uses a system thread to do most of the I/O processing. As a result, it spends very little time at DISPATCH_LEVEL IRQL and does not interfere as much with other system components. Code examples can be found on the CD that accompanies this book or on the book's Web site: www.W2KDriverBook.com.

How the Driver Works

Figure 14.6 gives a high-level view of the sample driver architecture. One of the first things to notice is that the driver has no Start I/O routine. When a user-mode I/O request arrives, one of the driver's Dispatch routines simply adds the IRP to a work queue associated with the Device object. Then the Dispatch routine calls **KeReleaseSemaphore** to increment a Semaphore object that keeps track of the number of IRPs in the work queue. A nonzero Semaphore count indicates the number of IRPs within the work queue yet to be processed.

Each Device object has its own system thread that processes these I/O requests. This thread is in an endless loop that begins with a call to **KeWaitForSingleObject** on the Semaphore. If the Semaphore object has a nonzero count, the thread removes an IRP from the work queue and performs the I/O

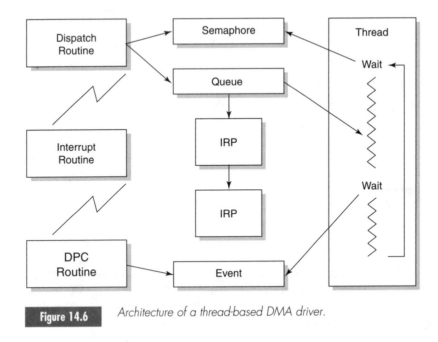

Figure 14.6   *Architecture of a thread-based DMA driver.*

operation. On the other hand, if the count is zero the thread goes into a wait state until the Dispatch routine inserts another IRP in the queue.

When the thread needs to perform a data transfer, it starts the device and then uses **KeWaitForSingleObject** to wait for an Event object. The driver's DpcForIsr routine sets this Event into the signaled state after an interrupt arrives. The Event object effectively synchronizes the interrupt service code (actually the DPC) with the worker thread that dequeues IRPs.

When the driver's RemoveDevice routine needs to kill the system thread, it sets a flag in the Device Extension and increments the Semaphore object. If the thread was asleep waiting for the Semaphore object, it wakes up, sees the flag, and terminates itself. If it is in the middle of an I/O operation, it won't see the flag until it completes the current IRP.

The DEVICE_EXTENSION Structure

This file contains all the usual driver-defined data structures. The following excerpt shows only additional fields that the driver needs in order to manage the system thread and its work queue. Other fields are identical to those in the packet-based slave DMA example of chapter 12.

```
typedef struct _DEVICE_EXTENSION {
    ...
    // Pointer to worker thread object
    PETHREAD pThreadObj;
```

```
        // Flag set to TRUE when worker thread should quit
        BOOLEAN bThreadShouldStop;

        // Event object signaling Adapter is now owned
        KEVENT evAdapterObjectIsAcquired;
        // Event signaling last operation now completed
        KEVENT evDeviceOperationComplete;

        // The work queue of IRPs is managed by this
        //    semaphore and spin lock
        KSEMAPHORE semIrpQueue;
        KSPIN_LOCK lkIrpQueue;
        LIST_ENTRY IrpQueueListHead;
} DEVICE_EXTENSION, *PDEVICE_EXTENSION;
```

The AddDevice Function

This portion of the example shows the initialization code for the Thread object, the work queue, and the various synchronization objects used to process an I/O request. Remember that **AddDevice** is called once for each Device object.

```
NTSTATUS AddDevice( IN PDRIVER_OBJECT pDriverObj,
                    IN PDEVICE_OBJECT pdo ) {
    ...
    // Initialize the work queue lock
    KeInitializeSpinLock( &pDevExt->lkIrpQueue );

    // Initialize the work queue itself
    InitializeListHead( &pDevExt->IrpQueueListHead );

    // Initialize the work queue semaphore
    KeInitializeSemaphore( &pDevExt->semIrpQueue,
                           0, MAXLONG);

    // Initialize the event for the Adapter object
    KeInitializeEvent(
            &pDevExt-> evAdapterObjectIsAcquired,
            SynchronizationEvent, FALSE );

    // Intialize the event for the operation complete
    KeInitializeEvent(
            &pDevExt->evDeviceOperationComplete,
            SynchronizationEvent, FALSE );

    // Initially the worker thread runs
    pDevExt->bThreadShouldStop = FALSE;

    // Start the worker thread
    HANDLE hThread = NULL;
```

```
status =
    PsCreateSystemThread( &hThread,
                          (ACCESS_MASK)0,
                          NULL,
                          (HANDLE)0,
                          NULL,
                          WorkerThreadMain,
                          pDevExt );        // arg
if (!NT_SUCCESS(status)) {
    IoDeleteSymbolicLink( &linkName );
    IoDeleteDevice( pfdo );
    return status;
}

// Obtain real pointer to Thread object
ObReferenceObjectByHandle(
    hThread,
    THREAD_ALL_ACCESS,
    NULL,
    KernelMode,
    (PVOID*)&pDevExt->pThreadObj,
    NULL );
ZwClose( hThread );        // don't need handle at all

...
}
```

The DispatchReadWrite Function

This routine responds to user requests to read or write the device. After checking for a zero-length transfer, it puts the IRP into the pending state and inserts it into the work queue attached to the target Device object. It then increments the count in the work queue's Semaphore object. Notice that there are no calls to **IoStartPakcet** because there is no Start I/O routine.

```
NTSTATUS DispatchReadWrite( IN PDEVICE_OBJECT pDO,
                            IN PIRP pIrp ) {
    PIO_STACK_LOCATION pIrpStack =
        IoGetCurrentIrpStackLocation( pIrp );

    PDEVICE_EXTENSION pDE = pDO->DeviceExtension;

    // Check for zero-length transfers
    if( pIrpStack->Parameters.Read.Length == 0 )
    {
        pIrp->IoStatus.Status = STATUS_SUCCESS;
        pIrp->IoStatus.Information = 0;
        IoCompleteRequest( pIrp, IO_NO_INCREMENT );
        return STATUS_SUCCESS;
```

```
    }

// Start device operation
    IoMarkIrpPending( pIrp );

    // Add the IRP to the thread's work queue
    ExInterlockedInsertTailList(
        &pDE->IrpQueueListHead,
        &pIrp->Tail.Overlay.ListEntry,
        &pDE->lkIrpQueue );

    KeReleaseSemaphore(
        &pDE->semIrpQueue,
        0,                      // No priority boost
        1,                      // Increment semaphore by 1
        FALSE );        // No WaitForXxx after this call

    return STATUS_PENDING;
}
```

Thread.cpp

This module contains the main thread function and the routines needed to manage the thread.

WorkerThreadMain

This is the IRP-processing engine itself. Its job is to pull I/O requests from the work queue in the Device Extension and perform the data transfer operation. This function continues to wait for new IRPs until the **RemoveDevice** routine tells it to shut down.

```
VOID WorkerThreadMain( IN PVOID pContext ) {
    PDEVICE_EXTENSION pDevExt = (PDEVICE_EXTENSION)
            pContext;

    PDEVICE_OBJECT pDeviceObj =
            pDevExt->pDevice;

    PLIST_ENTRY ListEntry;
    PIRP pIrp;
    CCHAR PriorityBoost;

    // Worker thread runs at higher priority than
    //    user threads - it sets its own priority
    KeSetPriorityThread(
        KeGetCurrentThread(),
        LOW_REALTIME_PRIORITY );

    // Now enter the main IRP-processing loop
```

```
while( TRUE )
{
    // Wait indefinitely for an IRP to appear in
    // the work queue or for the RemoveDevice
    // routine to stop the thread.
    KeWaitForSingleObject(
        &pDevExt->semIrpQueue,
        Executive,
        KernelMode,
        FALSE,
        NULL );

    // See if thread was awakened because
    // device is being removed
    if( pDevExt->bThreadShouldStop )
        PsTerminateSystemThread(STATUS_SUCCESS);

    // It must be a real request. Get an IRP
    ListEntry =
        ExInterlockedRemoveHeadList(
            &pDevExt->IrpQueueListHead,
            &pDevExt->lkIrpQueue);

    pIrp = CONTAINING_RECORD(
            ListEntry,
            IRP,
            Tail.Overlay.ListEntry );

    // Process the IRP. This is a synchronous
    // operation, so this function doesn't return
    // until it's time to get rid of the IRP.
    PriorityBoost =
        PerformDataTransfer(
            pDeviceObj,
            pIrp );

    // Release the IRP and go back to the
    // top of the loop to see if there's
    // another request waiting.
    IoCompleteRequest( pIrp, PriorityBoost );

} // end of while-loop
}
```

KillThread

This function notifies the thread associated with a particular Device object that it's time to quit. For simplicity, this function stops and waits until the target thread is gone. Consequently, it can be called only from PASSIVE_LEVEL IRQL.

```
VOID KillThread( IN PDEVICE_EXTENSION pDE ) {
    // Set the Stop flag
    pDE->bThreadShouldStop = TRUE;

    // Make sure the thread wakes up
    KeReleaseSemaphore(
        &pDE->semIrpQueue,
        0,              // No priority boost
        1,              // Increment semaphore by 1
        TRUE );         // WaitForXxx after this call

    // Wait for the thread to terminate
    KeWaitForSingleObject(
        &pDE->pThreadObj,
        Executive,
        KernelMode,
        FALSE,
        NULL );

    ObDereferenceObject( &pDE->pThreadObj );
}
```

Transfer.C

This portion of the example contains the support routines that perform I/O operations. This code is largely derived from the packet-based slave DMA driver in chapter 12. Consequently, only those features that differ significantly are described in detail.

The most notable detail is that very little actual work occurs within the Adapter Control or DpcForIsr routines. Instead of doing their usual jobs, these functions just set Event objects to signal the thread's data transfer routines that they can proceed.

PerformDataTransfer

This function moves an entire buffer of data to or from the device. This may include splitting the transfer over several device operations if there aren't enough mapping registers to handle it all at once. This routine runs at PASSIVE_LEVEL IRQL and doesn't return to the caller until everything is done.

```
CCHAR PerformDataTransfer(
    IN PDEVICE_OBJECT pDevObj,
    IN PIRP pIrp
    )
{
    PIO_STACK_LOCATION  pIrpStack =
        IoGetCurrentIrpStackLocation( pIrp );

    PDEVICE_EXTENSION pDE = (PDEVICE_EXTENSION)
        pDevObj->DeviceExtension;
```

```
PMDL pMdl = pIrp->MdlAddress;
ULONG MapRegsNeeded;
NTSTATUS status;

// Set the I/O direction flag
if( pIrpStack->MajorFunction == IRP_MJ_WRITE )
    pDE->bWriteToDevice = TRUE;
else
    pDE->bWriteToDevice = FALSE;

// Set up bookkeeping values
pDE->bytesRequested =
        MmGetMdlByteCount( pMdl );

pDE->bytesRemaining =
        pDE->bytesRequested;

pDE->transferVA = (PCHAR)
        MmGetMdlVirtualAddress( pMdl );

// Flush CPU cache if necessary
KeFlushIoBuffers(
    pIrp->MdlAddress,
    !pDE->bWriteToDevice,
    TRUE );

// Calculate size of first partial transfer
pDE->transferSize = pDE->bytesRemaining;

MapRegsNeeded =
    ADDRESS_AND_SIZE_TO_SPAN_PAGES(
        pDE->transferVA,
        pDE->transferSize );

if( MapRegsNeeded > pDE->mapRegisterCount )
{
    MapRegsNeeded =
        pDE->mapRegisterCount;

        pDE->transferSize =
            MapRegsNeeded * PAGE_SIZE -
            MmGetMdlByteOffset( pMdl );
}

// Acquire the adapter object.
status = AcquireAdapterObject(
            pDE,
            MapRegsNeeded );
if( !NT_SUCCESS( status )) {
    pIrp->IoStatus.Status = status;
    pIrp->IoStatus.Information = 0;
    return IO_NO_INCREMENT;
}
```

```
// Try to perform the first partial transfer
status =
    PerformSynchronousTransfer(
        pDevObj,
        pIrp );

if( !NT_SUCCESS( status )) {
    pDE->pDmaAdapter->DmaOperations->
        FreeAdapterChannel ( pDE->pDmaAdapter );
    pIrp->IoStatus.Status = status;
    pIrp->IoStatus.Information = 0;
    return IO_NO_INCREMENT;
}

// It worked. Update the bookkeeping information
pDE->transferVA += pDE->transferSize;
pDE->bytesRemaining -= pDE->transferSize;

// Loop through all the partial transfer
// operations for this request.
while( pDE->bytesRemaining >0 )
{
    // Try to do all of it in one operation
    pDE->transferSize = pDE->bytesRemaining;

    MapRegsNeeded =
        ADDRESS_AND_SIZE_TO_SPAN_PAGES(
                pDE->transferVA,
                pDE->transferSize );

    // If the remainder of the buffer is more
    // than we can handle in one I/O. Reduce
    // our expectations.
    if (MapRegsNeeded > pDE->mapRegisterCount) {
        MapRegsNeeded = pDE->mapRegisterCount;

        pDE->transferSize =
            MapRegsNeeded * PAGE_SIZE -
                BYTE_OFFSET(pDE->TransferVA);
    }

    // Try to perform a device operation.
    status =
        PerformSynchronousTransfer(
                pDevObj,
                pIrp );

    if( !NT_SUCCESS( status )) break;

    // It worked. Update the bookkeeping
    // information for the next cycle.
    pDE->transferVA += pDE->transferSize;
    pDE->bytesRemaining -= pDE->transferSize;
```

```
    }

    // After the last partial transfer is done,
    // release the DMA Adapter object .
    pDE->pDmaAdapter->DmaOperations->
                FreeAdapterChannel ( pDE->pDmaAdapter );

    // Send the IRP back to the caller. Its final
    // status is the status of the last transfer
    // operation.
    pIrp->IoStatus.Status = status;
    pIrp->IoStatus.Information =
                    pDE->bytesRequested -
                          pDE->bytesRemaining;
    // Since there has been at least one I/O
    // operation, give the IRP a priority boost.
    //
    return IO_DISK_INCREMENT;
}
```

AcquireAdapterObject AND AdapterControl

These two functions work together to give a thread a synchronous mechanism for acquiring ownership of the adapter object. **AcquireAdapterObject** runs in the context of a system thread so it can stop and wait for a nonzero time interval.

```
static NTSTATUS AcquireAdapterObject(
    IN PDEVICE_EXTENSION pDE,
    IN ULONG MapRegsNeeded
    ) {
    KIRQL OldIrql;
    NTSTATUS status;

    // We must be at DISPATCH_LEVEL in order
    // to request the Adapter object
    KeRaiseIrql( DISPATCH_LEVEL, &OldIrql );

    pDE->pDmaAdapter->DmaOperations->
        AllocateAdapterChannel (
            pDE->pDmaAdapter,
            pDE->pDevice,
            MapRegsNeeded,
            AdapterControl,
            pDE );

    KeLowerIrql( OldIrql );

    // If the call failed, it's because there
    // weren't enough mapping registers.
    if( !NT_SUCCESS( status ))
        return status;
```

```
        // Stop and wait for the Adapter Control
        // routine to set the Event object. This is
        // our signal that the Adapter object is ours.
        KeWaitForSingleObject(
            &pDE->evAdapterObjectIsAcquired,
            Executive,
            KernelMode,
            FALSE,
            NULL );

    return STATUS_SUCCESS;
}

IO_ALLOCATION_ACTION AdapterControl(
    IN PDEVICE_OBJECT pDevObj,
    IN PIRP pIrp,
    IN PVOID MapRegisterBase,
    IN PVOID pContext
    )
{
    PDEVICE_EXTENSION pDE = (PDEVICE_EXTENSION)
            pContext;

    // Save the handle to the mapping
    // registers. The thread will need it
    // to set up data transfers.
    //
    pDE->mapRegisterBase = MapRegisterBase;

    // Let the thread know that its Device
    // object the Adapter object
    KeSetEvent(
        &pDE->evAdapterObjectIsAcquired,
        0,
        FALSE );

        return KeepObject;
}
```

PerformSynchronousTransfer

Running in the context of the system thread, this function performs a single data transfer operation. It doesn't return to the caller until the transfer finishes. Notably, the function uses an Event object to wait for the arrival of a device interrupt.

```
NTSTATUS PerformSynchronousTransfer(
    IN PDEVICE_OBJECT pDevObj,
    IN PIRP pIrp
    ) {
    PDEVICE_EXTENSION pDE = (PDEVICE_EXTENSION)
```

```
        pDevObj->DeviceExtension;
// Set up the system DMA controller
// attached to this device.
pDE->pDmaAdapter->DmaOperations->
    MapTransfer(
            pDE->pDmaAdapter,
            pIrp->MdlAddress,
            pDE->mapRegisterBase,
            pDE->transferVA,
            &pDE->transferSize,
            pDE->bWriteToDevice );

// Start the device
WriteControl(
    pDE,
    CTL_INTENB | CTL_DMA_GO );

// The DPC routine will set an Event
// object when the I/O operation is
// done. Stop here and wait for it.
KeWaitForSingleObject(
    &pDE->evDeviceOperationComplete,
    Executive,
    KernelMode,
    FALSE,
    NULL );

// Flush data out of the Adapater
// object cache.
pDE->pDmaAdapter->DmaOperations->
    FlushAdapterBuffers(
            pDE->pDmaAdapter,
            pIrp->MdlAddress,
            pDE->mapRegisterBase,
            pDE->transferVA,
            pDE->transferSize,
            pDE->bWriteToDevice );

// Check for device errors
if( !STS_OK( pDE->DeviceStatus ))
    return STATUS_DEVICE_DATA_ERROR;
else
    return STATUS_SUCCESS;
}
```

DpcForIsr

When the device generates an interrupt, the Interrupt Service Routine (not shown here) saves the status of the hardware and requests a DPC. Eventually, **DpcForIsr** executes and just sets an Event object into the signaled state.

PerformSynchronousTransfer (which has been waiting for this Event object) wakes up and continues processing the current IRP.

```
VOID DpcForIsr(
    IN PKDPC pDpc,
    IN PDEVICE_OBJECT pDevObj,
    IN PIRP pIrp,
    IN PVOID pContext
    )
{
    PDEVICE_EXTENSION pDE = (PDEVICE_EXTENSION)
            pContext;

    KeSetEvent(
        &pDE->evDeviceOperationComplete,
        0,
        FALSE );

    return;
}
```

Summary

This chapter presented the use of system threads within drivers to accomplish specific tasks in parallel with others. Although not all drivers should utilize a multithreaded architecture, there are several scenarios where the technique is appropriate.

The next chapter deals with layering drivers to accomplish organization and reuse of code.

Layered Drivers

CHAPTER OBJECTIVES

The ability to break a large unit of work into several smaller pieces is the cornerstone of software development. The Windows 2000 device driver model supports this necessary abstraction by allowing the work of a driver to be implemented in multiple layers. Besides simplifying the overall job of writing a driver, this allows different vendors to supply different parts of the implementation.

Indeed, the WDM driver model is based upon layering *functional* drivers on top of *physical* drivers, with optional *filter* drivers surrounding the functional layer. In most cases, a physical driver (that interacts with a standard bus) is never written. And in many cases, only a filter driver must be written to affect the desired behavior from an existing functional driver.

This chapter describes the details of layering a driver design into a hierarchy.

An Overview of Intermediate Drivers

Before moving into the intricacies of the implementation of intermediate drivers, a few definitions are in order. This section also explores some of the trade-offs inherent in using a hierarchical driver architecture.

Intermediate Drivers Defined

For the purposes of this chapter, an *intermediate driver* is any kernel-mode driver that issues I/O requests to another driver. Intermediate drivers are often not responsible for any direct, register-level manipulation of hardware resources. Instead, they depend on a lower-level device driver, such as the physical driver, to perform hardware operations. In fact, intermediate drivers can assume a wide variety of forms.

The term "intermediate driver" is so generic that it must be classified in order to provide useful information. The possible classifications depend on whether or not the driver conforms to the WDM model.

For WDM-compliant driver implementations, there are three kinds of drivers:

- Bus drivers—Provide a hardware bus interface on a per slot basis and create one or more Physical Device Objects (PDOs).
- Function drivers—Provide read, write, and other functional logic for an individual device. They create and manage one or more Functional Device Objects (FDOs)
- Filter drivers—Provide modifications to an I/O request before presentation to lower layer drivers. Filters can be placed around the functional driver or on top of a bus driver.

Note the relationship between a bus driver and a physical device object. The bus driver constructs and manages PDOs and is therefore often called a physical driver.

Outside the WDM model, driver architectures can choose to use layered approaches in other ways:

- Filter drivers—A driver can be written to transparently intercept requests intended for some other driver. This allows behavior modifications of an existing driver.
- Tightly coupled drivers—This category includes drivers that define a private interface between them. The interface does not use the I/O Manager's calling mechanism for inter-driver communication.

With the exception of tightly coupled drivers, all intermediate drivers are a form of layered drivers. Later parts of this chapter explain how to develop drivers in each of these families.

When To Use a Layered Architecture

One early and important driver design issue is whether to implement the driver as a series of layers, or whether it should be structured as a single, monolithic unit. The following section provides the trade-offs of using a layered approach.

PROS OF LAYERED ARCHITECTURE

Depending on the goals, multiple driver layers can provide a number of benefits. Using layers allows the separation of higher-level protocol issues from management of the specific underlying hardware. This makes it possible to support a wider variety of hardware without having to rewrite large amounts of code. It also promotes flexibility by allowing the same protocol driver to plug into different hardware drivers at runtime. This is the approach taken by Windows 2000 network drivers.

If several different kinds of peripherals can all be attached to the same controller (as in the case of a SCSI adapter), layering allows the decoupling of the management of the peripheral from the management of the controller. To do this, a single device driver for the controller (the *port driver*) and separate higher-level *class drivers* for each type of attached peripheral must be written. The two main benefits are that the class drivers are smaller and simpler, and (assuming a well-defined protocol) the class and port drivers can come from different vendors.

The implementation of the USB and IEEE 1394 buses is based upon a layered approach for these exact reasons.

Layering also makes it possible to hide hardware limitations from users of the device, or to add features not supported by the hardware itself. For example, if a given piece of hardware can handle transfers only of a certain size, another driver that would break oversized transfers into smaller pieces might be stacked on top. Users of the device would be unaware of the device's shortcomings.

Inserting driver layers provides a transparent way to add or remove features from a product without having to maintain multiple code bases for the same product. Fault-tolerant disks are one example of this. They are implemented as a separate driver layer that is shipped with Windows 2000 Server but not with Windows 2000 Professional.

CONS OF LAYERED ARCHITECTURE

Of course, there is a downside to the use of a layered architecture. First, I/O requests incur extra overhead because each IRP has to take a trip through the I/O Manager every time it passes from one driver to another. To some extent, this overhead can be reduced by defining a private inter-driver interface that partially bypasses the I/O Manager.

It also takes somewhat more design effort to make sure that the separate driver components fit together seamlessly. In the absence of an external standard, this can be especially painful if some of the drivers are coming from different vendors.

Since the overall functionality is no longer contained in a single driver executable, there is somewhat more bookkeeping involved in managing the drivers. This also has some impact on maintaining version compatibility between various members of a hierarchy.

Finally, installing layered drivers is slightly more involved since each must provide proper installation procedures. In addition, it is necessary to set dependency relationships among the various drivers in the hierarchy to make sure they start in the proper order.

Writing Layered Drivers

Layered drivers are the most general type of intermediate driver. They depend on a well-defined inter-driver calling mechanism provided by the I/O Manager. The following three sections explain how this mechanism works and what a driver needs to do if it wants to use another driver as a component.

How Layered Drivers Work

As shown in Figure 15.1, a layered driver may expose one or more named Device objects to which clients send I/O requests. When an IRP representing one of these requests arrives, the layered driver can proceed in two different ways.

- Send the IRP directly to a lower-level driver.
- Hold the IRP in a pending state while it allocates additional IRPs and sends them to one or more lower-level drivers.

If the layered driver needs to regain control after a lower-level driver finishes with an IRP, it can attach an I/O Completion routine to the IRP. This routine executes when the lower driver calls **IoCompleteRequest**.

Initialization and Cleanup in Layered Drivers

Like every other kernel-mode driver, a layered driver must expose a main entry point called **DriverEntry**. It must also supply a corresponding **Unload** routine. As a WDM driver, a layered driver must support **AddDevice** and **RemoveDevice**, along with other PnP request handlers as appropriate. The following sections describe what these routines must do.

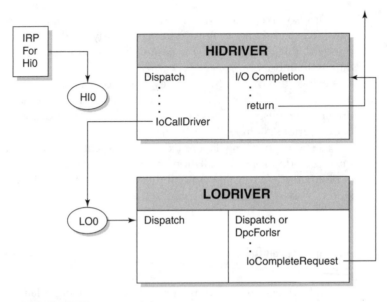

| **Figure 15.1** | *Layered driver operation.* |

DriverEntry

The initialization steps performed by a layered driver are similar to those of a regular driver. The prime difference is that a layered driver must determine which I/O requests it handles directly and which it passes through to lower-level drivers. The layered driver entry points are initialized to routines that perform the appropriate action on the various IRP requests.

AddDevice

The work performed by a layered driver is a variation of the work that any WDM driver must perform. It includes

1. Calling **IoCreateDevice** to build the upper-level device objects seen by the outside world. Like the device objects created by other drivers, the device name must be unique.

2. Calling **IoAttachDeviceToDeviceStack** to pile the layered driver's device on top of an existing stack of devices.

3. Normally, **AddDevice** saves the target Device object pointer in the Device Extension of the upper-level Device object at the time it stacks itself on top of the driver stack.

4. If the layered driver forwards incoming IRPs to the target Device object, **AddDevice** should set the layered Device object's **StackSize** field to a value one greater than the **StackSize** field of the target Device object.

This guarantees that there are enough stack slots for all the drivers in the hierarchy.

5. If the lower-level driver requires it, **AddDevice** fabricates an IRP with IRP_MJ_CREATE as its major function code and sends it to the target Device object.

6. If the Device object is exposed separately to Win32 applications, **Add-Device** calls **IoCreateSymbolicLink** to add its Win32 name to the \?? area of the Object Manager's namespace.

After these steps are performed, the layered driver can use the target Device object pointer to make calls to the lower-level driver.

RemoveDevice

When a layered driver is sent the PnP request for IRP_MN_REMOVE_DEVICE, the driver must reverse the work of **AddDevice**. Although the exact steps may vary, a layered driver's **RemoveDevice** routine generally performs the following:

1. It calls **IoDeleteSymbolicLink** to remove the upper-level Device object's Win32 name from the Object Manager's namespace.

2. If the lower-level driver requires it, an IRP with IRP_MJ_CLOSE as its major function code is fabricated and sent to the target Device object.

3. The target Device object's pointer reference count is decremented by calling **IoDetachDevice**. This effectively breaks the connection with the target Device object.

4. Finally, it destroys the upper-level Device object by calling **IoDelete-Device**.

Code Fragment: Connecting to Another Driver

The following code fragment shows how one driver might layer itself on top of another. In this example, the lower-level driver, LODRIVER, exposes a device called **LO0** and the layered driver, HIDRIVER, exposes **HI0**.

```
NTSTATUS AddDevice (
        IN PDRIVER_OBJECT pDriverObject,
        IN PDEVICE_OBJECT pdo ) {
  CUString hiDevName("\device\HI");
  PDEVICE_OBJECT pHiFdo;
  PDEVICE_EXTENSION pHiExt;

  NTSTATUS status;

  // Form the internal Device Name for the hi object
  ulHiDeviceNumber++;
  hiDevName += CUString(ulHiDeviceNumber);
```

```
// Now create the device
status =
    IoCreateDevice( pDriverObject,
                        sizeof(DEVICE_EXTENSION),
                        &(UNICODE_STRING)hiDevName,
                        FILE_DEVICE_UNKNOWN,
                        0, TRUE,
                        &pHiFdo );
if (!NT_SUCCESS(status))
    return status;

// Initialize the Device Extension
pHiExt = (PDEVICE_EXTENSION)pHiFdo->DeviceExtension;
pHiExt->pDevice = pHiFdo;      // back pointer
pHiExt->DeviceNumber = ulHiDeviceNumber;
pHiExt->ustrDeviceName = hiDevName;

// Pile this new fdo on top of the existing lower stack
pHiExt->pLowerDevice =         // downward pointer
    IoAttachDeviceToDeviceStack( pHiFdo, pdo);

// Since IRPs will be forwarded to the lower device,
//   room must be reserved within the IRP I/O Stack
//   locations for this higher Device object.
pHiFdo->StackSize = pHiExt->pLowerDevice->StackSize + 1;

// Finally, copy the characteristics of the lower device
// into the high device's "Flags" & "DeviceType" fields:
pHiFdo->Flags |=
    (pHiExt->pLowerDevice->Flags &
            (DO_BUFFERED_IO | DO_DIRECT_IO |
            POWER_INRUSH | POWER_PAGABLE ));
pHiFdo->DeviceType =
    pHiExt->pLowerDevice->DeviceType;
pHiFdo->Characteristics =
    pHiExt->pLowerDevice->Characteristics;

// Form the symbolic link name (if necessary), etc.
...
```

Other Initialization Concerns for Layered Drivers

Layered drivers operate, generically, in one of two modes: transparent or
virtual.

TRANSPARENT

Some layered drivers are intended to slip transparently between a lower-layer
driver and its clients. The layered driver would therefore need to mimic the
behavior of the lower driver, since clients are likely to be unaware of the in-

serted layer. Windows 2000 fault-tolerant disk driver is one example of a transparent layer.

To guarantee that the layered driver behaves in a transparent manner, the **DriverEntry** and **AddDevice** function needs to perform the following extra initialization:

- Within **DriverEntry**, the exact set of **MajorFunction** codes as the lower driver should be supported, either passing through IRP requests or overriding the behavior of the lower driver.
- Within **AddDevice**, copy the **DeviceType** and **Characteristics** fields from the target Device object into the layered Device object. This step is shown in the preceding code example.
- **AddDevice** should copy the DO_DIRECT_IO or DO_BUFFERED_IO bits from the target Device's **Flags** field. This ensures that the layered Device object uses the same buffering strategy as the target.

VIRTUAL OR LOGICAL DEVICE LAYER

The other possibility is that the layered driver exposes virtual or logical Device objects. It is possible to synthesize a device abstraction that bears little, if any, resemblance to the actual underlying physical implementation. For example, a named pipe object is a logical device that is far removed from the actual network hardware upon which it may be implemented.

In this case, the layered driver should choose appropriate values for the **Type** and **Characteristics** fields of the layered Device object. Also, the exact set of **MajorFunction** dispatch functions supported by the layered driver is the set appropriate to the logical Device object. Similarly, there is no requirement for the layered and target Device objects to use the same buffering strategy.

I/O Request Processing in Layered Drivers

Since layered drivers do not directly manage hardware, they do not need Start I/O, Interrupt Service, or DPC routines. Instead, most of the code in a layered driver consists of Dispatch routines and I/O Completion routines. Because they deserve extra attention, I/O Completion routines are discussed later in this chapter.

The sections below describe the operation of the layered driver's Dispatch routines. When one of these Dispatch routines receives an IRP, one of three actions can be taken: complete the IRP directly, pass down the IRP, or generate new IRP requests for lower layers. Each possibility is descried below.

COMPLETE THE ORIGINAL IRP

The simplest case is when the Dispatch routine is able to process the request all by itself and return either success or failure notification to the original caller. The Dispatch routine does the following:

1. It calls **IoGetCurrentStackLocation** to get a pointer to the driver's I/O stack slot.

2. The Dispatch routine processes the request using various fields in the IRP and the I/O stack location.

3. It puts an appropriate value in the **IoStatus.Information** field of the IRP.

4. The Dispatch routine also fills the **IoStatus.Status** field of the IRP with a suitable STATUS_XXX code.

5. Then it calls **IoCompleteRequest** with the priority-boost value of IO_NO_INCREMENT to send the IRP back to the I/O Manager.

6. As its return value, the Dispatch routine passes back the same STATUS_XXX code that it puts into the IRP.

This process is not magic. In fact, it is the same procedure any Dispatch routine follows when it wants to end the processing of a request.

PASS THE IRP TO ANOTHER DRIVER

The second possibility is that the layered driver's Dispatch routine needs to pass the IRP to the next lower driver. The Dispatch routine does the following:

1. It calls **IoGetCurrentIrpStackLocation** to get a pointer to its own I/O stack location.

2. The Dispatch routine also calls **IoGetNextIrpStackLocation** to retrieve a pointer to the I/O stack location of the next lower driver.

3. It sets up the next lower driver's I/O stack location, including the **MajorFunction** field and various members of the **Parameters** union.

4. The Dispatch routine calls **IoSetCompletionRoutine** to associate an I/O Completion routine with the IRP. At the very least, this I/O Completion routine is going to be responsible for marking the IRP as pending.

5. It sends the IRP to a lower-level driver using **IoCallDriver**. This is an asynchronous call that returns immediately regardless of whether the lower-level driver completed the IRP.

6. As its return value, the Dispatch routine passes back whatever status code is returned by **IoCallDriver**. This will be STATUS_SUCCESS, STATUS_PENDING, or some STATUS_XXX error code.

Notice that the Dispatch routine does not call **IoMarkIrpPending** to put the original IRP in the pending state before sending it to the lower driver. This is because the Dispatch routine does not know whether the IRP should be marked pending until after **IoCallDriver** returns. Unfortunately, by that time **IoCallDriver** has already pushed the I/O stack pointer in the IRP, so a call to **IoMarkIrpPending** (which always works with the current stack slot) would mark the wrong stack location. The solution is to call **IoMarkIrp-Pending** in an I/O Completion routine after the IRP stack pointer has been reset to the proper level.

ALLOCATE ADDITIONAL IRPs

Finally, the layered driver's Dispatch routine may need to allocate one or more additional IRPs, which it then sends to lower-level drivers. The Dispatch routine has the option of waiting for these additional IRPs to complete, or of issuing asynchronous requests to the lower driver. In the asynchronous case, cleanup of the additional IRPs occurs in an I/O Completion routine The technique of allocating IRPs within a driver is explained later in this chapter.

Code Fragment: Calling a Lower-Level Driver

The code fragment below shows how the Dispatch routine in one driver might forward an IRP to a lower-level driver. For purposes of the example, it also shows how the upper driver could store some context (in this case, a retry count) in an unused field of its own I/O stack location.

```
NTSTATUS DispatchRead(
                IN PDEVICE_OBJECT pDevObj,
                IN PIRP pIrp ) {
    PDEVICE_EXTENSION pDevExt = (PDEVICE_EXTENSION)
            pDevObj->DeviceExtension;

    PIO_STACK_LOCATION pThisIrpStack =
            IoGetCurrentIrpStackLocation( pIrp );

    PIO_STACK_LOCATION pNextIrpStack =
            IoGetNextIrpStackLocation( pIrp );

    // In this case, the upper driver copies the entire
    //      stack location from its slot into the stack
    //      of the next lower driver.
    // In other words - pass-thru to next lower driver
    *pNextIrpStack = *pThisIrpStack;

    // Choose a (now) unused field with the upper
    //      driver's IRP to store some context - in this
    //      case, a retry count.
    pThisIrpStack->Parameters.Read.Key =
            RETRY_COUNT_MAXIMUM_VALUE;

    // To recapture this IRP after the lower driver
    //      finishes, the upper driver attaches an
    //      I/O Completion routine: ReadCompletion.
    // Since the final 3 args of the following call are
    //      TRUE, ReadCompletion is called regardless
    //      of why the IRP completes.
```

```
IoSetCompletionRoutine(
        pIrp,
        ReadCompletion,
        NULL,
        TRUE, TRUE, TRUE );

// Now send the IRP to the lower driver.
// Return whatever the lower driver returns.
return IoCallDriver( pDevExt->pLowerDevice, pIrp );
```

Writing I/O Completion Routines

An I/O Completion routine is an I/O Manager callback that notifies a higher-level driver when the lower-level driver has finished work on an IRP. This section explains how to use I/O Completion routines in intermediate drivers.

Requesting an I/O Completion Callback

To regain control of an IRP after it has been processed by a lower-level driver, use **IoSetCompletionRoutine** (described in Table 15.1). This function puts the address of an I/O Completion routine in the IRP stack location associated with the next lower driver. When some lower-level driver calls **IoCompleteRequest**, the I/O Completion routine executes as the IRP bubbles its way back to the top of the driver hierarchy.

Except for the driver on the bottom, each driver in the hierarchy can attach its own I/O Completion routine to an IRP. This allows every level to re-

Table 15.1	*Function Prototype for IoSetCompletionRoutine*
VOID IoSetCompletionRoutine	**IRQL <= DISPATCH_LEVEL**
Parameter	**Description**
IN PIRP pIrp	Address of IRP the driver wants to track
IN PIO_COMPLETION_ROUTINE CompletionRoutine	Routine to call when a lower driver completes the IRP
IN PVOID pContext	Argument passed to I/O Completion routine
IN BOOLEAN bInvokeOnSuccess	Call routine if IRP completes successfully
IN BOOLEAN bInvokeOnError	Call routine if IRP completes with error
IN BOOLEAN bInvokeOnCancel	Call routine if IRP is canceled
Return value	- void -

ceive notification when an IRP completes. The I/O Completion routines execute in driver-stacking order, from bottom to top.

The three BOOLEAN parameters passed to **IoSetCompletionRoutine** allow the callback to be invoked based on the disposition of the IRP by the lower level. The I/O Manager uses the **IoStatus.Status** field of the IRP to decide whether to invoke the I/O Completion routine.

Execution Context

By the time an I/O Completion routine is called, the I/O Manager has already popped the I/O stack pointer, so the current stack location is the one belonging to the driver. Table 15.2 lists the arguments passed to an I/O Completion routine.

The execution context of an I/O Completion routine is the same as that of the caller of **IoCompleteRequest**. This could be either PASSIVE_LEVEL or DISPATCH_LEVEL, depending upon whether a DPC routine is used to complete the IRP. Since the design of the lower level is not likely to be under the control of the higher level, an I/O completion routine must assume the more restrictive context of DISPATCH_LEVEL IRQL.

When an I/O Completion routine is finished, it should return one of two status codes. Returning STATUS_SUCCESS allows the IRP to continue its journey back toward the original requester. Along the way, other I/O Completion routines attached to higher-level drivers execute. This is normally the appropriate return value when the IRP originated from a higher level.

To suspend further processing of the "completed" IRP, an I/O Completion routine can return STATUS_MORE_PROCESSING_REQUIRED. This value blocks the execution of any higher-level I/O Completion routines attached to the IRP. It also prevents the original caller from receiving notification that the IRP has completed. An I/O Completion routine should return this code if it either plans to send the IRP back down to a lower-level driver (as in the case of a split transfer) or if the IRP was allocated by this driver and the I/O Completion routine is going to deallocate it.

Table 15.2	*Function Prototype for an I/O Completion Routine*
NTSTATUS IoCompletion	**IRQL == PASSIVE_LEVEL or IRQL == DISPATCH_LEVEL**
Parameter	**Description**
IN PDEVICE_OBJECT pDevObj	Device object of the just completed request
IN PIRP pIrp	The IRP being completed
IN PVOID pContext	Context passed from **IoSetCompletionRoutine**
Return value	• STATUS_MORE_PROCESSING_REQUIRED • STATUS_SUCCESS

What I/O Completion Routines Do

An intermediate driver can attach an I/O Completion routine to any IRP it sends to another driver. This includes the original IRP the driver received from another caller, as well as any IRPs that the driver itself allocates. When an I/O Completion routine executes, there are three general kinds of tasks it may need to perform.

RELEASE THE ORIGINAL IRP

If the completed IRP is one that came from an outside caller, it may require some driver-specific cleanup. At the very least, the I/O Completion routine for one of these IRPs needs to do the following:

1. Test the value of the IRP's **PendingReturned** flag.
2. If this flag is TRUE, the I/O Completion routine puts the current I/O stack location into the pending state with a call to **IoMarkIrpPending**.
3. Finally, it returns a value of STATUS_SUCCESS to allow completion processing to continue.

DEALLOCATE THE IRP

If the IRP was allocated by the driver, the I/O Completion routine may be responsible for releasing it. Based on how the IRP was allocated, an appropriate deallocation technique must be employed. The next section explains the entire process.

RECYCLE THE IRP

Some intermediate drivers have to split a transfer into smaller pieces before sending it to a lower-level driver. Normally, the most efficient way to do this is to send each partial transfer to the lower driver by reusing the same IRP. To recycle an IRP, the I/O Completion routine does the following:

1. It checks the context information stored with the IRP to see if this was the last partial transfer. If the whole transfer is finished and the IRP came from an outside caller, the driver performs any necessary cleanup and returns STATUS_SUCCESS to allow further completion processing.
2. If the entire transfer is finished and the IRP is driver-allocated, the I/O Completion routine performs any necessary cleanup, frees the IRP, and returns STATUS_MORE_PROCESSING_REQUIRED to prevent any further completion processing.
3. If there is more work to be done, the I/O Completion routine calls **IoGetNextIrpStackLocation** and sets up the I/O stack slot for the next lower driver.

4. It uses **IoSetCompletionRoutine** to attach the address of this I/O Completion routine to the IRP.

5. It passes the IRP to the target Device object using **IoCallDriver**.

6. Finally, it returns STATUS_MORE_PROCESSING_REQUIRED to prevent any further completion processing of this IRP.

During each partial transfer, an intermediate driver must maintain the current transfer count. One clever way to maintain this context information is to store it in unused fields of the intermediate driver's I/O stack location. For example, the **Parameters.ByteOffset** and **Parameters.Key** fields of the IRP stack area are often unused fields for a higher-level driver. Three DWORDs of context data can be maintained within these fields.

Otherwise, the straightforward technique of allocating a private block from pooled memory that is passed as a context argument to the I/O Completion routine can always be used.

Code Fragment: An I/O Completion Routine

Listed below is a fragment of an I/O Completion routine. It complements the **DispatchRead** function presented in the last section. If the request completes normally, the IRP is sent back to the original caller. If something fails at a lower level, it retries the operation a fixed number of times.

```
NTSTATUS ReadCompletion(
            IN PDEVICE_OBJECT pDevObj,
            IN PIRP pIrp,
            IN PVOID pContext ) {
   PDEVICE_EXTENSION pDevExt = (PDEVICE_EXTENSION)
        pDevObj->DeviceExtension;

   PIO_STACK_LOCATION pThisIrpStack =
        IoGetCurrentIrpStackLocation( pIrp );

   PIO_STACK_LOCATION pNextIrpStack =
        IoGetNextIrpStackLocation( pIrp );

   // Set up a reference variable for the retryCount.
   // The variable uses the Parameters.Read.Key field.
   DWORD &retryCount =
      pThisIrpStack->Parameters.Read.Key;

   // If the lower level finshed successfully,
   //     or if we have exceeded our retry count,
   //     return normally.
   if ((NT_SUCCESS( pIrp->IoStatus.Status )) ||
      ( retryCount == 0 )) {
         // If the lower level requested that the
```

```
                    //    IRP be marked "pending", make it so.
                    if ( pIrp->bPendingReturned )
                        IoMarkIrpPending( pIrp );
                    return STATUS_SUCCESS;
        }

        // The lower level reported a failure, but we still
        //      have the patience to try again (for a while)
        retryCount--;       // patience counter

        // Copy down the stack (again)
        *pNextIrpStack = *pThisIrpStack;
        // Don't confuse lower level with our retry count
        *pNextIrpStack->Parameters.Read.Key = 0;

        // The I/O Completion routine must be reset each
        //      time the IRP is recyled.
        IoSetCompletionRoutine(
                    pIrp,
                    ReadCompletion,
                    NULL,
                    TRUE, TRUE, TRUE );

        // Send the IRP back to the lower level
        IoCallDriver( pDevExt->LowerDevice, pIrp );

        // Indicate to the I/O Manager that we're still
        //      working on the request.
        return STATUS_MORE_PROCESSING_REQUIRED;
}
```

Allocating Additional IRPs

There are some situations where an intermediate driver needs to allocate additional IRPs to send to another driver. For example, the initialization code in one driver might want to query the capabilities of a lower-level driver by issuing an IOCTL request. An example filter driver that implements this strategy is listed later in this chapter.

As another example, a fault-tolerant disk driver, implemented as an intermediate driver, might allocate an additional IRP to send to a second (mirror) driver. This second IRP would mirror the original request.

Yet a third example occurs when a higher-level driver exposes an abstract command to a client. The command itself is implemented through a series of lower-level calls, each requiring the allocation of a new IRP. The SCSI class driver implements this strategy when relying upon the lower-level SCSI port driver.

The IRP's I/O Stack Revisited

Before explaining the available IRP allocation techniques, it is important to have a clear understanding of the IRP stack operation. As already described, each driver that receives an IRP is supplied a unique IRP stack location that is easily obtained with a call to **IoGetCurrentIrpStackLocation**.

If an intermediate driver plans to pass an incoming IRP to a lower-level driver, it has to set up the I/O stack location for the next lower driver. To obtain a pointer to the lower driver's I/O stack slot, the intermediate driver uses **IoGetNextIrpStackLocation**. After setting up the lower stack slot (perhaps by copying the current slot into the next slot), the intermediate driver uses **Io-CallDriver** to pass the IRP down. This function, **IoCallDriver**, automatically pushes the I/O stack pointer so that when the lower driver calls **IoGet-CurrentIrpStackLocation**, it will get the right address (i.e., one lower than its caller).

When the lower driver calls **IoCompleteRequest**, the completed IRP's I/O stack is popped. This allows an I/O Completion routine belonging to the higher driver to call **IoGetCurrentIrpStackLocation** if it needs to access its own stack location. As the IRP bubbles its way back up to the original caller, the I/O stack is automatically popped again for each driver in the hierarchy. Table 15.3 summarizes the effects of these functions on an IRP's I/O stack pointer.

To maintain consistent behavior with driver-allocated IRPs, the I/O Manager initializes the new IRP's I/O stack pointer so that it points to a nonexistent slot one location before the beginning of the stack. This ensures that when the driver passes the IRP to a lower-level driver, **IoCallDriver**'s "push" operation sets the stack pointer to the first real slot in the stack. Thus, the higher-level driver must call **IoGetNextIrpStackLocation** to retrieve a pointer to the I/O stack slot intended for the target driver.

Table 15.3	*Effect of Functions on IRP's I/O Stack Pointer*

Working with the IRP Stack Pointer	
Function	**Effect on the IRP stack pointer**
IoGetCurrentIrpStackLocation	No change
IoGetNextIrpStackLocation	No change
IoSetNextIrpStackLocation	Pushes stack pointer by one location
IoCallDriver	Pushes stack pointer by one location
IoCompleteRequest	Pops stack pointer by one location

Controlling the Size of the IRP Stack

When a driver receives an IRP from an outside caller, the number of I/O stack slots is determined by the **StackSize** field of the driver's Device object. If the intermediate driver plans to pass incoming IRPs to a lower-level driver, it needs to increment this field to one more than the number of slots reserved by all lower drivers. That is, it must set the Device object's **StackSize** field to the value of the lower Device object's **StackSize** field plus one. This ensures that there are enough stack slots for all drivers within the hierarchy. Of course, the technique requires that drivers pile on top of each other, with the lower driver initialized prior to the higher driver.

The value of **StackSize** in a Device object represents the number of stack slots needed by all lower drivers, including one slot for itself. That is, it represents the maximum call depth *beneath* the current level plus one.

The I/O Manager constructs IRPs upon request of a driver when any of the following calls are made:

- IoBuildAsynchronousFsdRequest
- IoBuildDeviceIoControlRequest
- IoBuildSynchronousFsdRequest

The IRP constructed contains the number of stack slots specified in the *target* (where the IRP is being sent) Device object's **StackSize** field. The target Device object is passed as an argument to the three functions listed. These IRPs therefore contain sufficient stack slots for all calls to lower drivers, but *do not* contain a slot for the intermediate driver itself.

If an intermediate driver uses **IoAllocateIrp** or **ExAllocatePool** to create an IRP, the driver must explicitly specify the number of I/O stack slots in the new IRP. Of course, the common practice is to use the **StackSize** field of the target Device object to determine the proper number of slots.

Ordinarily, an intermediate driver does not need a stack slot for itself in the IRP it allocates. The exception occurs if the intermediate driver chooses to associate some per-request context within the IRP. In such a case, the driver allocates an IRP with one extra stack slot for itself, which is then used to hold private context data. The following code fragment shows how this technique is implemented:

```
pNewIrp = IoAllocateIrp( pLowerDevice->StackSize + 1 );

// Bearing in mind that a new IRP is allocated with
//    the stack pointer just before the beginning...
// Push the I/O stack pointer so that it points to
//    the first valid slot. Use this slot to hold
//    context information needed by the upper driver.
IoSetNextIrpStackLocation( pNewIrp );
pContextArea = IoGetCurrentIrpStackLocation( pNewIrp );
pNextDriverSlot = IoGetNextIrpStackLocation( pNewIrp );
```

```
// Set up the next driver's I/O stack slot:
pNextDriverSlot->MajorFunction = IRP_MJ_XXX;
...

// Attach an I/O Completion routine:
IoSetCompletionRoutine(
        pNewIrp,
        IoCompletion,
        NULL,
        TRUE, TRUE, TRUE );

// Send the IRP to someone else:
IoCallDriver( pLowerDevice, pNewIrp );
```

Creating IRPs with IoBuildSynchronousFsdRequest

The I/O Manager provides three convenience functions that simplify the process of building IRPs for standard kinds of I/O requests. The first one is **IoBuildSynchronousFsdRequest**, and it fabricates read, write, flush, or shutdown IRPs. See Table 15.4 for a description of this function.

The number of I/O stack locations in IRPs created with this function is equal to the **StackSize** field of the TargetDevice argument. There is no straightforward way to leave room in the I/O stack for the intermediate driver itself.

The Buffer, Length, and StartingOffset arguments to this function are required for read and write operations. They must be NULL (or 0) for flush or shutdown operations.

IoBuildSynchronousFsdRequest automatically sets up various fields in the **Parameters** area of the next lower I/O stack location, so there is rarely any need to touch the I/O stack. For read or write requests, this function also allocates system buffer space or builds an MDL, depending on whether the TargetDevice does Buffered or Direct I/O. For buffered outputs, it also copies the contents of the caller's buffer into the system buffer; at the end of a buffer input, data is automatically copied from the system buffer back to the caller's buffer.

As the function name suggests, **IoBuildSynchronousFsdRequest** operates synchronously. In other words, the thread that calls **IoCallDriver** normally blocks itself until the I/O operation completes. To conveniently perform the block, pass the address of an initialized Event object in the IRP that is allocated. Then, after sending the IRP to a lower-level driver with **IoCallDriver**, use **KeWaitForSingleObject** to wait for the Event object. When a lower-level driver completes the IRP, the I/O Manager puts this Event object into the signaled state, which awakens the intermediate driver. The I/O status block signifies whether everything worked.

Drivers that perform blocking I/O can degrade system performance because they prevent the calling thread from overlapping its I/O operations.

Table 15.4	Function Prototype for IoBuildSynchronousFsdRequest
PIRP **IoBuildSynchronousFsdRequest**	**IRQL == PASSIVE_LEVEL**
Parameter	**Description**
IN ULONG MajorFunction	One of the following: • IRP_MJ_READ • IRP_MJ_WRITE • IRP_MJ_FLUSH_BUFFERS • IRP_MJ_SHUTDOWN
IN PDEVICE_OBJECT pTargetDevice	Device object where IRP is sent
IN OUT PVOID pBuffer	Address of I/O buffer
IN ULONG Length	Length of buffer in bytes
IN PLARGE_INTEGER startingOffset	Device offset where I/O begins
IN PKEVENT pEvent	Event object used to signal I/O completion
OUT PIO_STATUS_BLOCK Iosb	Receives final status of I/O operation
Return value	• Non-NULL: address of new IRP • NULL: IRP could not be allocated

This is contrary to the philosophy of the Windows 2000 I/O architecture, so it should not be used without good reason.

Also, the Event object used to wait for I/O completion needs to be synchronized properly among multiple threads. Consider the case where two threads in the same process issue a read request using the same handle. The **DispatchRead** routine executes in the context of the first thread and blocks itself waiting for the Event object. Then, this same **DispatchRead** routine executes in the context of the other thread and reuses the same Event object to issue a second request. When the IRP for either request completes, the Event object signals. Both threads awaken, and neither thread knows which IRP really completed. One solution is to guard the Event object with a Fast Mutex. Perhaps a better solution is to allocate a new Event object with each IRP fabricated.

The I/O Manager automatically cleans up and deallocates IRPs created with **IoBuildSynchronousFsdRequest** after their completion processing is done. This includes releasing any system buffer space or MDL attached to the IRP. To trigger this cleanup, a lower-level driver simply has to call **IoCompleteRequest**.

Normally, there is no need to attach an I/O Completion routine to one of these IRPs unless some driver-specific postprocessing is needed. If an I/O Completion routine is attached, it should return STATUS_SUCCESS. This lets the I/O Manager free the IRP.

Creating IRPs with IoBuildAsynchronousFsdRequest

The second convenience function, **IoBuildAsynchronousFsdRequest**, is quite similar to the synchronous version. It builds read, write, flush, or shutdown requests without regard to many details. The main difference is that the IRPs fabricated by this call process asynchronously. There is no option to stop and wait for the I/O to complete. Table 15.5 contains the prototype for this function.

As with **IoBuildSynchronousFsdRequest**, the Buffer, Length, and StartingOffset parameters to **IoBuildAsynchronousFsdRequest** are required for read and write operations. They must be NULL (or 0) for flush or shutdown operations.

Notice that **IoBuildAsynchronousFsdRequest** can be called at or below DISPATCH_LEVEL IRQL. The synchronous version can be called only from PASSIVE_LEVEL.

Unlike the IRPs fabricated from the synchronous version, the ones from this function are not released automatically when a lower-level driver completes them. Instead, an I/O Completion routine *must* be attached to any IRP created with **IoBuildAsynchronousFsdRequest**. The I/O Completion routine calls **IoFreeIrp**, which releases the system buffer or MDL associated with the IRP and then deallocates the IRP itself. The return value of the I/O Completion routine should be STATUS_MORE_PROCESSING_REQUIRED.

Table 15.5	*Function Prototype for IoBuildAsynchronousFsdRequest*
PIRP **IoBuildAsynchronousFsdRequest**	**IRQL <= DISPATCH_LEVEL**
Parameter	**Description**
IN ULONG MajorFunction	One of the following: • IRP_MJ_READ • IRP_MJ_WRITE • IRP_MJ_FLUSH_BUFFERS • IRP_MJ_SHUTDOWN
IN PDEVICE_OBJECT pTargetDevice	Device object where IRP is sent
IN OUT PVOID pBuffer	Address of I/O buffer
IN ULONG Length	Length of buffer in bytes
IN PLARGE_INTEGER startingOffset	Device offset where I/O begins
OUT PIO_STATUS_BLOCK Iosb	Receives final status of I/O operation
Return value	• Non-NULL: address of new IRP • NULL: IRP could not be allocated

Creating IRPs with IoBuildDeviceIoControlRequest

The last convenience function, **IoBuildDeviceIoControlRequest** (described in Table 15.6) simplifies the task of building IOCTL IRPs. This is useful because it is fairly common for drivers to expose odd behavior through custom IOCTLs.

The InternalDeviceIoControl argument specifies the major function code in the target driver's I/O stack slot. FALSE produces an IRP with IRP_MJ_DEVICE_CONTROL, while TRUE causes it to be sent to IRP_MJ_INTERNAL_DEVICE_CONTROL.

Also, notice that either synchronous or asynchronous calls can be performed with IRPs returned by this function. To perform synchronous I/O control operations, simply pass the address of an initialized Event object when the IRP is allocated. Then, after sending the IRP to a lower-level driver with **IoCallDriver**, use **KeWaitForSingleObject** to wait for the Event object. When a lower-level driver completes the IRP, the I/O Manager puts this Event object into the Signaled state, which awakens the intermediate driver. The I/O status block reports the ultimate disposition of the IRP. As with **IoBuildSynchronousFsdRequest**, care must be taken when the Event object is used among multiple threads.

The I/O Manager automatically cleans up and deallocates IRPs created with **IoBuildDeviceIoControlRequest** after their completion processing is

Table 15.6	*Function Prototype for IoBuildDeviceIoControlRequest*
PIRP **IoBuildDeviceIoControlRequest**	**IRQL == PASSIVE_LEVEL**
Parameter	**Description**
IN ULONG IoControlCode	IOCTL code recognized by target device
IN PDEVICE_OBJECT pTargetDevice	Device object where IRP is sent
IN PVOID inputBuffer	Buffer passed to lower driver
IN ULONG inputLength	Length of input buffer in bytes
OUT PVOID outputBuffer	Buffer returned by lower driver
IN ULONG outputLength	Length of output buffer in bytes
IN BOOLEAN InternalDeviceIoControl	TRUE-Internal request FALSE-External request
IN PKEVENT pEvent	Event object used to signal I/O completion
OUT PIO_STATUS_BLOCK Iosb	Receives final status of I/O operation
Return value	• Non-NULL: address of new IRP • NULL: IRP could not be allocated

done. This includes releasing any system buffer space or MDL attached to the IRP. To trigger this cleanup, a lower-level driver simply has to call **Io-CompleteRequest**.

Normally, there is no need to attach an I/O Completion routine to one of these IRPs unless some driver-specific postprocessing is needed. If an I/O Completion routine must be used, it should return STATUS_SUCCESS when it is done. This lets the I/O Manager free the IRP.

The one idiosyncrasy with this function is the way it handles the buffering method bits embedded in the IOCTL code. If an IOCTL code contains METHOD_BUFFERED, **IoBuildDeviceIoControlRequest** allocates a nonpaged pool buffer and copies the contents of the InputBuffer. When the IRP completes, the contents of the nonpaged pool buffer are automatically copied to OutputBuffer. As just described, it behaves exactly like a Win32 **DeviceIoControl** call coming from a user-mode application.

But if an IOCTL code containing a Direct I/O method is specified, an interesting result occurs: **IoBuildDeviceIoControl** *always* builds an MDL for the output buffer address and *always* uses a nonpaged pool buffer for the Input Buffer address, regardless of whether the IOCTL code specifies METHOD_IN_DIRECT or METHOD_OUT_DIRECT.

Creating IRPs from Scratch

The I/O Manager routines just described are the most convenient way to work with driver-allocated IRPs. Occasionally, however, they may not be the appropriate vehicle for IRP allocation. For example, when issuing a request other than for read, write, flush, shutdown, or device I/O control, these functions do not help. The only option is to allocate a blank IRP and set it up manually. The following sections describe several ways to do this.

IRPs FROM IoAllocateIrp

The **IoAllocateIrp** function allocates an IRP from an I/O Manager zone buffer and performs certain basic kinds of initialization. A driver must fill the I/O stack location for the target driver and set up whatever kind of buffer the target driver is expecting to find. The following code fragment illustrates the use of this function.

```
PMDL pNewMdl;
PIRP pIrp;
PIO_STACK_LOCATION pNextIrpStack;

// Allocate the new IRP with enough stack locations to
//    hold the requirements of the drivers beneath us
pNewIrp = IoAllocateIrp( pLowerDevice->StackSize );

// Allocate the memory descriptor list for any driver
//    doing DMA beneath us
```

```
pNewMdl = IoAllocateMdl(
                MmGetMdlVirtualAddress(
                    pOriginalIrp->MdlAddress ),
                MAX_TRANSFER_SIZE,
                FALSE,     // Primary buffer
                FALSE,     // No quota charge
                pNewIrp );

IoBuildPartialMdl(
    pOriginalIrp->MdlAddress,
    pNewMdl,
    MmGetMdlVirtualAddress( pOriginalIrp->MdlAddress ),
    MAX_TRANSFER_SIZE );

// Place a request into the new IRP (in this case, Read)
//   The lower driver is being asked to perform a Read.
pNextIrpStack = IoGetNextIrpStackLocation( pNewIrp );

pNextIrpStack->MajorFunction = IRP_MJ_READ;

// Set any parameters appropriate for a Read request
pNextIrpStack->Parameters.Read.Length =
        MAX_TRANSFER_SIZE;

// Ensure that the lower driver knows what thread made
//   the original request (in case an error must be
//   reported - see text below)
pNewIrp->Tail.Overlay.Thread =
    pOriginalIrp->Tail.Overlay.Thread;

IoSetCompletionRoutine(
    pNewIrp,
    IoCompletion,
    NULL,
    TRUE, TRUE, TRUE );

// Finally, pass the new IRP request down:
IoCallDriver( pLowerDevice, pNewIrp );
```

If the new IRP is targeted at a disk device, or a device with removable media, the intermediate driver needs to provide information about the thread making the original request. This provides the lower-level driver with a target for any pop-up dialog box reporting a potential error using **IoSetHardError-OrVerifyDevice**. This thread information is contained in the original IRP's **Tail.Overlay.Thread** field and should be copied directly into the new IRP.

An intermediate driver is responsible for releasing any IRP created with **IoAllocateIrp**. It must also release other resources (MDLs or system buffers, for example) associated with the IRP. Normally, this cleanup occurs in the IRP's I/O Completion routine. The following code fragment provides an example.

```
NTSTATUS IoCompletion(
            IN PDEVICE_OBJECT pDevObj,
            IN PIRP pIrp,
            IN PVOID pContext ) {
    ...
    IoFreeMdl( pIrp->MdlAddress );
    IoFreeIrp( pIrp );

    return STATUS_MORE_PROCESSING_REQUIRED;
}
```

IRPs FROM ExAllocatePool

IRPs can also be allocated directly from a nonpaged pool using **ExAllocatePool**. The generic memory allocated must be initialized into an IRP using **IoInitializeIrp**. Setting up the I/O stack location, transfer buffers, and an MDL for DMA operations remain the responsibility of the driver.

The following is an example of a manually allocated IRP using **ExAllocatePool**. The lower Device object expects a nonpaged pool buffer rather than an MDL.

```
pNewIrp = ExAllocatePool(
            NonPagedPool,
            IoSizeOfIrp( pLowerDevice->StackSize ));

IoInitializeIrp(
    pNewIrp,
    IoSizeOfIrp( pLowerDevice->StackSize ),
    pLowerDevice->StackSize );

pNextIrpStack = IoGetNextIrpStackLocation( pNewIrp );

// Assuming a Read operation, set it up
pNextIrpStack->Parameters.Read.Length = BUFFER_SIZE;

// Instead of an MDL, use a custom buffer
pNewIrp->AssociatedIrp.SystemBuffer =
    ExAllocatePool( NonPagedPool, BUFFER_SIZE );

// As before, copy thread info of original caller
pNewIrp->Tail.Overlay.Thread =
    pOriginalIrp->Tail.Overlay.Thread;

IoSetCompletionRoutine(
    pNewIrp,
    IoCompletion,
    NULL,
    TRUE, TRUE, TRUE );
```

```
// Tell the fabricated IRP to "come on down"
IoCallDriver( pLowerDevice, pNewIrp );
```

Again, it is the job of the I/O Completion routine attached to the new IRP to perform cleanup and release the IRP. The following code fragment demonstrates.

```
NTSTATUS IoCompletion(
        IN PDEVICE_OBJECT pDevObj,
        IN PIRP pIrp,
        IN PVOID pContext ) {
    ...
    // Free the custom buffer used by the lower driver
    ExFreePool( pIrp->AssociatedIrp.SystemBuffer );

    // Free the manually allocated IRP
    IoFreeIrp( pIrp );

    return STATUS_MORE_PROCESSING_REQUIRED;
}
```

Notice that **IoFreeIrp** is used to free the IRP, even though it was allocated with **ExAllocatePool**. This is because the field in the IRP tells the I/O Manager whether this IRP came directly from the pool or whether it came from the I/O Manager's private zone buffer.

IRPs FROM DRIVER-MANAGED MEMORY

Finally, there are situations where a driver design chooses to maintain a private collection of IRPs allocated within a driver-specific zone buffer or a lookaside list. Such IRPs still need to be initialized using **IoInitalizeIrp**. However, since the I/O Manager knows nothing about the driver's memory management strategy for these IRPs, the **IoFreeIrp** function cannot be used. Instead, the I/O Completion routine needs to call whatever internal driver function is responsible for releasing the IRP.

Setting Up Buffers for Lower Drivers

The previous examples of the manually allocated IRPs demonstrate the need to initialize and clean up any buffers needed by those I/O requests. The actual technique utilized depends on whether the target Device object performs buffered or direct I/O.

BUFFERED I/O REQUESTS

In this case, the Dispatch routine in the intermediate driver has to call **ExAllocatePool** to allocate the buffer. It stores the address of this buffer in the **AssociatedIrp.SystemBuffer** field of the driver-allocated IRP. Later, an I/O

Completion routine attached to the IRP must release the buffer with a call to **ExFreePool**.

DIRECT I/O REQUESTS

Handling these requests means the intermediate driver must set up an MDL describing the I/O buffer. The intermediate driver's Dispatch routine performs the following:

1. It calls **IoAllocateMdl** to create an MDL large enough to map the buffer. It stores the address of this MDL in the **MdlAddress** field of the driver-allocated IRP.

2. The Dispatch routine fills the MDL. To map a portion of the buffer associated with the original caller's IRP, it calls **IoBuildPartialMdl**. To map system memory into the MDL, it uses **MmBuildMdlForNonPagedPool**.

3. It then attaches an I/O Completion routine to the driver-allocated IRP using **IoSetCompletionRoutine**.

4. Finally, the Dispatch routine sends the IRP to a lower-level driver with **IoCallDriver**.

When the lower-level driver completes the IRP, the intermediate driver's I/O Completion routine uses **IoFreeMdl** to release the MDL.

Keeping Track of Driver-Allocated IRPs

Intermediate drivers must be careful about the handling of incoming I/O requests that result in multiple IRPs being sent in parallel to lower drivers. In particular, it is vital for the original incoming IRP *not* to be completed until all the allocated IRPs have finished their work. Exactly how the intermediate driver does this depends on whether it performs synchronous or asynchronous I/O with the driver-allocated IRPs.

SYNCHRONOUS I/O

This is the simpler of the two cases since the intermediate driver's Dispatch routine just has to stop and wait until all the allocated IRPs have been completed. In general, the Dispatch routine does the following:

1. It calls **IoBuildSynchronousFsdRequest** to create some number of driver-allocated IRPs.

2. Next, the Dispatch routine calls **IoCallDriver** to pass all the driver-allocated IRPs to other drivers.

3. It then calls **KeWaitForMultipleObjects** and freezes until all the allocated IRPs have completed.

4. Finally, it calls **IoCompleteRequest** with the original IRP to send back to the caller.

Notice that since the original request is blocked inside the Dispatch routine itself, there is no need to mark the original IRP as pending.

ASYNCHRONOUS I/O

This is the more complex case because there is no central point of control where the driver can stop and wait for everything to finish. Instead, the intermediate driver must attach I/O Completion routines to each driver-allocated IRP, and the completion routine must decide whether it is time to complete the original caller's IRP.

The following steps are typical of work that is done in the Dispatch routine of intermediate drivers using Asynchronous I/O requests to lower drivers.

1. It puts the original caller's IRP in the pending state by calling **IoMarkPending**.

2. Next, the Dispatch routine uses one of the methods described in the previous section to allocate additional IRPs.

3. It attaches an I/O Completion routine to each of these IRPs with **IoSetCompletionRoutine**. When it makes this call, the Dispatch routine passes a pointer to the original caller's IRP as the pContext argument.

4. The Dispatch routine stores a count of outstanding allocated IRPs in an unused field of the original IRP. The **Key** field in the current I/O stack locations **Parameters** union is one possible context.

5. Next, it uses **IoCallDriver** to pass all the IRPs to other drivers.

6. Finally, the Dispatch routine passes back STATUS_PENDING as its return value. This is necessary because the original IRP is not yet ready for completion processing.

As each of the lower drivers complete each of their IRPs, the intermediate driver's I/O Completion routine executes. This routine does the following:

1. First, it performs whatever cleanup is necessary and deletes the driver-allocated IRP.

2. The I/O Completion routine calls **ExInterlockedDecrementLong** to decrement the count of outstanding IRPs contained in the original caller's IRP. A pointer to this original IRP is passed as its pContext argument.

3. If the count equals zero, then this indicates that the last outstanding driver-allocated IRP has completed. In this case, the I/O Completion routine completes the original IRP by calling **IoCompleteRequest**.

4. Finally, it returns STATUS_MORE_PROCESSING_REQUIRED to prevent any further completion processing of the driver-allocated IRP (which incidentally has just been deleted).

Writing Filter Drivers

A filter driver is a special type of intermediate driver. Filter drivers perform their work surreptitiously. They sit on top of some other driver and intercept requests directed at the lower driver's Device objects. Users of the lower driver are completely unaware that their requests are being preprocessed or intercepted by the filter driver. Some examples of the use of filter drivers include the following:

- Filters allow modification of some aspect of an existing driver's behavior without rewriting the entire driver. SCSI filter drivers work this way.
- Filters make it easier to hide the limitations of lower-level device drivers. For example, a filter could split large transfers into smaller pieces before passing them on to a driver with transfer size limits.
- Filters allow the addition of new features like compression or encryption to a device without modifying the underlying device driver or the programs that use the device.
- Filters allow the addition or removal of expensive behavior (like performance monitoring) a driver may not perform at all times. The disk performance monitoring tools in Windows 2000 work this way.

The remainder of this section explains how to write filter drivers. Bear in mind that driver-allocated IRPs and I/O Completion routines work the same in a filter driver as they do in a regular layered driver.

How Filter Drivers Work

The main distinction between filter drivers and other layered drivers is in the Device objects they create. Whereas a layered driver exposes Device objects with their own unique names, filter drivers' Device objects have no names at all. Filter drivers work by attaching one of these nameless Device objects to a Device object created by some lower-level driver. Figure 15.2 illustrates this relationship.

In the diagram, **FLTDRIVER** has attached a filter Device object to **FD0**, one of **FDODRIVER**'s Device objects. Any IRPs sent to **FD0** are automatically rerouted to the Dispatch routines in **FLTDRIVER**. It works as follows:

1. The **AddDevice** routine in the filter driver creates an invisible Device object and attaches it to a named Device object belonging to a driver beneath it.

2. A client of the lower-level driver opens a connection to **FD0**. This is typically done using the Win32 **CreateFile** method to obtain a handle, or a kernel-mode client can use **IoGetDeviceObjectPointer**. Regardless, the I/O Manager actually opens a connection between the client and the filter driver's invisible Device object.

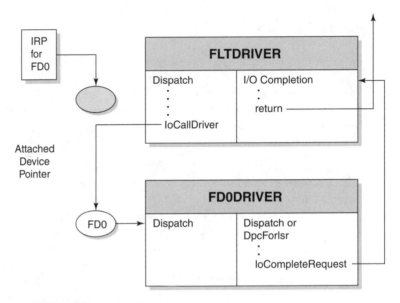

Figure 15.2   *Filter driver operation.*

3. When the client sends an I/O request to **FD0**, the I/O Manager sends it to the filter driver's unnamed Device object instead. The I/O Manager uses the **MajorFunction** table of the filter's Driver object to select an appropriate Dispatch routine.

4. The Dispatch routines in the filter driver either process the IRP on their own and complete immediately, or they send the IRP down to **FD0** with **IoCallDriver**. If the filter driver needs to regain control of the IRP when a lower-level driver completes it, the filter can associate an I/O Completion routine with the IRP.

Filters can also be layered above other filters. Attaching a new filter to an already filtered Device object results in the new filter simply getting layered on top of the highest existing filter. Essentially, any number of filter layers can exist for a single Device object.

Initialization and Cleanup in Filter Drivers

Like every other kernel-mode driver, a filter driver must have a main entry point called **DriverEntry**. Like other WDM drivers, it must export an **Add-Device**, **RemoveDevice**, and **Unload** routine. The following sections describe what these routines must do.

AddDevice ROUTINE

The initialization sequence in a filter driver for the PnP request to add a device is straightforward.

1. The filter calls **IoCreateDevice** to create a filter Device object for this target device. The filter Device object has no internal name, nor does it have a symbolic link name.

2. It calls **IoAttachDeviceToDeviceStack** (as usual) to stack itself on top of the lower driver and obtain a pointer to the target Device object.

3. It stores the address of the target device object in the Device Extension of the filter Device object. Other parts of the filter driver use this pointer to call the target driver.

4. Next, **AddDevice** copies the **DeviceType** and **Characteristics** fields from the target Device object to the filter Device object. It also copies the DO_DIRECT_IO, DO_BUFFERED_IO, DO_POWER_INRUSH, and DO_POWER_PAGABLE bits from the target Device object's **Flags** field. This guarantees that the filter looks the same and has the same buffering strategy as the target driver.

RemoveDevice ROUTINE

A filter driver's **RemoveDevice** routine must disconnect the filter and target Device objects. It does this by calling **IoDetachDevice** and passing a pointer to the target Device object. Once the filter Device object has been detached, the **RemoveDevice** routine calls **IoDeleteDevice** to delete the unnamed object.

Making the Attachment Transparent

Once a filter has attached itself to the target driver, any I/O requests sent to the target must pass through the Dispatch routines of the filter driver first. If the **MajorFunction** table of the filter Driver object does not support the same set of IRP_MJ_XXX codes as the target driver, clients of the target may experience problems when the filter is attached. Specifically, some types of requests that work without the filter are rejected as illegal operations when the filter is in place.

To avoid this inconsistency, the filter driver's **MajorFunction** table must contain a Dispatch routine for every IRP_MJ_XXX function supported by the target driver. Even if the filter is not interested in modifying a particular **MajorFunction** code, it still must supply the Dispatch routine that simply passes the IRP on to the target driver.

The most straightforward way for the filter driver to avoid the inconsistency problem is to provide a pass-through Dispatch routine for every slot within the **MajorFunction** table of the filter Driver object. For each **Major-Function** entry that the filter wishes to override, a non-pass-through function is provided. The sample driver in the next section demonstrates this technique.

Code Example: A Filter Driver

This example demonstrates a basic filter driver, called the HIFILTER, that intercepts all requests intended for a lower-level driver (LODRIVER). The purpose of the filter is to hide the lower driver's limited output transfer size. To do this, it breaks large transfer requests into smaller pieces. It also overrides an IOCTL from the lower driver that returns the maximum size of an output buffer. All other major function codes supported by the lower driver are passed through from the filter.

The code for this example is included on the accompanying disk and at the book's Web site: *www.W2KDriverBook.com.*

The DEVICE_EXTENSION Structure

The declarations of the Device Extension for the filter driver are minimal; the filter driver has few direct responsibilities.

```
    // BUFFER_SIZE_INFO is a driver-defined structure
    // that describes the buffers used by the filter
typedef struct _BUFFER_SIZE_INFO
{
    ULONG MaxWriteLength;
    ULONG MaxReadLength;
} BUFFER_SIZE_INFO, *PBUFFER_SIZE_INFO;

typedef struct _DEVICE_EXTENSION {
    PDEVICE_OBJECT pDeviceObject;    // Back pointer

    PDEVICE_OBJECT pTargetDevice;    // Lower device

    BUFFER_SIZE_INFO bufferInfo;
} DEVICE_EXTENSION, *PDEVICE_EXTENSION;
```

The DriverEntry Function

The **DriverEntry** function for a filter is unique in that its Dispatch routine announcement must closely follow the functionality exposed by the lower driver. If the lower driver supports a Dispatch entry, the filter must expose it as well. For those entries that the filter is modifying (overriding), the filter installs its own Dispatch function address. For entries that the filter does not override, a pass-through dispatch function is installed.

```
NTSTATUS DriverEntry(
        IN PDRIVER_OBJECT pDrvObj,
        IN PUNICODE_STRING pRegPath ) {
    // Export other driver entry points
    pDrvObj->DriverUnload = DriverUnload;
    pDrvObj->DriverExtension->AddDevice = AddDevice;

    // Assume (initially) nothing is overridden
```

```
for (int i=0; i<=IRP MJ MAXIMUM_FUNCTION; i++)
    if (i!=IRP MJ POWER)
        pDriverObject->MajorFunction[i] = DispatchPassThru;

// Export the overridden MajorFunctions
pDrvObj->MajorFunction[ IRP_MJ_WRITE ] =
        OverriddenDispatchWrite;
pDrvObj->MajorFunction[ IRP_MJ_DEVICE_CONTROL ] =
        OverriddenDispatchIoControl;
:
return STATUS_SUCCESS;
}
```

The AddDevice Function

This portion of the example shows the code executed each time a filter device attaches to the target device.

```
NTSTATUS AddDevice( IN PDRIVER_OBJECT pDrvObj,
                    IN PDEVICE_OBJECT pdo ) {
    NTSTATUS status;
    PDEVICE_OBJECT pFilterDevObj;
    PDEVICE_EXTENSION pDevExt;

    // Create the un-named filter device
    status =
        IoCreateDevice( pDrvObj,
                        sizeof(DEVICE_EXTENSION),
                        NULL,       // no name
                        FILE_DEVICE_UNKNOWN,
                        0, TRUE,
                        &pFilterDevObj );
    if (!NT_SUCCESS(status))
      return status;

    // Initialize the Device Extension
    pDevExt = (PDEVICE_EXTENSION)
      pFilterDevObj->DeviceExtension;
    pDevExt->pDevice = pFilterDevObj;     // back pointer

    // Pile this new filter on top of the existing target
    pDevExt->pTargetDevice =          // downward pointer
      IoAttachDeviceToDeviceStack( pFilterDevObj, pdo);

    // Copy the characteristics of the target into the
    //       the new filter device object
    pFilterDevObj->DeviceType =
            pDevExt->pTargetDevice->DeviceType;
    pFilterDevObj->Characteristics =
            pDevExt->pTargetDevice->Characteristics;
    pFilterDevObj->Flags |=
```

```
            ( pDevExt->pTargetDevice &
                ( DO_BUFFERED_IO | DO_DIRECT_IO |
                  DO_POWER_INRUSH | DO_POWER_PAGABLE));

    // Explore the limitations of the target device's
    // buffer. Save the results in the bufferInfo struct
    GetBufferLimits( pDevExt->pTargetDevice,
                     &pDevExt->bufferInfo );

    return STATUS_SUCCESS;
}
```

GetBufferLimits

This is a helper function that queries the lower-level driver for information about its buffer size limits. It shows how to make a synchronous IOCTL call from one driver to another.

```
VOID GetBufferLimits(
                IN PDEVICE_OBJECT pTargetDevObj,
                OUT PBUFFER_SIZE_INFO pBufferInfo ) {
    KEVENT keIoctlComplete;
    IO_STATUS_BLOCK Iosb;
    PIRP pIrp;

    // Initialize the event that is signaled when the
    // IOCTL IRP completes (by the target device)
    KeInitializeEvent(
        &keIoctlComplete,
        NotificationEvent,
        FALSE );

    // Construct the IRP for the private IOCTL request
    pIrp = IoBuildDeviceIoControlRequest(
        IOCTL_GET_MAX_BUFFER_SIZE,
        pTargetDevObj,
        NULL,
        0,
        pBufferInfo,
        sizeof(BUFFER_SIZE_INFO),
        FALSE,
        &keIoctlComplete,
        &Iosb );

    // Send the new IRP down to the target
    IoCallDriver( pTargetDevObj, pIrp );

    // Wait for the target to complete the IRP
    KeWaitForSingleObject(
        &keIoctlComplete,
        Executive,
        KernelMode,
```

```
        FALSE,
        NULL );
}
```

The OverriddenDispatchWrite Function

The **DispatchWrite** function of the target (lower) driver is overridden by the filter. Since the lower driver has a limit on the maximum size of a write request, the filter breaks client requests for larger transfers into smaller pieces. This **OverriddenDispatchWrite** routine, along with an I/O Completion routine, performs the work of the split transfer.

```
NTSTATUS OverriddenDispatchWrite(
        IN PDEVICE_OBJECT pDevObj,
        IN PIRP pIrp ) {

   PDEVICE_EXTENSION pFilterExt = (PDEVICE_EXTENSION)
        pDevObj->DeviceExtension;

   PIO_STACK_LOCATION pIrpStack =
        IoGetCurrentIrpStackLocation( pIrp );

   PIO_STACK_LOCATION pNextIrpStack =
        IoGetNextIrpStackLocation( pIrp );

   ULONG maxTransfer =
        pFilterExt->bufferInfo.MaxWriteLength;

   ULONG bytesRequested =
        pIrpStack->Parameters.Write.Length;

   // We can handle the request for 0 bytes ourselves
   if (bytesRequested == 0) {
      pIrp->IoStatus.Status = STATUS_SUCCESS;
      pIrp->IoStatus.Information = 0;
      IoCompleteRequest( pIrp, IO_NO_INCREMENT );
      return STATUS_SUCCESS;
   }

   // If the request is small enough for the target
   // device, just pass it thru...
   if (bytesRequested < maxTransfer)
   return DispatchPassThru( pDevObj, pIrp );

   // Set up the next lower stack location to xfer as
   // much data as the lower level allows.
   pNextIrpStack->MajorFunction = IRP_MJ_WRITE;
   pNextIrpStack->Parameters.Write.Length = maxTransfer;

   // It turns out that the lower driver doesn't use the
   // ByteOffset field of the IRP's Parameter.Write block
   // so we use it for context storage.
```

```
        // HighPart holds the remaining transfer count.
        // LowPart holds the original buffer address.
        pIrpStack->Parameters.Write.ByteOffset.HighPart =
                bytesRequested;
        pIrpStack->Parameters.Write.ByteOffset.LowPart =
                (ULONG) pIrp->AssociatedIrp.SystemBuffer;

        // Set up the I/O Completion routine. Since there is
        // no external context (beyond the IRP's Parameters)
        // no context is passed to the Completion routine.
        IoSetCompletionRoutine(
                pIrp,
                WriteCompletion,
                NULL,               // no context
                TRUE, TRUE, TRUE );

        // Pass the IRP to the target
        return IoCallDriver(
                pFilterExt->pTargetDevice,
                pIrp );
}
```

The OverriddenDispatchDeviceIoControl Function

To further hide the limitations of the lower-level driver, the filter intercepts the IOCTL queries about the driver's maximum transfer size. Instead of returning the lower-level driver's limit values, it lies and says there are no limits. Any other kind of IOCTL function is passed through.

```
NTSTATUS OverriddenDispatchDeviceIoControl(
        IN PDEVICE_OBJECT pDevObj,
        IN PIRP pIrp ) {

    PIO_STACK_LOCATION pIrpStack =
        IoGetCurrentIrpStackLocation( pIrp );

    PBUFFER_SIZE_INFO pBufferInfo;

    // Here is the interception
    if (pIrpStack->Parameters.DeviceIoControl.IoControlCode
                == IOCTL_GET_MAX_BUFFER_SIZE ) {
      // The buffer passed by the user (by mutual
      // agreement) is treated as BUFFER_SIZE_INFO type.
      pBufferInfo = (PBUFFER_SIZE_INFO)
          pIrp->AssociatedIrp.SystemBuffer;
      pBufferInfo->MaxWriteLength = NO_BUFFER_LIMIT;
      pBufferInfo->MaxReadLength = NO_BUFFER_LIMIT;

      // Complete the IRP by announcing the size of
      // the returned BUFFER_SIZE_INFO information.
      pIrp->IoStatus.Information =
              sizeof(BUFFER_SIZE_INFO);
```

```
        pIrp->IoStatus.Status = STATUS_SUCCESS;
        IoCompleteRequest( pIrp, IO_NO_INCREMENT );
        return STATUS_SUCCESS;
        } else
        // not the IOCTL we're supposed to intercept,
        // just pass it thru to the "real" device.
        return DispatchPassThru( pDevObj, pIrp );
}
```

The DispatchPassThru Function

If the IRP request (intercepted by the filter) is not a write or an IOCTL with IOCTL_GET_MAX_BUFFER_SIZE code, it is passed down to the target device without modification. The filter driver attaches a generic I/O Completion routine to the request to handle the case of marking the IRP pending when the target requires.

```
NTSTATUS DispatchPassThru(
            IN PDEVICE_OBJECT pDevObj,
            IN PIRP pIrp ) {

    PDEVICE_EXTENSION pFilterExt = (PDEVICE_EXTENSION)
            pDevObj->DeviceExtension;

    PIO_STACK_LOCATION pIrpStack =
            IoGetCurrentIrpStackLocation( pIrp );

    PIO_STACK_LOCATION pNextIrpStack =
            IoGetNextIrpStackLocation( pIrp );

    // Copy args to the next level
    *pNextIrpStack = *pIrpStack;

    // Set up a completion routine to handle the bubbling
    // of the "pending" mark of an IRP
    IoSetCompletionRoutine(
            pIrp,
            GenericCompletion,
            NULL,
            TRUE, TRUE, TRUE );

// Pass the IRP to the target.
return IoCallDriver(
            pFilterExt->pTargetDevice,
            pIrp );
}
```

The I/O Completion Routines

The filter driver example uses two I/O Completion routines. One handles the completion of write requests. The other handles the pass-through completion.

WriteCompletion

This somewhat involved function performs all the additional work required after a partial transfer has occurred. If any partial transfer results in an error, the entire transfer is aborted. Otherwise, it sets up the IRP for another small chunk and sends it to the target device. When the entire transfer finishes, the routine completes the original IRP.

```
NTSTATUS WriteCompletion(
               IN PDEVICE_OBJECT pDevObj,
               IN PIRP pIrp,
               IN PVOID pContext ) {

   PDEVICE_EXTENSION pFilterExt = (PDEVICE_EXTENSION)
          pDevObj->DeviceExtension;

   PIO_STACK_LOCATION pIrpStack =
          IoGetCurrentIrpStackLocation( pIrp );

   PIO_STACK_LOCATION pNextIrpStack =
          IoGetNextIrpStackLocation( pIrp );

   ULONG transferSize =
                pIrp->IoStatus.Information;

   ULONG bytesRequested =
                pIrpStack->Parameters.Write.Length;

   ULONG bytesRemaining = (ULONG)
          pIrpStack->Parameters.Write.ByteOffset.HighPart;

   ULONG maxTransfer =
          pFilterExt->bufferInfo.MaxWriteLength;

   NTSTATUS status = pIrp->IoStatus.Status;

   // If the last transfer was successful, reduce the
   // "bytesRemaining" context variable.
   if (NT_SUCCESS( status ))
      bytesRemaining -= transferSize;
   pIrpStack->Parameters.Write.ByteOffset.HighPart =
       bytesRemaining;

      // If there is still more data to transfer, do it.
   if ( NT_SUCCESS( status ) && (bytesRemaining > 0) ) {

      // Bump the buffer address to next chunk.
      pIrp->AssociatedIrp.SystemBuffer =
             (PUCHAR) pIrp->AssociatedIrp.SystemBuffer +
                          transferSize;

      // Update the new transferSize:
      transferSize = bytesRemaining;
      if ( transferSize > maxTransfer )
```

```
        transferSize = maxTransfer;
// Build the IRP stack beneath us (again)
    pNextIrpStack->MajorFunction = IRP_MJ_WRITE;

    pNextIrpStack->Parameters.Write.Length =
        transferSize;

    // Set up so we get called again:
    IoSetCompletionRoutine(
            pIrp,
            WriteCompletion,
            NULL,
            TRUE, TRUE, TRUE );

    // Now pass it down:
    IoCallDriver(
        pFilterExt->pTargetDevice,
        pIrp );

    return STATUS_MORE_PROCESSING_REQUIRED;

} else {
    // There was either an error on the last xfer, or
    // we're done. Either way, complete the IRP.

    // Restore the original system buffer address:
    pIrp->AssociatedIrp.SystemBuffer = (PVOID)
        pIrpStack->Parameters.Write.ByteOffset.LowPart;

    // Show the total number of bytes xfered:
    pIrp->IoStatus.Information =
        bytesRequested - bytesRemaining;

    // See if the pending mark should be bubbled:
    if ( pIrp->PendingReturned )
        IoMarkIrpPending( pIrp );

    return STATUS_SUCCESS;
    }
}
```

GenericCompletion

When a pass-through request completes, this completion routine checks the IRP returned by the lower level to see if it has been marked Pending-Returned. If so, it marks the (now current) filter IRP stack location as pending.

```
NTSTATUS GenericCompletion(
            IN PDEVICE_OBJECT pDevObj,
            IN PIRP pIrp,
            IN PVOID pContext ) {
```

```
if ( pIrp->PendingReturned )
  IoMarkIrpPending( pIrp );

return STATUS_SUCCESS;
}
```

Writing Tightly Coupled Drivers

Unlike layered and filter drivers, tightly coupled drivers do not use the I/O Manager's **IoCallDriver** function to communicate with each other. Indeed, tightly coupled drivers do not need to conform to the strict stacking architecture that the WDM model constructs. Instead, they define a private calling interface. The advantage of this approach is that it is usually faster than the IRP passing model supported by the I/O Manager. In trade for improved performance, the mechanics of the interface between tightly coupled drivers is left as an implementation detail. As a result, it is difficult for tightly coupled drivers from different vendors to interoperate.

How Tightly Coupled Drivers Work

Since the interface between two tightly coupled drivers is completely determined by the driver designer, it is impossible to provide a single, unified description of how all tightly coupled drivers work. Instead, this section presents some general architectural guidelines. Figure 15.3 shows one common method of tightly coupling a pair of drivers.

In Figure 15.3, the lower driver has exposed an interface. During the upper driver's initialization, the interface is retrieved from the lower driver using the PnP request IRP_MN_QUERY_INTERFACE. The interface is returned as a structure of data and function pointers. When the upper driver needs the services of the lower driver, it calls one of the functions in this structure directly, rather than using **IoCallDriver**. Before unloading, the upper driver calls another function in the interface, **InterfaceDereference**, to disconnect it from the lower driver.

Initialization and Cleanup in Tightly Coupled Drivers

The following sections describe in general terms how a pair of tightly coupled drivers might initialize and unload. Of course, the exact steps vary depending upon the driver design.

LOWER AddDevice ROUTINE

The "lower" driver acts as a server for the upper driver, exposing an interface that is used by this "client." The following steps describe the work performed by the lower driver.

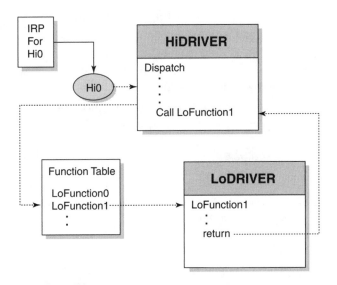

Figure 15.3   *Tightly coupled driver operation.*

1. Using the technique discussed in chapter 9, the lower driver exposes an interface using **IoRegisterDeviceInterface**. The interface exposed has a unique GUID and the interface structure is known to all clients a priori, including the higher driver.

2. The lower driver enables the exposed interface by calling **IoSetDeviceInterfaceState**.

3. The lower driver performs normal operations, awaiting the connection to its interface by the upper driver.

UPPER AddDevice ROUTINE

The upper driver, acting as a client of the server lower driver, performs the following steps:

1. It calls **IoGetDeviceObjectPointer** to obtain a reference to the lower device object. Since this routine also returns a corresponding File object pointer that is "counted," the File object pointer is usually dereferenced by using **ObDereferenceObject**.

2. Using the Device object pointer returned by **IoGetDeviceObjectPointer**, a call to **IoGetDeviceInterface** confirms the existence of the requested interface, by GUID, in the lower driver.

3. Using **IoCallDriver**, an IRP is sent to the lower device with IRP_MJ_PNP, minor subcode IRP_MN_QUERY_INTERFACE, to obtain

the requested interface. The interface is returned as a structure of data and function pointers.

4. The higher driver calls **InterfaceReference**, a required function pointer entry within the interface. This function allows the lower driver to keep track of clients of its exposed interface.

5. The higher driver calls any other method of the interface, or may choose to read or write data exposed by the interface.

UPPER RemoveDevice ROUTINE

When the upper driver no longer requires use of the interface, typically during **RemoveDevice**, the higher driver calls **InterfaceDereference** to release its use of the interface on the lower driver.

LOWER RemoveDevice ROUTINE

The lower driver must call **IoSetDeviceInterfaceState** to announce that its interface is no longer available for clients. If any clients are connected to an interface at the time **RemoveDevice** is invoked, the lower driver must determine an appropriate course of action. For example, it may need to forcibly disconnect clients by freeing resources reserved on their behalf. Otherwise, the lower driver can reject the **RemoveDevice** request.

Summary

The layered architecture of Windows 2000 allows the simplified design of device drivers. Breaking a monolithic driver into smaller, logically distinct pieces makes implementation and maintenance easier, reduces debugging time, and increases the likelihood that some of the software will be reusable.

In this chapter, different methods of stacking drivers on top of one another were presented. Most of the techniques depend on the I/O Manager's standard calling mechanism to send IRPs from one driver to another. When this mechanism proves insufficient, a private interface can be defined between a pair of drivers. In general, private interfaces make the design more fragile and harder to maintain.

The next chapter describes the details necessary to professionally install device drivers.

Driver Installation

CHAPTER OBJECTIVES

The convenient, automated, and trouble-free installation of a device driver is an essential step for users and support personnel. For Plug and Play drivers, the installation process is fundamental in providing the user with effortless device management.

This chapter focuses on the details necessary to ensure proper device driver installation.

Installation of a Driver

The automated installation of a device driver is controlled by a text file with the INF extension. The INF format resembles the old-style .INI files of Windows 3.x fame, but is deceptively more complex. An INF file, properly stored on a Windows 2000 system, allows for an automated or dialog-assisted installation of driver files.

It is important to understand that the end result of a driver installation consists of two persistent changes to a system:

- System registry entries describing the driver, its load order, and any appropriate configuration data
- Driver files, copied to a suitable system directory

While the INF file is the standard mechanism for affecting these changes, it is also true that a custom installation program can be provided, if appropriate, to force the same resulting system changes. The next section deals with the syntax and operation of an INF file.

Auto-Install Using INF Files

INF files are typically provided with the hardware and driver on diskette or CD. The structure and content of the INF file is the responsibility of the driver author.

INF File Structure

An INF file is a simple text file divided into sections, with each section designated by an identifier within closed braces ([ ]). Some section names are required, while others are driver-specific. Entries beneath each section control some installation action, or they link or enumerate other sections.

The order that sections appear in a file is unimportant, since each section is named and linked. A section continues until either another section or the end-of-file is encountered. The unique name that specifies a section is case-insensitive and should be limited to 28 characters in length to maintain compatibility with Windows 98. Section names can include spaces, but only if the entire name is quoted. The underscore and dot characters are allowed.

The general format of section entries is

```
entry = value [, value…]
```

where *entry* is a directive, keyword, or filename, and *value* is the attribute that is to be applied to *entry*.

An illustration of the linkage of section names is shown in Figure 16.1.

The *entry* or *value* names can be specified as a *string token*, which is a substitution string enclosed within percent signs (%). A separate INF section, **[Strings]**, provides the string token values for a given language ID.

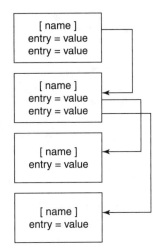

Figure 16.1   *INF file section linkage.*

Version Section

A valid INF file begins with a section named **[Version]**, which acts as a header and signature for the entire INF file. The allowed and required entries within the **[Version]** section are listed in Table 16.1.

Manufacturers Section

Another required section is the **[Manufacturers]** entries. Each entry within this section lists the devices and their drivers that are installed by the INF file. The form of each entry is

```
manufacturer=model
```

where the *manufacturer* lists an INF-unique name for the producer of one or more models of hardware being installed. The *model* value points to another INF section name that lists the further direction for driver installation of the hardware model.

Models Section

For each model listed within the **[Manufacturers]** section, a corresponding section must appear as specified by *model*. The form of each model entry is

```
device-description=install-section-name,hw-id[,compatible-
id...]
```

where *device-description* represents a human-readable listing of the device model and a short description. This string is presented to the user in a dialog box during some installations, so it may need to be provided in multiple languages as a string token.

Table 16.1	[Version] Section Entries

[Version] Section

Entry	Value
Signature	One of • "$Windows NT$" • "$Windows 95$" • "$Chicago$"
Class	A class name for an entire family of drivers. Some names, such as Net or Display, are predefined.
ClassGuid	The unique GUID for a class.
Provider	Provider of the INF file; organization name.
LayoutFile	Used only by system-supplied INF files; OEM-supplied files must use SourceDisksNames and SourceDisksFiles instead.
CatalogFile	Specifies a file (with .CAT extension) to validate drivers files; use only after validation by Microsoft HW Quality Lab.
DriverVer	mm/dd/yyyy[,x,y,v,z]; Required entry includes optional version numbers after date.

The value of *install-section-name*, also referred to as the **[DDInstall]** section, represents yet another INF section that directs further installation. The *hw-id* value is the PnP identifier returned by the hardware device during its announcement on a PnP-compatible bus. For example, USB\VID_045E&PID_00B identifies the Microsoft HID (Human Input Device) keyboard device on a USB. Any number of *compatible-id* values can be appended signifying that the same install script is to be used for any device contained in the list.

DDInstall Section

Near (but not quite at) the bottom of this linked list of INF section names is the **[DDInstall]** section, whose name is actually specified uniquely for each model of each manufacturer from the **[Models]** sections. The allowed and required entries within the **[DDInstall]** section are listed in Table 16.2.

While only the *AddReg* entry is syntactically required, the *CopyFiles* entry is an essential directive for **[DDInstall]** sections. It takes the form

```
CopyFiles=file-list-section[,file-list-section...] or
CopyFiles=@filename
```

The former version is more common in that it allows an indirect pointer to another section that contains a list of files to be installed. However, for

Table 16.2	[DDInstall] Section Entries

[DDInstall] Section	
Entry	**Value**
DriverVer	mm/dd/yyyy[,x,y,v,z]; required entry includes optional version numbers after date.
CopyFiles	Either another section name specifying a list of files to copy for this installation, or an individual filename, prefixed with the @ character.
AddReg	Required. Lists other section names that contain system registry information to be added by this installation.
Include	INF filename pointer list to other INF files (and directives) needed by this install.
Needs	Subsets the Include entry (above) listing the sections needed within the INF files.
DelFiles	Specifies other section names that list files to be removed from target (typically for upgrade purposes).
RenFiles	Specifies other section names that list files to be renamed on target prior to installation (typically to save previous installation state).
DelReg	Lists other section names that contain system registry information to be removed by this install.
ProfileItems	Lists other sections that contain modifications to the Start menu on the target system.

simple driver installations, the direct filename approach gets the job done. Both the *AddReg* and *CopyFiles* directives are explained in further detail in the next two sections.

CopyFiles Section

The **[CopyFiles]** sections of an INF file are uniquely named and referenced from *CopyFiles* directives in the **[DDInstall]** sections. Each entry within the section takes the form

```
destination-filename[,source-filename,temp-filename,flag]
```

where *destination-filename* is the ultimate target name for the file to be copied. If the source filename is not the same, *source-filename* must be specified. The *temp-filename* value is an anachronism (though still required for Windows 98) that specifies an intermediate filename for the new file until the next system reboot. For Windows 2000, the value is ignored.

The *flag* value specifies the disposition of the new target file and is described in Table 16.3. The bits within the *flag* value are ORed to effect multi-

Table 16.3	*CopyFiles* flag *Definition*

CopyFiles *flag* Definition

Bit value	Symbolic Name	Description
0x0400	COPYFLG_REPLACEONLY	Copy if source already present
0x0800	COPYFLG_NODECOMP	Copy without decompressing
0x0008	COPYFLG_FORCE_FILE_IN_USE	Copy source to temp name; force reboot; rename temp
0x0010	COPYFLG_NO_OVERWRITE	Do not replace existing source
0x1000	COPYFLG_REPLACE_BOOT_FILE	File is part of system loader; force reboot
0x2000	COPYFLG_NOPRUNE	Force copy operation, even if installer believes unnecessary.
0x0020	COPYFLG_NO_VERSION_DIALOG	Do not overwrite newer file (ignored if install package is digitally signed)
0x0004	COPYFLG_NOVERSIONCHECK	Always overwrite target file
0x0040	COPYFLG_OVERWRITE_OLDER_ONLY	Overwrite older target file
0x0001	COPYFLG_WARN_IF_SKIP	Warn if the user skips file
0x0002	COPYFLG_NOSKIP	Do not allow user to skip file

ple actions. Several actions are mutually exclusive (e.g., WARN_IF_SKIP and NOSKIP) and the documentation should be checked when in doubt.

Since the syntax for the **[CopyFiles]** entry does not include an option to specify a disk or path for the source file, other INF sections, **[SourceDisksNames]** and **[SourceDisksFiles]** must be used. The files copied by the entries within the **[CopyFiles]** section are targeted by yet another INF section, **[DestinationDirs]**.

AddReg Section

The **[AddReg]** sections of an INF file are uniquely named and referenced from *AddReg* directives in the **[DDInstall]** sections. The purpose of the section is to provide directives that add or modify entries in the target system registry. Each entry within the section takes the form

```
reg-root[,subkey,value-name,flags,value]
```

where *reg-root* is an abbreviation for one of the Registry hives, as listed in Table 16.4. The value designates the hive being modified. The *subkey* value represents the key name beneath the hive, with subkeys separated in the hierarchy

Table 16.4	AddReg reg-root Abbreviations

AddReg *reg-root* Abbreviations

Value	Description
HKCR	HKEY_CLASSES_ROOT
HKCU	HKEY_CURRENT_USER
HKLM	HKEY_LOCAL_MACHINE
HKU	HKEY_USERS
HKR	The hardware subkey for the device being installed

by the backslash (\) character. For example, Software\W2KDriverBook\ Driver\Setting is a valid subkey in either the HKCU or HKLM hive.

The *value-name* designates the Registry value being added or modified. Each system Registry key contains zero or more values that hold different types of data. The Registry Editors list values of a subkey in the right-hand pane. Both the *value name* and the *value data* appear in this pane. The left pane lists only subkeys. Figure 16.2 illustrates the relationship between Registry terms.

The *flags* specify the type of data that is to be stored and the possible bit values for *flags* is listed in Table 16.5.

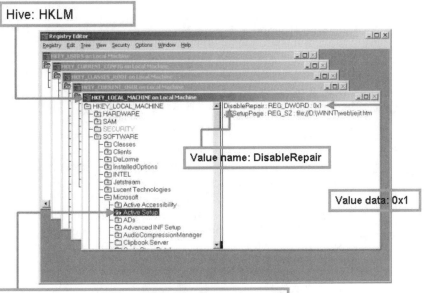

Figure 16.2	System Registry terminology.

Table 16.5	AddReg flags Definition

AddReg *flags* Definition

Bit value	Symbolic Name	Description
0x00000	FLG_ADDREG_TYPE_SZ	Null-terminated string
0x00001	FLG_ADDREG_BINVALUETYPE	Binary data
0x00002	FLG_ADDREG_NOCLOBBER	Do not replace existing value
0x00004	FLG_ADDREG_DELVALUE	Delete subkey or value-name
0x00010	FLG_ADDREG_KEYONLY	Create subkey, ignore value
0x00020	FLG_ADDREG_OVERWRITEONLY	If value exists, replace it, else do nothing
0x10000	FLG_ADDREG_TYPE_MULTI_SZ	REG_MULTI_SZ data (array)
0x00008	FLG_ADDREG_APPEND	Append to existing REG_MULTI_SZ array
0x20000	FLG_ADDREG_TYPE_EXPAND_SZ	REG_EXPAND_SZ data
0x10001	FLG_ADDREG_TYPE_DWORD	DWORD data
0x20001	FLG_ADDREG_TYPE_NONE	REG_NONE data

The significance of system Registry entries to a driver installation is discussed in a later section of this chapter.

SourceDisksNames Section

If the distribution of the driver files controlled by the INF file spans more than a single disk (diskette or CD), the INF file must include a **[SourceDisksNames]** section. This section includes one entry for each disk within the distribution set. The entry takes the form

```
diskid=disk-description[,tagfile,unused,path]
```

where *diskid* is a unique number within the distribution set. Typically, disks are numbered starting at 1. The *disk-description* tag is a human-readable text string that can be used to prompt the user for the proper disk as needed.

The *tagfile* value assumes a dual role. To ensure that the user supplies the correct disk during the installation process, the *tagfile* value is verified as existing on the inserted media before the install process continues. If the *tagfile* file is missing, the user is reprompted to insert the correct disk. If the *tagfile* value contains a .CAB extension, the file is further assumed to be a collection of compressed files for the source of driver files on the disk.

The *path* value is a root-relative disk path value for the source of driver files on the disk. Like the *tagfile* value, *path* is optional. If omitted, the root directory is assumed to be the source of the files.

SourceDisksFiles Section

A driver INF file must also contain a section named **[SourceDisksFiles]**. This section lists the filenames used during installation of the driver. Each file corresponds to one entry within the section and takes the form

```
filename=diskid[,subdir,size]
```

Naturally, the *diskid* value specifies a disk within the **[SourceDisks-Names]** section where the *filename* is to be found. The optional *subdir* value specifies a path on the disk for the file. The optional *size* value specifies the uncompressed size of the file in bytes. An installation process can use the size to determine if the source file fits on the target system prior to attempting the copy.

DestinationDirs Section

This required section in an INF file specifies the target directory for source files. Without knowledge of this section, an installation program or process would have no target directory in which to copy files. The entries in the **[DestinationDirs]** section take the form

```
file-list-section=dirid[,subdir] or
DefaultDestDir=dirid[,subdir]
```

where *file-list-section* specifies a section called out in a **[CopyFiles]** directive. It specifies that all the files copied by a directive install into the specified directory. For the entry **DefaultDestDir**, the specification applies to all **[CopyFiles]** directives that do not otherwise associate with a *file-list-section* within the **DestinationDirs** section.

The *dirid* value specifies an enumerated value for a destination directory according to Table 16.6. If the value *subdir* is supplied, it specifies a relative path beneath the directory called out by *dirid*.

DDInstall.Services Section

In order to actually have the copied file(s) act as a driver on the target system, the Service Control Manager (SCM) must be notified. As discussed in chapter 6, entries are made in the Registry under **HKLM\System\Current-ControlSet\Services** for each driver installed under Windows 2000. A **ServiceType** value of 1 signifies a kernel-mode device driver. **StartType** designates at what point in the boot process the driver loads (3 denotes on-demand or manual start). The **ErrorControl** value determines what happens during the driver load if an error is encountered. A **ServiceBinary** value points to the location of the driver file (.SYS file), but may be omitted if the binary is located in the %windir%\system32\drivers directory and has the same name as the subkey name underneath **HKLM\...\Services**.

Table 16.6	DestinationDirs *dirid* Definition

DestinationDirs *dirid* Definition

Value	Meaning
12	%windir%\system32\drivers for Windows 2000 %windir%\system\IoSubsys for Windows 98
10	%windir%
11	%windir%\system32 for Windows 2000 %windir%\system
30	Root directory of the boot drive
54	Boot directory for Windows 2000
01	Directory of this INF file
17	INF file directory
20	Fonts directory
51	Spool directory
52	Spool drivers directory
55	Print processors directory
23	Color (ICM)
-1	Absolute path
21	Viewers directory
53	User Profile directory
24	Applications directory
25	Shared directory
18	Help directory
16406	All Users\Start Menu
16407	All Users\Start Menu\Programs
16408	All Users\Start Menu\Programs\Startup
16409	All Users\Desktop
16415	All Users\Favorites
16419	All Users\Application Data
16422	Program Files
16427	Program Files\Common
16429	All Users\Templates
16430	All Users\Documents

Table 16.7	*AddService* flags *Definition*

AddService *flags* Definition

Bit value	Symbolic Name –SPSVCINST_	Description
0x0002	ASSOCSERVICE	Driver is an FDO (function driver), not a filter
0x0008	NOCLOBBER_DISPLAYNAME	Do not overwrite friendly name
0x0100	NOCLOBBER_DESCRIPTION	Do not overwrite description
0x0010	NOCLOBBER_STARTTYPE	Do not overwrite start type
0x0020	NOCLOBBER_ERRORCONTROL	Do not overwrite error control

The entries of the **DDInstall.Services** section include an entry of the form

```
AddService=ServiceName,[flags],service-install-section[,eventlog-install-section]
```

where *ServiceName* represents the name of the service, typically the name of the driver, sans the .SYS extension. The *flags* value is described in Table 16.7.

The *service-install-section* and optional *eventlog-install-section* values call out additional INF section names that control service value entries (such as **ServiceType** and **StartType**).

ServiceInstall Section

The **[ServiceInstall]** section, whose name is actually specified uniquely for each AddService entry within the DDInstall.Services sections, controls the installation of a driver into the Service Control Manager. The allowed entries within the **[ServiceInstall]** section are listed in Table 16.8.

INF Example

If the preceding explanation of INF files appears overly complex, a simple example may clarify. In the following example, a two-file driver is controlled by the INF file. The driver binary, Launcher.SYS, is copied into the system's driver directory (e.g., WINNT\System32\Drivers). A separate help file, Launcher.HLP, is copied into the help directory of the system (e.g., WINNT\Help).

```
[Version]
Signature="$Windows NT$"
Class=Missiles
ClassGUID={C9B3D080-6889-11d4-93FC-444553540000}
Provider=W2KDriverBook
DriverVer=07/04/2000,1.00.2468.1
```

Table 16.8	*ServiceInstall Section Entries*

[ServiceInstall] Section	
Entry	**Value**
DisplayName	Friendly name of driver, displayed in Device Manager
Description	Short description of purpose of driver or service, displayed by Device Manager
ServiceType	Type of driver: 0x01 – kernel driver 0x02 – file system driver
StartType	Specifies when driver loads: 0 – Boot time 1 – System start 2 – Auto start after system 3 – Demand start 4 – Disabled
ErrorControl	Disposition of errors during driver load: 0 – Ignore all errors 1 – Display errors to user 2 – Restart with "last known good," ignore further errors 3 – Restart with "last known good," bugcheck if further errors
ServiceBinary	Full path name of driver, which may include *dirid* values (see Table 16.6)

```
; Comments follow a semicolon

[DestinationDirs] ; Specify where files are copied to
DefaultDestDir=12 ; %windir%\system32\drivers
CopyLaunchHelp=18 ; standard help directory

[Manufacturer]
W2KDriverBook=MyMfgName   ; call out a model section

[MyMfgName] ; begin a Models section
; Our list of devices follows:
"ISA Missile Launcher"=InstallLauncher,ISA\Launcher

[InstallLauncher]  ; begin a DDInstall section
CopyFiles=CopyLaunchFiles ; call out a CopyFiles sec.
CopyFiles=CopyLaunchHelp ; and one for the help files
AddReg=LaunchRegSection   ; call out an AddReg section

[CopyLaunchFiles]  ; begin a CopyFiles section
Launcher.sys

[CopyLaunchHelp]   ; a second CopyFiles for Help file
```

```
Launcher.hlp

[LaunchRegSection] ; begin an AddReg section
; Provide a DWORD registry value of 0 for our device:
HKR,"Parameters","Coordinates",FLG_ADDREG_TYPE_DWORD,0

[SourceDisksNames]
; This section is not really required because we have
; only two files and they probably fit on one disk.
1="Missile Launcher Driver Files"

[SourceDisksFiles]
; Similarly, since everything came from one disk,
; we don't really need this section either.
Launcher.sys=1
Launcher.hlp=1

[InstallLauncher.Services] ; DDInstall.Services sec.
AddService=Launcher,2,LaunchService

; Setup the SCM registry entries so driver can start
[LaunchService]
ServiceType=1         ; driver
StartType=3           ; on-demand (manual)
ErrorControl=1        ; report errors
ServiceBinary=%12%\Launcher.sys     ; path to driver
```

Validating INF Syntax

The DDK includes a rudimentary tool, CHKINF, in the Tools directory of the DDK. It relies upon the Perl scripting engine, available for download from *www.perl.com*. While the tool is not without merit, it reports numerous errors when checking standard Microsoft INF files. The output from the tool is in the form of an HTML file.

The DDK Tools directory also contains a utility to simplify the construction of an INF file, GENINF.EXE. The tool must also be classified as rudimentary but may assist first-time authors.

Finally, a simple tool supplied with the DDK, STAMPINF.EXE, provides a quick mechanism to add or modify the version information in an INF file.

Using a Driver INF File

Once the driver's INF file is created, it must be processed for it to take effect. Obviously, the strict adherence to INF syntax suggests that an engine exists for just such a purpose. This section describes the mechanics of running the engine, either automatically or manually.

Manual Installation

To process an INF file manually, simply use the Windows Explorer file manager to select the INF file. Right-clicking the file offers the option to Install (process) the file.

In a true Plug and Play environment, the insertion or removal of a device triggers the installation, load, and unload of an appropriate driver. Therefore, the use of manual installation is reserved for initial testing and debugging of a driver.

Automatic Installation

When a PnP device is inserted into a system, several subsystems interact to force the loading of a new driver, if necessary. The steps are outlined below.

1. When the device is inserted, the hardware, using auto-detection and notification, alerts the bus driver that the device is present. Depending on the bus hardware, this might involve notifying the bus driver that a change has occurred that warrants a new enumeration of bus devices. Regardless, at the end of this step, the bus driver is aware that the new device is present and that it has a specific device ID.

2. The kernel-mode PnP Manager notifies the user-mode PnP Manager that a new device with a specific ID is present in the system.

3. The user-mode PnP Manager, using the Setup API library of Windows 2000, constructs a likely list of drivers for the new device. The INF directory of the system (e.g., WINNT\INF) is searched using the class and model information from the new device for a suitable match.

4. If a suitable INF file cannot be located, the system delays further action until a privileged user logs on. Then the user is presented with a dialog-driven New Hardware wizard. The user supplies the location of the drivers (CD, diskette, Web location, etc.) and the appropriate INF file is located.

5. Once the INF file is found, it is processed using the CfgMgr API library. The driver files and Registry entries are installed and modified. This step is primarily carried out by the kernel-mode PnP Manager.

6. Based on the directives of the INF file, the kernel-mode PnP Manager loads any lower filter drivers, then the functional driver, and finally any upper filter drivers for the device. The top driver in the stack is then sent appropriate PnP messages, including IRP_MN_START_DEVICE.

The Add/Remove Hardware Wizard

As just explained, the user must sometimes interact with even an automated installation. The prime interface for this interaction is the New Hardware wizard. A typical screen shot from this (all too) familiar tool is shown in

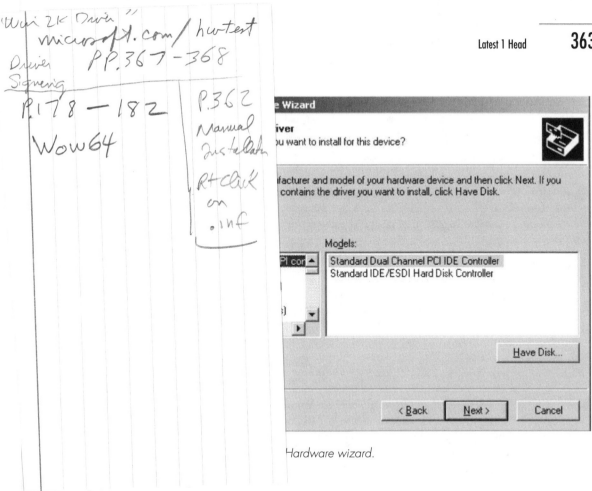

Hardware wizard.

Figure 16.3. Notice that there is a column for Manufacturers (listed from INF files **[Manufacturers]** section), and for Models (listed from INF files **[Models]** sections).

In general, the user manually selects the appropriate driver to install and load. If the driver survives installation, its DriverEntry and AddDevice routines must still validate that the hardware they are being asked to drive satisfies their set of code assumptions. In other words, a manual selection process can succeed the installation, but still fail initialization.

Class Names and Device IDs

The automated process of installation of a Plug and Play device depends largely on the ability of the Setup program to locate an *appropriate* INF file and section for the driver. The purpose of this section is to explain the source for Device IDs and Class Names, as well as explain the matching process that is used to locate an INF file section.

Every Plug and Play device should have an identifier that uniquely specifies the model of hardware. This Device ID must be provided to the Plug and Play bus hardware and, therefore, to a bus driver upon request. Of course, the bus driver requests the Device ID shortly after a new device is inserted. The form of a Device ID varies somewhat with the hardware bus type, but generally appears as

```
<enumerator>\<enumerator-specific-device-ID>, (for example,
PCI\VEN_1000&DEV_0001&SUBSYS_00000000&REV_02)
```

to driver code. A given hardware device can report more than one Device ID, which is a statement that the device is functionally compatible with numerous models. Since the **[Models]** section of an INF file includes an *hw-id* value, it is a simple matter to look for a direct match between an entry in the INF file with the Device ID returned by a newly installed device. The same INF entry allows for the specification of a list of (hopefully) compatible hardware, in the form of additional Device IDs. If an exact match cannot be located with the INF file for the Device ID, a compatible match is used as recourse.

Another key element used in locating appropriate drivers for a device is the notion of a *Setup Class*. A group of related devices can share layers of drivers (e.g., upper or lower filters) even though individual drivers within the stack vary. Setup Classes are uniquely identified by GUID and name. Microsoft defines a series of driver classes, listed in Table 16.9. New classes can be defined for new hardware groupings, with the same benefits bestowed to drivers that participate in the group membership. To create a new group, a new GUID and class name must be chosen.

Customizing an Installation

There are generally two things that a driver author can provide to customize the installation of a driver. First, a custom installation program can be provided that essentially replaces the work of the New Hardware wizard. To provide this functionality, the custom program must utilize the library routines provided by SETUPAPI.DLL. Each of the functions within this library begins with the name **SetupDiXxx**. The DDK provides the laborious details of the use of this DLL.

Second, a driver can provide a custom wizard page to allow the specification of custom device settings. Just prior to the completion of its work, the setup process sends a DIF_NEWDEVICEWIZARD_FINISHINSTALL request that offers the opportunity for a driver to display the custom page. Again, the DDK provides the details for this process.

Controlling Driver Load Sequence

Sometimes, the order in which a driver loads is important. Perhaps one driver depends on another to complete its initialization. When such dependencies arise, the Service Control Manager can be informed with the Registry entries **LoadOrderGroup** and **Dependencies**. These values can also be specified in the **[ServiceInstall]** section of an INF file.

Table 16.9	Setup Classes: Names and GUIDs	

Setup Classes

Class Name	Description	GUID
1394	1394 Host Bus Controller	{6bdd1fc1-810f-11d0-bec7-08002be2092f}
Battery	Battery Devices	{72631e54-78a4-11d0-bcf7-00aa00b7b32a}
CDROM	CD-ROM Drives	{4d36e965-e325-11ce-bfc1-08002be10318}
DiskDrive	Disk Drives	{4d36e967-e325-11ce-bfc1-08002be10318}
Display	Display Adapters	{4d36e968-e325-11ce-bfc1-08002be10318}
FloppyDisk	Floppy Disk Controllers	{4d36e980-e325-11ce-bfc1-08002be10318}
HDC	Hard Disk Controllers	{4d36e96a-e325-11ce-bfc1-08002be10318}
HIDClass	Human Input Devices	{745a17a0-74d3-11d0-b6fe-00a0c90f57da}
Image	Imaging Devices	{6bdd1fc6-810f-11d0-bec7-08002be2092f}
Infrared	IrDA Devices	{6bdd1fc5-810f-11d0-bec7-08002be2092f}
Keyboard	Keyboard	{4d36e96b-e325-11ce-bfc1-08002be10318}
MediumChangers	Medium Changers	{ce5939ae-ebde-11d0-b181-0000f8753ec4}
MTD	Memory Technology Driver	{4d36e970-e325-11ce-bfc1-08002be10318}
Media	Multimedia	{4d36e96c-e325-11ce-bfc1-08002be10318}
Modem	Modem	{4d36e96d-e325-11ce-bfc1-08002be10318}
Monitor	Monitor	{4d36e96e-e325-11ce-bfc1-08002be10318}
Mouse	Mouse	{4d36e96f-e325-11ce-bfc1-08002be10318}
Multifunction	Multifunction Devices	{4d36e971-e325-11ce-bfc1-08002be10318}

(continued)

Table 16.9	*Setup Classes: Names and GUIDs (continued)*	
	Setup Classes	
Class Name	**Description**	**GUID**
MultiportSerial	Multi-port Serial Adapters	{50906cb8-ba12-11d1-bf5d-0000f805f530}
Network	Network Adapter	{4d36e972-e325-11ce-bfc1-08002be10318}
NetClient	Network Client	{4d36e973-e325-11ce-bfc1-08002be10318}
NetService	Network Service	{4d36e974-e325-11ce-bfc1-08002be10318}
NetTrans	Network Transport	{4d36e975-e325-11ce-bfc1-08002be10318}
PCMCIA	PCMCIA Adapters	{4d36e977-e325-11ce-bfc1-08002be10318}
Ports	Ports (COM & LPT)	{4d36e978-e325-11ce-bfc1-08002be10318}
Printer	Printer	{4d36e979-e325-11ce-bfc1-08002be10318}
SCSIAdapter	SCSI and RAID Controllers	{4d36e97b-e325-11ce-bfc1-08002be10318}
SmartCardReader	Smart Card Readers	{50dd5230-ba8a-11d1-bf5d-0000f805f530}
Volume	Storage Volumes	{71a27cdd-812a-11d0-bec7-08002be2092f}
System	System Devices	{4d36e97d-e325-11ce-bfc1-08002be10318}
TapeDrive	Tape Drives	{6d807884-7d21-11cf-801c-08002be10318}
USB	USB	{36fc9e60-c465-11cf-8056-444553540000}

The **LoadOrderGroup** identifies by name a single group in which the specified driver is a member. The **Dependencies** value specifies which other groups must load prior to this driver loading successfully.

The need for such interdependencies is not common, nor should it be. In a truly device-centric environment (which Plug and Play purports), drivers should be in a position to load and unload with few strings attached. On the other hand, heavily layered driver implementations may have legitimate needs for such specifications.

Driver Stack Order

A related issue concerns the order in which drivers stack. In a layered driver environment, any number of drivers can stack on top of each other to distribute and reuse code. In a typical WDM model, driver stacks exist that contain a PDO (Physical Device Object) at the bus level, a possible bus filter object, an FDO (Functional Device Object), and surrounding upper and lower filter devices. (refer to chapters 1 and 15.)

In such environments, it is the Registry entries (once again) for each driver layer that determine the order in which drivers stack. Notice that the *load* order is independent of the *stack* order. When a driver invokes **IoAttach-DeviceToDeviceStack**, it is the responsibility of the I/O Manager to link drivers appropriately, independently of their load order.

The Registry entries for a driver may contain values named **UpperFilters** and **LowerFilters**. These are REG_MULTI_SZ string arrays, each containing the names of drivers that stack above and below the given driver. The order of the string array determines the stack order for multiple upper or lower filters.

A segment of an INF file appears below to demonstrate the installation of a filter driver. Notice that the upper filter is installed as a *demand start* driver. Even though it has announced that it stacks on top of the functional device, the driver may not load and insert itself into the stack until it is manually loaded.

```
...
[upperFilter_install]     ; DDInstall section
CopyFiles = @upperFilter.SYS
AddReg = upperFilter_addreg

[upperFilter_addreg]       ; AddReg section
; append this filter to the list of filters
HKR,,"UpperFilters",0x10008,"upperFilter"

[upperFilter_install.Services]  ; DDInstall.Services
AddService = Launcher,0x2,Launcher_Service
AddService = upperFilter,,upperFilter_Service

[upperFilter_Service]
DisplayName = "Upper Filter Service for Launcher"
ServiceType = 1       ; kernel-mode driver
StartType = 3         ; demand start
ErrorControl = 1
ServiceBinary = %12%\upperFilter.SYS
```

Digital Signing of a Driver

Many third-party drivers ship with the Microsoft Windows 2000 CD distribution. In order to participate in this program, several requirements must be met.

Additionally, whenever a naive attempt to install a driver on Windows 2000 is made, a warning message is issued stating that the device driver is not *digitally signed* and its authenticity cannot be verified by Microsoft.

This section explains the role of Microsoft in verifying driver authenticity and the burden placed on a driver author and hardware manufacturer to certify their package for inclusion into future Windows 2000 CD distribution.

Why Microsoft Verifies Drivers

It is in Microsoft's best interest to promote two (conflicting) goals.

- Provide or promote as much interoperability for Windows 2000 and varied hardware devices as possible through the convenient distribution of device drivers.
- Ensure that device drivers are stable and do not compromise the integrity of the system.

Since device drivers operate in kernel mode, they have the capability to slowly or quickly crash a system. Since instability of the system will often be blamed on the kernel itself, it is clearly in Microsoft's interest to maintain a list of *certified* vendors and drivers for their operating systems.

Of course, stating that Windows 2000 interoperates with more hardware devices than other OSs is a strong selling feature. Therefore, Microsoft often works with hardware vendors to ensure timely release of compatible drivers.

To accomplish the two goals, Microsoft has established a specialized group, the Windows Hardware Quality Labs (WHQL), that provides a certification of hardware and the device driver. The participation benefits for hardware vendors include

- Use of the Windows logo on the certifying hardware and software
- Inclusion in the official list of supported and certified hardware for the various Microsoft operating system offerings (see *www.microsoft.com/hcl*)
- The opportunity to distribute the driver with future releases of the OS
- A digital signature that ensures tamper-proof code and allows customers to obtain the latest versions of drivers through Microsoft's Windows Update site

To participate in the program, visit the site *www.microsoft.com/hwtest* for procedures and pricing.

Digital Signatures

As part of the WHQL program, a certified driver obtains a digital signature that permits Windows 2000 to install the driver without the unprofessional warning of "imminent danger." The digital signature consists of several components.

- A catalog file (.CAT) that is included with the distributed driver package. It contains the actual digital signature assigned by Microsoft.
- An INF file entry in the **[Versions]** section that references the .CAT file.
- Windows 2000 policy that restricts whether or not an unsigned driver can be installed.

The digital signature is allegedly tamper-proof and ensures that the driver being installed is the original code supplied by the vendor. It uses cryptographic technology to achieve this goal. The signature itself does not alter the code in any way.

Summary

For those familiar with the installation of drivers into earlier implementations of Windows, the automated process of Windows 2000 and Windows 98 is a great step forward for users. However, the step requires additional work on the part of the driver author in that, at a minimum, an INF file must be supplied. In the end, all parties benefit from the common, standardized mechanism of driver installation.

The final chapter in the book deals with the necessary subject of debugging device drivers using Microsoft tools.

Testing and Debugging Drivers

*I*n many ways, this chapter should be first in the book. After all, it is not possible to design software (that works, anyway) without considering a testing and debugging strategy from the very beginning. Of course, since the purpose of the book is to present the Windows 2000 driver architecture, the focus has been to explain the way drivers work, not fail.

The purpose of this chapter is to introduce the concept of writing *defensive* driver code. By considering the ways in which code can fail, the design and implementation of the driver can facilitate the isolation and reporting of the error. The techniques covered in this chapter include a presentation of trace methods and procedures.

The chapter also presents some tools provided by Microsoft with the DDK and elsewhere. For example, the very useful WinDbg debugger operation is explained.

And, by placing this chapter at the end, it does make for easy reference whenever it is needed.

Guidelines for Driver Testing

In many ways, driver testing is like all software testing: develop test cases that exercise boundary and stress conditions and measure the results. At a more practical level, however, driver testing requires innovation, real-time skills, hardware knowledge, and above all, patience.

A Generalized Approach to Testing Drivers

No complex body of code can ever be bug-free. Everyone is familiar with the phenomena that fixing bugs introduces new bugs. Bugs cannot be stopped; they can only be contained. This is especially true when software interacts with other vendors' software and hardware. Further, as software design occurs in layers and components, the actual mix of software and hardware versions may never have been tested as a system. This classic problem appears time and again with DLLs. Vendors test their code with one version of DLLs, but by the time the product is deployed en masse, the DLL versions have changed on the end users' systems.

Therefore, every test plan must be reasonable—searching for the knee in the curve beyond which diminishing returns on the testing effort occur. The real point is that test design is every bit as challenging as software design.

WHEN TO TEST

Experience shows that incremental testing of software components as they are developed is far more effective than waiting until the entire system is constructed. Although incremental testing requires a large number of small tests, bug isolation makes the technique worthwhile. Additionally, predicting the ship date of progressively tested software is more reliable than predicting the ship date of code that has never been tested.

The small test programs developed for this strategy also form the basis of a more formal regression test. As future changes are made to the code base, the small tests help ensure that new bugs are not introduced.

Yet another advantage of incremental testing throughout the driver development phase is that hardware design flaws are identified early. This is especially important for new hardware under design. Nothing kills a schedule more than identifying another spin on a custom ASIC late in the development phase.

WHAT TO TEST

Generally, driver tests can be categorized as follows:

- **Hardware tests** verify the operation of the hardware. These tests are essential when the device and driver are being developed in parallel.
- **Normal response tests** validate the complete and accurate functionality of the driver. Does the driver respond to each command as promised?
- **Error response tests** check for appropriate action when a bad stimulus is applied to the driver. For example, if the device reports an error, does the driver respond by reporting and logging the error? The error stimulus can also be bad data from a user response.
- **Boundary tests** exercise the published limits of the driver or device. For example, if there is a maximum transfer size, does the driver deal appropriately when presented with one more byte? Speed boundaries are also addressed in this category.
- **Stress tests** subject the driver and device to high levels of sustained activity. The amount of stimulus is ideally just beyond what will be encountered in the real world. Within this category, different subcategories of stress can be applied. For example, limited CPU availability, limited memory, and heavy I/O activity are all dimensions where stress can be applied.

HOW TO DEVELOP THE TESTS

For optimum scheduling and to ensure a dedicated effort, a separate test design team should be established. However, it is often difficult enough to staff a driver development team, let alone attempt to find specialists in driver testing. As mentioned, the skill set required for the testing effort is every bit as rare as the driver development set. Few organizations can realistically afford the luxury of separate development and test teams.

Thus, the driver author must often write the incremental tests in parallel with the development code. One advantage of the singleton approach is that the author implicitly knows the boundary conditions of the code just developed. Tests to exercise arbitrary software limits are therefore well known.

Regardless, a good discipline must be established to ensure that the scheduling process allocates sufficient time to both development and testing efforts. Reducing test time to enhance a schedule is a "fools gold" approach to any development effort.

HOW TO PERFORM THE TESTS

The test procedure should be as automated as possible. Besides eliminating the boredom and opportunity for missed tests or errors, an automated test script ensures that if (when) an error occurs, the opportunity to reproduce it is high.

Also, after each round of bug fixes is applied to code, the entire suite of incremental tests should be rerun. This is called *regression testing* and it ensures that one bug fix doesn't introduce others.

All test runs should be logged and it is a good idea to keep statistics on the number of bugs found versus lines of development code added. Beyond the simple value of a management metric, it provides hard evidence of techniques that provide diminishing returns. For example, is it really productive to have developers work 14 hour days to "meet" the schedule?

WHO SHOULD PERFORM THE TESTS

The code author often has a vested interest in keeping some bugs hidden. Perhaps bugs are suspected but the developer is not yet ready to confirm their presence. Perhaps a questionable design must be defended. Perhaps simple ego prevents honest observation of a result. For all of these reasons, the test author is the better choice to run regression tests. A code author simply cannot be expected to be objective about his or her own code and design.

Of course, if the team does not have separate development and test personnel, an alternative must be accepted. When more than one developer makes up the team, the operating procedure can be to have different members test code written by other members.

The Microsoft Hardware Compatibility Tests

Microsoft provides a hardware compatibility test suite (or simply, the HCTs) that is the official test for a hardware platform's ability to run Windows 2000. The suite contains a number of different components, including

- General system tests that exercise the CPU, the onboard serial and parallel ports, the keyboard interface, and the HAL.
- Tests that exercise drivers for specific kinds of hardware, such as video adapters, multimedia devices, network interface cards, tape drives, SCSI devices, and so on.
- General stress tests that put unusually high loads on system resources and I/O bandwidth.
- A GUI-based test manager that automates test execution and data collection.

Even if the class of hardware for the driver being developed is not covered by the HCTs, the suite can still serve as a tool to place system-level stress on custom driver tests.

The HCT suite is shipped as a separate disk within the DDK. It should be installed on the target machine, not on the development machine. A complete set of documentation is included on the HCTs CD.

Why Drivers Fail

While testing uncovers the *presence* of bugs, the more serious challenge is to analyze, isolate, and correct the source of the bug. The goal of this section is to provide the basis for the analysis of driver bugs. Drivers fail for specific reasons and some up-front thought about the ways in which they fail can start the elusive search for a bug in an orderly fashion.

Categories of Driver Errors

Drivers can fail in any number of interesting ways. Although it is not possible to give a complete list, the following sections describe some of the more common types of driver pathology.

HARDWARE PROBLEMS

It goes without saying (to a software developer, anyway) that there is always an even chance that the hardware itself is the source of a problem. In fact, when developing drivers for new, undeployed, untested hardware, the chances of a hardware problem rise significantly. Symptoms of hardware problems include

- Errors occur during data transfer.
- Device status codes indicate an error (when a device reports an internal error, it is the equivalent of a confession).
- Interrupts do not arrive or they arrive spuriously.
- The device does not respond properly to commands.

The cause might be as simple as undocumented behavior in the device, and hardware designers have been known to alter documentation after witnessing the results of their work. There might be a restriction on command timing or sequencing. The firmware on the device might be faulty. There could be a bus protocol problem resulting in sporadic failures as other devices on the bus engage. Then again, the device might just be broken.

Because attempting to debug a problem whose ultimate source is hardware is so frustrating, it is best to eliminate (within reason) this category of fault before proceeding.

The best approach to validate a hardware problem is to employ a logic analyzer or hardware emulator. Hardware and software designers should work closely on unstable platforms until the first level of fault isolation can be determined.

SYSTEM CRASHES

Because driver code operates in kernel mode, it is straightforward for such code to kill the entire system. While many driver logic errors produce a crash, the most common stem from access violations (e.g., referencing a logical address that has no physical memory behind it) through use of a bad C pointer. Among the more difficult-to-trace scenarios within this category is setting DMA addresses incorrectly into the mapping registers. The device scribbles into random memory with a resulting crash seemingly caused by another entire subsystem.

A later section in this chapter deals with analyzing system crashes to determine the ultimate source.

RESOURCE LEAKS

Because kernel-mode driver code is trusted code, the system does not perform any tracking or recovery of system resources on behalf of a driver. When a driver unloads, it is responsible for releasing whatever it may have allocated. This includes both memory from the pool areas and any hardware the driver manages.

Even while a driver is running, it can leak memory if it regularly allocates pool space for temporary use and then fails to release it. High-layered drivers can leak IRPs by failing to free those fabricated and passed to lower levels. Resource leaks force sluggish system performance and, ultimately, a system crash.

Windows 2000 allows memory allocated by kernel-mode code to be tagged with an ID. When analyzing system memory after a crash, the tags help determine where the blocks are located, their size, and most importantly, which subsystem allocated them. Tools such as GFLAGS, supplied with the Platform SDK, enable the pool tagging feature globally for the system.

Resource leaks in progress can sometimes be determined by careful monitoring of system objects. Tools such as WINOBJ (supplied with the Platform SDK or by *www.sysinternals.com*) assist in this monitoring.

Tracking resource leakage can be an arduous process. Considerable patience must be exercised when analyzing and isolating such problems.

THREAD HANGS

Another failure mode is caused by synchronous I/O requests that never return. The user-mode thread issuing the request is blocked forever and remains forever in its wait state. This type of behavior can result from several causes.

First, an explicit bug might be failing to ever call **IoCompleteRequest,** thus never sending the IRP back to the I/O Manager. Not so obvious is the need to call **IoStartNextPacket**. Even if there are no pending requests to be processed, a driver must call this function because it marks the Device object as idle. Without this call, all new IRPs are placed in the pending queue, never arriving at the Start I/O routine.

Second, a logic error can hang a thread in a Dispatch routine. Perhaps the driver is attempting recursively to acquire a Fast Mutex or an Executive resource. Perhaps another code path has acquired a mutex but failed to release it. Subsequent requests for the mutex hang indefinitely.

Similarly, DMA drivers can hang while awaiting ownership of the Adapter object or its mapping registers. The IRP request is therefore never processed, which in turn queues all further IRPs. For slave DMA devices, the offending driver might cause other drivers using the same DMA channel to freeze.

Drivers that manage multiunit controllers can effect similar problems by not releasing the Controller object. New IRPs sent to any Device object using the locked Controller object queue indefinitely.

Unfortunately, there is no convenient way to see who currently owns Adapter or Controller objects, Mutexes, or Executive resources. It is sometimes helpful to maintain a resource management structure for tracking purposes. Each owner of a synchronization object should register its use within the structure, clearing it when the object is released. Of course, this technique requires a manual coding effort; the act of adding the code often reveals the source of the problem.

Another hit or miss attempt to isolate thread hang problems is the use of the checked build of the Windows 2000 kernel. The checked build reports the use of system synchronization objects through **DbgPrint** statements that appear on an attached debugger.

SYSTEM HANGS

Occasionally, a driver error causes the entire system to lock up. For example, a deadly embrace involving multiple spin locks (or attempts to acquire the same spin lock multiple times on a single CPU) can freeze system operation. Endless loops in a driver's Interrupt Service Routine or DPC routine cause a similar failure.

Once this kind of system collapse occurs, it is difficult, if not impossible, to regain control of the system. The best approach is usually to debug the driver interactively, using WinDbg, and attempt to duplicate the failure.

Reproducing Driver Errors

One key to isolating a driver bug is the ability to reproduce the problem. Intermittent errors are the bane of a driver author's existence. By meticulously recording the *exact* sequence of events leading up to the failure, the possibility of reproduction increases. The causes of intermittent failures are numerous.

TIME DEPENDENCIES

Some problems occur only when a driver is running at full speed (or worse, at some exact slower speed). This could produce an unusually high I/O request rate or data transfer rate. Stress testing is usually a good way to attempt reproduction of this type of failure.

MULTIPROCESSOR DEPENDENCIES

If the driver is certified for multiprocessor operation, it *must* be tested on a multiprocessor platform. Numerous timing conditions present themselves only within the MP environment. For example, ISR, DPC, and I/O Timer routines can run simultaneously on an SMP machine. One warning: SMP debugging is very painful, so it is best to start with a single processor environment.

MULTITHREADING DEPENDENCIES

If a driver manages sharable Device objects, the test strategy must access a single Device object from multiple threads. IRPs that flow from multiple threads often provoke unintended results.

OTHER CAUSES

A computer system involves many components. Sometimes behavior appears non-deterministic due to system load conditions, combinations of installed hardware and drivers, or other configuration differences. A detailed log is perhaps the best tool to assist in identifying this category of problem.

Defensive Coding Strategies

Any good software design anticipates problems. To facilitate the detection and isolation of failures, several coding techniques should be employed.

- Maximize the generation of *intermediate output* within the driver code. Intermediate output, also known as *trace* output, should be sprinkled liberally within the driver code. Using the function **DbgPrint** (described later in this chapter), intermediate output is directed at a connected interactive debugger such as WinDbg. Sysinternals also produces a utility, DebugView, that captures this trace output on a single system.
- Use assertions (described later in this chapter) liberally to validate internal consistency within driver code.
- Debug code can remain with the driver source, properly bracketed by **#ifdef** and **#endif** statements. When needed, a debug version of the driver can be used to track particularly elusive bugs.
- Faithfully maintain version information for each driver shipped. Often, bugs follow a particular version of a driver, yielding major clues to its cause.
- Use version control software throughout the development process. This allows code changes to be easily backed out to test for failure modes on older code bases.

Keeping Track of Driver Bugs

Research has shown that bugs are not evenly distributed throughout code. Rather, they tend to cluster in a few specific routines, proportional to the routine's complexity. A carefully maintained bug log identifies the routines that deserve special attention.

A good bug log allows patterns that highlight configuration-related failures to be spotted. It can also highlight holes within the testing design and strategy itself.

Good failure logs should contain at least the following:

- An exact description of the failure.
- As much detail as possible about the prevailing conditions at the time of the failure. For example, the OS version and service pack, the drivers installed and their versions, and so on.
- The exact configuration of the system at the time of failure.
- Bug severity (from showstopper to cosmetic).
- Current status of the bug.

Reading Crash Screens

System crashes, which Microsoft euphemistically terms "STOP messages," are a dramatic sign that a driver has failed. This section describes how STOP messages are generated and explains how they provide useful information.

What Happens When the System Crashes

Despite its name, a system crash is quite orderly. The OS is reporting that it has detected an internal state that is inconsistent with continued operation. As a result, the OS believes it is better to shutdown *now* rather than continue operation with the illegal state. This is appropriate in many cases since the illegal state could cause real damage, perhaps to the file system. Continuing operation under such circumstances could also breach security.

Two different sequences of events can lead to a system crash. First, some kernel-mode component can be the detector of an illegal state and elect to force a system STOP. For example, if the I/O Manager discovers that a driver is passing an already completed IRP to **IoCompleteRequest**, the I/O Manager forces a system STOP.

The second scenario is more indirect. A kernel-mode component is the direct source of the failure, generating an exception within its code operation. For example, a memory access violation or integer division by zero result in an exception being generated. Referencing paged memory at an elevated

IRQL level is also an exception. If the kernel-mode routine that performs the illegal operation does not trap the exception directly, the result is an *unhandled exception* within kernel mode.

When this occurs, a standard exception handler within the kernel responds and initiates a system STOP.

Regardless of which kernel subsystem initiates the system STOP, one of two calls actually performs the operation.

```
VOID KeBugCheck( Code );
VOID KeBugCheckEx( Code, Arg1, Arg2, Arg3, Arg4 );
```

Either function generates the STOP screen and optionally saves a crash dump file to disk. Depending on the system administrator's choice, the system either halts, reboots, or starts the kernel's debug client.

The *Code* argument to the **KeBugCheck** routines specifies the cause of the crash as a simple DWORD value. It is also known as a *bugcheck* code. The additional four arguments to **KeBugCheckEx** appear within the STOP message screen as further information for the user to report (and hopefully assist in isolating the source of the STOP).

Bugcheck codes are either defined by Microsoft (see BUGCODES.h within the DDK and Appendix B of this book) or are driver-specific.

Calls to either **KeBugCheck** function can be made from a driver. In fact, it is common for a debug version of a driver to force system STOPs at various points of interest.

The Blue Screen of Death

A system STOP message appears on an entire screen of blue background, earning it the name *Blue Screen of Death*, or BSOD. In versions of NT prior to Windows 2000, the STOP message filled the screen with information of questionable value. In Windows 2000, the STOP message is simplified, containing the most relevant information about the cause and location of the crash. A sample BSOD is illustrated in Figure 17.1.

The STOP message contains three lines of information. The bugcheck code, along with the four arguments passed to **KeBugCheckEx** if it initiated the STOP, is supplied on the first line. Depending on the bugcheck code, the four extra arguments contain meaningful information (see Appendix B for a description).

The second line identifies the bugcheck code symbolically. In this case, the bugcheck code of 0xD1 specifies DRIVER_IRQL_NOT_LESS_OR_EQUAL. Appendix B states that code 0xD1 indicates that a driver caused a page fault at or above DISPATCH_LEVEL IRQL. Also, the four **KeBugCheckEx** arguments for this code specify

Arg1: The paged address referenced: 0

Arg2: IRQL level at the time of the reference: 2

```
*** STOP: 0x000000D1 (0x00000000,0x00000002,0x00000000,0xFCE10796)
DRIVER_IRQL_NOT_LESS_OR_EQUAL

*** Address FCE10796 base at FCE10000, DateStamp 398aeb8f - Driver.sys

Beginning dump of physical memory
Physical memory dump complete. Contact your system administrator or
technical support group.
```

| Figure 17.1 | The STOP message screen (Blue Screen of Death). |

Arg3: Type of access: 0 means "read"

Arg4: Address of instruction that caused the fault: 0xFCE10796.

Thoughtfully, the third line of the STOP message information looks up the failing instruction address and specifies the module that contains the instruction. In this example, Driver.sys was responsible for the page fault.

An Overview of WinDbg

WinDbg (affectionately pronounced *wind bag*) is a hybrid kernel-mode and user-mode debugger that can be used to analyze crash dump files, executing driver code, and application dump files created by the Dr. Watson utility. This section provides an overview of the WinDbg capabilities. The DDK documentation provides additional details on the use of WinDbg in various debugging scenarios.

WinDbg is a hybrid debugger in that it serves a purpose in both kernel mode and user mode. It also combines the look and feel of a GUI (graphical) debugger with a window for entering old-style keyboard commands.

WinDbg is supplied from several sources, including the DDK and Platform SDK. Additionally, it is supplied on the Customer Support and Diagnostics Tools CD of the Windows 2000 distribution.

The Key to Source Code Debugging

One of WinDbg's most powerful features is its ability to debug kernel-mode components at the source-code level. Source code and symbol files must be available to WinDbg during the debug session to allow this mode of operation.

SYMBOL DIRECTORIES

Symbol files are optionally generated with the compile and link process of a project. They include names for local and global variables, linked function addresses, and typedef information. Line number information is also provided by symbol files so that compiled machine instructions can be associated with source code lines. Microsoft tools can supply symbol files in several formats including an older (but more standard) COFF format (Common Object File Format) and the PDB format (Program Database). Compiler and linker switches determine the format of the symbols generated.

The Windows 2000 operating system itself is supplied with associated symbol files. They are optionally installed from the Customer Support and Diagnostics Tools CD. Since symbol files change with each build, a service pack distribution of the operating system requires that the symbol files be updated.

Access to driver and OS symbols is essential for any serious debugging attempt. They provide intelligible call stack information and display of source code. Trying to isolate a bug from screens of disassembly is an exercise in frustration.

Once symbols are installed, WinDbg must be informed of their install location. This is accomplished by using the Symbols tab of the Options dialog box under the View menu. Operating system symbols are usually installed in the %SystemDir%\Symbols directory. Symbol files for a driver (.DBG or .PDB extension) are often kept with the binary .SYS file.

SOURCE CODE DIRECTORIES

Besides the symbol files, WinDbg needs access to the source code (.C and .H) for the driver in order to display it during debugging. A path for the source code directories can be supplied through the Source Files tab of the Options dialog under the View menu in WinDbg.

Some WinDbg Commands

Although WinDbg is a GUI program, its most useful operations are initiated from a command-line window. The command set is similar to other command-line debuggers supplied by Microsoft (e.g., NTSD and KD), so knowledge of the command set is leveraged. Table 17.1 provides a quick overview of the more

Table 17.1	Common WinDbg Commands and Extensions

WinDbg Common Commands and Extensions

Command	Description
Help	Display list of basic WinDbg commands
k, kb, and kv	Display stack trace
dd *address*	Dump the contents of memory
ln	Display symbol names to the break point
r	Display or modify CPU register(s)
p	Trace over
t	Trace into
g	go (continue execution)
.reboot	Reboot target computer
!help	Display help for WinDbg extension commands
!handle	Display information about process handle(s)
!process 0 0	Display list of current processes
!process *pid flags*	Display information about specific process
!thread *tid*	Display information about specific thread
!vm	Display virtual memory statistics
!sysptes	Display information of system page table usage
!drivers	List currently loaded drivers
!drvobj *address*	Display information about driver object
!devobj *address*	Display information about device object
!exr *address*	Display the exception record at given address
!cxr *address*	Display the context record at given address
!irp *address* [verbose]	Dump an IRP
!irpfind	Display list of IRPs allocated
!errlog	Display list of pending error log entries
!trap	Display contents of a trap frame
!poolfind *tag*	Locate instances of a pool tag
!poolused	Display memory usage summary based on tag
!reload *module*	Reload module symbols
!load *name*	Load an extension DLL
!unload *name*	Unload an extension DLL

common WinDbg commands. The WinDbg Help option provides more detailed information. Also, see the DDK for driver-specific (kdextx86.DLL) extension command help. Extension commands begin with a bang (!).

Analyzing a Crash Dump

When a crash occurs, Windows 2000 can save the state of the system in a dump file. To enable this feature, the System Control Panel applet (Advanced tab, Startup and Recovery) must be configured. Crash dumps allow an immediate reboot of the system without losing the state of memory at the moment of failure. This section explains how to analyze a system crash dump.

Goals of the Analysis

With WinDbg and a crash dump file, the state of the failed system can be examined. It is possible to find out almost as much information as if it were still running or if a live debugger were attached at the moment of failure. This kind of forensic pathology can help develop a convincing explanation of what led to the crash. Some of the questions that should be asked during the analysis include

- Which drivers were executing at the time of the crash?
- Which driver was responsible for the crash?
- What was the sequence of events leading to the crash?
- What operation was the driver trying to perform when the system crashed?
- What were the contents of the Device Extension?
- What Device object was it working with?

Starting the Analysis

To begin the analysis, the crash dump file must be obtained. If WinDbg is available on the target system (the system that crashed), the file is present wherever the Control Panel configuration specified (e.g., WINNT\Memory.DMP). If the system that crashed is at a remote site, the dump file must be transported. Since dump file sizes range from large to *very* large, be sure to use appropriate techniques for transport (e.g., compression and/or CD-R media).

On the analyzing machine, invoke WinDbg. Then choose the menu option File and select Open Crash Dump. Choose the dump file name to open. After the dump file loads, information is displayed as shown in the following excerpt:

```
Kernel Debugger connection established for D:\WINNT\MEMORY.DMP
Kernel Version 2195 Free loaded @ ffffffff80400000
```

```
Bugcheck 0000001e : c0000005 f17a123f 00000000 00000000
Stopped at an unexpected exception: code=80000003 addr=8045249c
Hard coded breakpoint hit
...
Module Load: CRASHER.SYS (symbol loading deferred)
```

The initial information reveals the same STOP message information from the original blue screen. The bugcheck code is 0x1E, signifying KMODE_EXCEPTION_NOT_HANDLED. The second bugcheck argument is the address where the problem occurred (0xF17A123F). To see where this instruction falls within the source code, choose Edit, then Goto Address and enter the address from the bugcheck information. If symbol information is located (don't forget to set the symbol path from the Options dialog of the View menu), the source file is opened. For this example, a function that purposefully generates an unhandled exception, **TryToCrash**, is displayed with the cursor placed on the line of code that was executing. The screen shot of Figure 17.2 displays this remarkably helpful feature.

The first parameter for bugcheck 0x1E is the unhandled exception code, 0xC0000005. This signifies an access violation, which is not surprising given the code of **TryToCrash**. Dereferencing a NULL pointer is never a great idea.

Do not be misled by the message about the unexpected exception with code 0x80000003. This is just the breakpoint used by **KeBugCheck** itself to halt the system, so it has no significance.

Figure 17.2 *Crash dump analysis screen shot.*

Tracing the Stack

The stack trace is one of the most important steps in analyzing a crash dump. The stack state at the time of the crash is a record of the calls made from the oldest frame (at the stack bottom) to the crash point itself (at the top).

Unfortunately, finding the right stack to trace is often quite involved. This is due to the fact that systems operate with many threads, each with their own context (which includes a private stack). At the time of an unhandled exception (as in the example), control is transferred to a system routine that switches to a safe context. (After all, the unhandled exception could have been caused by a corrupt stack. Further processing within that context would be unsafe.) The Windows 2000 kernel routine that performs the unhandled exception processing for most driver operations is **PspUnhandledExceptionInSystemThread**.

HIGH IRQL CRASHES

If the system crashed while it was running at or above DISPATCH_LEVEL IRQL, a straightforward stack trace is in order.

To obtain a stack trace from a crash dump under analysis by WinDbg, the Call Stack option can be selected from the View menu, or the k command can be used directly. To continue the example, the following is displayed:

```
> k
f79a6678 8045251c f79a66a0 8045cc77 f79a66a8
  NTOSKRNL!PspUnhandledExceptionInSystemThread+0x18
f79a6ddc 80465b62 80418ada 80000001 00000000 NTOSKRNL!Psp-
  SystemThreadStartup+0x7a (EBP)
00000000 00000000 00000000 00000000 00000000
  NTOSKRNL!KiThreadStartup+0x16 (No FPO)
>
```

Each line shows the address of the stack frame, the return address of the function, and the first three arguments passed to the function. (The kb stack backtrace command can be used instead of k to better format the display.)

CRASHES BELOW DISPATCH_LEVEL

As demonstrated, the function **PspUnhandledExceptionInSystemThread** indeed was called to handle the NULL pointer dereference, but there is no obvious linkage back to the faulty driver code itself.

The first input parameter to **PspUnhandledExceptionInSystemThread** is a pointer to a structure that contains the exception and context records. The !exr and !cxr extension commands can be used to format and display these vital records.

After the !cxr command executes, the very useful !kb command displays a stack trace using the context of the last !cxr command. This should be the call stack that was in context at the time of the unhandled exception.

```
> dd f79a66a0 l 2   ; this is a lowercase L, not a 1
0xF79A66A0 f79a6b28 f79a6780
> !exr f79a6b28
Exception Record @ F79A6B28:
ExceptionAddress: f17a123f (TryToCrash+0xf)
  ExceptionCode: c0000005
 ExceptionFlags: 00000000
NumberParameters: 2
   Parameter[0]: 00000000
   Parameter[1]: 00000000

> !cxr f79a6780
CtxFlags: 00010017
eax=00000001 ebx=00000000 ecx=01000100 edx=f79a6dcc esi=e1eba118 edi=fcdb8c38
eip=f17a123f esp=f79a6bf0 ebp=f79a6bf4 iopl=0    nv up ei pl zr na po nc
vip=0    vif=0
cs=0008  ss=0010  ds=0023  es=0023  fs=0030 gs=0000          efl=00210246
0000123F

> !kb
ChildEBP RetAddr  Args to Child
f79a6bf4 f17a11b5 00000001 00000000 7cdb3738 CRASHER!TryToCrash+0xf
f79a6c78 f17a102e fcdb3750 00000000 804a43c4 CRASHER!CreateDevice+0x162
f79a6c90 804a4431 fcdb3750 fcd67000 f79f2d08 CRASHER!DriverEntry+0x2e
f79a6d58 804d9281 0000035c fcd67000 f79f2d08 NTOSKRNL!_NtSetInformationFile@20+0x5a0
f79a6d78 80418b9f f79f2d08 00000000 00000000 NTOSKRNL!_NtSetInformationFile@20+0x7e1
f79f2d58 80461691 00f1f784 00000000 00000000 NTOSKRNL!_ExpWorkerThread@4+0xae
f79f2d58 77f9a31a 00f1f784 00000000 00000000 NTOSKRNL!_KiSystemService+0xc4
f79a6bec 01000100 f79a6c78 f17a11b5 00000001 +0xffffffff
00f1f794 00000000 00000000 00000000 00000000 +0xffffffff
```

Indirect Methods of Investigation

If a driver was not the direct cause of the crash, it still cannot be ruled out as an indirect cause. Perhaps a device DMA operation scribbled into memory. To analyze such situations, considerable information must be gathered. This can involve creativity and imagination (a.k.a. snooping and patience).

FINDING I/O REQUESTS

A good starting point is to identify any IRPs that the driver was processing at the time of the crash. Begin by obtaining a list of the active IRPs on the entire system with the !irpfind command.

```
> !irpfind
Searching NonPaged pool (8090c000 : 8131e000) for Tag: Irp
8097c008 Thread 8094d900 current stack belongs to \Driver\Crasher
8097dec8 Thread 8094dda0 current stack belongs to \FileSystem\Ntfs
809861a8 Thread 8094dda0 current stack belongs to \Driver\symc810
```

```
809864e8 Thread 80951ba0 current stack belongs to \Driver\Mouclass
80986608 Thread 80951ba0 current stack belongs to \Driver\Kbdclass
80986728 Thread 8094dda0 current stack belongs to \Driver\symc810
```

From this list, select the IRP belonging to the driver under test. Then the !irp command is used to format the specific IRP.

```
> !irp 8097c008
Irp is active with 1 stacks 1 is current
 No Mdl System buffer = ff593d88 Thread 80987da0:  Irp stack trace.
 cmd flg cl Device  File   Completion-Context
> 4  0  1  809d50d0  00000000 00000000-00000000  pending
            \Driver\Crasher
                     Args: 0000000C 00000000 00000000 00000000
```

The **cmd** field shows the major function, and the **Args** field displays the **Parameters** union of the I/O stack location. The **flg** and **cl** fields show the stack location flags and control bits, defined in NTSTATUS.H.

For this example, the IRP major function code is 4, signifying IRP_MJ_WRITE, with a **Parameters.Write.Length** of 12 (0xC). Further, no completion routine is associated with the IRP and it has been marked pending at the time of the crash.

There is a system buffer associated with the IRP (at location 0xFF593D88), which can be examined with the dd command or the Memory option in the View menu. This device is performing buffered I/O.

To examine the Device object the IRP was sent to, use the !devobj command on the address specified by the IRP.

```
> !devobj 809d50d0
Device object is for:
 Crash0 \Driver\Crasher DriverObject ff53e1d0
 Current Irp 8097c008 RefCount 1 Type 00000022 DevExt ff58bc58
 DeviceQueue:
```

The Device Extension can also be dumped using the dd command. Later in this chapter, a WinDbg extension that makes the Device Extension easier to display is demonstrated.

Of course, the IRP may not yield as much information as the stack trace, but it does reveal some possibly relevant information. For example, the IRP reveals that the driver was performing buffered I/O and that the request was passed to the Start I/O routine, since it was marked as pending. Detective work does not always yield a quick path to the truth.

EXAMINING PROCESSES

Sometimes, it is helpful to know what processes were running on a system at the time of a crash. This can help spot patterns of system usage or even specific user programs that trigger a driver to fail. For general information, the !process command is used.

```
> !process 0 0
**** NT ACTIVE PROCESS DUMP ****
PROCESS 80a02a60 Cid:   0002   Peb:    00000000   ParentCid: 0000
    DirBase: 00006e05   ObjectTable: 80a03788   TableSize: 150.
    Image: System
PROCESS 80986f40 Cid:   0012   Peb:    7ffde000   ParentCid: 0002
    DirBase: 000bd605   ObjectTable: 8098fce8   TableSize: 38.
    Image: smss.exe
PROCESS 80958020 Cid:   001a   Peb:    7ffde000   ParentCid: 0012
    DirBase: 0008b205   ObjectTable: 809782a8   TableSize: 150.
    Image: csrss.exe
PROCESS 80955040 Cid:   0020   Peb:    7ffde000   ParentCid: 0012
    DirBase: 00112005   ObjectTable: 80955ce8   TableSize: 54.
    Image: winlogon.exe
PROCESS 8094fce0 Cid:   0026   Peb:    7ffde000   ParentCid: 0020
    DirBase: 00055005   ObjectTable: 80950cc8   TableSize: 222.
    Image: services.exe
PROCESS 8094c020 Cid:   0029   Peb:    7ffde000   ParentCid: 0020
    DirBase: 000c4605   ObjectTable: 80990fe8   TableSize: 110.
    Image: lsass.exe
PROCESS 809258e0 Cid:   0044   Peb:    7ffde000   ParentCid: 0026
    DirBase: 001e5405   ObjectTable: 80925c68   TableSize: 70.
    Image: SPOOLSS.EXE
```

For more information, the CID number of a specific process can be used to increase the level of verbosity.

```
> !process 0 7
**** NT ACTIVE PROCESS DUMP ****
PROCESS fb667a00 Cid: 0002 Peb: 00000000 ParentCid: 0000
  DirBase: 00030000 ObjectTable: e1000f88 TableSize: 112.
  Image: System
  VadRoot fb666388 Clone 0 Private 4. Modified 9850. Locked 0.
  FB667BBC MutantState Signalled OwningThread 0
  Token                 e10008f0
  ElapsedTime               15:06:36.0338
  UserTime              0:00:00.0000
  KernelTime            0:00:54.0818
  QuotaPoolUsage[PagedPool]     1480
Working Set Sizes (now,min,max) (3, 50, 345)
  PeakWorkingSetSize        118
  VirtualSize           1 Mb
  PeakVirtualSize        1 Mb
  PageFaultCount        992
  MemoryPriority         BACKGROUND
  BasePriority          8
  CommitCharge          8

  THREAD fb667780 Cid 2.1 Teb: 00000000 Win32Thread: 80144900 WAIT:
          (WrFreePage) KernelMode Non-Alertable
    80144fc0 SynchronizationEvent
```

```
Not impersonating
Owning Process fb667a00
WaitTime (seconds)  32278
Context Switch Count 787
UserTime     0:00:00.0000
KernelTime   0:00:21.0821
Start Address Phase1Initialization (0x801aab44)
Initial Sp fb26f000 Current Sp fb26ed00
Priority 0 BasePriority 0 PriorityDecrement 0 DecrementCount 0

ChildEBP RetAddr Args to Child
fb26ed18 80118efc c0502000 804044b0 00000000 KiSwapThread+0xb5
fb26ed3c 801289d9 80144fc0 00000008 00000000 KeWaitForSingleObject+0x1c2
```

For multithreaded processes, this form of the !process command lists thread information, including objects on which they might be waiting. It also provides information about the I/O requests issued by a given thread, which may help in resolving deadlock conditions.

Interactive Debugging

Post mortem analysis is a necessary skill, but many driver problems are easier to diagnose while the driver is actively running. This section briefly describes how to debug driver code interactively.

Starting and Stopping a Debug Session

WinDbg is the primary tool for interactive debugging. To use it, two machines are needed: the target (machine under test) and the host (development machine running WinDbg). Appendix A describes the basics of making the connection between machines, but essentially a serial link is used to control and monitor activity on the target. Figure 17.3 shows the positioning of the host and target machines and files.

The first secret to successful interactive debugging is to ensure that the necessary files are installed on the proper machines. The steps are outlined below.

1. Install the binary driver file (.SYS) on the target. The target does not need symbol files or source code.

2. The host requires symbol information for both the driver and the operating system of the target. For simplicity, it is a good idea to ensure that both target and host are running the same version (including service pack) of Windows 2000, but this is not strictly required.

3. On the host, launch WinDbg. Set up the symbols and source directory options to include a path to the appropriate information. Remember,

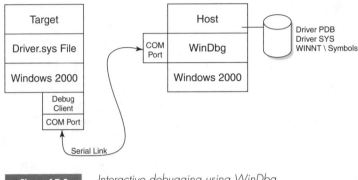

Figure 17.3   *Interactive debugging using WinDbg.*

the symbols and source information must match the target's binary file.

4. Select kernel mode debugging from the View menu under the Options Kernel Debugger tab of WinDbg.

5. Select the appropriate COM port and baud rate from this dialog box.

6. Choose the GO toolbar button, or type g in the command window. This places WinDbg into a mode where it waits to connect to the target.

7. Reboot the target machine with the kernel's debug client enabled. (Details are included in Appendix A.) As the system boots, a connection between host and target is established. Once connected, the command window of WinDbg displays considerable information.

The host is now in complete control of the target. The interactive version of a WinDbg session is a superset of the post mortem mode of crash dump analysis. Breakpoints can be established, even on top of code that has yet to be loaded into kernel memory.

To disconnect a debug session, perform the following steps:

1. Pause the target by typing Ctrl-C in the WinDbg command window. You can also press the SYSREQ key on the target.

2. Choose Edit, then Breakpoints, from the WinDbg menu and choose Clear All. It is important to clear breakpoints before breaking the connection between host and target.

3. From the Run menu, choose Go (or use the toolbar button) to release the target for continued execution.

4. From WinDbg, choose File, then Exit.

The target may still run sluggishly for a time after disconnecting from the host, but should recover shortly. This may be due to the fact that **Kd-Print** and **DbgPrint** routines no longer have a connected debugger to which they can send output.

Setting Breakpoints

Setting breakpoints in live code is often the most attractive way to chase bugs in drivers. The technique is actually overblown in that stopping the system for a breakpoint is a remarkably invasive action. Frequently, intermediate or trace output judiciously placed in driver code yields superior results. However, there is comfort in the knowledge that this incredibly fast system has completely paused while the slow human takes time to sort things out and poke around.

To set a breakpoint with WinDbg, perform the following:

1. If the target machine is running, type Ctrl-C in the WinDbg command window to pause the target and regain control. Breakpoints cannot be set if the target is running.

2. From the File menu, choose Open. This allows any source code module to be opened within the host's WinDbg session.

3. Move the cursor onto a source code line where the desired breakpoint is to be set. If choosing a multiline C statement, choose a position that includes the statement's semicolon.

4. Click on the breakpoint button in the toolbar. (It resembles a raised hand.) If the driver is currently loaded into memory, the source code line turns red. Otherwise, the line is colored magenta.

5. Resume the target by clicking the Go button on the toolbar. Just prior to the source-code line executing, control is returned to the host and the breakpoint source code line turns green.

To remove a breakpoint, pause the target, select the source code line, and click on the breakpoint button. The Edit, Breakpoints menu item allows the removal of multiple breakpoints.

Setting Hard Breakpoints

Given WinDbg's interactive capabilities, there are not many reasons for putting hard breakpoints into driver code. When the need arises, the following two calls can be used:

```
VOID DbgBreakPoint();
VOID KdBreakPoint();
```

KdBreakPoint is just a macro that wraps a conditional compilation directive around a call to **DbgBreakPoint**. The macro generates no call if the driver is built for release (free build).

Beware: Windows 2000 crashes with a KMODE_EXCEPTION_NOT_HANDLED STOP message if a driver encounters a hard-coded breakpoint and the kernel's debug client is not enabled. If a driver hits a breakpoint and there is no debugger connected to the serial line, the target hangs. Sometimes, this situation can be rectified by launching WinDbg on the host, after the fact.

Table 17.2	*DbgPrint and KdPrint Function Prototype*
ULONG DbgPrint or KdPrint	
Parameter	**Description**
PCHAR formatString	**printf**-like string to control format of remaining arguments
…arguments	*vararg* list of arguments, **printf** style

Intermediate Output

Debugging code by sprinkling **printf** statements throughout has a long and honored tradition. The technique is sometimes called *generating intermediate output*. In fact, there is probably no bug that cannot be found by sufficient and proper use of intermediate output.

The technique lacks the glamour of breakpoint debugging, but is often better suited for chasing timing-sensitive bugs. The two routines to generate trace messages **DbgPrint** and **KdPrint** are described in Table 17.2. Both send a formatted string generated on the target to WinDbg on the host.

Since **KdPrint** is actually a macro (defined in NTDDK.H), an extra set of parentheses is required in order to pass a variable-length list of arguments. The **KdPrint** macro becomes a no-op in retail (free) builds of a driver.

Writing WinDbg Extensions

One of WinDbg's strengths is that its capabilities can be expanded by writing custom extension commands. This can be quite convenient, particularly for formatting the display of driver-specific data structures. This section explains the process of adding extension commands to WinDbg.

How WinDbg Extensions Work

A WinDbg extension is just a user-mode DLL that exports various commands in the form of DLL functions. The extension DLL also contains several support routines that perform initialization and version-checking operations.

The linkage between target system memory (whether crash file dump or a live target) is established with callback routines that the extension DLL uses to reference the debug target. This means the DLL has the same view of the target system's memory as WinDbg. In particular, extension commands cannot reference memory that was paged out at the time a crash or breakpoint occurs.

Initialization and Version-Checking Functions

To write an extension DLL for WinDbg (or NTSD or KD, for that matter), two DLL export functions are required for initialization. Optionally, a third version-checking function can be provided. These functions are described below.

WinDbgExtensionDllInit

WinDbg calls this function when the user loads the extension DLL. Its job is to save the address of the callback table so that other parts of the DLL can use it. This function (described in Table 17.3) is required.

ExtensionApiVersion

WinDbg calls this function when it attempts to load an extension DLL. Its purpose is to validate version compatibility between WinDbg and the extension. It does this by returning a pointer to the version structure associated with the extension DLL. This function (shown in Table 17.4) is required.

CheckVersion

Each time WinDbg executes a command in the DLL, it calls this function before calling the command routine. CheckVersion's job is to ensure that the version of the extension DLL is compatible with the version of Windows 2000 being debugged. If not, an error message should inform the user of the problem. The function (described in Table 17.5) is optional.

Writing Extension Commands

Each command in an extension DLL is implemented as a separate function. A macro, DECLARE_API, facilitates the declaration of each extension function.

Table 17.3	Function Prototype for WinDbgExtensionDllInit
VOID WinDbgExtensionDllInit	
Parameter	**Description**
PWINDBG_EXTENSION_APIS pExtensionApis	Address of table containing pointers to WinDbg callback functions
USHORT MajorVersion	0xF for free build of Windows 2000 0xC for checked build
USHORT MinorVersion	Build number of Windows 2000
Return value	- void -

Table 17.4	*Function Prototype for ExtensionApiVersion*

LPEXT_API_VERSION ExtensionApiVersion	
Parameter	**Description**
Void	None
Return value	Address of the DLL's EXT_API_VERSION structure

```
DECLARE_API( command_name )
{
    //
    // code goes here...
    //
    ...
}
```

DECLARE_API provides the function with the prototype shown in Table 17.6. The names of commands must be provided in complete lowercase; otherwise WinDbg cannot find them.

The work that an extension command might perform is boundless. Any operation that makes debugging easier, such as formatting and displaying driver-specific data structures, is appropriate.

If an extension command takes (or could take) a long time to execute, or if considerable output is involved, it should periodically check to see if the WinDbg user has typed Ctrl-C. Otherwise, the user has no way to interrupt the command. One of the WinDbg helper functions described in the next section performs this check.

WinDbg Helper Functions

An extension DLL gains access to the system being debugged by invoking helper functions exported by WinDbg. These functions also provide access to the WinDbg command window for input and output. Table 17.7 contains a brief description of these helper functions.

Table 17.5	*Function Prototype for CheckVersion*

VOID CheckVersion	
Parameter	**Description**
Void	None
Return value	None

Table 17.6	*Extension Command Function Prototypes*

VOID command_name

Parameter	Description
IN HANDLE hCurrentProcess	Handle of current process on target
IN HANDLE hCurrentThread	Handle of current target thread
IN ULONG dwCurrentPc	Current value of program counter
IN ULONG dwProcessor	Number of current CPU
IN PCSTR args	Argument string passed to the command
Return value	void

Table 17.7	*WinDbg Helper Functions Available to Extension DLLs*

WinDbg Helper Functions

Function	Description
dprintf	Print formatted text in WinDbg command window
CheckControlC	See if WinDbg user has typed Ctrl-C
GetExpression	Convert a C expression into a DWORD value
GetSymbol	Locate name of symbol nearest a given address
Disassm	Generate string representation of machine instruction
StackTrace	Return stack-trace of current process
GetKDContext	Return current CPU number and count of CPUs
GetContext	Return CPU context of process being debugged
SetContext	Modify CPU context of process being debugged
ReadControlSpace	Get platform-specific CPU information
ReadMemory	Copy data from system virtual space into buffer
WriteMemory*	Copy data from buffer to system virtual space
ReadIoSpace*	Read I/O Port
WriteIoSpace*	Write I/O port
ReadIoSpaceEx*	Read I/O port on specific bus-type and number (Alpha only)
WriteIoSpaceEx*	Write I/O port on specific bus-type and number (Alpha only)
ReadPhysical	Copy data from physical memory into buffer
WritePhysical*	Copy data from buffer to specific physical addresses

The documentation for these helper functions is contained within the DDK help files. Look for the section entitled "Routines Called From Debugger Extensions."

Building and Using an Extension DLL

A WinDbg extension is just a user-mode DLL, and, therefore, Visual Studio is an appropriate vehicle for its construction. Interestingly, because a driver-specific extension relies on driver structures (and perhaps some DDK structures), some unusual #include statements appear. Otherwise, the build process is quite routine for an extension DLL.

To load and use an extension DLL with WinDbg, it must be loaded using the !load command. After that, the commands are directly accessible by preceding them with a bang (!), using the form *!command*. The !unload command allows the unloading of an extension DLL.

WinDbg allows up to 32 extension DLLs to be loaded simultaneously. When executing a *!command*, WinDbg searches DLLs starting with the most recently loaded. Thus, it is possible to override the functionality of an existing extension command.

Code Example: A WinDbg Extension

This example shows how to write a simple WinDbg extension DLL. The code is contained on the accompanying CD and on the book's web site: *www.W2KDriverBook.com*. The purpose of the extension is to provide one command: !devext that formats and displays the driver's Device Extension data structure.

DBG.C

All the code for this extension resides in a single source file. Of course, the file #includes other files, but they are sourced from elsewhere, such as the driver.

HEADER

This part of the code contains the definitions for the extension DLL.

```
// The ordering of #include files is important
#include <ntddk.h>
#include <windef.h>

// The following items are from WINBASE.H
// in the Win32 SDK. (WINBASE.H itself can't
// coexist with NTDDK.H, yet we need to be
```

```
// able to get at DDK and driver-defined data
// structures and types.)
#define LMEM_FIXED          0x0000
#define LMEM_MOVEABLE       0x0002
#define LMEM_NOCOMPACT      0x0010
#define LMEM_NODISCARD      0x0020
#define LMEM_ZEROINIT       0x0040
#define LMEM_MODIFY         0x0080
#define LMEM_DISCARDABLE    0x0F00
#define LMEM_VALID_FLAGS    0x0F72
#define LMEM_INVALID_HANDLE 0x8000


#define LPTR (LMEM_FIXED | LMEM_ZEROINIT)


#define WINBASEAPI


WINBASEAPI
HLOCAL
WINAPI
LocalAlloc(
    UINT uFlags,
    UINT uBytes
    );


WINBASEAPI
HLOCAL
WINAPI
LocalFree(
    HLOCAL hMem
    );


#define CopyMemory RtlCopyMemory
#define FillMemory RtlFillMemory
#define ZeroMemory RtlZeroMemory


// Now we can bring in the WINDBG extension
// definitions...
#include <wdbgexts.h>


// Other header files...
#include <stdlib.h>
#include <string.h>


// Driver-specific header file...
#include "..\driver\xxdriver.h"
```

GLOBALS

These global variables are necessary for the proper operation of the extension library.

```
// Structure passed back from ExtensionApiVersion
static EXT_API_VERSION
     ApiVersion = { 3, 5, EXT_API_VERSION_NUMBER, 0 };

// Holds callback function table from WinDbgExtensionDllInit
static WINDBG_EXTENSION_APIS ExtensionApis;

// Holds Windows 2000 build info - Major & Minor numbers
static USHORT SavedMajorVersion;
static USHORT SavedMinorVersion;
```

REQUIRED FUNCTIONS

These functions perform the required initialization interaction with WinDbg.

```
VOID
WinDbgExtensionDllInit(
    PWINDBG_EXTENSION_APIS lpExtensionApis,
    USHORT MajorVersion,
    USHORT MinorVersion
    )
{
    // Save pointer to the table of utility
    // functions provided by WinDbg
    ExtensionApis = *lpExtensionApis;

    // Save information about the version of
    // NT that's being debugged
    SavedMajorVersion = MajorVersion;
    SavedMinorVersion = MinorVersion;

    return;
}

VOID CheckVersion( VOID ) {

    // Your version-checking code goes here
    //
    dprintf(
        "CheckVersion called... [%1x;%d]\n",
        SavedMajorVersion,
        SavedMinorVersion
        );
}

LPEXT_API_VERSION
ExtensionApiVersion( VOID ) {
    return &ApiVersion;
}
```

COMMAND ROUTINES

The one command supported by this sample DLL prints the contents of the
Device Extension for an associated driver. It illustrates how to access memory
on the system being debugged.

```
DECLARE_API(devext)
{
    DWORD dwBytesRead;
    DWORD dwAddress;

    PDEVICE_OBJECT pDevObj;
    PDEVICE_EXTENSION pDevExt;

    // Get memory for Device object buffer
    if(( pDevObj = (PDEVICE_OBJECT) malloc (
                    sizeof( DEVICE_OBJECT ))) == NULL )
    {
        dprintf( "Can't allocate buffer.\n" );
        return;
    }

    // Get address of Device object from command line
    dwAddress = GetExpression( args );

    if( !ReadMemory(
            dwAddress,
            pDevObj,
            sizeof( DEVICE_OBJECT ),
            &dwBytesRead ))
    {
        dprintf( "Can't get Device object.\n " );
        free( pDevObj );
        return;
    }

    // Get memory for Device Extension buffer
    if( (pDevExt = (PDEVICE_OBJECT) malloc (
                    sizeof( DEVICE_EXTENSION ))) == NULL )
    {
        dprintf( "Can't allocate buffer.\n" );
        free( pDevObj );
        return;
    }

    // Use Device object to get Device Extension
    if( !ReadMemory(
            (DWORD)pDevObj->DeviceExtension,
            pDevExt,
            sizeof( DEVICE_EXTENSION ),
            &dwBytesRead ))
```

```
    {
        dprintf( "Can't get Device Extension.\n " );
        free( pDevExt );
        free( pDevObj );
        return;
    }

    // Print out interesting values
    dprintf(
            "BytesRequested: %d\n"
            "BytesRemaining: %d\n"
            "TimeoutCounter: %d\n"
            "DeviceObject: %8x\n",

            pDevExt->BytesRequested,
            pDevExt->BytesRemaining,
            pDevExt->TimeoutCounter,
            pDevExt->DeviceObject
            );

    // Clean up and go
    free( pDevExt );
    free( pDevObj );
}
```

SAMPLE OUTPUT

Here is a sample of the output produced by the DBG extension DLL.

```
> !load dbg        ; dbg.DLL must be in the standard DLL
;path for Windows 2000
Debugger extension library [dbg] loaded

> !devext ff58bc40
 CheckVersion called... [f;2195]
BytesRequested: 0
BytesRemaining: 0
TimeoutCounter: 0
DeviceObject: ff58bc40


> !unload dbg
> Extension DLL dbg unloaded
```

Miscellaneous Debugging Techniques

Often the main problem in correcting driver bugs is just getting enough information to make an accurate diagnosis. This section presents a variety of techniques that may help.

Leaving Debugged Code in the Driver

In general, it is a good idea to leave debugging code in place, even after the driver is ready for release. That way, it can be reused if the driver must be modified at some later date. Conditional compilation makes this easy.

The BUILD utility defines a compile-time symbol called **DBG** that can be used to conditionally add debugging code to a driver. In the checked BUILD environment, **DBG** has a value of 1; in the free environment, it has a value of 0. Several of the macros described below use this symbol to suppress the generation of extraneous debugging code in free versions of drivers. When adding debugging code to a driver, it should be wrapped in **#if DBG** and **#endif** directives.

Catching Incorrect Assumptions

As in real life, making unfounded assumptions in kernel-mode drivers is a dangerous practice. For example, assuming that some function argument will always be non-NULL, or that a piece of code is only called at a specific IRQL level can lead to disaster if these expectations are not met.

To catch unforeseen conditions that could lead to driver failure, two things must be done. First, the explicit assumptions made by code must be documented. Second, the assumptions must be verified at runtime. The **ASSERT** and **ASSERTMSG** macros help with both these tasks. They have the following syntax:

```
ASSERT( Expression );
ASSERTMSG( Message, Expression );
```

If *Expression* evaluates to FALSE, **ASSERT** writes a message to WinDbg's command window. The message contains the source code of the failing expression, plus the filename and line number of where the **ASSERT** macro was called. It then provides the option of taking a breakpoint at the point of the **ASSERT**, ignoring the assertion failure, or terminating the process or thread in which the assertion occurred.

ASSERTMSG exhibits the same behavior, except that it includes the text of the *Message* argument with its output. The *Message* argument is just a simple string. Unlike the debug print functions described earlier, **ASSERTMSG** does not allow **printf**-style substitutions.

It should be noted that both assertion macros compile conditionally and disappear altogether in free builds of the driver. This means it is a very bad idea to put any executable code in the *Expression* argument.

Also, the underlying function used by these macros, **RtlAssert**, is a no-op in the free version of Windows 2000 itself. So, to see any assertion failures, a checked build of a driver must be run under a checked version of Windows 2000.

Finally, a warning is in order. The checked build of Windows 2000 crashes with a KMODE_EXCEPTION_NOT_HANDLED error if an assertion fails and the Kernel's debug client is not enabled. If the debug client is enabled, but there is no debugger on the other end of the serial line, the target machine simply hangs if an assertion fails. Recovery can be attempted by starting WinDbg on the host machine, but the text of the assertion that failed is lost.

Using Bugcheck Callbacks

A bugcheck callback is an optional driver routine that is called by the kernel when the system begins to crash. These routines provide a convenient way to capture debugging information at the time of crash. They can also be used to place hardware in a known state before the system goes away. They work as follows:

1. In **DriverEntry**, use **KeInitializeCallbackRecord** to set up a KBUGCHECK_CALLBACK_RECORD structure. The space for this opaque structure must be nonpaged and must be left untouched until it is released with a call to **KeDeregisterBugCheckCallback**.

2. Also in **DriverEntry**, call **KeRegisterBugCheckCallback** to request notification when a bugcheck occurs. The arguments to this function include the bugcheck callback record, the address of a callback routine, the address and size of the driver-defined crash buffer, and a string that is used to identify this driver's crash buffer. As with the bugcheck-callback record, memory for the driver's crash buffer must be nonpaged and left untouched until the driver calls **KeDeregisterBugCheckCallback**.

3. Call **KeDeregisterBugCheckCallback** in a driver's Unload routine to disconnect from the bugcheck notification mechanism.

4. If a bugcheck occurs, the system calls the driver's bugcheck-callback routine and passes it the address and size of the driver's crash buffer. The job of the Callback routine is to fill the crash buffer with any information that would not otherwise end up in the dump file (like the contents of device registers).

5. When analyzing a crash dump with WinDbg, use the !bugdump command to view the contents of the crash buffer.

There are some restrictions on what a bugcheck callback is allowed to do. When it runs, the Callback routine cannot allocate any system resources (like memory). It also cannot use spinlocks or any other synchronization mechanism. It is allowed to call kernel routines that don't violate these restrictions, as well as the HAL functions that access device registers.

Catching Memory Leaks

A memory leak is one of the harder kinds of driver pathology. Drivers that allocate pool space and then forget to release it may just degrade system performance over time, or they can lead to actual system crashes. Using the Windows 2000 built-in pool-tagging mechanism can help determine if a driver leaks memory. Here is how it works.

1. Replace calls to **ExAllocatePool** with **ExAllocatePoolWithTag** calls. The extra four-byte tag argument to this function is used to mark the block of memory allocated by the driver.

2. Run the driver under the checked build of Windows 2000. Keeping track of pool pages is an expensive activity, so it only works under the checked version of the OS. Optionally, the **GFLAGS** utility, supplied with the Platform SDK, can be used to enable the feature for the retail version of Windows 2000.

3. When analyzing a crash, or when a driver stops at a breakpoint, use the !poolused or !poolfind commands in WinDbg to examine the state of the pool areas. These commands sort the pool areas by tag value and display various memory statistics for each tag.

One easy way to use pool tagging is to replace the **ExAllocatePool** function with **ExAllocatePoolWithTag** inside of conditional compilation directives. This way, tagging can be enabled and disabled without considerable effort. Even better, a driver macro can be used for all pool allocations. The macro itself can contain the conditional compilation directives. For example:

```
#define ALLOCATE_POOL( type, size )                        \
#if DBG==1                                                  \
  ExAllocatePoolWithTag( (type), (size), 'DCBA' )          \
#else                                                       \
  ExAllocatePool( (type), (size) )                         \
#endif
```

The tag argument to **ExAllocatePoolWithTag** consists of four case-sensitive ANSI characters. Because of the byte-ordering phenomena of little-endian machines, the tag must be specified as characters in reverse order. Hence, the DCBA tag in the example becomes ABCD in the pool tag display.

In this example, the same tag value is used for all the allocations made by a single driver. For some situations, it may be appropriate to use different tag values for different kinds of data structures, or for allocations made by different parts of a driver. These kinds of strategies may help identify memory leaks caused by a driver.

The POOLMON utility that ships with the DDK allows dynamic observation of pool tags without the need for WinDbg. This command-line utility runs on the target machine and it outputs a continuously updated display of the pool tags. The tool is also supplied with the Windows 2000 Resource Kit.

Using Counters, Bits, and Buffers

There is no question that interactive driver debugging is a wonderful feature. Unfortunately, some bugs are time-dependent, and they disappear when breakpoints or single-stepping is used. This section presents several techniques that may help under these circumstances.

SANITY COUNTERS

Pairs of counters can be used to perform several kinds of sanity checks in a driver. For example, they might count how many IRPs arrive at a driver and how many are sent to **IoCompleteRequest**. Or, in a higher-level driver, the number of IRPs allocated versus the number released could be tracked. Checks like these can help find subtle inconsistencies in the behavior of a driver. The only disadvantage of sanity counters is that they do not necessarily pinpoint the location of the problem.

Implementing a counter is very simple. Declare a ULONG variable within the Device Extension for each counter, and then add appropriate code to increment the counters throughout the driver. As with all debugging support, it is a good idea to wrap sanity-counter code in conditional compilation statements that depend on the **DBG** symbol.

A somewhat ambitious plan would be to write a WinDbg extension command to display all of a driver's counters. As a simple alternative, a driver can force a bugcheck after it has collected enough data and simply use a bugcheck callback to save the counter values.

EVENT BITS

Another useful technique is to keep a collection of bit flags that track the occurrence of significant events in a driver. Each bit represents one specific event, and when that event happens, a driver sets the corresponding bit. Where sanity counters track global driver behavior, event bits provide information about what parts of code have executed.

One of the design decisions for event bits is whether to clear the event variable during **DriverEntry**, during the **AddDevice** or Dispatch routines, or when processing begins on each new IRP. Each of these options provides useful information in different situations.

TRACE BUFFERS

The problem with event bits and counters is that they do not provide information about the sequence of execution of code. As an alternative, a simple tracing mechanism can be added that makes entries in a special buffer as different parts of a driver execute.

Trace buffers can be very useful for tracking down unexpected interactions in asynchronous or full-duplex drivers. On the downside, this extra information is not free. Trace buffers use more CPU time than counters or event bits, and this can have invasive results on time-sensitive bugs.

Implementing a trace buffer mechanism takes more work than the other techniques already presented. Here are the basic steps to follow.

1. Add trace buffer data structures to the driver. Normally, the structures should appear in the Device Extension so that tracing can occur on a device-by-device basis. Occasionally, there may be merit in providing a global buffer that traces the entire driver.

2. Define a macro to make entries in the trace buffer. As with other debug code, it is a good idea to bracket the trace macro with conditional compilation statements.

3. Insert calls to the trace macro at various strategic places in the driver.

4. Write a debugger extension to dump the contents of the trace buffer.

The trace buffer is just an array coupled with a counter that keeps track of the next free slot. The following code fragment illustrates the structure of the basic trace buffer:

```
typedef _DEVICE_EXTENSION {
    :
#if DBG==1
    ULONG traceCount;
    ULONG traceBuffer[ TRACE_BUFFER_SIZE ];
#endif
    :
} DEVICE_EXTENSION, *PDEVICE_EXTENSION;
```

Again, depending upon the data being sought, the **traceCount** field can be initialized once in the **DriverEntry** routine, or each time an IRP arrives.

Adding entries to the buffer is just a matter of storing an item in the array and incrementing the counter. The code fragment below demonstrates how to implement a basic trace macro.

```
#if DBG==1
#define DRVTRACE( pDE, Tag )                       \
  if (pDE->traceCount >= TRACE_BUFFER_SIZE)        \
    pDE->traceCount = 0;                           \
  pDE->traceBuffer[ pDE->traceCount++ ] =          \
    (ULONG) (Tag);
#else
#define DRVTRACE( pDE, Tag )
#endif
```

Notice that this implementation ignores all the synchronization issues that can arise when DRVTRACE is used from multiple IRQL levels (potentially on multiple CPUs). Since the whole purpose of using trace buffers is to catch errors that are sensitive to timing, putting synchronization mechanisms into DRVTRACE would probably render it useless.

One solution is to call DRVTRACE only from places in a driver where synchronization will not be a problem. For example, when calling DRV-TRACE from DPC routines, synchronization is inherently handled as part of the larger structure of the driver itself. Similarly, if it is called from an ISR and a SyncCritSection routine, synchronization is already guaranteed. If these restrictions cannot be met, explicit synchronization must be added to DRV-TRACE.

Summary

When kernel-mode drivers execute, few limits are placed on what can be done to the system. With such power comes the heavy burden of ensuring that a driver does not compromise system integrity. Driver failures that overtly crash the system, as well as failures that cause more suble damage, must be detected and corrected. This chapter has presented some techniques for detection, isolation, and elimination of driver failures, both early in the development cycle and later when the driver is distributed to the world.

The Driver Debug Environment

CHAPTER OBJECTIVES

The standard Microsoft tools for debugging device drivers require that two systems be used: a host *and* target. *The purpose of this appendix is to describe the details required to successfully set up this debugging environment.*

Hardware and Software Requirements

The terminology of the debug environment for drivers should be clear. The target machine executes the driver under test. The host machine, sometimes referred to as the *development system,* runs the debugger (e.g., WinDbg) and therefore controls the operation of the target. The two machines are connected together using a null-modem serial cable.

Another important but confusing term is *debug client*. The target machine must be booted into a special environment whereby it installs the debug client between the serial port and its operating system code. The debug client is the small block of code that allows the host debugger, via the serial port, to control the operation of the target system. The term can be confusing because the target installs and executes the debug client, yet the code makes the target a slave of the host.

For convenience, a network connection between machines is usually established. This ensures that files can be quickly exchanged—providing that both machines are operational. (Never forget that while the target is paused by WinDbg, it cannot participate in network operations.)

Host System

The host system is typically used to compile and link the test driver, and it runs WinDbg as a kernel debugger. Therefore, if a choice exists, choose the machine with the more powerful set of hardware resources as the host system. The list of software that a host should contain follows:

- Windows 2000 retail build
- Visual C++
- Platform SDK
- Windows 2000 DDK
- Symbol files for target OS build(s)
- Driver source code
- Driver symbol file(s)

The host does not necessarily need to execute the same OS version as the target, but it is more convenient. The host requires the symbol file for the OS version running on the target (and it cannot be networked from the target). Thus, if the host and target OS versions do not match, two versions of OS symbols may conceivably be present on the host system. With each launch of WinDbg, thought must be given to which OS symbol file set to use for the session.

Target System

The target system provides the execution environment for the test driver. It is typically configured with the following:

- Windows 2000 retail *and* checked builds with debugging enabled for both
- Driver executable (e.g., .SYS file)
- Driver's hardware
- Full crash dump enabled
- Some tools from the Platform SDK (e.g., WinObj)
- Hardware compatibility tests (HCTs) from the DDK

As explained later in this chapter, the BOOT.INI file on the target must be configured to allow selection of the appropriate Windows 2000 kernel (retail or checked). The checked version runs with considerable assertion and

Table A.1	*Null-Modem Cable Pin Assignments*	

Null-Modem Cable Pin Assignments

Connector A DB9 or DB25	Signal	Connector B DB9 or DB25
2	Transmit to Receive	3
3	Receive to Transmit	2
7	Ground	7

debug code enabled (at the cost of reduced OS performance). The extra code can produce intermediate output that is helpful for tracing some driver or driver-related bugs.

Connecting the Host and Target

To debug a driver interactively with WinDbg, the host and target must be connected using serial ports on each machine. A standard null-modem cable can be used. Since COM ports come in two flavors of connectors, DB-9 and DB-25 (both male on the computer), a dual-headed cable (Y DB-9 and DB-25 female connectors at each end) is the preferred accessory.

For the do-it-yourselfer, Table A.1 shows the necessary connections. The debug client does not use the flow control mechanisms of RS-232, but the universal jumpering scheme of DTR to DSR (Data Terminal Ready to Data Set Ready) and RTS to CTS (Request To Send to Clear To Send) is a good idea and cannot hurt. Table A.2 shows the signal assignments for the different cable connectors.

Table A.2	*Flow Control Jumpers for Null-Modem Cable*			

Flow Control Jumpers on Null-Modem Cable

DB9	DB25	Signal	DB25	DB9
1	20	DTR to DSR	6	6
6	6	DSR to DTR	20	1
8	4	RTS to CTS	5	7
7	5	CTS to RTS	4	8

Debug Symbol Files

One of the more puzzling aspects of debugging is the role of symbol files. Symbol files falls into two categories: OS and driver.

Operating System Symbols

With the release of each version (i.e., service pack) of Windows 2000, Microsoft releases the public symbols for that build. Public symbols are essentially the information that could have been gleaned from the linker's load map, except that they are in debugger-readable format. The information is read, used, and displayed by the debugger during a stack trace operation, a trace or step operation, or when evaluating and setting breakpoints.

Microsoft does not publish private symbol information for its operating systems. Such information is deemed proprietary, and unless a bug were being chased in the OS itself, it is not particularly helpful. The public symbol information, however, is quite useful and is a recommended installation for application as well as driver debugging.

OS symbols are unique to each build (service pack) of an OS. Always install the symbols for the base OS first by using the Windows 2000 Customer Support Diagnostics CD. Then, after a service pack is applied to the OS, locate the symbol file for the service pack (the location varies based on where the update is obtained) and install it *over* the existing OS symbols.

By default, OS symbols install into a directory %SystemRoot%\Symbols. The debugger must point to appropriate directories for a given debug session. For WinDbg, the symbol path can be configured from the Options dialog of the View menu, Symbols tab.

Driver Symbols

The driver symbols are created when the driver source compiles and links. The symbols for a driver (as for the OS itself) fall into public and private categories. The public symbols provide link map information (correlating function names and addresses), while the private symbols information includes source-line linkage, data type definitions (e.g., typedefs), and static declarations (functions and data).

To generate public symbol information for a driver, the link switch /pdb:"filename" can be used. To generate private symbol information, the compiler switch /Zi is used. The slick Edit and Continue feature should not be used for driver development. Linker and compiler switches can be set for a command-line build (e.g., using the BUILD utility) or from Visual Studio if the IDE is used.

Incidentally, the *generation* of public and private symbols is a separate issue from the *inclusion* of symbol data into a binary distribution file. While it is obvious that a debug (checked) build of a driver should include symbol generation, it is less obvious, but nonetheless critical, that symbol information be generated for a release build. The symbol information (.PDB or .DBG files) should then be archived, but not distributed, with the released binary driver. (The REBASE utility's –x switch can be used to strip a binary (.SYS) file of its symbol data.)

As with the OS symbol data, the debugger must be informed of the path of the driver symbol data.

Enabling Crash Dumps on the Target System

As presented in Chapter 17, crash dumps that occur after a driver failure can be very helpful in isolating and locating bugs. To enable this feature on a target machine, the following steps are required:

1. From the Control Panel, select the System applet.
2. Select the Advanced tab.
3. Choose the Startup and Recovery button.
4. Select either Complete Memory Dump or Kernel Memory Dump from the Write Debugging Information group. It is prudent to also select Overwrite any existing file.
5. Note (or change) the location and filename of the crash dump file. By default, it is %SystemRoot%\MEMORY.DMP.
6. Select OK.
7. Reboot the system, as the changes made to this reconfiguration take effect only with the next boot.

When a crash occurs, the system copies an image of physical memory into the paging file of the root partition. During the next boot, the image is copied into the file specified with Control Panel.

Forcing a Memory Dump With a Keystroke Sequence

By modifying a registry entry, Windows 2000 allows the user to generate a keystroke sequence, Ctrl-Scroll Lock (twice), to force a system Stop with the message:

```
*** STOP: 0x000000E2 (0x00000000,0x00000000,0x00000000,
0x00000000)
The end-user manually generated the crashdump.
```

The Registry entry is located in the key:

```
HKLM\System\CurrentControlSet\Services\i8042prt\Parameters
```

By adding the value with the name, type, and data shown below, the feature is enabled. For obvious reasons, it is not enabled by default.

Value Name:	CrashOnCtrlScroll
Data Type:	REG_DWORD
Value:	1

Enabling the Target System's Debug Client

Both the retail and checked (debug) versions of Windows 2000 include a debugging client that allows the kernel to communicate over a serial line with the WinDbg debugger. The debug client must be enabled on the target system during the boot process.

To enable the debug client, select the OS for the target machine with cursor keys while the system boot screen is displayed. Press F8 and select (with cursor keys) the option for Debugging Mode. Press Enter twice to boot the system.

By default, the debug client uses the COM2 port, configured for 19200 baud. These are the same defaults used by WinDbg. To use a different port or baud rate, the BOOT.INI file located on the boot partition root must be modified.

Modifying BOOT.INI

The BOOT.INI file is a read-only, hidden file located on the boot partition's root directory. To edit it, these attributes must be removed. Windows Explorer works well, or the ATTRIB utility of the command prompt can be used.

```
attrib -s -h -r BOOT.INI
```

Then the file is modified using any familiar text editor, such as Notepad. The file is similar in structure to an INI file and contains a section labeled **[operating systems]**. Each entry (line) within this section is displayed on the system boot screen as a choice for user selection. (A timeout value located in the **[boot loader]** section specifies how long the user has to make this choice.)

The format of each line of the **[operating systems]** section includes an ARC-style path to a specific drive, partition, and directory, which holds kernel files. An ="Description" value specifies the text shown to the user on the boot screen for the selection.

An example of a BOOT.INI file is

Table A.3	*Debugging Options for BOOT.INI*

BOOT.INI Options	
Option	**Description**
/DEBUG	Enables kernel debug client
/NODEBUG	Disables debug client (default)
/DEBUGPORT=*PortName*	Specifies COM*n* port to use
/BAUDRATE=*BaudRate*	Specifies baud rate for COM port
/CRASHDEBUG	Causes debugger to activate only upon system bugcheck
/SOS	Displays list of modules loaded while system starts
/MAXMEM=*MBSize*	Specifies maximum memory available to this boot (for testing with smaller memory configurations)

```
[boot loader]
timeout=30
default=multi(0)disk(0)rdisk(0)partition(2)\WINNT

[operating systems]
multi(0)disk(0)rdisk(0)partition(2)\WINNT="W2K Pro" /fastdetect
C:\="Microsoft Windows"
```

To specify a boot option for debugging, switches are added to an existing or new **[operating systems]** entry. The relevant switches for debugging are listed in Table A.3.

An example entry to allow the user to select a debug client on COM port 4, with a baud rate of 38.4 KBaud, would be:

```
multi(0)disk(0)rdisk(0)partition(2)\WINNT="W2K Debug" /debugport=COM4 /baudrate=38400
```

If two different kernels are installed on the same system, they must reside in different directories. The **[operating systems]** entry would specify the appropriate directory instead of WINNT.

Bugcheck Codes

System Stop messages, also known as bugchecks, display as codes, which designate the reason for the system panic. Depending upon the bugcheck code, up to four parameters provide additional information about the cause and location of the problem. The purpose of this appendix is to provide a list of the more common bugcheck codes that a driver author may encounter. The meanings and common causes of the codes, along with the meanings of the additional parameters, are listed.

Bugcheck 0x0A	IRQL_NOT_LESS_OR_EQUAL
The driver accessed paged memory at DISPATCH_LEVEL or above.	
Parameter	**Description**
1	Memory referenced
2	IRQL at time of reference
3	0: Read operation 1: Write operation
4	Address that referenced memory

Bugcheck 0x1E   KMODE_EXCEPTION_NOT_HANDLED

A kernel-mode program generated an unhandled exception.

Parameter	Description
1	Exception Code
2	Address where exception occurred
3	Parameter 0 of exception
4	Parameter 1 of exception

Bugcheck 0x24   NTFS_FILE_SYSTEM

A problem occurred in ntfs.sys.

Parameter	Description
1	Source file and line number
2	Address of the exception record (optional)
3	Address of the context record (optional)
4	Address where the original exception occurred (optional)

Bugcheck 0x2E   DATA_BUS_ERROR

Typically indicates that a parity error in system memory has been detected; usually a hardware problem.

Parameter	Description
1	Virtual address that caused the fault
2	Physical address that caused the fault
3	Processor status register (PSR)
4	Faulting instruction register (FIR)

Bugcheck 0x35   NO_MORE_IRP_STACK_LOCATIONS

The IoCallDriver packet has no remaining stack locations.

Parameter	Description
1	Address of the IRP
2–4	Reserved

Bugcheck 0x3F	NO_MORE_SYSTEM_PTES
A fragmented system page table exists.	

Parameter	Description
1–4	Reserved

Bugcheck 0x50	PAGE_FAULT_IN_NONPAGED_AREA
Invalid system memory has been referenced.	

Parameter	Description
1	Memory address referenced
2	0: Read 1: Write
3	Address that referenced memory (if known)
4	Reserved

Bugcheck 0x58	FTDISK_INTERNAL_ERROR
System booted from the wrong copy of a mirrored partition.	

Parameter	Description
1–4	Reserved

Bugcheck 0x76	PROCESS_HAS_LOCKED_PAGES
A driver failed to release locked pages after an I/O operation.	

Parameter	Description
1	0
2	Process address
3	Number of locked pages
4	0, or pointer to driver stacks

Bugcheck 0x77   **KERNEL_STACK_INPAGE_ERROR**

The requested page of kernel data from the paging file could not be read into memory.

Parameter	Description
1	Status code or 0
2	Value found in stack where signature should be or I/O status code
3	0 or page file number
4	Address of signature on kernel stack or offset into page file

Bugcheck 0x79   **MISMATCHED_HAL**

The Hardware Abstraction Layer (HAL) revision level or configuration does not match that of the kernel or the machine.

Parameter	Description
1	1: PRCB release-level mismatch 2: Build type mismatch 3: Micro Channel mismatch
2	1: Release level of ntoskrnl.exe 2: Build type of ntoskrnl.exe 3: Machine type detected during boot
3	1: Release level of hal.dll 2: Build type of hal.dll 3: Machine type supported by HAL
4	Reserved

Bugcheck 0x7A   **KERNEL_DATA_INPAGE_ERROR**

The requested page of kernel data from the paging file could not be read into memory.

Parameter	Description
1	Lock type that was held or page table entry address
2	I/O status code
3	If lock type is 1 or 2: current process If lock type is 3: virtual address
4	Virtual address that could not be paged into memory

Bugcheck 0x7B	INACCESSIBLE_BOOT_DEVICE

Windows 2000 has lost access to the system partition during startup. This error always occurs while the system is starting and cannot be debugged because it generally occurs before the operating system has loaded the debugger.

Parameter	Description
1	Address of the device object that could not be mounted
2	0
3	0
4	0

Bugcheck 0x7F	UNEXPECTED_KERNEL_MODE_TRAP

A trap, which the Kernel did not catch, was generated by the Intel CPU.

Parameter	Description
1–4	Reserved

Bugcheck 0x9F	DRIVER_POWER_STATE_FAILURE

The driver is in an inconsistent or invalid power state.

Parameter	Description
1	1: The device object being freed still has an outstanding power request that it has not completed
	2: The device object completed the IRP for the system power state request, but failed to call PoStartNextPowerIrp
	3: The device driver did not properly set the IRP as pending or complete the IRP
	100: The device objects in the devnode were inconsistent in their use of DO_POWER_PAGABLE
	101: A parent device object has detected that a child device has not set the DO_POWER_PAGABLE bit
2	1: Pointer to the device object
	2: Pointer to the target device object
	3: Pointer to the target device object
	100: Pointer to the nonpaged device object
	101: Child device object (FDO)

(continued)

(continued)

Bugcheck 0x9F	DRIVER_POWER_STATE_FAILURE

The driver is in an inconsistent or invalid power state.

Parameter	Description
3	1: Reserved 2: Pointer to the device object 3: Pointer to the device object 100: Pointer to the target device object 101: Child device object (PDO)
4	1: Reserved 2: Reserved 3: The IRP 100: Pointer to the device object to notify 101: Parent device object

Bugcheck 0xBE	ATTEMPTED_WRITE_TO_READONLY_MEMORY

A driver attempted to write to a read-only memory segment.

Parameter	Description
1	Virtual address of attempted write
2	PTE contents
3–4	Reserved

Bugcheck 0xC1	SPECIAL_POOL_DETECTED_MEMORY_CORRUPTION

The driver wrote to an invalid section of the special memory pool.

Parameter 1	Parameter 2	Parameter 3	Parameter 4	Description
Address that the driver tried to free	Reserved	0	0x20	Attempt to free pool that was not allocated
Address that the driver tried to free	Bytes requested	Bytes calculated	0x21, 0x22	Attempt to free a bad address

(continued)

(continued)

Bugcheck 0xC1		SPECIAL_POOL_DETECTED_MEMORY_CORRUPTION		

The driver wrote to an invalid section of the special memory pool.

Parameter 1	Parameter 2	Parameter 3	Parameter 4	Description
Address that the driver tried to free	Address where bits are corrupted	Reserved	0x23	Freeing an address when nearby bytes on same page have been corrupted
Address that the driver tried to free	Address where bits are corrupted	Reserved	0x24	Freeing an address when bytes after end of allocation have been overwritten
Current IRQL	Pool type	Number of bytes	0x30	Attempt to allocate pool at incorrect IRQL
Current IRQL	Pool type	Address that the driver tried to free	0x31	Attempt to free pool at incorrect IRQL

Bugcheck 0xC2		BAD_POOL_CALLER		

The current thread is making a bad pool request.

Parameter 1	Parameter 2	Parameter 3	Parameter 4	Description
0x01, 0x02, or 0x04	Pointer to pool header	First part of pool header contents	0	Pool header has been corrupted
0x06	Reserved	Pointer to pool header	Pool header contents	Attempt to free pool that was already freed
0x07	Reserved	Pointer to pool header	0	Attempt to free pool that was already freed

(continued)

(continued)

Bugcheck 0xC2			**BAD_POOL_CALLER**	
The current thread is making a bad pool request.				
Parameter 1	**Parameter 2**	**Parameter 3**	**Parameter 4**	**Description**
0x08	Current IRQL	Pool type	Size of allocation	Attempt to allocate pool at an invalid IRQL
0x09	Current IRQL	Pool type	Address of pool	Attempt to free pool at an invalid IRQL
0x40	Starting address	Start of system address space	0	Attempt to free Kernel pool at user-mode address
0x41	Starting address	Physical page frame	Highest physical page frame	Attempt to free a nonallocated nonpaged pool address
0x50	Starting address	Start offset in pages from beginning of paged pool	Size of paged pool, in bytes	Attempt to free a nonallocated paged pool address
0x99	Address being freed	0	0	Attempt to free pool with invalid address (or corruption in pool header)

Bugcheck 0xC5	**DRIVER_CORRUPTED_EXPOOL**
A driver has probably corrupted the system pool.	
Parameter	**Description**
1	Memory referenced
2	IRQL at time of reference
3	0: Read 1: Write
4	Address that referenced memory

Bugcheck 0xC6   **DRIVER_CAUGHT_MODIFYING_FREED_POOL**

A driver attempted to access a freed memory pool.

Parameter	Description
1	Memory referenced
2	0: Read 1: Write
3	0: Kernel mode 1: User mode
4	4

Bugcheck 0xC7   **TIMER_OR_DPC_INVALID**

A kernel timer or delayed procedure call (DPC) object was freed while it was still queued for activation.

Parameter	Description
1	0: Timer object 1: DPC object 2: DPC routine
2	Address of object
3	Beginning of memory range checked
4	End of memory range checked

Bugcheck 0xCA   **PNP_FATAL_ERROR**

The PnP Manager encountered a severe error, probably as a result of a flawed Plug and Play driver.

Parameter 1	Parameter 2	Parameter 3	Parameter 4	Description
0x01	Address of newly reported PDO	Address of older PDO which has been duplicated	Reserved	Duplicate PDO. A specific instance of a driver has enumerated multiple PDOs with identical device and unique IDs.

(*continued*)

(continued)

Bugcheck 0xCA			PNP_FATAL_ERROR	

The PnP Manager encountered a severe error, probably as a result of a flawed Plug and Play driver.

Parameter 1	Parameter 2	Parameter 3	Parameter 4	Description
0x02	Address of purported PDO	Reserved	Reserved	Invalid PDO. An API that requires a PDO has been called with random memory, an FDO, or a PDO which hasn't been initialized.
0x03	Address of purported PDO	Reserved	Reserved	Invalid PDO. An API that requires a PDO has been called with random memory, an FDO, or a PDO that hasn't been initialized.
0x04	Address of PDO with DOE_ DELETE_ PENDING set	Address of ID buffer	1: DeviceID 2: UniqueID 3: HardwareIDs 4: Compatible IDs	Invalid ID. An enumerator has returned an ID that contains illegal characters or isn't properly terminated. (IDs must contain only characters in the ranges 0x20 to 0x2B and 0x2D to 0x7F.)

(continued)

(continued)

Bugcheck 0xCA			PNP_FATAL_ERROR	

The PnP Manager encountered a severe error, probably as a result of a flawed Plug and Play driver.

Parameter 1	Parameter 2	Parameter 3	Parameter 4	Description
0x05	Address of PDO	Reserved	Reserved	PDO freed while linked in devnode tree. The object manager reference count on a PDO dropped to zero while the devnode was still linked in the tree. (This usually indicates that the driver is not adding a reference when re turning the PDO in a query IRP.)

Bugcheck 0xCB	DRIVER_LEFT_LOCKED_PAGES_IN_PROCESS

A driver failed to release locked pages after an I/O operation.	

Parameter	Description
1	Calling address in driver that locked the pages
2	Caller of the calling address in driver that locked the pages
3	Pointer to MDL containing the locked pages
4	Guilty driver's name (pointer to Unicode string)

Bugcheck 0xCC   **PAGE_FAULT_IN_FREED_SPECIAL_POOL**

The system has referenced memory that was earlier freed.

Parameter	Description
1	Memory address referenced
2	0: Read 1: Write
3	Address that referenced memory (if known)
4	Reserved

Bugcheck 0xCD   **PAGE_FAULT_BEYOND_END_OF_ALLOCATION**

The system accessed memory beyond the end of some driver's pool allocation.

Parameter	Description
1	Memory address referenced
2	0: Read 1: Write
3	Address that referenced memory (if known)
4	Reserved

Bugcheck 0xCE   **DRIVER_UNLOADED_WITHOUT_CANCELLING_
PENDING_OPERATIONS**

A driver failed to cancel pending operations before unloading.

Parameter	Description
1	Memory address referenced
2	0: Read 1: Write
3	Address that referenced memory (if known)
4	Reserved

Bugcheck 0xCF	TERMINAL_SERVER_DRIVER_MADE_INCORRECT_ MEMORY_REFERENCE

A driver has been incorrectly ported to the terminal server.

Parameter	Description
1	Memory address referenced
2	0: Read 1: Write
3	Address that referenced memory (if known)
4	Reserved

Bugcheck 0xD0	DRIVER_CORRUPTED_MMPOOL

A driver has corrupted the system pool.

Parameter	Description
1	Memory referenced
2	IRQL at time of reference
3	0: Read 1: Write
4	Address that referenced memory

Bugcheck 0xD1	DRIVER_IRQL_NOT_LESS_OR_EQUAL

A driver attempted to access pageable memory at a process IRQL that was too high.

Parameter	Description
1	Memory referenced
2	IRQL at time of reference
3	0: Read 1: Write
4	Address that referenced memory

Bugcheck 0xD3   **DRIVER_PORTION_MUST_BE_NONPAGED**

A driver has incorrectly marked code or data as pageable.

Parameter	Description
1	Memory referenced
2	IRQL at time of reference
3	0: Read 1: Write
4	Address that referenced memory

Bugcheck 0xD4   **SYSTEM_SCAN_AT_RAISED_IRQL_CAUGHT_IMPROPER_
DRIVER_UNLOAD**

A driver did not cancel pending operations before unloading.

Parameter	Description
1	Memory referenced
2	IRQL at time of reference
3	0: Read 1: Write
4	Address that referenced memory

Bugcheck 0xD5   **DRIVER_PAGE_FAULT_IN_FREED_SPECIAL_POOL**

A driver has referenced memory that was earlier freed.

Parameter	Description
1	Memory address referenced
2	0: Read 1: Write
3	Address that referenced memory (if known)
4	Reserved

Bugcheck 0xD6   **DRIVER_PAGE_FAULT_BEYOND_END_OF_ALLOCATION**

A driver accessed memory beyond the end of its pool allocation.

Parameter	Description
1	Memory address referenced
2	0: Read 1: Write
3	Address that referenced memory (if known)
4	Reserved

Bugcheck 0xD7   **DRIVER_UNMAPPING_INVALID_VIEW**

A driver is trying to unmap an address that was not mapped.

Parameter	Description
1	Virtual address to unmap
2	0: system is not terminal server 1: system is terminal server
3	0
4	0

Bugcheck 0xD8   **DRIVER_USED_EXCESSIVE_PTES**

There are no remaining system page table entries.

Parameter	Description
1	Pointer to the guilty driver's name (Unicode string), or 0
2	Number of PTEs used by the guilty driver (if Parameter 1 is nonzero)
3	Total free system PTEs
4	Total system PTEs

Bugcheck 0xDB	DRIVER_CORRUPTED_SYSPTES

An attempt was made to touch memory at an invalid IRQL, probably due to corruption of system PTEs.

Parameter	Description
1	Memory referenced
2	IRQL
3	0: read 1: write
4	Address in code which referenced memory

Bugcheck 0xDC	DRIVER_INVALID_STACK_ACCESS

A driver accessed a stack address that lies below the stack pointer of the stack's thread.

Parameter	Description
1 - 4	Reserved

Bugcheck 0xDE	POOL_CORRUPTION_IN_FILE_AREA

A driver corrupted pool memory used for holding pages destined for disk.

Parameter	Description
1 - 4	Reserved

Bugcheck 0xE1	WORKER_THREAD_RETURNED_AT_BAD_IRQL

A worker thread completed and returned at IRQL DISPATCH_LEVEL or above.

Parameter	Description
1	Address of the worker routine
2	IRQL (should have been 0)
3	Work item parameter
4	Work item address

Bugcheck 0xE2	MANUALLY_INITIATED_CRASH

The user deliberately initiated a crash dump from either the kernel debugger or the keyboard.

Parameter	Description
1–4	Reserved

Bugcheck 0xE3	RESOURCE_NOT_OWNED

A thread tried to release a resource it did not own.

Parameter	Description
1	Address of resource
2	Address of thread
3	Address of owner table (if it exists)
4	Reserved

Bugcheck 0xE4	WORKER_INVALID

An Executive worker item was found in memory that must not contain such items.

Parameter	Description
1	Code position indicator
2	Address of worker item
3	Start of pool block
4	End of pool block

Building Drivers

CHAPTER OBJECTIVES

There is nothing magical about the build process for a driver. Like any piece of "real" (i.e., noninterpreted) code, it must be compiled and linked into a binary file before it can be used. The issues that arise when building drivers concern notifying the build tools (compiler and linker) that the environment for the code being generated is that of kernel mode.

Although it sometimes may appear otherwise, Microsoft supplies a single compiler and linker. Whether the tools are invoked from a command-line prompt or from an elaborate Integrated Development Environment (IDE) such as Visual Studio, the resulting binary files are the same. In many ways, Visual Studio is merely a GUI interface for the build and editing tools. Clicking on the menu option for Project, then Settings, provides a convenient dialog-based interface to the tool switches.

The DDK provides a utility, BUILD, that is convenient for batch and production builds of device drivers (as well as other production-level binaries). With proper environment settings, however, the driver author may successfully use Visual Studio. Indeed, it may be appropriate to use Visual Studio throughout the development phase and introduce BUILD during the later release stages of the project.

The purpose of this appendix is to provide background material on the BUILD utility, as well as provide the Visual Studio settings necessary for successful driver builds.

The Build Utility

The DDK-supplied BUILD utility is ideal for production releases because it works from a single "makefile" concept to batch-build a variety of targeted binaries. For example, a single set of source files can be used to generate driver binaries for both Intel x86 platforms and Alpha platforms. Similarly, both the retail (free) and checked (debug) versions can be built from a single procedure.

What BUILD Does

The BUILD utility is just an elaborate wrapper around NMAKE. (NMAKE is Microsoft's attempt at the Unix *make* utility.) A batch file of instructions provides a recipe for the construction of one or more target configurations (e.g., checked and free).

Using a set of keywords, a source file list, and miscellaneous switches, BUILD constructs an appropriate *makefile* and then invokes NMAKE to actually perform the build to produce one or more BUILD *products*. Figure C.1 shows how this process works.

BUILD itself is actually a rather simple-minded program. Most of the build process is controlled by a set of standard command files that BUILD passes to NMAKE. These files contain all the platform-specific rules and option settings needed to create a BUILD project. By separating the rules from the utilities, there is less version interdependency.

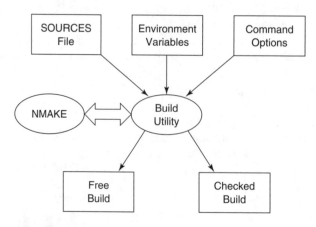

Figure C.1   *The BUILD utility process.*

BUILD uses several command files (located in the DDK's binary directory, \BIN:).

- MAKEFILES.DEF is the master control file. It references other files to perform its work.
- MAKEFILE.PLT selects the platform for a build operation.
- i386MK.INC, ALPHAMK.INC, and ia64mk.inc contain platform-specific compiler and linker switches for Intel, Alpha, and 64-bit Intel Itanium processors, respectively.

BUILD helps manage multiplatform projects by separating binary files according to their platform type. To do this, it uses different directories for different platforms. So long as cross-hosted compilers and linkers are available, a single BUILD process can generate binaries for all the supported platforms. The directory structure for the output files takes the form shown in Figure C.2.

Notice that BUILD uses separate directories for the checked and free versions of the generated binaries. The **DBG** symbol is defined as 1 when performing the checked build.

How to Build a Driver with BUILD

Once the source code is ready for compilation, the use of the BUILD utility requires that the following steps be followed:

1. In the source file directory, create a file called SOURCES that identifies the components that comprise the driver. A description of the format of this file follows in the next section.

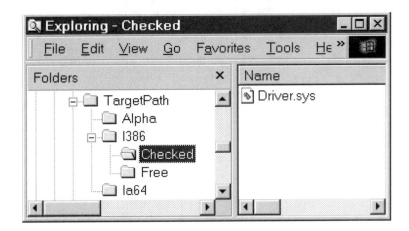

Figure C.2   *Directory structure for BUILD products.*

2. In the source directory, create a file called MAKEFILE that contains only the following line:

```
!INCLUDE $(NTMAKEENV)\MAKEFILE.DEF
```

This stub invokes the standard makefile needed by all drivers created with BUILD. Do not add source files to this makefile. Instead, use the SOURCES file.

3. Use Windows Explorer or the MKDIR command to set up the directory tree for the BUILD products. Refer to Figure C.2.

4. In the Program Manager group for the Windows 2000 DDK, select either the Checked Build Environment or the Free Build Environment. A command window appears with the appropriate BUILD environment variables set.

5. Navigate (using the CD command) to the source file directory for the driver.

6. Run the BUILD utility (i.e., type BUILD) to create the driver executable.

The binary output is created in the CHECKED or FREE directory of the appropriate platform. Any on-screen errors are also written to the BUILD log file.

Writing a SOURCES File

The BUILD operation is controlled by a series of keywords. These keywords specify the type of driver to be generated, the source files that comprise the product, and the directories for various files. While some keywords can be passed as command-line options to BUILD, the more useful procedure is to place the keywords into the SOURCES file. The following general rules apply to the SOURCES file:

- The filename must be SOURCES (no extension).
- The file contents are of the form
  `keyword=value`
- A single BUILD command can be extended over multiple lines by using the backslash (\) character at then end of a line.
- The value of a BUILD keyword must be simple text. BUILD itself does little processing of NMAKE macros and does not handle conditional statements.
- Ensure that there is no white space between a BUILD keyword and the equal sign (=) character. White space *after* the equal sign is acceptable.
- Comments in a SOURCE file line start with a sharp (#) character.

| Table C.1 | Common BUILD Utility Keywords |

<table>
<tr><td colspan="2" align="center">**Common BUILD Keywords**</td></tr>
<tr><td align="center">**Keyword**</td><td align="center">**Meaning**</td></tr>
<tr><td>INCLUDES</td><td>List of paths containing header files</td></tr>
<tr><td>SOURCES</td><td>List of source files making up BUILD product (required)</td></tr>
<tr><td>TARGETPATH</td><td>Top-level directory for BUILD product tree (required)</td></tr>
<tr><td>TARGETNAME</td><td>Name of BUILD product, sans extension</td></tr>
<tr><td>TARGETEXT</td><td>File extension for the BUILD product</td></tr>
<tr><td>TARGETTYPE</td><td>Case sensitive keyword describing BUILD
● DRIVER
● GDI_DRIVER
● MINIPORT
● LIBRARY
● DYNLINK (for DLLs)</td></tr>
<tr><td>TARGETLIBS</td><td>List of libraries to be linked with driver</td></tr>
<tr><td>LINKER_FLAGS</td><td>Linker switches of the form –flag:value</td></tr>
<tr><td>PRECOMPILED_INCLUDE</td><td>File containing precompiled #include directives</td></tr>
</table>

Table C.1 lists the common SOURCES keywords for building drivers. The DDK includes additional keywords and details regarding these keywords.

The following is an example of a minimal SOURCES file for building a kernel-mode driver:

```
TARGETNAME= DRIVER

TARGETTYPE= DRIVER
TARGETPATH= .
SOURCES= init.c dispatch.c driver.c \
         pnp.c
```

Log Files Generated by BUILD

In addition to screen output, the BUILD utility generates several text files that can be used to determine the status of a BUILD product.

- **BUILD.LOG** lists the commands invoked by NMAKE.
- **BUILD.WRN** contains warnings generated during the build.
- **BUILD.ERR** contains a list of errors generated during the build.

BUILD generates these files in the same directory as the SOURCES files. The warning and error files appear only if needed.

Recursive BUILD Operations

BUILD can be used to maintain an entire source code tree by creating a file called DIRS. This file is placed in a directory containing other subdirectories. Each subdirectory can be a source directory (containing a SOURCES file) or the root of another source tree (containing another DIRS file). When BUILD runs from the topmost DIRS directory, it creates all the BUILD products described in the now linked SOURCES files.

The rules for writing a DIRS file are the same as those for a SOURCES file, with the restriction that only two keywords are allowed.

- **DIRS** lists subdirectories that should always be built. Entries in the list are separated by spaces or tabs.
- **OPTIONAL_DIRS** lists subdirectories that should be built only if they are named on the original BUILD command line.

Besides performing multiplatform builds, the recursive BUILD feature can be used to generate a kernel-mode and user-mode component at the same time.

Using Visual Studio to Build Drivers

Although Visual Studio is quite obviously promoted as an application development tool for C++ (and several other languages), it is nonetheless an IDE for the standard compiler and linker. Therefore, using the proper compile and link switch settings, the tool can be used to build kernel-mode device drivers.

The DDAppWiz Tool

The CD that accompanies this book includes an App Wizard that conveniently provides the necessary compile and link switch settings for Visual Studio to build a device driver. The file, **DDAppWiz.AWX**, must be copied into the Visual Studio path: ...\Microsoft Visual Studio\Common\MSDev98\Template. Thereafter, a new Project type appears in the New Project dialog box: W2K Device Driver.

The use of the App Wizard is straightforward and described in Chapter 6. This section lists the Visual Studio environment settings modified or added by the wizard.

Preprocessor Symbols Modification

The table below shows the compiler preprocessor symbols removed from the standard Win32 project, normally generated by Visual Studio.

Preprocessor Symbol	Modification	Reason
WIN32	Deleted	Driver is not a Win32 application
_WINDOWS	Deleted	Driver is not a Windows application
_MBCS	Deleted	Driver uses Unicode, not multibyte character set
_DEBUG	Deleted	Driver is not Win32 debug target
DBG	Added	Driver's standard debug symbol definition (1=checked, 0=free)
_X86_	Added	DDAppWiz produces driver for Intel platform
WIN32_WINNT=0x500	Added	Version of Windows 2000

Compiler Switch Modifications

Several compile switches are required for driver builds, as shown in the following table:

Compiler Switch	Modification	Reason
/GX and –GX	Deleted	Do not enable synchronous exception handling
/GZ	Deleted	Do not attempt to catch release build errors
-Gz	Added	Use __stdcall calling convention

Compiler Include Directories

The Device Driver App Wizard adds two include directories to the set of compiler options (-I switch). The paths are listed below.

```
\NTDDK\inc     and
```

```
\NTDDK\inc\ddk
```

These may require modification, depending upon choices specified when the DDK is installed.

Link Modifications

All of the standard Win32 libraries are removed from linker input and replaced with the following list of libraries:

- int64.lib
- ntoskrnl.lib
- hal.lib

The /nodefaultlib linker option is selected. Depending on the configuration (Debug or Release), a library path is added of either

```
/libpath:\NTDDK\libchk\i386 or
```

```
/libpath:\NTDDK\libfre\i386
```

Either of these link settings may require manual modification based on where the DDK is actually installed.

The remaining linker switch modifications are as follows:

Link Option	Modification	Reason
/subsystem:windows	Deleted	Driver is not a Win32 application
-driver	Added	Link for kernel-mode driver
-subsystem:NATIVE,5.00	Added	Required for driver build
-base:0x10000	Added	Drivers specify load of 0x10000, kernel relocates
-entry:DriverEntry	Added	Entry point for all drivers

No MFC

To ensure that the driver project is not MFC based (for obvious reasons), the option is removed by the App Wizard.

Anderson, Don. *FireWire System Architecture*. Reading, Masschusetts, Addison-Wessley, 1999. ISBN 0-201-48535-4

Solomon, David. *Inside Windows NT—Second Edition*. Redmond, Washington, 1998. ISBN 1-57231-677-2

Richter, Jeffrey. *Advanced Windows*. Redmond, Washington, Microsoft Press, 1997. ISBN 1-57231-548-2

Brain, Marshall. *Win32 System Services*. Upper Saddle, New Jersey, Prentice Hall PTR, 1995. ISBN 0-13-324732-5

Anderson, Don, and Mindshare Inc. *Universal Serial Bus System Architecture*. Reading Massachusetts, Addison Wesley Longman 1997. ISBN 0-201-46137-4

IEEE 1394 Specifications and white papers. (*http://www.1394ta.org*)

USB Specifications and white papers (*http://www.usb.org*)

Windows 2000 DDK (*http://www.microsoft.com/ddk*)

Windows 2000 Platform SDK
(*http://msdn.microsoft.com/library/psdk/portals/mainport.htm*)

Windows 2000 IFS Kit (*http://www.microsoft.com/ddk/IFSKit*)

About the CD-ROM

The CD-ROM included with *The Windows 2000 Device Driver Book* contains the following:

Sample device drivers and tools demonstrating the Windows 2000 device driver model, including Plug and Play.

The CD-ROM can be used on Microsoft Windows 2000® platforms with the following prerequisites:

- Visual C++ 6.0 Professional or Enterprise
- Windows 2000 DDK
- Windows 2000 Platform SDK
- Parallel Port Loopback connector (CheckIt® compliant)

License Agreement

Use of the software accompanying The Windows 2000 Device Driver Book is subject to the terms of the License Agreement and Limited Warranty, found on the previous page.

Installation Instructions:

1. It is important that Visual C++ (Visual Studio) be installed BEFORE installing the Platform SDK or the DDK. Also, be sure to check the box "Register Environment Variables" near the end of the Visual C++ installation.

2. Once the Microsoft products are successfully installed, copy the file:

   `DDAppWiz.awx`

   from the Tools directory of this CD to the system's directory:

   `...\Microsoft Visual Studio\Common\MsDev98\Template`

   Typically, this directory is located under the system's "Program Files" directory. Once copied, a new App Wizard (for creating projects for Windows 2000 device drivers) is available from the Visual C++ IDE (File...New...Project).

3. Copy the directories "ChapNN" from this CD to the Windows 2000 system, to the directory of your choice. Also, copy the Tools directory.

Technical Support

Additional information regarding troubleshooting suggestions and updated files may be found on the following web site:

http://www.W2KDriverBook.com

Prentice Hall does not offer technical support for any of the programs on the CD-ROM. However, if the CD-ROM is damaged, you may obtain a replacement copy by sending an email that describes the problem to: *disc_exchange@prenhall.com*.